Indigenous Knowledge

Indigenous Knowledge

Philosophical and Educational Considerations

Kai Horsthemke

LEXINGTON BOOKS
Lanham • Boulder • New York • London

Published by Lexington Books
An imprint of The Rowman & Littlefield Publishing Group, Inc.
4501 Forbes Boulevard, Suite 200, Lanham, Maryland 20706
www.rowman.com

6 Tinworth Street, London SE11 5AL, United Kingdom

Copyright © 2021 by The Rowman & Littlefield Publishing Group, Inc.

All rights reserved. No part of this book may be reproduced in any form or by any electronic or mechanical means, including information storage and retrieval systems, without written permission from the publisher, except by a reviewer who may quote passages in a review.

British Library Cataloguing in Publication Information Available

Library of Congress Control Number: 2020948151

ISBN 978-1-7936-0416-3 (cloth)
ISBN 978-1-79360-418-7 (pbk)
ISBN 978-1-7936-0417-0 (electronic)

Imfihlakalo yasemhlabeni iqiniso.

("The truth is the world's secret."—IsiZulu proverb)

Contents

Preface		ix
Introduction		1
1	The Idea of Indigenous Knowledge	9
2	Relational Epistemology and the Idea of Epistemological Diversity	27
3	An Analysis of Knowledge and Epistemology	43
4	A Critique of Indigenous Knowledge	97
5	Ethnomathematics	135
6	Indigenous Science	165
7	Traditional Ecological (or Environmental) Knowledge	183
8	Morality, Knowledge, and Local Values	205
9	Epistemic Justice, Recognition, and Rights	221
10	An Applied Epistemology for the Real World	237
References		247
Index		271
About the Author		281

Preface

Many of the thoughts and arguments captured in this book were formed in conversation with my teachers and, later, my colleagues. I wish, therefore, to express my sincere appreciation to Mary Tjiattas, Shirley Pendlebury, Penny Enslin, Mike Kissack, David Bensusan, Krassimir Stojanov, Michael Pendlebury, Graeme McLean, and Mark Leon. I have also benefited from countless exchanges with my dear friends Thomas Kölble, Marc Schäfer, Peter Krause, Alison Elgin, Carola Steinberg, Carlotta von Maltzan, Paul Hendler, Martin Noll, Jürgen Risser, and Michael Woitynek. I am deeply grateful, further, to Hella Rabbethge-Schiller, for permission to use Stefaans Samcuia's gouache painting "Moons and Stars" (from her collection of !Xun and Khwe art, and for which she holds sole copyright) as the cover image for this book. Hella not only enabled members of a severely marginalized community to create these works, by providing the opportunity and raw materials, but also purchased the works from the artists, thereby ensuring their livelihood, and recorded the biographies and the stories behind the works. I am indebted also to Harvey Siegel and David Bridges for inspiration and encouragement along the way, and to Holly Buchanan at Lexington Books. Finally, as always, if it weren't for the love and support of Edda and our wonderful boys (and critical scrutinizers) Tau and Vusi, I don't think I would have been able to write all this.

Some of the material contained in this book has been published previously and is reprinted here with minor modifications and with the kind permission of the publishers and/or editors, as noted. I am grateful to

- the *Journal of Education* (Horsthemke, K. 2004, 'Indigenous knowledge': Conceptions and misconceptions. *Journal of Education* 32: 31–48; Horsthemke, K. 2005, Redress and reconciliation in South African education:

The case for a rights-based approach. *Journal of Education* 37/Kenton 2004 Special Edition: 169–187; Horsthemke, K. 2010, 'Knowledge diversity', truth and schooling: In (cautious) defence of realism. *Journal of Education* 48: 1–22);
- the *South African Journal of Higher Education*, and especially Yusef Waghid and Anel de Beer (Horsthemke, K. 2004, 'Indigenous knowledge', truth and reconciliation in South African higher education. *South African Journal of Higher Education* 18(3): 65–81; Horsthemke, K. 2006, The idea of the African university in the twenty-first century: Some reflections on Afrocentrism and Afroscepticism. *South African Journal of Higher Education* 20(4): 449–465; Horsthemke, K. 2008, Scientific knowledge and higher education in the 21st century: The case against 'indigenous science'. *South African Journal of Higher Education* 22(2): 333–347);
- Taylor and Francis, and Paul Smeyers, the editor of *Ethics and Education* ("Of ants and men: Epistemic injustice, commitment to truth, and the possibility of outsider critique," Horsthemke, K., Ethics and Education, 2014, Taylor and Francis, reprinted by permission of the publisher (Taylor & Francis Ltd, http://www.tandfonline.com); "Epistemic empathy in childrearing and education," Horsthemke, K., Ethics and Education, 2015, and Taylor and Francis, reprinted by permission of the publisher (Taylor & Francis Ltd, http://www.tandfonline.com); "#FactsMustFall"?—Education in a post-truth, post-truthful world," Horsthemke, K., Ethics and Education, 2017 and Taylor and Francis, reprinted by permission of the publisher (Taylor & Francis Ltd, http://www.tandfonline.com);
- Berghahn Journals, and especially Sherran Clarence, the managing editor of *Theoria* (Parts of chapters 2, 4, and 7 first appeared as Horsthemke, K. 2010. "African and Afrikaner 'ways of knowing': Truth and the problems of superstition and 'blood knowledge'." *Theoria: A Journal of Social and Political Theory* 57(123): 27–51 and is printed with the permission of Berghahn Journals);
- *Quest*, and the editor, Wim Van Binsbergen (Horsthemke, K. 2014, Some doubts about 'indigenous knowledge', and the argument from epistemic injustice. *Quest* 25/1–2 (special issue), ed. T. Metz in collaboration with W. Van Binsbergen, "Engaging with the Philosophy of D.A. Masolo": 49–76);
- Springer Nature (reprinted by permission from Springer Nature: Springer Nature, *Science and Engineering Ethics*, "'Diverse epistemologies', truth and archaeology: In defence of realism," Horsthemke, K., © Springer Science+Business Media B.V. 2010; Horsthemke, K. 2017, "Africanisation and diverse epistemologies in higher education discourses: Limitations and possibilities," reprinted/adapted by permission from Springer Nature: Rotterdam, Boston & Taipei: Sense Publishers, *Knowledge and change in*

the African universities: Volume 1— Current debates, ed. M. Cross & A. Ndofirepi, All rights reserved © 2017 Sense Publishers, 2017);
- FLM Publishing, and especially Susan Oesterle, the managing editor of *for the learning of mathematics* (Horsthemke, K. 2006, Ethnomathematics and education: Some thoughts. *For the Learning of Mathematics* 26(3): 15–19);
- The South African Comparative and History of Education Society (SACHES) and the *South African Review of Education* with *Education with Production*, and especially Azeem Badroodien and Jo-Anne Koch (Parts of chapters 3 and 4 first appeared as an article in *Southern African Review of Education (SARE) with Education with Production*, Vol. 13, No. 1 (2007): pp.19–30, and are reprinted with minor modifications and with the kind permission of SARE);
- *Education Sciences* (Horsthemke, K. 2016, 'Way-centred' versus 'truth-centred' epistemologies. *Education Sciences* 6(1)/8: 1–11; published online 4 March: doi:10.3390/educsci6010008),
- Isaac Scientific Publishing, and especially J.W. Good, the editor of the *Journal of Advances in Education Research* (Horsthemke, K. 2017, Access, parentalism and justice: Epistemological reflections on integration and inclusion in education. *Journal of Advances in Education Research* 2/3: 145–156);
- *Forum Pedagogiczne*, Poland, and especially the editor, Dariusz Stępkowski (Horsthemke, K. 2017, Epistemological diversity in education: Philosophical and didactic considerations. *Forum Pedagogiczne* 1: 265–282; Horsthemke, K. 2020, Global citizenship education and the idea of diverse epistemologies. *Forum Pedagogiczne* x/2020: xx–xx);
- *On_Education*, and especially Johannes Drerup (Horsthemke, K. 2020, The provincialization of epistemology: Knowledge and education in the age of the postcolony. *On Education. Journal for Research and Debate*, 3/7: 1–5. https://doi.org/10.17899/on_ed.2020.7.6);
- Palgrave Macmillan (Horsthemke, K., *Animals and African Ethics*, 2015, Palgrave Macmillan, reproduced with permission of Palgrave Macmillan; Horsthemke, K. "Indigenous (African) knowledge systems, science, and technology." In *The Palgrave Handbook of African Philosophy*, ed. A. Afolayan & T. Falola: 585–603, 2017, Palgrave Macmillan, reproduced with permission of Palgrave Macmillan; Horsthemke, K. "Free-roaming animals, killing, and suffering: The case of African elephants." In *The Palgrave Handbook of Practical Animal Ethics*, ed. A. Linzey & C. Linzey: 525–543, 2018, Palgrave Macmillan, reproduced with permission of Palgrave Macmillan).

My book was completed during a time of severe global uncertainty, when our lives and thoughts were (and continue to be) challenged by three substantial crises that are somehow all connected. As if the omnipresent threat of climate change, imminent ecological disaster, and the loss of biodiversity were not enough to keep us both alert and humble, the start of the new decade also saw the outbreak of a new pandemic, the seemingly unlimited edition of the new Corona virus, that catapulted societies and economies into a lockdown the end of which is not yet in sight. But instead of a sense of global solidarity, nurtured by the realization that all of us are in this together, many societies drifted further and further apart, polarized by the martial rhetoric of bungling politicians, strong-arm posturing by nondemocratic governments, and a spate of undoubtedly racially motivated killings by those in charge of actually protecting the people they end up harming. As a result, the *Fridays for Future* protests that had been the expression of public indignation and outrage were replaced by the *Black Lives Matter* movement in recent months, and also by (frequently conspiracy-based) anti-lockdown protests.

My friend Sean Fitzpatrick was among the first in England to contract the virus and be admitted to the intensive care unit of a nearby hospital. During the induced coma, with subsequent intubation and tracheotomy, he suffered not only kidney failure but also a stroke. Miraculously (we had all but given up hope), he survived and is gradually adjusting to his situation of circumscribed mobility. When he described to me his first attempts at using his numb legs again after weeks and weeks of enforced inactivity, he said, "I actually walked today—and I know I was walking because I could see my legs moving!" I could not help but respond, "Well, you've now given epistemic justification a new kind of twist." Seanie, this one's for you.

Introduction

I came across the following story some time ago. Although it is contrived (unsurprisingly—it is in the nature of jokes that they tend to be contrived), I repeat it here, because it arguably resonates with some of the central ideas this book is concerned with.

It was October and the Indigenous Americans on a remote northern reservation asked their new Chief whether the coming winter was going to be cold or mild. Since the Chief grew up in a modern society, he had never been taught the old ways and secrets. When he looked up at the sky, he could not tell what the winter was going to be like. Nevertheless, to be on the safe side he told his people that the winter was indeed going to be cold and that the members of the tribe should collect firewood in anticipation of the cold season ahead. But, being a practical leader, after several days he had an idea. He went to the next phone booth and called the National Weather Service and asked, "Is the coming winter in this area going to be cold or mild?"

The meteorologist responded, "It looks like this winter is going to be quite cold."

So the Chief went back to his people and instructed them to collect even more wood in order to be prepared.

A week later he called the National Weather Service again, "Does it still look like it's going to be a cold winter?"

"Yes," the meteorologist replied, "it's actually going to be a very cold winter."

So the Chief went back to his people and instructed them to go and find every scrap of wood they could find. Two weeks later he called the National Weather Service again: "Are you absolutely sure that the winter is going to be very cold?"

"Absolutely," the man said, "it's looking more and more like it is going to be one of the coldest winters ever."

"How can you be so sure?" the Chief asked.

The weatherman replied, "Our satellites have reported that the people on the reservations are collecting firewood like crazy, and that's always a sure sign."

I have not been able to determine the original source of this story, of which several versions have circulated over the past few years. Nor have I been able to verify whether a Chief who has not been educated in or initiated into the 'old ways' or traditions can be designated or elected leader of an aboriginal community. (This *does* seem rather unlikely.) What is noteworthy about this story is that the traditional, rural community (i.e., the Chief speaking for the indigenous people) and the scientific establishment (i.e., the meteorologist speaking for the weather bureau) appear to rely on each other, with regard to their epistemic justification. Each takes the assumed 'knowledge' of the other as the basis for their own predictions—which not only raises something like the 'chicken-or-the-egg' question but also causes one to doubt whether or not we are actually dealing with *knowledge* here. The joke is derived from the implication that, at least in this instance, it is *both* indigenous truth claims *and* scientific truth claims that constitute myths.

I want to argue the following: science (e.g., meteorology) can—with some degree of accuracy, on the basis of available evidence—make predictions (e.g., about the impending seasons). Similarly, nonscientists (i.e., people not formally schooled or trained in science) can—with some degree of accuracy, on the basis of their own and others' experiences—make certain predictions (e.g., about the weather). But can one really, and meaningfully, distinguish between 'mainstream' and 'indigenous' knowledge? I do not think so—and I will attempt to show in this paper why not.

A further set of questions arises with the definition of, say, 'coldness'—not to mention individual and communal experiences of coldness. These questions do not seem to be immediately relevant to the present concerns—but it may still be illustrative how one might try to address them. While it is clear that experiences of coldness, warmth, and heat vary, it can nonetheless be stated that temperature is objectively measurable. Not only that, but one might also say that (as far as weather is concerned) anything below 0° Celsius is cold, while anything above 40° Celsius is at least very warm. Of course, what is 'cold' to members of a San community is not what is so to members of an Inuit community, and the same thing can be said about experiences and perceptions of what is 'hot'. In fact, our individual perceptions change all the time. Does this mean that everything is relative, that there are only subjective 'truths'? No, because our personal and communal perceptions and experiences relate in some way or other to the way the world is, to how things are.

For example, it is possible for me to perceive (at the same time) the same body of lukewarm water as 'cold' and as 'hot'—depending on where I have previously had my hands. If I place one of my hands in hot water, the other hand in cold water, and then place both in a bucket filled with lukewarm water, the water will feel cold to one hand and very warm (if not hot) to the other. Yet, I *know* the water is lukewarm. It just *seems* cold or hot.

THE NOTION OF INDIGENOUS KNOWLEDGE

Although the manifestation of what is taken to be indigenous knowledge could presumably be traced back roughly to the origins of humankind, the idea of indigenous knowledge is a relatively recent phenomenon. It has arguably gained conceptual and discursive currency only over the past half century, with a veritable slew of conferences, workshops, special journal editions, and anthologies devoted to the topic. Yet, there has been no treatise that offers a comprehensive, critical examination of this notion. Accounts of indigenous knowledge usually focus on explanations of 'indigenous', 'local', 'traditional, 'African' and the like—but to date not a single defense of indigenous knowledge has bothered to explain the particular understanding of 'knowledge' the authors are working with. I have no idea why there has, as yet, been no extensive treatment of the epistemological assumptions, problems, and concerns at work here. I can imagine that it is only a matter of time until other theorists tackle the subject of indigenous knowledge from this less comfortable, counter-current perspective.

I have published in this field since 2004, on indigenous or local knowledge (systems), African ways of knowing, and related fields like knowledge diversity and culturally distinctive epistemologies. My (admittedly ambitious) endeavor in writing this book is to pull all these concerns, ideas, and arguments together in one key work that no future defense of indigenous knowledge (and related ideas) ought to be able to ignore. My hope is that it will provide those who share my concerns with some conceptual and argumentational tools with which to defend their position. Correspondingly, I hope that those who disagree with me will seize the opportunity to attempt to strengthen their position by reflecting on and interrogating the kinds of arguments I advance here—first and foremost, by providing an understanding of knowledge, knowing, and truth, and indeed of epistemology, that is both coherent and compelling. My critique of the idea of indigenous knowledge should in no way be understood as an endorsement of the evils of colonial conquest and (ongoing) exploitation, oppression, and subjugation. Nor should it be taken as an indication of a failure on my part to sympathize with the struggle of indigenous peoples the world over for a dignified and sustainable way of life, for personal and communal space, and for self-determination. My aim is to provide especially 'indigenous' educators with theoretical tools for critical reflection and interrogation of their own and others' preconceptions, assumptions, and epistemic practices and customs.

There are several approaches to the notion of indigenous knowledge:

- Radical culturalist and/or feminist: All knowledge is 'local'. But, given that so-called academic (mainstream, Western, or Northern) or scientific knowledge is irrevocably perverted by power relations (Prakash 1999: 163; Maurial 1999: 64) and tainted by a history of oppression and subjugation, the preferred if not the only 'valid' or 'legitimate' (untainted) knowledge is that emanating from indigenous or native sources, traditional, cultural, and ethnic groups, and subgroups within these groups. Examples of such a position are certain Afrocentric (Asante 1987, 2003, 2005, 2017; Ani 1994; Kunnie 2000: 159, 164, 168), "Africanist" and "Africanization" (Matos 2000: 18; Makgoba and Seepe 2004; Kwaa Prah 2004), and radical feminist approaches (Harding 1987, 1991, 1996, 1998, 2002) that, respectively, privilege Africans' and women's knowledge systems and epistemological standpoints. Proponents of this approach commonly refer to the incommensurability of, or fundamental difference or incompatibility between, "modern knowledge systems," and "other [that is, indigenous] knowledge systems" (Prakash 1999: 160, 167–168; see also Reynar 1999: 301fn.2), and "pyramids of knowledge" (Ramose 1998; Teffo 2000: 106).
- Compatibilist: All knowledge is 'local'. Indigenous knowledge is compatible and should be integrated with so-called 'academic' (mainstream, Western or Northern) or scientific knowledge, which is of course also 'local' (Aikenhead 1996, 2001; Aikenhead and Jegede 1999; Aikenhead and Elliott 2010; Makgoba 1997: 177, 199; Semali and Kincheloe 1999: 28; Le Grange 2004, 2007, 2016: 6; Abdullah and Stringer 1999: 150; Teffo 2000: 106; Odora Hoppers 2002b: 7; Vergès 2002: 174; Fatnowna and Pickett 2002b: 211–212, 2002c: 270; Wallner 2005; Turnbull 2009: 2, 3). An example of indigenous knowledge working hand-in-glove with modern, mainstream digital technology is that of a San hunter being fitted with an electronic tracking device.
- 'Academic right'[1]: All so-called 'indigenous knowledge' is fictitious and therefore scientifically worthless, little more than epistemic and scientific pretense. For example, Africa's contribution to 'world' or 'global' knowledge has been negligible, as have been other indigenous and aboriginal contributions. The verdict, among other things, is that in "the nascent literature of Afrocentric science," for example, there is "an enormous amount of Afrocentrism" and a "remarkable paucity of science" (Gross and Levitt 1998: 205). The classic dismissals of African thought are, of course, those

provided by Immanuel Kant and Georg Wilhelm Friedrich Hegel—articulated with a kind of brazenness that is all but inconceivable today outside of the social media.
- My own (context-sensitive realist) approach: Although it deserves to be taken seriously, as a significant item in postcolonialist reclamation discourses, 'indigenous knowledge' has at best limited applicability, in that it might plausibly be taken to range over various kinds of practical and acquaintance-type knowledge—but not over theoretical (factual or propositional) knowledge. Thus, it is doubtful whether the case of the San hunter offers an example of 'indigenous' knowledge in anything other than an acquaintance-, practical or skill-sense. 'Knowledge diversity' in the relevant sense can be explained in terms of epistemic priorities that emanate from certain living conditions, socioeconomic situations, and particular geographical and historical contexts.

In this book, I argue the following: (1) 'indigenous knowledge' involves at best an incomplete, partial or at worst a questionable understanding or conception of knowledge; and (2) as a tool in anti-discrimination and anti-repression discourse, 'indigenous knowledge' is largely inappropriate. I show, however, that in the development of 'knowledge', following some necessary conceptual readjustments in our understanding of this term, and acknowledging knowers' contexts and epistemic priorities, there is considerably greater common ground than theorists usually admit. It is this acknowledgment, not adherence to a popular concept of debatable coherence and plausibility, that also has profound political, ethical, and educational consequences.

CHAPTER OUTLINE

The first chapter explains the idea of 'indigenous knowledge', as well as the motivation that exists for it, and provides a brief history. 'Indigenous knowledge' is generally taken to cover local, traditional, non-Western beliefs, practices, customs, and worldviews, and frequently also to refer to alternative, informal forms of knowledge. Although some writers reject this contraposition, 'indigenous knowledge' is commonly contrasted, implicitly or explicitly, with 'knowledge from abroad', a 'global', 'cosmopolitan', 'Western', 'academic', 'formal', or 'world' (systems of) knowledge. What the emphasis on indigenous knowledge is meant to achieve includes reclamation of cultural or traditional heritage; decolonization of mind and thought; recognition and acknowledgment of self-determining development; protection against further colonization, exploitation, appropriation, and/or commercialization; legitimation or validation of indigenous practices and worldviews; and condemnation of, or at least caution against, the subjugation of nature and general oppressiveness of nonindigenous rationality, science, and technology.

What is arguably characteristic of African (and other traditional or indigenous) conceptions of knowledge, which are examined in the second chapter, is a strongly relational element that is also found in African ontology and ethics. Coming to know is understood as a process of persons developing insights in relation with one another and with all that exists. This indicates not only an intimate relationship between knower and known, between what it is to know and what it is to be known, but in effect also a communalist understanding of knowledge: *I know because we know.* Or, *A knower is a knower because of other knowers.* This understanding of knowledge relations and knowledge communities then serves to validate indigenous insights and multitudinous ways of knowing, alternative conceptions of knowledge and epistemological diversity. 'Epistemological diversity' embodies the idea that diverse cultural and ethnic groups, and subgroups within these groups—marking differences in gender, sexual orientation, and the like, have their own characteristic epistemologies and distinct ways of knowing.

The third chapter offers definitions of the key terms, 'knowledge' and 'epistemology'. A distinction is made between three distinct senses of knowledge (propositional, theoretical or factual; practical or skill-type; and finally, acquaintance- or familiarity-type knowledge). I then introduce and defend a modified version of the traditional philosophical definition of theoretical knowledge (the three components being belief, truth, and appropriate/suitable justification, with a strong emphasis on the significance of 'context' in justification and in knowledge claims). I conclude the chapter by problematizing constructivism as a theory of knowledge.

With this modified philosophical definition of knowledge in place, which is demonstrably not an exclusively Western construct, I attempt to make sense of the idea of indigenous knowledge in chapter 4. A tentative conclusion is that this notion faces at least two potential problems, those of relativism and superstition. Similar problems are encountered by the notion of 'epistemological diversity'. After providing what is generally taken to be the proper philosophical understanding of 'epistemology', as distinct from other conceptions of epistemology, I examine how one might make sense, in this regard, of the notion of 'diversity'.

Chapters 5, 6, and 7 examine special applications of 'indigenous knowledge' and 'epistemological diversity' in educational contexts and elsewhere. Thus, 'ethnomathematics' and 'indigenous science' (and subcategories like 'indigenous archeology', 'ethnoastronomy', or 'ethnobotany'), respectively, have been invoked in a quest for both relevance and epistemological access in teaching and learning. A careful analysis reveals both phenomena to be conceptually problematic, insufficiently plausible on a theoretical level, and practically confused—as exemplified by the invocation of 'feminist algebra'. Traditional ecological or environmental knowledge seeks to straddle the traditional divide between the empirical and the normative, by bringing indigenous values to bear on scientific practice, especially on questions of sustainability. Like 'ethnomathematics' and 'indigenous science', however, it is revealed to be conceptually problematic. Some doubts can also be raised about the values at work here, which are predominantly anthropocentric and often even tend to be ethnocentric.

Chapter 8 discusses the subject of moral knowledge and examines the application of 'indigenous knowledge' to ethics, values, and considerations of social justice, and in particular the proximity of indigenous knowledge to questionable meta-ethical theories like cultural and moral relativism. After I discuss, and dismiss, the case for the latter kinds of particularity and perspectivalism, I advance the argument that, like the ideas of 'knowledge' and 'truth', ethical values have universal purchase. What ultimately seems to unite the plausible meta-ethical views (e.g., ethical objectivism, moral realism, and universal prescriptivism) is an acknowledgment of the requirements of rationality and impartiality as well as an objective notion of reasons for action. Moral facts are perceived to be those objective or external factors that provide individuals with a reason or reasons for action.

Chapter 9 deals with the important idea of 'epistemic justice'. It also includes recommendations, regarding rectification of past injustices and so-called 'epistemic marginalization', that is, of the nonrecognition and misrecognition of indigenous people's contributions to 'world' or 'global' knowledge. These recommendations take the form of a hybrid approach that combines a justice/rights orientation with one that foregrounds empathetic and sympathetic understanding, by advocating what might be called epistemic empathy.

Postcolonial theory presumably errs in postulating the existence of diverse knowledges and truths. Nonetheless, the diversity in question is conceivably generated by (characteristically) practical epistemic priorities—priorities that emanate from different lived experiences, individual as well as social and cultural. A plausible view, examined and defended in chapters 4 and 10, appears to be that knowledge and truth do not fluctuate, that they remain invariant across individuals, societies, and cultures, but that there may well be idiosyncratic sets of epistemic concerns that emerge from personal, historical, and sociopolitical circumstances. If it is correct to assume that practical epistemic and educational priorities will arise from life experiences and from the ways these are socially articulated, then one might reasonably assume that, given the different life experiences of people across the globe, the practical epistemic, and educational priorities will also differ.

The promise of an applied epistemology for the real world, then, has in part to do with locality and context-specific relations—but not in terms of any exclusionist, 'hands-off' approach. Rather, it appears to be plausible that the particular historical, geographic, and sociocultural experiences of people give rise to particular priorities that shape their epistemic theory and practice—and also yield conceptual and epistemological tools that are likely to enrich education and educational research as a whole.

Although the chapters in this book follow a certain narrative, sequential structure, they are also meant to be readable and intelligible when studied on their own, that is, as more or less self-contained essays. It is therefore inevitable that there will be some repetition of ideas and variation of arguments. I trust that this will not be deemed patronizing but seen, rather, as a series of well-intentioned reminders of the elements, or fibers, of the red thread running through this book.

NOTE

1. I have based this somewhat tendentious label on Paul Gross and Norman Levitt's (1998) disparaging and equally tendentious reference to "the academic left", a diverse group that includes various kinds of postmodernists and constructivists, ethnoepistemologists, bricoleurs, culturalists, and feminists. (I have borrowed the notions of "bricoleurs"/"bricolage" and "culturalists"/"culturalism" from Claude Lévi-Strauss [1979] and Elizabeth Rata [2012a and 2012b], respectively).

Chapter 1

The Idea of Indigenous Knowledge

THE SAN-*HOODIA* CASE

In 2003, after decades of marginalization, nonrecognition, and dispossession, the fate of the Southern African San[1] finally seemed to take a turn for the better. A deal had been signed between South Africa's Council of Scientific and Industrial Research (CSIR) and the South African San Council (representing the Khomani, !Xun and Khwe tribes) to share royalties accruing from commercial sales of *Hoodia gordonii*. This plant, a spiny, leafless succulent, is called *!Khoba* by the San communities and has been used for countless generations, not only because of its ability to treat stomach aches and eye infections but also because of its thirst-quenching and appetite-suppressant properties, especially during their long and energy-sapping hunting excursions in the Kalahari Desert. In 1977, the CSIR conducted research to isolate the ingredient responsible for the plant's appetite-suppressant effect and patented this ingredient, which became known as P57, in 1996.[2] A license was then granted to UK-based Phytopharm, who collaborated with Pfizer, in order to synthesize and later market the active ingredients as a wonder drug against obesity. Following publication of the uninformed remark by a Pfizer representative, Richard Dixey, to the effect that *Hoodia* had been used as an appetite-suppressant by a now-extinct ethnic group, intervention by a team of lawyers acting on behalf of the San secured them intellectual property rights over the plant and a percentage of the royalties, profits, and any spin-offs emanating from the commercial use, marketing, and sales of the plant (Wynberg et al. 2009). South African human rights lawyer Roger Chennels, who took up the San's case, said they immediately challenged the CSIR. "The negotiations were tough," according to the lawyer (ibid.),

9

but the San had the moral high ground. Once their moral ownership of the intellectual property rights was recognized, and once they wisely agreed to enter into a partnership, the dealings became reasonable.

Following the signing of the agreement on March 24, 2003, in Molopo (South Africa), the chairman of the San Council, Petrus Vaalbooi, said,

> We are thankful that the traditional knowledge of our forefathers is acknowledged by this important agreement, and that we are making it known to the world. As San leaders we are determined to protect all aspects of our heritage. (Wynberg and Chennells 2009: 88).

As Kxao Moses ‡Oma, Chairperson of the Board of Trustees of the Working Group for Indigenous Minorities in Southern Africa (WIMSA), noted at the celebration of the agreement,

> For years the San culture—including our traditional knowledge—has been put to use by external parties for multiple purposes, with little or no benefit accruing to the San . . . The international interest that the agreement between the San and the CSIR has aroused has helped the San umbrella body, WIMSA, to raise awareness of the need to protect and control San intellectual property.[3]

Chennells, who had also been fighting the San's legal battle for restitution of their traditional land, said in the CSIR press release[4] that he believes the deal represents notable recognition and acknowledgment of the importance of the traditional knowledge and heritage of the San peoples:

> This groundbreaking, benefit-sharing agreement between a local research council and the San represents enormous potential for future bioprospecting successes based on the San's extensive knowledge of the traditional uses of indigenous plants of the area. We are optimistic that this case will serve as a sound foundation for future collaboration, not only for the San but also for other holders of traditional knowledge.

Pfizer later stopped development, owing to difficulties encountered in the synthesizing process. Apparently, there were indications of side effects on the liver caused by other components that were difficult to remove from the manufactured product. The resultant slack was picked up by Unilever who entered into an agreement with Phytopharm in 2004 to begin marketing *Hoodia* in a variety of diet drinks and energy bars. Apart from the bandwagon effect, with all kinds of products flooding the market claiming to contain the active ingredient when they evidently did not, an additional problem was that the appetite-suppressant properties could not be established conclusively. Unilever pulled out of the agreement with Phytopharm in 2008, and in 2010, Phytopharm relinquished the patenting rights to South Africa. The clinical study that led to this decision was published in 2011 and revealed that the active ingredient's effect can be compared to that of a placebo. Although public demand has diminished a little over the years, it continues to this day, and *Hoodia* products are currently marketed largely in the form of diet pills.

The *Hoodia* deal and the expected financial benefits have been widely acknowledged to be instrumental in reconstructing San identity, society, and culture, especially through publicizing the tribal elders' 'traditional knowledge'—the 'knowledge of the old ways'.

'INDIGENOUS KNOWLEDGE'

Although the manifestation of what is generally taken to be indigenous knowledge could presumably be traced back roughly to the origins of humankind, the notion of indigenous knowledge is a fairly recent phenomenon. It has gained conceptual and discursive currency, arguably, only during the last forty years. Especially in the new millennium, it has been the subject of congresses, conferences, workshops, as well as countless essays, articles, opinion pieces, and reports. Among many other things, it constitutes part of a challenge to 'Western' (or 'Northern') education. Proponents of traditional or local knowledge and indigenous knowledge systems maintain that its study has a profound effect on education and educational curricula (see Semali 1999: 97; Crossman and Devisch 2002: 110), on what is being taught and how learning is to be stimulated and enriched.

'Indigenous knowledge' is generally taken to cover local, traditional, non-Western beliefs, worldviews, skills, practices, and customs, and frequently also to refer to alternative, subaltern, or informal forms of knowledge. Thus, U.S.-based academics Ladislaus Semali and Joe Kincheloe (1999: 12) refer to "the skills to function in the traditional society" and to the "knowledges that manifest themselves in local history, traditional stories, and folklore" (49). With "the body of unofficial knowledge" Tanzania-born Semali (1999: 98) also associates "anecdotal memories of customary law, inheritance rights, beliefs about witchcraft, taboos, and rituals, which form the wisdom of how things were [and still continue to be] done." When speaking of indigenous or "African knowledge systems," Pitika Ntuli (2002: 54, 55), South African sculptor, poet, writer and academic, has in mind "natives'['] . . . worldviews and belief systems." Sometimes a distinction is made between knowledge and practice or skills. "For Africans," says Semali (1999: 95), "indigenous knowledge is about what people know and do, and what they have done and known for generations—practices that developed through trial and error and proved flexible enough to cope with change." Later in his chapter, he emphasizes both "the authority of elders" and "practical knowledge" (101), "prior knowledge," as well as "indigenous literacy skills" (106, 107). Based at the Aboriginal Education Unit and Curtin Indigenous Research Centre in Western Australia, Scott Fatnowna and Harry Pickett (2002c: 270), too, speak of both "indigenous knowledge and practices," which seems to indicate an understanding of indigenous knowledge as encompassing both knowledge-that and knowledge-how. I will examine the distinction between propositional and practical knowledge in chapter 3.

Although some writers reject this contraposition,[5] 'indigenous knowledge' is commonly contrasted, implicitly or explicitly, with 'knowledge from abroad', 'mainstream', 'global', 'cosmopolitan', 'Western', 'colonial', 'formal', 'academic', or 'world' (systems of) knowledge (see Semali 1999: 114; Mwadime 1999: 247; Viergever 1999: 334, 335; Odora Hoppers 2002b: 14; Fatnowna and Pickett 2002b: 217). According to Semali and Kincheloe (1999: 51),

> If the discourse of Western science is mechanistic, exact, hypothesis driven, and in search of laws, universal generalizations, and ground theories, the discourse of many indigenous knowledge systems is metaphysical, based on the forces that connect people to one another, and inseparable from religion. Often agricultural, culinary, medical, architectural knowledges in indigenous discourses are intricately intertwined with the theological realm.

Brazil-based development coordinator Marcel Viergever (1999: 334-335) claims that "there can be no doubt that traditional communities possess another type of knowledge than urban communities in Western or Westernized societies." Quoting from the International Labour Organization document, 'Convention 169', IKS ('indigenous knowledge systems') specialist Catherine Odora Hoppers (2005: 2) describes 'indigenous knowledge' as

> knowledge that is held and used by a people who identify themselves as indigenous of a place on a combination of cultural distinctiveness and prior territorial occupancy relative to a more recently arrived population with its own distinct and subsequently dominant culture.

According to legal theorist Luvuyo Dondolo (2005: 116), similarly:

> Local Knowledge is a complex system of knowledge that is local and unique to a particular population within a specific geographical area. Local Knowledge ... manifests itself in various aspects of social life. ... [It] is socially constructed

and resides in living memories, practises, and expressions of the practicing communities. . . . In post-colonial and post-apartheid Africa, aspects of Local Knowledge have been recognized and revitalized. . . . Local Knowledge is characterized by its own epistemology and its own organisational structures for the creation of knowledge. *Ways of knowing vary with cultures, locations, historical periods, and gender.* (emphasis added)

The attributes of social construction and cultural variance are significant here (see also Semali and Kincheloe 1999: 47) and will be discussed in detail in the chapters that follow. David Turnbull (2009: 3) of the Australian Center for Science Innovation and Society has provided a lengthy account of his understanding of indigenous or local knowledge that is worth quoting also for what it leaves out, namely a conception or definition of knowledge:

Local knowledge . . . is a generic term referring to knowledge generated through observations of a particular environment or at a particular site and produced by a specific group of people with specific practices and tools. Indigenous knowledge is local knowledge held by indigenous peoples, or local knowledge unique to a given culture or society based in particular relationships to the land or place, rather than in the special sense of descent from original or pre-conquest inhabitants. It is a way of life, a way of knowing, as noted by Berkes and Berkes (2009: 8). This blurs the distinction between indigenous and non-indigenous, since in some sense we are all indigenous and all knowledge including science is local. But, it reveals the inherent tension in conceptions of scientific knowledge as universal and placeless which are nonetheless thoroughly place-based.

Turnbull notes that traditional knowledge is "a cumulative body of knowledge and beliefs" that evolves "by adaptive processes" and is "handed down through generations by cultural transmission that may be held by particular groups or professions":

So rather than restrict cultural diversity to language or [indigenous knowledges], it should also embrace the entire range of local knowledges such as the knowledge of gardeners, herbalists, sailors, farmers, artists, translators and so on. It should also include knowledge and practices from the past such as the earlier inhabitants of the Amazon who were able to sustain an urban population in the rainforest. (Ibid.)

Turnbull takes this "'localist' perspective on knowledge traditions" to reveal "their multiple performative and practice-based dimensions." He considers this "performative understanding" to reveal that knowledges are dynamic, heterogeneous, social, and distributed, they are not unified, coherent or located in the heads of individuals, rather they are experimental, messy, inconsistent, collective, and in the process of continuous adaptation and negotiation. Their assemblage requires considerable work in coordinating commensurability and creating equivalences. (Ibid.)

"Not unified," "not coherent," "messy," "inconsistent"—what makes them *knowledges*, then, over and above accumulations of performative skills, practices, or of mere beliefs, and how could their 'commensurability' possibly be 'coordinated'? Odora Hoppers (2005: 2), who also considers all knowledge to be locally anchored, refers to traditional knowledge as

> the totality of all knowledges and practices, whether explicit or implicit, used in the management of socio-economic, spiritual, and ecological facets of life. In that sense, it can be contrasted with 'cosmopolitan knowledge' that is culturally anchored in Western cosmology, scientific discoveries, economic preferences, and philosophies.

The focus on indigenous knowledge has several purposes: reclamation of cultural or traditional heritage; decolonization of mind and thought; recognition and acknowledgment of self-determining development; protection against further colonization, exploitation, appropriation and/or commercialization; legitimation or validation of indigenous practices and worldviews; and condemnation of, or at least caution against, the subjugation of nature and general oppressiveness of nonindigenous rationality, science, and technology. A common (and certainly justified) complaint is that multinational corporations make substantial profits from indigenous biodiversity but do not share these with the local communities who discovered, stored, and transmitted the relevant knowledge.[6]

Advocates of indigenous knowledge (systems) emphasize its significance in anti-racist, anti-sexist, and postcolonialist discourse, in general, and in terms of the 'African Renaissance', in particular (I return to this idea later). South African academic and newspaper columnist Sipho Seepe writes:

> Africanization of knowledge . . . refers to a process of placing the African worldview at the centre of analysis . . . [and] advocates for the need to foreground African indigenous knowledge systems to address [Africa's] problems and challenges. . . . Apart from the fact that one can be pro-African and not necessarily anti-White, the concept of Afrocentric orientation is pre-eminently about how one views data/information. (Seepe 2000: 119)

He continues (120), "Afrocentrists . . . do not claim that historians, sociologists, literary critics, philosophers do not make valuable contributions, but rather that by using the Eurocentric approach they often ignore an important interpretive key to the African experience." Seepe goes on to say (ibid., 132),

> Starting with indigenous knowledge systems would encourage learners to draw on their cultural practices and daily experiences as they negotiate and grapple with new situations and unfamiliar terrain. . . . According to Ubiratan D'Ambrosio . . ., who coined the term *ethnomathematics*, mathematical practices refer not only to formal symbolic systems but also to concrete physical activities that illustrate the difference in quantities. Similar understanding can be extended to ethnoscience.

Ntuli suggests that the call to "decolonize the mind" be acted on. He contends that the African "renaissance as a rebirth requires us to re-examine our knowledge system anew" (Ntuli 2002: 54). He states further, "To invoke African knowledge systems as a basis upon which to build new knowledge systems, for the purposes of contributing to the task of bringing about Africa's rebirth, requires us to embark on a journey of reclamation (of) . . . African culture, religion and values for an African development" (55).

These, then, are perhaps the key questions:

- What kind of understanding of 'knowledge' do appeals to 'indigenous knowledge', 'Africanization of knowledge', diverse and/or multicultural epistemologies, and so forth involve? Writers are commonly rather unclear and vague about their understanding of 'epistemology' and whether they mean skills, beliefs, or worldviews, or familiarity ('practical', 'factual or propositional', or 'acquaintance-type' knowledge; see chapter 3), and, indeed, seem to vacillate between these three.[7]
- What does the 'knowledge' in question cover? It ranges over all kinds of indigenous and traditional worldviews and skills, as well as disciplines that have now been called 'ethnomathematics' (see chapter 5), 'indigenous science', 'traditional medicine', 'ethnozoology', 'ethnobotany', and so on (see chapter 6), and also traditional, indigenous people's familiarity with each other's customs, their environment and the terrain as well as with the local flora and fauna (see chapter 7).
- What is the function of the terms 'indigenous', 'local', 'traditional', or 'Southern' in this regard? They are usually meant to set this type of knowledge apart, often by way of criticism, from so-called 'Western' ('Northern'), 'international', 'global' or 'world' knowledge, commonly also to signal that—for example—Aboriginal, Māori, San, Dogon, Palikur, and Mexica knowledge are unique, and distinct (perhaps even fundamentally different) from all other knowledge or knowledges. Coupled with the demands for 'decolonization', 'reclamation', 'recognition', 'legitimization'

or 'validation' of traditional knowledge and diverse knowledge systems is the call to protect these from exploitation.

RECLAMATION

The etymological origin of the concept of reclamation is interesting, in that its original Latin meaning *reclamare* is 'to cry out against'. The implication of past injustice is also captured in the common sense understanding, seeking the return of (e.g., one's property). Speaking about African knowledge systems, in particular, as the basis for building "new knowledge systems, for the purposes of contributing to Africa's rebirth," Ntuli (2002: 55) considers it mandatory "to embark on a journey of reclamation." After illustrating the "long and varied provenance" of the term, he settles on its definition as "the action of claiming the return of something taken away," in this case "African culture, religion, and values for African development." Yet, he is aware that the "reclamation project" he is suggesting "acknowledges that no past can be recovered in its pristine form" (66). Similarly, president of the (South African) Human Sciences Research Council Mokubung Nkomo (2000: 54) urges that "formerly silenced indigenous knowledge systems should be brought back to life through a renewed African research in education process informed by the scientific method of inquiry." American Africana Studies scholar Julian Kunnie (2000: 170) emphasizes the "revalorization of indigenous philosophies and their insertion into the socio-educational fabric of post-apartheid society." The physical domain of reclamation is articulated by American associate professor of geography Joe Bryan (2009: 24, 25, 27), when he describes the power dynamics that are implicit in efforts by indigenous peoples to reclaim their territory and to fight for corresponding rights. On a similar note, according to North American Indigenous Studies scholars Jeff Corntassel and Tiffanie Hardbarger (2019: 89), "As a reframing of decolonization, Indigenous resurgence is about reclaiming relationships grounded in land, culture and community that promote the health and well-being of Indigenous Nations."

DECOLONIZATION

'Decolonization' refers essentially to the liberation (of a colony) from dependency. Linda Tuhiwai Smith, the leading theorist on Māori decolonization in New Zealand, argues that the business of colonialism is far from being unfinished, however. She considers 'decolonization' a euphemism that only describes the formal handing over of the instruments of government, when in reality it is a long-term process involving the cultural, linguistic, and psychological dismantling of colonial parameters. Among many other things, it covers epistemological decolonization or desuperiorization of Western or Northern knowledge (see also Hall and Tandon 2017; Mbembe n.d.; Ndlovu-Gatsheni 2018: 3, 60–64; Freter 2020; De Sousa Santos and Meneses 2020), and also methodological decolonization, or decolonization of research methods (see Chan-Tiberghien 2010; Keane et al. 2016; Khupe and Keane 2017; Keane et al. 2017; Mataira 2019; Nelson-Barber and Johnson 2019; Sumida Huanan 2019). After identifying the following elements of decolonization: deconstruction and reconstruction; self-determination and social justice; ethics, language, internationalization of indigenous experiences, history and critique, Smith (1999) introduces the concept of Kaupapa Māori as a new way of thinking about Māori indigenous research: "We have a different epistemological tradition which frames the way we see the world, the way we organize ourselves in it, the questions we ask and the solutions we seek" (187–188). Māori indigenous research is research with a strong anti-positivistic stance, primarily concerned with the issues of social justice and of relevance to the Māori community. Research should set out to make a positive difference for the researched, and the participation of nonindigenous researchers is either squarely ruled out or accepted only under certain conditions (183–193). A more conciliatory, less exclusive or 'hands-off' approach is manifest in the writing of Réunion-born European Studies specialist Françoise Vergès (1999: 174), who refers to a "process of decolonization—that is, of retrieving and developing indigenous systems of thought" that fosters "a search for hybrid systems of knowledge that weave European and non-European forms of thought together" (see also Aikenhead and Elliott 2010; Le Grange 2016).

Fatnowna and Pickett (2002a: 75) note that it "is not just knowledge itself that needs to be decolonized, but also the systems of knowledge production and legitimation." Coupled with the call for decolonization is very often an emphasis on relevance in education (Matos 2000: 16). As Narciso Matos, rector at the Universidade Polytécnica in Maputo (Mozambique), puts it (18):

> Rethinking the content of higher education in Africa must . . . begin with valorizing, seeking to understand, and transmitting to students and to the community at large the knowledge base on which African societies are organized. It requires an understanding of the mathematical and geometrical concepts involved in building houses and granaries, in weaving baskets or painting walls, in designing elaborate patterns on pottery and cloth. It involves a willingness to further the current understanding of the pharmacological and medicinal properties of plants and other materials used in traditional African medicine. It challenges academicians to study the traditional processes of land irrigation and the biological foundations on which the common popular practices of crop rotation

and the selection and combination of certain types of crops are based. Modern African . . . education needs to recognize the value and the wisdom informing the provision of local justice, the laws governing land tenure and inheritance, as well as the systems of government and succession of leadership. In sum, science [and] education—and in particular higher education—need to acknowledge African traditions and practices, and work towards eliciting and understanding their fundamentals, so as to include these in the education provided to new generations of children, students, and thinkers.

One could go on: one should include in the curricula "the knowledge present in African society" in children's and students' mother-tongue, "[l]iterature, poetry, art in all forms and manifestations, history, religion, cosmogony, and in general culture" (19).

Thus, decolonization is frequently given a regional interpretation. As the previous set of examples indicates, it is often treated as synonymous or at least as closely allied with Africanization. Associated with reclamation, Kunnie (2000: 164, 170) also invokes a decolonization movement within advocacy of indigenous education and knowledge, which he connects with "re-Africanization." According to U.S. Afrocentrist scholar Molefi Kete Asante (2005: 40),

> the critique of Western and Westernized epistemologies constitutes an important part of African epistemology. Moreover, in the postcolonial era world, where the limitations of the dominant Western concepts have become obvious, it is imperative . . . to decolonize knowledge, by exploring different ways of knowing.

Asante goes on to explain that "African epistemology comprises four basic African ways of *knowing* that can be separated into three categories, the supernatural, the natural, and the paranormal paths to knowledge." The supernatural mode "includes divination . . . and revelation (i.e., messages revealed in dreams and visions)" (ibid.). These two "cognitive modes" involve "the intervention of supernatural beings—spirits, ancestors, dead relatives, gods, goddesses—who impart knowledge" to living humans "directly through a dream or vision," or "indirectly through mediums, diviners, animals, extraordinary life events, or natural phenomena that require a special kind of information" (ibid.). In the natural way of knowing, writes Asante, "human beings gain knowledge by using their natural faculties and abilities, including intuition . . . , which consists of the work of the human heart (i.e., feeling and insight), and reason, which consists of a natural investigation of reality through the human intellect and logical thought process" (ibid.). The third category, the paranormal mode, comprises "extrasensory perception (ESP), which includes such modes as clairvoyance and telepathy" (41). Divination is not only "a trusted means of decision making" but is also "a basic source of vital knowledge" (ibid.): "through a healthy decolonization of knowledge, postcolonial scholarship has shown that divination is not an irrational practice by some charlatan or obtuse superstitious mystificators, but rather a powerful epistemological approach by men and women of exceptional wisdom and high personal character" (ibid.).

In some instances, authors invoke Kenyan author Ngũgĩ wa Thiong'o's notion of "decolonization of the mind," a kind of reconceptualization and anti-colonial reclamation process involving thought and language (Wa Thiong'o 1986; see Smith 1999: 59, 108; Ntuli 2002: 53; Ndlovu-Gatsheni 2018: 43, 58). For example, this notion has been adapted and deepened by Ghanaian philosopher Kwasi Wiredu (2008). The reasoning is as follows: Africa, and in particular education on the African continent, is to be transformed through a process of decolonization of the mind. During and after colonization, Africans' own thinking and educational systems were eclipsed by the thinking and policies of the dominant minorities. Eventually, writes Wiredu (2008), the very philosophy of Africans was written by foreigners employing the conceptual framework of foreigners. Inevitably, there have been distortions. Africans have been brought up on foreign literature and foreign thinking, so their own thinking is in terms of the conceptual framework brought from abroad. Africans, according to Wiredu, need to be clear about their own traditional thought, which has to be recovered by removing several layers of foreign, imposed conceptualization. They ought to try to think through their own language again, to formulate and test their own theorizing in their own languages.

The emphasis on the importance of language and the idea of decolonization of the mind are both appealing and plausible. Given that language is a system of symbolization for ideas and, at a deeper level, used to conceptualize ideas which are then symbolized: if all learning is done in a foreign language, those symbols—and the very ideas they symbolize—are conceptualized in a foreign language. When people learn about the world and to philosophize in in a foreign language, Wiredu contends (ibid.), they become fixated on manners of conceptualization that are not congruent with our own. The solution is to go back to one's own language and examine one's own ways of conceptualization, and then to make critical comparisons with those of other people. At the deeper conceptual levels, says Wiredu, colonization has led to subservience in thinking. Having a foreign framework imposed on that conceptualization results in intellectual subservience and an unconscious adherence to foreign concepts.

The importance of mother-tongue education can certainly not be overemphasized. But does mental or intellectual decolonization mean rejecting every foreign influence? In the 1970s, Wa Thiong'o, together with his colleagues, Taban lo Liyong and Henry Uwuor-Anyumba, motivated for the abolition of the department of English at the University of Nairobi, in favor of a department of African Literature: "To orientate ourselves toward placing Kenya at the center. All other things are to be considered in their relevance to our situation" (Wa Thiong'o 1986: 145). Drawing on Wiredu, former vice-chancellor of the University of KwaZulu-Natal in South Africa William Malegapuru Makgoba claims that for South African universities to achieve transformation and, indeed, mental decolonization, "this means discarding the English-speaking and liberal images" (Makgoba 1997: 187). Apart from wanting to replace (Latin) mottos and hymns (see Makgoba 2003)—which makes good sense, as does the dismantling of symbols of colonialism like the statue of Cecil John Rhodes (see chapter 2)[8]—Makgoba appears to advocate discarding the English language as an instructional medium. Indeed, in a 1998 copresentation at the University of the Witwatersrand with Pretoria-based researcher Console Tleane, Makgoba, and Tleane (1998) pleaded for a replacement of the colonial languages by four basic African language groups, Nguni, Sotho, Venda, and Pondo. (A considerably less radical plea is made in Makgoba and Seepe 2004.)

It is unclear whether this is likely to enable (South) Africa to be internationally competitive (Makgoba 2003: 2) or to contribute to "world knowledge." There is also the concern that the invention of new terminology is an avoidably forced and artificial process that replaces one form of foreign intellectual framework with another. Given young and adolescent learners' well-known capacity for language acquisition, any talk of 'abolition' and 'replacement' is likely to promote mental decolonization at the expense of a kind of educational impoverishment in other respects. Beninese philosopher Paulin Hountondji (2000: 43) proceeds a little more subtly:

> It is up to the African elites and decision makers to initiate new language policies that promote African languages as means for scientific expression and communication, instead of the exclusive use of their colonizers' languages . . . (T)he idea that some languages are too poor to express the subtleties of modern science and though is a prejudice which, like many commonplace prejudices, has also been unfortunately defended and elaborated on by some scholars and theoreticians. This prejudice does not resist the slightest scrutiny.

Unfortunately, Hountondji fails to provide examples. That the categorical imperative, the theory of general and special relativity, the concept of entropy, and so forth, cannot be done justice in traditional African languages may well be a prejudice, but Hountondji would do well to demonstrate this via translation, and without inventing a new vocabulary.

According to Macedo (1999: xv), "It is only through the decolonization of our minds, if not our hearts, that we can begin to develop the necessary political clarity . . . to begin to humanize the meaning and usefulness of indigeneity." In this regard, South African educational theorist Lesley Le Grange (2016: 9) draws on the relational ontology embodied by the African principle of humanness ("I am because we are") and argues that a "decolonized curriculum is evidenced by a shift in subjectivity from the arrogant 'I' (of Western individualism) to the humble 'I'—to the 'I' that is embedded, embodied, extended and enacted." Whether or not the association of (Western) individualism with arrogance and selfishness is tenable is an issue that is deferred to later chapters.

RECOGNITION AND ACKNOWLEDGMENT

Recognition is commonly seen as a vital human need and contrasted with nonrecognition and misrecognition. It is associated with acknowledgment of self-determining development. Nonrecognition involves the denial or active thwarting of such development, while misrecognition frequently involves well-meaning aid and assistance that ends up stifling any sense of autonomy and corresponding development.

"Indigenous knowledge systems, according to Fatnowna and Pickett (2002c: 263), "require protocols of recognition and protection, acknowledgement of ways of self-determining development, and negotiated processes of relationship with other knowledge systems." Social anthropologists Peter Crossman and René Devisch from Belgium (2002: 98, 99) articulate their preference for the term 'endogenous' over 'indigenous': "While the term indigenous might well comprise the site-specific character of knowledges . . . , it does not comprise that all-important nuance borne by endogenous: development determined by innate resources." This indicates a refusal on the part of the authors to solely "situate indigenous knowledge in an archaic, ahistorical or even 'primitive' past—as often happens when one uses the term tradition." The distinction between indigenous and endogenous certainly merits consideration—but Crossman and Devisch fail to make more of their preferred concept. That is, they might have contrasted endogenous with exogenous knowledge, knowledge that is foreign to or outside of a particular locality. For the purposes of my argument here, then, I merely note the authors' emphasis on the function of knowledge in self-determining development.

Perhaps three forms of recognition can be identified: emotional (love, devotion, or affection), legal (acknowledgment of rights, legal claims and entitlements, liberties, and immunities), and social/moral estimation or esteem (respect, solidarity). Misdirecting, ignoring, stifling, or thwarting any of these can result in serious harm to the individuals or groups concerned.

LEGITIMIZATION AND VALIDATION

Connected, both conceptually and practically, with recognition and acknowledgment is the call for the legitimization and validation of indigenous knowledge (systems). Thus, Crossman and Devisch (2002) speak of the failure of anthropology to legitimize indigenous knowledge, while U.S. educationalist Frances Rains (1999: 328–329) emphasizes that it is "essential that indigenous knowledge be acknowledged as legitimate and valuable, but just as importantly, it is crucial to understand how it can be denied, for therein lies the power to consider change, to consider social justice, as well the social and political ramifications of a hegemony composed of historical amnesia and intellectual authority." Fatnowna and Pickett (2002a: 75), as we saw, stress the decolonization not only of knowledge but also of "the systems of knowledge production and legitimation." Xhosa-born U.S.-based scholar Ivy Goduka (2000: 63) questions the exclusion and marginalization of "other ways of knowing" by "a view of reason" and "methods for making judgements (, . . .) a method of investigation in which valid knowledge is thought to be rationally determined." Other scholars who refer to the legitim(iz)ation, validation and reliability of indigenous knowledge (systems) are Kunnie (2000: 165), Seepe (2000: 134), Zimbabwean educational scholar Edward Shizha (2006: 27–29), and South African political economist Sabelo Ndlovu-Gatsheni (2018: 3, 137–157) (see also Smith 1999: 63; Keane et al. 2016: 177).

For Odora Hoppers (2002b: 12), one of the key policy issues that the study of indigenous knowledge systems addresses is "the knowledge legitimation and, and accreditation culture and procedures." Semali and Kincheloe (1999: 34, 35) list as one of the educational benefits of the study of indigenous or subjugated knowledges the focusing of "attention on the ways knowledge is produced and legitimated." For example, they say, educators "begin to understand the social construction of knowledge and truth" and thus "are able to uncover the socially created hierarchies that travel incognito as truth." I will argue later not only that talk of 'legitimate' and 'valid' knowledge presupposes that there could be 'illegitimate' or 'invalid' knowledge—'legitimated' knowledge as opposed to what?—and that such talk therefore involves a tautology, but also that the truth of the claim that all knowledge and truth are socially constructed must also be a social construct, and therefore cannot be universally valid, which will give rise to all kinds of problems (logical as well as practical) of coherence and consistency.

PROTECTION

The San-*Hoodia* case discussed at the beginning of this chapter illustrates the urgent need for protection of indigenous resources and the importance of a revised understanding of intellectual property rights. Thus, Viergever (1999: 333, 334) considers it to be "of critical importance to the survival of indigenous communities" to "preserve their knowledge," to "identify strategies to conserve the social structures through which that knowledge is generated, and to protect it from appropriation by others," for example, by "pharmaceutical industries." Fatnowna and Pickett (2002c: 263), as we saw, emphasize the requirement of "protocols of recognition and protection" for indigenous knowledge systems, "and negotiated processes of relationship with other knowledge systems."

Margarita Flórez Alonso (2007) articulates the imperative of protecting the "traditional knowledge associated with biological diversity" (251) and that is threatened by the Western (Northern) biotechnological industrial complex. The latter seeks immunity via a particular understanding and interpretation of environmental legislation, intellectual property rights, and 'ownership' that do not tally with the understanding and interpretation of indigenous communities. Traditional peoples and communities' own internal customs and mores, contends Flórez Alonso, should set the parameters for protection and prevail over competing Western interests and legal constructs. For

> us, the citizens of developing nations, the patenting of animals, plants, or microorganisms is unacceptable, because they are part of our genetic and biological heritage. We cannot allow these resources to become—even temporarily—the monopoly of individuals or companies, since they are our heritage, our legacy, and have been given to us by physical, biological, social, and cultural conditions. They are to be used for our benefit, and shared with others. We should valorize the knowledge of a culture with a lifestyle different from ours, and it is the lifestyle that should receive priority, rather than the culture's possible skills in conserving and maintaining biological diversity, or any use that is made of its knowledge. (268)

Tewolde Egziabher (2007), of the Environmental Protection Authority of Ethiopia, cautions against both the introduction of genetically modified crops and plants and the global imposition of a Eurocentric (or 'North-centric') legal monoculture of intellectual property rights. He maintains that both indigenous interests and biodiversity are best promoted and safeguarded via the introduction of a global regime of community rights. I will pay closer attention to traditional ecological knowledge, local values, and the challenge of cultural relativism in chapters 7 and 8.

CRITIQUE AND CONDEMNATION OF WESTERN OR NORTHERN EPISTEMOLOGIES AND RATIONALITY

By some distance, the largest part of the literature on indigenous knowledge and related issues and ideas is devoted to the critique and condemnation of Western or Northern epistemologies (just insofar as these have been articulated at the expense of indigenous or Southern epistemologies, or in terms of rejecting or belittling indigenous science and rationality), as a survey of only a few of the available anthologies and collections of essays shows (see, e.g., Semali and Kincheloe, eds. 1999; Higgs et al., eds. 2000; Odora Hoppers, ed. 2002; Higgs et al., eds. 2004; and De Sousa Santos, ed. 2007). Only a few examples of such critique must suffice here, although I will return to these (frequently valid) objections and concerns throughout this book.

Semali (in Semali and Kincheloe 1999: 9, 10) recounts his own experience of how "indigenous education, history, and multiple ways of knowing" are commonly replaced by or subjugated to "the new and 'superior' knowledge" that "preferred the morals, customs, and ways of knowing brought by missionaries as well as colonial rulers." Odora Hoppers (2002a: vii) targets "the arrogance of practice . . . still rife in formal institutions that are confidently, and without qualms, determined to continue with the monochrome logic of Western epistemology," while "the works of Le Grange and Aikenhead have been essentially concerned with critiquing the marginalization, denigration and decimation of indigenous knowledges" (Le Grange and Aikenhead 2017: 32[9]).

Rather perplexingly, while a lot has been said and continues to be said about the idea of indigeneity (see Semali and Kincheloe, eds. 1999 *passim*; Odora Hoppers, ed. 2002 *passim*; and De Sousa Santos, ed. 2008 *passim*), there have been very few writers or authors willing to furnish an explanation of their understanding or concept of 'knowledge'. Although (or because?) the notion of 'knowledge' is used in liberal abundance, no account is given of the actual meaning(s) of this idea. Thus, there is a general failure among theorists to appreciate and engage with the ramifications of this concept. Instead, 'indigenous knowledge' is unquestioningly employed as an umbrella concept to cover a large variety of practices, skills, customs, worldviews, perceptions, beliefs, as well as theoretical and factual understandings. I will argue later that what proponents call indigenous (African, Māori, aboriginal, and so forth) knowledge *either* refers to indigenous (African, Māori, aboriginal, and so forth) customs, skills, and worldviews or beliefs, *or* is not clearly and distinctly 'indigenous' ('African', 'Māori', 'aboriginal' and so forth). I next turn to the ideas of relational epistemology and epistemological diversity, respectively.

NOTES

1. The San are southern Africa's oldest human inhabitants, having lived in the deserts and on the plains and mountains of the subcontinent for at least the past 20,000 years and possibly going back 40,000 years. Only about 100,000 remain, predominantly in Angola, Botswana, Namibia, South Africa, and Zambia.

2. Since then, a large number of patents on African plants have been filed, for example, for *brazzeine*, a protein said to be 500 times sweeter than sugar from a plant in Gabon; *teff*, the grain used in Ethiopia's flat *injera* bread; thaumatin, a natural sweetener from a plant in western Africa; the African soap berry and the Kunde Zulu cowpea; as well as genetic material from the west African cocoa plant. (https://www.culturalsurvival.org/news/sharing-secrets-hoodia-san-reap-financial-benefits-traditional-knowledge; retrieved 6 May 2020).

3. https://www.culturalsurvival.org/news/sharing-secrets-hoodia-san-reap-financial-benefits-traditional-knowledge (retrieved 6 May 2020).

4. Ibid. See also Robins 2008: 19, 51, 52.

5. Thus, Arun Agrawal (1995) argues that no substantial difference exists between indigenous and scientific knowledge. Donaldo Macedo (1999: xi, xii) speaks of "the reductionisticbinarism of Western versus indigenous knowledges systems" and of "a false dichotomy between Western and indigenous knowledge" (xv). Semali and Kincheloe (1999: 23, 24), too, caution against "forms of essentialism" such as that manifest in the "binary opposition between local knowledge and academic knowledge," before endorsing "a counter-essentialist understanding": "there may be some common threads running through many indigenous knowledge systems." Fatnowna and Pickett (2002b: 211–212) appeal to the complementarity of different knowledge systems, which, "considered together, promise a knowledge that begins to engage the richness and subtleties of what together we are able to begin to see and engage as a fuller reality." Bryan McKinley Jones Brayboy and Emma Maugham (2009: 5) emphasize that their "purpose is not to reify a sense of binaries," to "set up a dichotomy between Western and Indigenous knowledge": indigenous knowledge, they maintain, is substantially "more than the binary opposite of Western knowledge." Deborah Barca and Alberto Arenas (2010: 5; see also 6, 9–15, 18) consider the belief that "knowledge can be neatly divided into indigenous versus Western worldviews," and that these "worldviews not only represent distinct and even opposite epistemologies but are also irreconcilable," to be mistaken.

6. http://www.thenewhumanitarian.org/feature/2002/08/30 (retrieved 7 May 2020). See also Wilder et al. 2016.

7. An exception is constituted by Brian Yazzie Burkhart's account (2009), which indicates a keen awareness of the three kinds of knowledge distinguished here and adds a fourth kind of knowledge, as understood by American Indians, namely "knowledge in experience" (20), "knowledge gained from experience and used in it" (21): "Knowledge is what we put to use. Knowledge can never be divorced from human action and experience" (ibid.). I am not convinced, however, that this adds a new dimension beyond the propositional and practical senses. Rata argues (2102b: 103), moreover, that "experiential knowledge limits access to a powerful class resource;

that of conceptual knowledge required for critical reasoning and political agency": "Knowledge that comes from experience limits the knower to that experience."

8. An interesting parallel is constituted by the removal of statues of controversial figures, for example, in the United States and in England, as a result of the flaring up of the 'Black Lives Matter' protests.

9. This is a response to Enslin and Horsthemke 2015.

Chapter 2

Relational Epistemology and the Idea of Epistemological Diversity

What is arguably characteristic of African (and other traditional or indigenous) conceptions of knowledge is a strongly relational element that is also found in African ontology and ethics. This is also captured in the verdict, "Indigenous knowledge has a trans-generational, communal and cultural nature."[1] Semali and Kincheloe (1999: 51) refer to the 'metaphysicality' of indigenous knowledge systems, "based on the forces that connect people to one another." Tanzanian academic R. Sambuli Mosha (1999: 214) asserts that "Whatever is known, and passed on as knowledge, is known in the context of its relationship to life and the world." American social scientist Rodney Reynar (1999: 290–291) points out that indigenous knowledge "is indigenous precisely because it is incorporated in a way of life." It "does not derive its origins from the individual but, rather, in the collective epistemological understanding of the community." Coming to know is understood as a process of persons developing insights in relation with one another and with all that exists. This indicates not only an intimate relationship between knower and known, between what it is to know and what it is to be known, but in effect also a communalist understanding of knowledge: *I know because we know*. Or, *A knower is a knower because of other knowers*. This understanding of knowledge relations and knowledge communities then serves to validate indigenous insights and multitudinous ways of knowing, alternative conceptions of knowledge, and epistemological diversity.

A slightly different take on the relational understanding of indigenous knowledge is captured in the following remarks by Greek legal scholar and diplomat Erica-Irene Daes (1997: 3; see also Marker 2003: 105–106):

> Indigenous peoples regard all products of the human mind and heart as interrelated and as flowing from the same source: the relationship between people

and their land, their kinship with other living creatures that share the land and with the spirit world. Since the ultimate source of knowledge is the land itself, all of the art and science of a specific people are manifestations of the same underlying relationships, and can be considered as manifestations of the people as a whole.

According to Turnbull (2009: 1), such a relational understanding of indigenous knowledges would seem to "set them apart from scientific and non-indigenous knowledge," "which is usually taken to consist in formalized propositions that, . . . in some way independent of culture, correspond to reality" (see also Green 2009). I will return to the relational environmental understanding and related notions in chapter 7. I next turn to the idea of 'knowledge in the blood', worldviews and experiences transmitted faithfully as 'knowledge' from one generation to the next.

'BLOOD KNOWLEDGE'

How is it that young Afrikaners, white South African students born around the time of Nelson Mandela's release from prison, entertain intense beliefs about a past they never lived, rigid ideas about black people, and fatalistic thoughts about the future? How is it that young African 'born-frees', black South African students born after the official end of apartheid and the first democratic election in the country, hold firm beliefs about a past they never experienced, hostile ideas about white people, and militant thoughts about the future?

In 2010, four white former students of the University of the Free State in Bloemfontein, South Africa (a traditionally Afrikaans university, where black students now make up 60 percent of the 25,000-strong student body) pleaded guilty to humiliating black workers in an infamous Internet video. The case of the "Reitz Four"—named after their *koshuis*, or university dormitory—has been one of the most incendiary in South Africa's convoluted journey toward racial reconciliation. The video, filmed in 2007, showed five middle-aged campus workers, four women, and a man, participating in mock initiation rites for students, which involved having to eat while on their knees, drink beer, and perform athletic tasks. The workers clearly knew and trusted the students in the video, laughing as they tried to eat the food. But according to the video footage, one of the students appeared to have urinated on the food beforehand. The workers expressed their dismay and hurt at the video and said they had been unaware of what they were re-enacting, believing they were participating in some kind of competition. "We feel pain," said Emma Koko, who had been working for the university for twenty years and whose son was also a student there. "It's not something we were expecting. We regard [the students] as our children."[2] In what was considered to be a surprise development at the Bloemfontein magistrate's court hearings, the former students pleaded guilty to unlawfully and willfully injuring another person's dignity. In the apology issued in the statement, two of the students said they had been "crucified as racists" and regretted making the film, meant as a "satirical slant" on the university's policy of racially integrating the student residences years after the end of apartheid.[3] The video, which emerged on the web in 2008, triggered a new wave of anger and soul-searching in South Africa. There was further controversy in 2009 when Jonathan Jansen, the first black vice-chancellor of the university, dropped disciplinary action against the former students. The move was condemned by leaders across the political spectrum as an "abortion of justice," but won support from Archbishop of Cape Town Desmond Tutu, who chaired the country's Truth and Reconciliation Commission (TRC).[4]

The '#RhodesMustFall' movement on South African university campuses was the initial 2015 campaign by South African students and a few likeminded academics to decolonize the curriculum at universities "by ending the domination of Western epistemological traditions, histories and figures" (Molefe 2016: 32). In particular, participants demanded the end of domination by "white, male, Western, capitalist, heterosexual, European worldviews" in higher education and incorporation of other African and subaltern "perspectives, experiences [and] epistemologies" as the central tenets of university curricula, teaching, learning, and research in the country (Shay 2016; see also Heleta 2016; Ramoupi and Ntongwe 2017; Ndlovu-Gatsheni 2018: 60, 64, 188–190, 221–239). These demands were reiterated in the 2015/2016 '#FeesMustFall' movement, which demanded free, decolonized education for black people, and during which demonstrations and protests striking students across the country caused temporary shutdowns of universities. While the grievances and demands of the students and their leaders were certainly reasonable, the same could not be said for much of the ensuing or accompanying behavior, more often than not characterized by "unreason" (Jansen 2017: 127), a refusal to enter into rational dialogue with politicians and university management. Apart from causing considerable damage to property, students and student leaders displayed an aggressive, often racist (and sometimes overtly patriarchal) hostility toward university staff and even fellow students, culminating in the wearing of 'Fuck whites' T-shirts.

"Knowledge in the blood" is the title of Jansen's captivating book.[5] The phrase in question is taken from a poem by Macdara Woods. In response to Jansen's request, the Irish poet explained "knowledge in the blood" as the sum total of what we learn (or have to learn—from experience), of love, disappointment, age, loss, and how this knowledge can both make the necessary ongoing human reaffirmation of life and hope possible and at the same time hinder it. . . . It is almost as though we are carrying psychological antibodies inside us. The knowledge in the blood, however it got there, is as ingrained as a disease—although at the same time it can be truly benign. In this sense the knowledge (which we have been gathering since childhood, as well as having it handed down from before) can be—even at its best—as pitilessly indifferent, as ultimately powerful, and as random in why it propels us in any particular direction, as a microbe. (Woods; quoted in Jansen 2009: 170–171)

With Jansen, the phrase "knowledge in the blood" receives a rather specific application. For him, it means

knowledge embedded in the emotional, psychic, spiritual, social, political, and psychological lives of a community. Such is the knowledge transmitted faithfully to the second generation of Afrikaner students. It is not, therefore, knowledge that simply dissipates like the morning mist under the pressing sunshine of a *new regime of truth*; if it were, then curriculum change would be a relatively straightforward matter. (Jansen 2009: 171; emphasis mine[6])

"Knowledge in the blood," adds Jansen, "is habitual." By this, he means a "knowledge that has long been routinized in how the second generation sees the world and themselves, and how they understand others" (ibid.). It is a

knowledge that reacts against and resists rival knowledge, for this *inherited truth* was conceived and delivered in the face of enemies—the English imperialists, the barbarous blacks, the atheistic communists . . . The phrase draws attention to *deeply rooted knowledge* that . . . is not easily changed. (Ibid.; emphasis added)

With regard to curriculum change in particular, Afrikaner[7] "responsiveness to the new authorities," to "the formal demands of reconstruction," should not be construed as a change in "deep-rooted assumptions and beliefs about history, identity, knowledge, and change: the curriculum is, at base, an institutional subject." Apart from seeing it as inscribed in the course syllabus, this also entails regarding the curriculum as involving

an understanding of knowledge encoded in the dominant beliefs, values and behaviors deeply embedded in all aspects in all aspects of institutional life. Knowledge therefore becomes both what is formally designated for learning, such as the course syllabus, and what are widely understood within the institution to be *acceptable forms of knowledge* and *recognized ways of knowing* that distinguish one university type (such as the Afrikaans universities) from others. (171, 172; emphasis added).

Jansen's project in the book is to attempt to understand the "indirect knowledge" that continues to guide the attitudes and behavior of young Afrikaners, with no direct, personal experience of the events of the (preapartheid and apartheid) past. What accounts for white Afrikaans-speaking people, born around the time of the unbanning of political organizations like the ANC and Mandela's release from prison, having "firm knowledge" about a past they never experienced, holding "rigid views about the present" (especially with regard to black people), and conveying "fatalistic views about the future" (51)? Jansen refers to the received, "racial knowledge of the Apartheid state" (115) also as "bitter knowledge" (114–144 passim). Respectful disruption of this received, "indirect" knowledge is connected, among other things, with the necessity to understand its power, says Jansen (260–262). This constitutes a key element of the second part of his project: to understand how a postconflict pedagogy contributes to change.

Compelling though they are, what interests me is not so much Jansen's ideas in the latter regard, but rather his use (one might also call it 'misuse' or at least 'overuse') of 'knowledge' and 'truth'. He employs the terms 'knowledge' and 'knowing' in such a vast and varied number of ways that one is ultimately unsure what, for Jansen, constitutes knowledge proper and what, if anything, distinguishes it from (mere) belief, assumption, prejudice, dogma, and the like. On this account, everything is broadcast as 'knowledge'—only the adjectives and other descriptors change: this makes for a fairly comprehensive dilution of the idea in question. Equally disconcertingly, his reference to 'truth' appears to involve the assumption that there exist, either consecutively or concurrently, different regimes of truth, that one people's truth is not necessarily (indeed, is frequently not) that of another—which, it turns out (I will address this point in the following chapter) is a rather hazardous epistemological position to occupy, to say the least. Are the "forms of knowledge" acceptable to, and the "ways of knowing" recognized by, Afrikaners really *knowledge* and ways of *knowing*? The same question can be asked about "knowledge in the blood." The analysis in the chapters to follow will go some way towards accounting for my misgivings about Jansen's overly generous bestowal of epistemic (i.e., cognitive) status.

Definitions of "African ways of knowing" characteristically focus on 'African' or 'indigenous' (see, for example, Mudimbe 1988; Bakari 1997; Owuor 2007; Dei 2004[8])—as if these were the difficult or controversial terms. They are commonly coupled with 'traditional', 'local', and the like, and contrasted with 'universal', 'global', 'world', 'cosmopolitan', 'Western', 'Eurocentric', and so forth. To date, no pertinent policy document, statement, or article has yielded the understanding of 'knowing' or 'knowledge' the respective authors are working with—as if these concepts were simple and uncontroversial. I contend that they are not, and that a careful account of 'knowing' and 'knowledge' will reveal different 'indigenous', 'African', or 'alternative' 'ways of knowing' to be something of a misnomer.

DIFFERENT 'WAYS OF KNOWING'

With postcolonialist and antiracist discourse characterizing, if not most then certainly the latter half of, the twentieth century, there has been a 'back-to-the-roots' celebration of 'the African', in Africa as elsewhere. In postcolonial southern Africa especially, it has been coupled with invocation of a particular idea. The 'African Renaissance'[9] is understood, among other things, as a process of reclamation of indigenous or traditional African 'ways'—of knowing, seeing, doing and valuing, a process of promotion of 'African culture'.

Following George J. Sefa Dei's argument (2002: 1, 2, 10; 2004) for the place of spirituality in education and schooling, Constantine Ngara (2007: 14–16) illustrates the need for a spirituality centered thought and wisdom as a definite paradigm of knowing in Africa. Examples of "ways of knowing" applicable to modern life in Africa are *taboo-based knowing*, "herbal knowledge" or *indigenous healing wisdom, faith-based knowing,* and *political wisdom* (coupled with *prophetic wisdom*) (Ngara 2007: 14–16). Nashon, Anderson, and Wright (2007: 1, 2) refer to these ways of knowing as "knowing through taboos, through collective wisdom and experience, knowing through faith, and knowing through communication (spiritual wisdom)," respectively. "African spiritual ways of knowing," writes Dei (2004: 340; see also Dei 2002: 4),

> are intimately bound up with the affirmation of self and indigenous subjectivity. Many African ways of knowing affirm that personal subjectivity and emotionality must be legitimized[, t]hereby asserting that the subjectivity/objectivity and rationality/irrationality splits are false. In fact, while spiritual knowledge challenges subject-object dualism, it simultaneously upholds 'objectivity' to the subjective experience and similarly some 'subjectivity' to the objective reality. The subjective is capable of comprehending the 'objective universe'.

To sum up, then, these appear to be the most significant characteristics of "African ways of knowing": epistemic and conceptual decolonization; self-affirmation; inclusion or reintroduction of spirituality and faith in education and schooling; emphasis on intuition in knowledge production; and emphasis on relationality—not only between human beings, and between human beings and ancestors, spirits, gods and goddesses, but also between subject and object, the rational and the irrational and so forth. The first of these, epistemic and conceptual decolonization, arguably entails all the other characteristics, while the last three appear to constitute different senses of 'holism' in epistemic activity.

Dutch educational philosopher Claudia Ruitenberg provides some reasons for concern about the plausibility of the notion of "ways of knowing" (2012: 101, 102). Drawing on the work of R.S. Peters (1970) and analytic philosophers Gilbert Ryle (1963) and Richard Robinson (1971), she argues (2012: 103, 104) that the phrase is not only vague but also fraught with all kinds of linguistic and conceptual difficulties. She questions the continuing use of this 'ambiguous' and 'vague' phrase, for example, by feminist and Africanist scholars, especially when "more precise descriptions are available, such as 'sources of knowledge', 'forms of representation', 'ways of learning', and 'regimes of truth'" (101–102).

Why is reference to 'ways of knowing' problematic? In essence, 'know' and 'knowledge' signal states, rather than activities. Knowledge, according to Robinson (1971: 17),

> is never an act, or any kind of event. [. . .] Although [it] is not an event, it has events closely connected with itself, notably its origin, that is the coming to know or learning, and its ending, that is the being forgotten or otherwise ceasing, and its recalls or realizations whenever we bring to mind or remember what we know. [. . .] there is no actual as opposed to habitual present tense of the verb 'to know' in English.

In a related move, Peters employs Ryle's distinction between "achievement words" and "task words" (Ryle 1963: 143–147, 155). The latter refer to activities, while the former designate the results of these activities. Thus, 'teaching' and 'learning' are task words, while education is the (possible) result of these, that is, an achievement word (Peters 1970: 26). Similarly, knowledge is not a task word. It *may be* the result of both teaching and learning, just as it may result from 'reading', 'listening', 'seeking', and so forth. But, even if these difficulties are acknowledged, does the linguistic and conceptual awkwardness of a phrase (in the English language) suffice to threaten the validity of the idea it expresses?

Ruitenberg is careful not to leap to this conclusion. Instead, she examines the idea of 'ways of knowing' and asks what it is meant to convey and to do, that is, what claims or demands it is used to "make (and possibly mask)" and what effects it is meant to bring about (Ruitenberg 2012: 110). It appears, she says, that "the phrase 'ways of knowing' often addresses issues far beyond epistemology" (ibid.). Indeed, a conflation of ontology and epistemology is manifest not only in some appeals to 'women's ways of knowing' but also in Asante's assertion (2005: 42), "African ontology involves the interconnectedness of all reality, thus African epistemology is grounded in holistic reason." Similarly, although less explicitly than Asante, Dei (2004: 338) speaks of "the struggle to affirm diverse forms of knowledge as a way to transform education at the school site into learning experiences that are interconnected with the individual and collective reality or realities of the learner in a locality."[10] Ruitenberg argues (2012: 114), correctly I believe, that the phrase "ways of knowing" covers[11] various ideas, like "spiritual beliefs, beliefs about the individuality or relationality of human beings, and beliefs about the relation between reason and emotion . . . under a single verb with a long history in Western philosophy." "The use of an epistemological-sounding phrase such as 'ways of knowing'," she says (117, 116),

> can have the effect of legitimating a discussion that might otherwise be dismissed. However, epistemological-sounding discourse not only legitimates but also obscures the other questions at stake [i.e., more ontological or metaphysical concerns].

There are arguably two ways of framing claims about different 'ways of knowing': the first considers these as "shorthand for the larger worldviews of which epistemologies are a part" (111), while the second treats claims about different 'ways of knowing' as claims about "epistemological diversity" (101, 114). However, while this would enable the distinction between epistemology, on the one hand, and ontology and metaphysics, on the other, the idea of 'epistemological diversity' is anything but uncontroversial.

A problem with Ruitenberg's analysis is that her favored substitutes for 'ways of knowing' are every bit as problematic—if not more so. Thus, she approvingly quotes Michel Foucault's "critique of epistemological hegemony," his analysis of "how knowledge and truth are always part of systems of power" (115):

> Each society has its own regime of truth, its 'general politics' of truth: that is, the types of discourse which it accepts and makes function as true; the mechanisms and instances which enable one to distinguish true and false statements, the means by which each is sanctioned; the techniques and procedures accorded value in the acquisition of truth; the status of those who are charged with saying what counts as true. (Foucault 1984: 73)

At least two concerns arise in this regard. The ideas of "regimes of truth" and "'general politics' of truth" not only indicate a category mistake (in treating epistemological matters as necessarily inseparable from matters of social justice), but they also involve relativism about truth. Is Foucault able to make these sorts of assertions consistently? If he is correct, then this is so only on the basis of his particular society's regime or "general politics" of truth—in which case the question arises why others (i.e., those who do not belong to his particular society) ought to find his analysis compelling. If he is saying, however, that this particular truth holds transsocietally, then he has in effect opened the door to the (strong) possibility of there being *other* truths that are not confined to the contexts of society or culture. Either way, then, this account loses much of its intended force.

The other descriptions offered by Ruitenberg may be less contentious, conceptually, but they cannot work as substitutes for 'ways of knowing'. '*Sources* of knowledge', for example, are different from '*kinds* of knowledge'. The former include observation, sensation, reasoning, testimony, memory, and the like, while the latter include theoretical (or propositional), practical, and acquaintance-type knowledge—clearly not the same (see chapter 3 for a detailed exploration of these issues). What about "ways of learning"? 'Ways of learning' may also be, but are not necessarily, ways of acquiring knowledge. 'Learning how' may be said to lead to 'knowing how', but the same is not true for 'learning that' and 'knowing that'. What is learned may be false, or insufficiently justified. *Learning that* God created the universe does not imply *knowing that* he did. (In addition, assuming the plausibility of Peters's analysis, 'learning' designates a task, unlike 'knowledge'—which constitutes an achievement; see also Ryle 1963: 28–32.) "Forms of representation," similarly, is hardly a "more precise" phrase than 'ways of knowing'—over and above the consideration that 'representation' and 'knowing' can hardly be treated as synonyms. Apart from these problems of substitution, Ruitenberg fails to consider the ramifications of referring to, for example, 'women's sources of knowledge', 'indigenous ways of learning' or 'African forms of representation', let alone women's or indigenous or African regimes, or 'general politics', of truth.

The response, then, could simply be the following. It appears to be possible to understand the admittedly awkward phrase 'ways of knowing' in an extra-epistemological (and extra-ontological), more practical way—especially given the fact that 'ways of knowing' and 'knowledge (systems)' are usually treated as conceptually distinct, mentioned separately.[12] 'Ways of knowing' would then refer not to 'systems/forms of belief', 'worldviews', 'ways of being' and the like, but to 'ways of doing', practices, skills, and so forth. Either that—or one might simply refer to 'African knowledge (systems)' and, if need be, distinguish between practical and theoretical knowledge: between skills or practices, on the one hand, and knowledge proper, on the other—where the latter also appears to underlie claims about 'ecologies of knowledges', 'diverse epistemologies' or 'epistemological diversity' (see

Horsthemke 2017c, 2017e, 2019, 2020a, b). If one opts for this interpretation, however, there are additional problems, as I will show in chapter 4.

EPISTEMOLOGICAL DIVERSITY

The strongly relational element that is arguably characteristic of African conceptions of knowledge is also captured in Portuguese sociologist Boaventura De Sousa Santos's idea of "ecologies of knowledges" (2014: 188): "The ecology of knowledges assumes that all relational practices involving human beings . . . entail more than one kind of knowledge." The notions of "pluralist epistemologies" (189) and 'epistemological diversity' embody the idea that diverse cultural and ethnic groups, and subgroups within these groups—marking differences in gender, sexual orientation, and the like—have their own characteristic epistemologies and distinct ways of knowing. In their defense of what they call the "ecology of knowledges" De Sousa Santos, João Arriscado Nunes, and Maria Paula Meneses speak of the immense "epistemological diversity of the world" (De Sousa Santos et al. 2008: xix, xlviii). However, on the basis of the premise that "there is no global social justice without global cognitive justice" (xix; see also De Sousa Santos 2014: 42; Chan-Tiberghien 2004: 196; De Oliveira Andreotti 2011: 381), they relate this appeal not to different normative theories of knowledge (which are concerned with establishing what makes something 'knowledge'), but rather to diversity across ethnicities and cultures, as well as to gender differences:

> Over the last decades, there has been a growing recognition of the cultural diversity of the world, with current controversies focusing on the terms of such recognition. But the same cannot be said of the recognition of the epistemological diversity of the world, that is, of the diversity of knowledge systems underlying the practices of different social groups across the globe. (De Sousa Santos *et al.* 2008: xix)

Beginning with the assumption that "cultural diversity and epistemological diversity are reciprocally embedded," the authors' intention is to show that "the reinvention of social emancipation is premised upon replacing the 'monoculture of scientific knowledge' by an 'ecology of knowledges'." In other words, "far from refusing science," the "alternative epistemology" envisaged here "places the latter in the context of diversity of knowledges existing in contemporary societies" (xx):

> The ecology of knowledges is an invitation to the promotion of non-relativistic dialogues among knowledges, granting 'equality of opportunities' to the

different kinds of knowledge engaged in ever broader epistemological disputes aimed both at maximizing their respective contributions to build a more democratic and just society and at decolonizing knowledge and power. (Ibid.)

This exemplifies the recent but widespread view that ethnic or cultural groups have their own distinctive epistemologies, that epistemologies are also gendered, and that these have been largely ignored by the dominant social group. A corollary of this view states that educational research is pursued within a framework that represents particular assumptions about knowledge and knowledge production that reflect the interests and historical traditions of this dominant group. For example, in opposition to "the monochrome logic of Western epistemology" (Odora Hoppers 2002a: vii), Odora Hoppers (2002b: 18) draws attention to the existence of "plural manifestations of epistemology" and endorses both indigenous knowledge systems and indigenous theories of knowledge. In her book *Technofeminism* Judy Wajcman (2004) makes a similar plea for "epistemological diversity" and for the coexistence of a multitude of truths. In his introduction to a special journal edition on the "Futures for indigenous knowledges" Turnbull (2009: 2) refers to "the diversity of knowledges" as "autonomous differing knowledges," which he hopes can be "enabled to find ways to interact and work with their differences." This "diversity and plurality of knowledges is fundamental to the dynamism of knowledges systems and the survival of communities over time" (Brayboy and Maugham 2009: 5). Other popular, related terms include "democratic epistemology" (Nkomo 2000: 54), "multicultural epistemologies" (Banks 1998), "African"/"Afrocentric epistemology" (Asante 1990, 2005; Bakari 1997; Teffo 2000: 112; Zulu 2006), "feminist epistemology" (Harding 1987, 1996, 2002; Code 2012; Schumann 2016), "Chicana feminist epistemology" (Delgado Bernal 1998), "Afrocentric feminist epistemology" (Hill Collins 1990), and so forth—alongside references to "sexist"/"androcentric" and "racist epistemologies" (Braidotti 1991, 1993, 2006; Scheurich and Young 1997, respectively), as well as "ecology of knowledges" or "ecologies of knowledge" (De Sousa Santos et al. 2008; De Sousa Santos 2014; Visvanathan 2002: 49), "women's" or "gendered ways of knowing" (Belenky et al. 1986; Harding 1996), "Islamization of knowledge" (Dangor 2005; I will discuss this notion in chapter 4), and "African" or "native ways of knowing" (Dei 2002, 2004; Barnhardt and Kawagley 2005, respectively).

KNOWLEDGE, EPISTEMOLOGY, AND EDUCATION

Education is a prime terrain for the transmission, facilitation, development, and production of knowledge. This is a truism bordering on platitude.

Universities, in particular, are literally defined in terms of the generation of knowledge. Given the intimate relationship between education and educational institutions, on the one hand, and epistemology and knowledge, on the other, it should come as no surprise that the decolonization discourses around indigenization of education should have come to include talk of indigenization of epistemology.

What exactly do educational and epistemological democratization and decolonization, and indigenization of knowledge involve? And what is it about so-called 'Western' or 'Eurocentric' education, epistemology, and knowledge that must be decentered, or shifted from the center (Le Grange 2016: 10; Ndlovu-Gatsheni 2018: 80)? The most plausible response is that knowledge that had been 'colonized', appropriated, disowned and/or suppressed is now being reclaimed, reappropriated, and repossessed. In this process, the view that is vilified is the following (and here we notice a move from social justice to epistemology): achievement of reliable knowledge through objective, dispassionate inquiry can occur only when knowers are understood as separate from the objects of knowledge, and operate freely from subjective distortion and from the influence of society or culture. The maligned universalist view holds that this constitutes the pathway to truth, a universal method leading to a universal, value-neutral system of knowledge about life, the universe and (just about) everything. Knowledge not only renders possible prediction of how nature will behave, but it also yields the power to impose order on it and control it. By contrast, advocates of indigenization emphasize ecologies of knowledge (see also Ndlovu-Gatsheni 2018: 81), epistemic diversity, different/diverse epistemologies (Andreotti et al. 2011: 40) or epistemological pluralism (De Oliveira Andreotti et al. 2011: 236), indigenous knowledge (systems) (Ahenakew et al. 2014: 220; Le Grange 2016: 3), and alternative ways of knowing (Mackenthun 2016). The demand for cognitive justice (see Le Grange 2016: 4; Ndlovu-Gatsheni 2018: 4) usually goes hand in hand with condemnation of epistemic injustice and the "coloniality of knowledge" (Masaka 2017b: 73–75).

Key tenets are the following (see Hall and Tandon 2017: 6):

- The concepts of cognitive justice and democratization of knowledge acknowledge the significance of diverse epistemologies and organic, spiritual, and land-based knowledge systems, epistemological frameworks arising from social movements and the knowledge of the marginalized or excluded. They are about both institutional and epistemological access, making the sharing of knowledge a powerful tool in the struggle to deepen democracy and for a healthier and more just world.
- Higher education institutions today exclude many of the diverse knowledge systems in the world, such as those of indigenous peoples and marginalized

ethnic and racial groups, and those marginalized because of gender and sexual orientation.
- Such exclusion often involves "epistemicide" (see also Lebakeng 2004; De Sousa Santos 2014; Le Grange 2016; Masaka 2017a, b, 2018), which refers to the killing of knowledge systems, of "indigenous people's knowledges" (Ndlovu-Gatsheni 2018: 3).

One of the major problems with decolonization and indigenization discourses is that the ideas of epistemology and knowledge have characteristically been used by advocates in a variety of tendentious and even sloganeering ways. 'Epistemology' is a domain or division within philosophy that investigates the nature, origins, and conditions of knowledge. It further means 'theory of knowledge', that is, theory of the nature, origins, and conditions of knowledge. Thus, the very least one would expect from advocates is a theory of the nature of knowledge—including articulation of the concept of knowledge they are working with.

CONCLUSION

The ideas of indigenous knowledge and epistemological diversity have arguably gained conceptual and discursive currency only over the past half century, with a veritable slew of conferences, workshops, special journal editions, and anthologies devoted to these and related topics. Yet, there has been no treatise that offers a comprehensive, critical examination of these notions. Accounts of indigenous knowledge usually focus on explanations of 'indigenous', 'local', 'traditional, 'African' and the like—but to date not a single defense of indigenous knowledge has bothered to explain the particular understanding of 'knowledge' the authors are working with. Similarly, accounts of epistemological diversity or diverse epistemologies have tended to focus extensively and exclusively on 'diversity'—and not at all on the respective understanding of 'epistemology'. In other words, there has as yet been no extensive treatment of the epistemological assumptions, problems, and concerns at work here. The following chapter endeavors to provide an analysis of the pertinent concepts.

NOTES

1. http://www.thenewhumanitarian.org/feature/2002/08/30 (retrieved 7 May 2020). See also Gwaravanda 2019.
2. https://www.breakingnews.ie/world/south-africa-students-say-sorry-for-racist-video-351113.html (retrieved 29 May 2020).

3. Kemp J. Kemp, the defense lawyer, said that although the accused realized that it had degraded their victims, the employees participated voluntarily in the mock ritual. He insisted that the former students used a bottle and put it in their pants to make it look like they urinated into the mixture of orange squash, garlic, and protein powder. https://www.theguardian.com/world/2010/jul/27/bloemfontein-students-black-staff-campus (retrieved 29 May 2020).

4. Ibid. See chapters 8 and 9, where I discuss the TRC in more detail.

5. At the time of writing the book, and before accepting the position of rector and vice-chancellor of the University of the Free State, Jansen was the dean of the University of Pretoria's Faculty of Education.

6. It is worth noting the Foucaultian phrase here, to which I will return in this and later chapters.

7. Note, again, that the term "Afrikaner" refers to white and predominantly Afrikaans-speaking (South) Africans.

8. Dei (2004: 339) employs the following account:

Indigenous knowledge is knowledge arising with the long-term occupancy of place. . . . It is knowledge unique to a given culture or society characterized by the common sense ideas, thoughts, values of people formed as a result of the sustained interactions of society, nature and culture[,]

before quoting Roberts's definition of indigenous knowledge as knowledge "'accumulated by a group of people, not necessarily indigenous, who, by centuries of unbroken residence, develop an in-depth understanding of their particular place in their particular world'" (ibid.; Roberts 1998: 59).

9. Several kinds of response to the idea in question might be noted. Lesiba Joe Teffo (2000: 115) points out that 'Renaissance' ('rebirth of the knowledge of the past') is wholly appropriately used with regard to Africa: "Historically, . . . the European [R]enaissance . . . has nothing European about it because the knowledge, if truth be told, was learned from the African civilization and culture" (amendment mine; see also Teffo 1999; Kwaa Prah 1999; Ntuli 1999). Second, one might distinguish between 'Renaissance' and 'renaissance', the latter connected only incidentally and loosely to the former (with a capital 'R'), and appeal to the usefulness of the French term (with a small 'r') or the English equivalent 'renascence', insofar as they denote 'rebirth', 'regeneration', while rejecting the use of the name 'Renaissance'. The third kind of response is the contention that even the latter understanding is inapplicable, since Africa never died. Fourth, of course, one might reject the use of the terms 'African' and 'Africa' as being themselves European constructs and monikers and opt for 'Azania(n)', for example (see Ramose 2004). Finally, Mogobe Ramose (2002c: 608) writes that the

marriage between African and 'renaissance' is an uneasy one . . . full of historical and philosophical problems. The attempt to implant the 'renaissance' into Africa is an implicit denial of Africa's right to choose from her experience terms and concepts that can be used to understand and interpret African history and politics.

10. Given that Dei is referring here to *traditional* African forms of knowledge, I am unsure to what extent they could contribute toward *trans*formation—that is, as opposed to '*retro*formation'.

11. Ruitenberg uses the words "hides" and, elsewhere, "masks." I am not sure whether these apply to the accounts of "African ways of knowing" provided by Asante, Dei, and others. I suspect not—hence my preference for the broader (and perhaps more equivocal) term 'covers'.

12. Dei (2004: 339), for example, speaks of a transformation of education and schooling that includes "diverse forms of knowledge and ways of knowing."

Chapter 3

An Analysis of Knowledge and Epistemology

THE DIFFERENT MEANINGS OF KNOWLEDGE

The common sense understanding of knowledge is captured in the following exchange between a father and his two young sons, around some question of fact, with one of them—James—saying:

> 'I know it is!' His father replied, 'But perhaps you might be wrong!' Denis, 4 years, 7 months, then joined in, saying: 'But if he knows he can't be wrong! *Thinking*'s sometimes wrong, but *knowing*'s always right!' (reported in Matthews 2009: 163)

Little Denis is making a philosophically compelling point here about what it is to know something. If something genuinely constitutes knowledge, then it is infallible: in knowing something, one cannot be wrong.

In this chapter, I examine the traditional (or original philosophical) definition of knowledge and discuss the conditions of propositional, factual, or theoretical knowledge, before offering a modified definition. With this definition in place, I attempt to make sense of the ideas of 'indigenous knowledge' and 'epistemological diversity' in chapter 4. Some of the main problem clusters that will be addressed in the present chapter are the following:

- What are the different meanings or senses of knowledge? What is the relationship between epistemological concepts like knowledge and belief and educational concepts like teaching and learning?
- What constitutes knowledge in the propositional (and epistemologically relevant) sense? Are the criteria for knowledge jointly sufficient, or at

best individually necessary? Under what conditions are knowledge claims justified?
- What makes a belief 'strong'? What should we do about conflicting or rebellious beliefs within our web of belief?
- What are the sources of knowledge and justification? What kind of justification is at work in the natural sciences, in mathematics and logic, and in ethics and politics? What does trustworthiness comprise?
- How can an understanding of the nature of knowledge and justification improve our evaluations and help us to make better assessments, provide better explanations, ask better questions, and get people to change their minds?
- What is epistemic responsibility? How ought conflicts between different kinds of obligations, epistemic, and nonepistemic, to be resolved?
- Do knowledge and truth vary between individuals and/or groups? Are conceptions and theories of knowledge relative to a particular community, society or culture?

By working through these problems, this chapter will provide a framework for examining and evaluating different conceptions of and assumptions about knowledge, belief, truth, and justification in current educational and political debates. In order to indicate how these questions might be answered and what the answers would entail, it is necessary to distinguish between different senses of knowledge and to look more closely at the nature of one of these, namely propositional knowledge.

The view of knowledge articulated, however teasingly, by little Denis has a long and distinguished pedigree and goes back to ancient Greece.[1] The traditional (or classical philosophical) understanding of propositional knowledge can be traced back to Socrates, through Plato, whose dialogues *Meno* (99c–100a) and *Theaetetus* (200e–202d) contain the essence of this definition. It has proved very influential, and there is hardly any text on epistemology and education that has been able to bypass or ignore it. According to Socrates, in Plato's *Meno* (1970a: 65),

> True opinions, as long as they stay, are splendid and do all the good in the world, but they will not stay long—off and away they run out of the soul of mankind, so they are not worth much until you fasten them up with the reasoning of cause and effect. . . . When they are fastened up, first they become knowledge, secondly they remain; and that is why knowledge is valued more than right opinion, and differs from right opinion by this bond.[2]

And in Plato's *Theaetetus* (1978: 909), Socrates asks, "how can there ever be knowledge without an account and right belief?"[3] The classical philosophical definition of knowledge, then, is the following: S knows that p if and only if (1) S believes that p, (2) S is justified in believing that p, and (3) p (that is, p is true, or: It is the case that p). Socrates, of course, famously claimed *not* to know—but that knowing that he did not know put him in a position of advantage over (and arguably made him wiser than) those who claimed to know when they evidently did not. A corollary of the Socratic understanding is that in questioning what others believed to be true he would at least be able to learn to avoid falsehoods and error and, in so doing, get closer to the truth.

In everyday English, we distinguish between different senses of knowledge:

1. Knowledge of a person, place or thing: 'I know the feeling.'
2. Knowledge how: 'I know how to plan and organize my teaching.'
3. Knowledge that: 'I know that Humpty Dumpty was pushed.'
4. Knowledge what: 'I know what *agnotology* means.'
5. Knowledge who: 'I know who pushed Humpty Dumpty.'
6. Knowledge about: 'I know about the life.'[4]
7. Knowledge of the way: 'I know the way to San José.'
8. Knowledge how to be: 'I know how to be quiet.'
9. Knowledge why: 'I know why she cries at night,' and so on.

The senses of knowledge listed and exemplified here can be reduced to three:

- knowledge-by-acquaintance or familiarity-type knowledge, such as 'How well I know them!' or 'I only know Humpty Dumpty by name' (see examples 1, 6, and 7 above)
- practical or skill-type knowledge, as in 'I know how to play *Donna Lee* on the bass' (see examples 2 and 8)
- theoretical, factual or propositional knowledge, as in 'I know that *agnotology* means the study of ignorance', 'that Humpty Dumpty was pushed by the security police', 'that she cries at night because she is homesick' (see examples 3, 4, 5, 6, and 9).

Occasionally, the different senses of knowledge may overlap. Thus, language skills may be characterized both in terms of practical knowledge and acquaintance: if I know (i.e., if I am acquainted or familiar with) a particular language, then this implies that I can speak and/or read it. Similarly, if I know how to bake bread, then I know that I require certain ingredients and utensils, and that I am familiar with certain facts about the dough, baking temperature and duration, and so forth. The English-language reference to acquaintance or familiarity as a form of knowledge is not widely shared. In German and French, for example, a distinction is made between *Wissen* or *savoir*, both of which are used in the senses of both knowledge-that and knowledge-how, and *Kennen* or *connaissance*, respectively, which signal knowledge-by-acquaintance or familiarity-type knowledge. In Spanish, *saber* is used for all three senses of knowledge, including 'knowing the way', but *conocer* is also used for knowing a person. Likewise in Italian: *sapere* and *conoscenza*, and Dutch: *weten* and *kennis*. A further distinction is made, for example, between realist, constructivist, and relativist conceptions of knowledge. (I will return to these distinctions towards the end of this chapter.)

THE CLASSICAL PHILOSOPHICAL DEFINITION OF KNOWLEDGE

It is important to recognize that propositional knowledge, or knowing-that, is the crucial sense of knowledge with which epistemology is concerned. What, then, is propositional knowledge? What does it mean when a person claims to know that something is the case? Take the knowledge-claim, 'Humpty Dumpty was pushed.' First of all, it is clear that the speaker in question has to believe (or have an opinion about) something before he can claim to know it. In this instance, he has to believe that the individual known as Humpty Dumpty did not fall or jump but was relocated by force. But is belief really necessary for knowledge? Consider the statement made by Arnold Schwarzenegger's character in the film *True Lies*, "I don't believe it: my wife is having an affair." Does he *know* this without *believing* it? Or consider my reaction after seeing my exam marks on the noticeboard: "I don't believe it: I've actually passed!" Of course we know—and we have corresponding beliefs, although we may find it difficult to come to terms with these beliefs. No reasonable account denies that believing-that is necessary for knowing-that.

Merely believing that something is the case, though necessary, is not sufficient for knowledge. After all, what a person believes could be false. It may be the result of the speaker's prejudice or political bias that he holds the belief he does. The second condition, therefore, is truth. A person's beliefs must be true in order to qualify as knowledge. Truth, like belief, is necessary for knowledge. The speaker's belief that Humpty Dumpty was forcibly dislodged from the wall must be true in order for him to be able to know. 'Although I know that Humpty Dumpty was pushed, it is not the case that he was pushed' cannot literally be true. It is important to note that truth is not a subjective matter. No matter what a person believes or what all of his or her friends and colleagues believe, or what most people in his or her society or culture believe, the truth of something being the case is independent of thinking or believing that it is. The fact that beliefs are subjective or relative (to a particular society, culture and so on) does not undermine the objectivity of the truth of those beliefs.

Are belief and truth jointly sufficient for knowledge? No. The speaker's belief that Humpty Dumpty was pushed could turn out to be true, could turn out to reflect what is actually the case, but it may just be guesswork or the result of the speaker's strong prejudice or antipathy towards organs of the state (or of state power). It may be wholly unjustified. Something else is required. The third condition is justification (having evidence, proof, or a reason—there being grounds for believing that something is the case). The learner must be justified in believing that Humpty Dumpty was not an unfortunate accident. What might such justification look like? There may be photographic evidence or video footage of the incident. The speaker may personally have seen the event unfold—or listened to a witness produce a reliable account. Or there may be circumstantial evidence, implicating the security police in similar incidents in the recent past, Humpty Dumpty having been targeted by state organs before because of his criticism of the regime, for having been a dissident, and so forth.

Together these three conditions add up to the qualification that knowledge is true, justified belief. This is what is known as the traditional philosophical definition of knowledge. Whether or not these three conditions are not only necessary but also jointly sufficient has been subject to considerable debate. It is generally accepted, as it has been since the days (the 'tradition') of Socrates and Plato, that each of these conditions needs to be present for the claim I am making to be considered knowledge. Until the publication of American philosopher Edmund Gettier's influential article (Gettier 1963), it was also accepted that this is all there is to knowledge. I will provide a modified definition of propositional knowledge later, in the hope of circumventing Gettier-type objections. However, my critique of 'indigenous knowledge' and the like focuses on justification and truth as necessary conditions of knowledge. Such an account need not agree with the traditional analysis of sufficient conditions for propositional knowledge. Before I focus my attention on belief, truth, and justification, I will look briefly at the relationship between cognitive and educational terms.

COGNITIVE AND EDUCATIONAL CONCEPTS

How are the cognitive notions of 'knowing' and 'believing' related to the educational notions of 'learning' and 'teaching'? 'Learning that' seems to imply 'believing that', but not 'knowing that'. Successful teaching involves the learner coming to believe something. The converse does not apply. It is possible to come to learn something without having been taught. What makes teaching successful is not merely that the learner believes what the educator takes to be true, but that the subject matter is true. As I have indicated earlier, 'knowing' not only has a propositional or factual sense ('knowing that') but also a practical or skill sense ('knowing how'). Believing, on the other hand, is only propositional ('believing that'). According to educational philosopher Israel Scheffler (1965: 7), 'knowing' thus has a larger range than 'believing', and 'learning' and 'teaching' are at least as large in range as 'knowing'. Both also have a practical or skill sense ('teaching how', 'learning how'), in addition to being used propositionally ('teaching that', 'learning that'), unlike believing. The acquaintance or familiarity sense of knowing is neither shared by believing nor by the educational concepts in question, which accounts for its educational irrelevance.

Yet, the range of education also goes beyond that of knowledge: we also employ these concepts in terms of 'learning to' and 'teaching to', unlike knowing. The same goes for learning and teaching, but not knowing, with regard to the appreciation of music and/or the development of understanding. It is important to note that 'teaching how' and 'learning how' arguably involve 'knowing how', whereas 'teaching that' and 'learning that' do not necessarily involve 'knowing that'. 'Teaching that' does not even imply 'believing that', although 'learning that' seems to. This serves to explain, among other things, how indoctrination takes place. I return to this idea later in the chapter.

KNOWLEDGE AND BELIEF

The concept of belief is central to epistemology. Both truth and justification refer to beliefs in the theory of knowledge. Any (body of) knowledge, whether scientific or nonscientific, incorporates belief. Any kind of enquiry that aims at yielding knowledge must involve belief. What, then, are beliefs? Every one of us holds on to a multitude of beliefs every day of our lives. For example, we believe that there will be an increase in pandemics in the future, that the choice of hosts for both the last and the coming soccer world cups has involved irregularities and corruption, that our students are making good progress, that we have a good grasp of what is important in education, and that the recently dethroned "leader" of the free world has the cognitive and empathic competence of a spoilt child. Beliefs pertain both to places and events, which are often fairly easy to verify, and also to mental states, which are much more difficult to establish and prove. Education involves and, indeed, depends on beliefs that extend across both terrains, beliefs about the here and now (and of course about the past) as well as beliefs that are more speculative.

"Educationally," says British educational philosopher John White (2002: 57), "belief belongs to the mental *equipment* which we both draw on as teachers and want children to acquire." When he claims that the "education of belief is many-sided" (59), he is in the main referring to children's acquisition of "true beliefs about the natural and social worlds" (ibid.) as well as the acquisition of true beliefs about a person's place in these worlds. This indicates two important responsibilities on the part of parents and educators:

- the socialization or acculturation of children into a multitude of new ideas (empirical or scientific, logical, ethical, and interpersonal), which will facilitate ever-increasing 'webs of beliefs' both in terms of number and complexity;
- providing children or learners with the tools for distinguishing between true and false beliefs.

What is important, says White, is that—as rational parents and educators—we do not want children to have mere beliefs: we want them to have knowledge (59, 60). "Beliefs do not exist independently" of each other (60). They form a "web," to use an image introduced by American philosophers Willard Van Orman Quine and Joseph S. Ullian (1978); they constitute (a) map/s "by which we steer" (White 2002). However, it is possible to have a perfectly coherent and consistent web or set of beliefs that are all false (like the East German ardent communist mother's web of beliefs in the 2003 German film *Goodbye Lenin!*). So it is not only coherence and mutual support that are important but also (the provision of) justification, or "good reasons" (White 2002: 61).

With regard to beliefs proper, White distinguishes between three main kinds, on the basis of their duration: transient or fleeting beliefs, longer-lasting beliefs and permanent or life-long beliefs. Education has to do essentially with the inculcation of longer-lasting beliefs and permanent or life-long beliefs, in other words, "continuants" rather than "occurrences" (56).

Given these distinctions, it is somewhat puzzling that White claims that (all) beliefs "are continuants, not occurrences" (ibid.). For one thing, some beliefs (namely transient beliefs) appear to be not continuants, but occurrences. They exist presently and disappear as soon as we cease to be aware of them. (Moreover, do beliefs not accompany occurrent phenomena like fear, pain, and so on?) For another, the verdict that beliefs, being continuants, are not "conscious events" appears to be contradicted by common sense. Certainly, it is a characteristic feature of longer-lasting and life-long beliefs that they exist even when we are not aware of them, but surely they can also be occurrent (namely when we are aware of them). Or is White saying something like, "Beliefs are continuants and frequently also occurrences"? Why does he not simply postulate the existence of, and distinguish between, continuant beliefs and occurrent beliefs?

Many factors influence our beliefs and their reliability. What we, as individuals, can believe and do believe is influenced by our upbringing and education as well as by our cultural and social circumstances. All of these constitute our frame of reference, our system of values, and the concept or image each one of us has of ourselves. This makes for considerable variations among people's beliefs and belief systems. That does not mean, however, that there are variations in individual knowledge. Because it has truth as its objective component, knowledge does not vary from individual to individual, from society to society or from culture to culture. (As I will argue later in this chapter, people can at best be credited with different levels of knowledge, and different priorities in their quest for knowledge, given their different social, political, geographic, and historical contexts.)

Belief, unlike truth and—indeed—unlike knowledge, is a matter of degree. A person may half-heartedly accept something as being the case, he or she may have an ungrounded opinion about something, or he or she may have a strong belief, and even be totally convinced, that something is the case. It is generally thought that knowledge requires at least strong belief.

White asserts that beliefs "can differ in degree of strength" (60). Strength of belief should not be confused with intensity of belief. Strength of belief depends on evidential grounds. A strong belief is one that is based on strong evidence or on good reasons. Intensity of belief is a psychological attribute and is, in principle, acceptable only if fervor is guided by reason. This is why superstition does not qualify as knowledge. We would hardly describe the security guard who kicked a black cat to death during a soccer match in South Africa some time ago as being justified in believing that black cats bring bad luck, let alone as having acted rationally. Conditions of rationality and conditions of knowledge are closely related. Sexist and racist beliefs, however intense, are generally indicative of irrational prejudice. They have little, if anything, to do with knowledge. Not being willing to seek justification is a sign of not being willing to be rational.

Although belief is necessary for knowledge, it is not a sufficient condition for knowledge. The presence of belief is not enough for knowledge. Belief on its own does not guarantee knowledge. A person's beliefs may be false or completely unfounded. In order for them to constitute knowledge, they must at least also be true and justified. Beliefs are evaluated in terms of truth-conditions and supporting evidence as well as in relation to each other. It is possible to evaluate our beliefs by checking on whether they are mutually supporting. But what happens when two beliefs conflict? In clear-cut cases, we tend to drop one of the beliefs. Of course, much depends on the type of people we are, on our other beliefs, and on the importance of the belief or beliefs in question, but people generally do not relinquish or abandon what they believe to be true. It frequently happens that we ignore new evidence responsible for a potentially disruptive or rebellious belief and rationalize the beliefs we have. We might also try to accommodate these beliefs without any major rearrangement within our web of belief. Or we might push threatened beliefs into the background without actually giving them up. Finally, we might relinquish or abandon beliefs that conflict with the new evidence where this evidence is overwhelming. I will say more about this below. People do not readily abandon what they believe to be true just because a new government or some other authority tells them to. Deeply seated beliefs (which we take to range over both intense and strong beliefs), too, are unlike clothes: they cannot be changed just to suit the occasion. Many of these beliefs have been acquired over a long time and held for a long time. People often feel secure because of their beliefs, so why should they relinquish something that gives them a sense of security and comfort? This emphasizes some of the difficulties involved in teaching, where one of the central aims is to get people to give up poor and inadequate beliefs and replace them with better ones. The task obviously is to convince them of the inadequacy of their beliefs, which can be a major challenge. When a person changes a set of beliefs, the change is motivated by the quest for these beliefs to band together in a way that they support each other. Obviously, a belief that supports other beliefs would not contradict them. This is as true for science as it is for everyday activities involving knowledge claims. A person's questioning and (re)shuffling of beliefs usually ends when she is satisfied with the consistency or coherence of her beliefs.

True belief is necessary, but not sufficient for knowledge. The truth of a belief does not entail that it is justified. Nor is feeling or thinking that my belief is justified equivalent to being justified. If my reasons for a belief are bad, then the belief is unjustified, even if I think my reasons are good. If I do not think that I have good reasons for believing something, I give up the belief. The source of a belief—what causes or prompts it—may not be the same as the source of its justification. Someone who comes to believe something purely on the basis of prejudice might later come across good evidence for the belief. On the other hand, justification does not entail truth or correctness. For example, Newton was justified in his belief that time and space constitute an absolute frame of reference. Although based on observation, Newton's belief lacked the evidence of relativity that Einstein would later provide. His belief, although justified, was false.

PRIMARY AND SECONDARY SOURCES OF KNOWLEDGE

I suggested earlier that strength of belief depends on evidential grounds and that a strong belief is one that is based on strong evidence or on good reasons. 'Good reasons' signals three distinct, albeit related focus points: appropriate kinds of reasons (or justification), the degree of justification required for knowledge, and reference to context of knowledge attribution and knowledge claims. With regard to the first, we generally distinguish between primary, immediate or direct kinds (reason, observation, sense experience, self-evidence, and introspection) and secondary, mediate, or indirect kinds (testimony, authority, memory, deductive reasoning, and nondeductive reasoning) of reasons, or justification. One way of establishing or demonstrating the strength of your justification is through the quality of your reasoning. This is as true for educators as it is for anyone working with knowledge and justification. Note that reasons (as in 'good reasons') are not identical to either 'reason' or 'reasoning'. 'Reason' refers both to a mental faculty (and is intimately linked with 'rationality') and to one of the two candidates for the basis of knowledge (the other being 'evidence'). 'Reasoning' is one source or kind of justification, among several such sources or kinds.

Philosophers as well as educators have enumerated several sources of knowledge, ranging from introspection and intuition to authority. As I will show, different sources of knowledge are connected with different kinds of justification. A distinction is frequently made between primary or original sources (factors that directly yield knowledge or justification) and secondary or derived sources (factors that indirectly yield knowledge or justification).

Two primary sources of knowledge and justification that concern us here have to do with sense experience and reason. Usually, we claim to know something from sense experience on the basis of what we have seen, heard, touched, tasted, or smelled. Sense experiences in the form of what we see, hear, touch, and so on, should be distinguished from mental events such as thoughts, intentions, beliefs, or desires. The argument is often advanced that our direct senses of things offer more reliable contact with the world than thoughts or beliefs. Sense experience therefore appears to be necessary for knowledge of the external world. A person knows that there is a keyboard in front of him or her because he or she can see it, touch it, and hear the clicking sounds it emits when that person types. We are thus crucially guided by our sense experiences in gaining knowledge of the world. In fact, there is no other source of information about the world that can claim to be as reliable as sense experience, even though some think that intuition might also have a claim to reliability. In spite of this, however, sense experience does not appear to be sufficient for knowledge. After all, sense experiences sometimes deceive us and often involve illusions or hallucinations. Consider the simple example of a straight stick that looks bent when immersed in water. More difficult cases occur when a person reports an event, especially one of historical importance. We know that observers bring with them to an occasion conceptions and beliefs that often cloud their ability to see and observe it clearly.

So, although we need to trust our senses, we also need to be aware that our senses can deceive us.

The other important source of knowledge is reason. Unlike sense experience, reason does not usually begin with observation of things in the world, but by working with logical arguments. From these, it tries to derive certain conclusions that follow with absolute certainty. If the three angles of a triangle are equal to 180°, we are able to reason that if a triangle has two angles of 90° and 40°, the third angle must be of 50°. We discover this not by looking at or even measuring different triangles, but by deducing from certain initial principles that are given to us in advance. Mathematical and geometric truths are prime examples of this kind of reason. Similarly, so-called 'analytical truths' are good examples, like 'Green is a color' and 'Bachelors are unmarried'. These happen to be true, not because every time we see green we also see (a) color or because we have counted how many bachelors are unmarried, but because they are defined in this way. Logical truths, too, fall into this category: 'Either I have passed the entrance examination, or I haven't.' When we reason in this way, we do not observe or perceive things. We rely on truths that depend on logical form and on logical terms. However, in spite of the appeal of reason, which works to establish certainty, there is a sharp disagreement over the question of whether or not reason can yield substantial knowledge about the external world in the absence of sense experience.

This, incidentally, reflects the debate between empiricists and rationalists. Both empiricism and rationalism are foundational epistemologies—that is, they take sense experience and reason, respectively, to be the foundation of knowledge. Nonfoundational epistemologies deny that knowledge has any such foundation. I return to these and related issues later.

EVIDENCE AND BELIEF: THE CENTRAL ROLE OF OBSERVATION

Although evidence is frequently taken to be identical with justification, there are some limits to the concept of evidence. In the natural sciences, that is, in physics, chemistry, and biology, it is wholly appropriate to refer to evidence. However, in the case of mathematical knowledge, we speak of proof rather than evidence, while in the case of moral, legal, and political deliberation, we refer to reasons, albeit often guided by evidence (Scheffler 1965: 58, 59; see also White 2002: 61, for a similar set of distinctions). For attributions of knowledge to a person regarding his pains or perceptual experiences, the request or demand for evidence appears similarly inappropriate, as it is in the case of feelings or moods (Scheffler 1965: 59).

Justification, like belief (but unlike truth), is a matter of degree. What degree of justification must a true belief have in order to constitute knowledge? Clearly, there are instances when demands made on justification are simply too ambitious. Consider two extremes: logically conclusive justification and minimal justification. Both are problematic: the first because it requires too much, the second because it requires too little. On the one hand, logically conclusive justification would guarantee the truth of a knowledge-claim. A belief with such a justification is objectively certain. (A belief that is merely subjectively certain, on the other hand, is one that is held with total conviction. This is what I characterized as an 'intense' belief earlier. Religious beliefs arguably belong in this category.) But logical or objective certainty seems too much to require, as it would rule out all kinds of knowledge claims that seem to be true. For example, the statements 'I know that my friend died on 28 November' and 'There is a keyboard in front of me' do not meet the requirements of objective certainty, yet it seems rather harsh to rule them out as legitimate knowledge claims. On the other hand, minimal or weak justification is plainly not enough.

Observation is one source of justification (and indeed of evidence), even if not the only primary source. I mentioned earlier that belief is the subjective component of knowledge, while truth is its objective component. What we believe is one thing. What is actually the case, what is true, is another. This is where working with evidence, and more specifically with observations (and observation statements), becomes significant. Quine and Ullian claim that our beliefs ultimately rely on observations, including observations of what we as well as others have noted or written down. Whatever evidence we have consists ultimately of what we have accessed and internalized through the use of our senses (see Quine and Ullian, 1978: 21). Our observations pertain to external objects and different people can observe the same things. In other words, multiple witnesses can attest to our observation statements, or what we claim to observe or have observed.

Two additional points need to be made about observations. First, we often claim to have knowledge about things that we might not be able to observe. We do, however, build instruments such as microscopes and cameras to do the work for us. On this basis, we claim to have 'seen' things and places we are normally incapable of seeing. Second, much of what we observe occurs against the backdrop of some or other theory we have about what it is we are looking at. When we immerse a stick in water, we do not jump to the conclusion, on the basis of our observation, that a liquid substance such as water affects the stick's physical properties, in other words, causes it to bend. As Quine and Ullian put it (31ff.), we "find it second nature to edit observation."

Observation, then, has an important role in justification. Much of the evidence we give to justify our beliefs comes from observation. But observation alone can be misleading. Our observations take place in the context of a web of belief. People do not have beliefs in isolation from each other. (This is the essence of the notion of relational epistemology I discussed in chapter 2.) Our beliefs about any one event are intimately tied up with related beliefs that support each other in what Quine and Ullian (1978), and also White (2002), refer to as a web of beliefs. The more support the beliefs give to each other, the stronger and more reliable the web is. By contrast, if any belief undermines others, then the whole web is likely to suffer, as it depends on the combined support of all of the beliefs acting harmoniously. Although justification does not entail truth or correctness, the best (perhaps even the only) way to maximize truth and minimize falsehood among beliefs is to attempt to ensure that our belief system as a whole is as justified as possible.

Earlier, I discussed ways of dealing with a web of belief being disrupted by an anomalous event or new evidence. Such an anomalous event might lead to a new belief that we will accommodate in our web. Sometimes this new belief leads to a conflict in our beliefs.

Rational procedures of belief acquisition are fundamental or central to the acquisition of knowledge. We aim for consistency and coherence among our beliefs by virtue of the fact that we are rational beings. A justified belief is often justified by other beliefs that support it.

This leads us to an important but difficult question: what justifies the supporting beliefs?

There are arguably some beliefs that can be regarded as basic or privileged (I return to this point later in the chapter), either because they are self-evident or because they rest immediately on experience and direct observation (e.g., 'I feel dizzy'). Those beliefs most closely associated with immediate experience are privileged, even though they are not infallible. Sensory experience and observations are often deceptive and are therefore not a completely reliable basis for beliefs. But here we need to draw some subtle distinctions.

OBSERVATION AND SENSATION
(OR SENSE EXPERIENCE)

Events of sensation (or sense experience) and events of observation share certain important features. They are among the most obvious sources of justification and knowledge. They involve engaging and relying on our senses. They also require our physical presence in order for us to be able to make appropriate knowledge claims. But are they identical? A careful reading of Quine and Ullian (1978) reveals that the authors do not think so. They consider sense experience, like introspection, to be essentially private and characteristically to involve privileged access. In other words, although the description of our sensations conveys information to others and also has a distinctly explanatory function, others will never be able to know whether what we have said is actually true, unlike accounts of our observations. When I say something like 'I seem to see blue now', this can be understood by others—but they will not be able to contradict me: after all, they do not have access to my personal, private, and immediate sense experience. On the other hand, when I state that the sky is blue, this is something others will be able to agree or disagree with. The same goes for statements reporting pain perception. My feelings of pain remain essentially my own, that is, private—although others may reasonably agree (or disagree) that I look like I am in pain. (See Quine and Ullian 1978: 22ff., 33–34.) Observation clearly involves sense experience in that observations are made by means of our senses, but it also goes beyond mere events of sensation. Observations are characteristically (or can in principle be) made by several observers, who can attest to the veracity of a particular observation statement. Observation does not involve privileged access.

A problem that pertains to observation, but not to sensation, is that of fallibility. Yes, it is possible for a person to be mistaken about the actual object of his or her sense experience, but that person cannot be mistaken about his or her sensation as such. It just is the way it appears to that person. Unlike events of sensation, however, observations are frequently unreliable or deceptive (as in illusions or hallucinations). They are also partial and subject to perceptual relativism. In other words, there is also the possibility of different interpretations of, or our vantage points affecting, what we observe. Indeed, we may focus on different aspects of a given observed event, which explains why the accounts of several eyewitnesses often diverge from each other, if they do not actually contradict each other.

Furthermore, what we observe frequently also depends on the particular theory we have about what it is we are looking at. Take the wave-particle duality of light: when we expect to see waves in examining light patterns, we see waves; when we expect to see particles, this is what we see. That is, theory or theoretical knowledge frequently guides our observations, but not our sensations. Although geometry, chemistry, art, music, and the like evidently engage the senses, it is their observational content that renders them teachable or subject to facilitation. Why? In what way? It is not possible for a music teacher to make learners 'feel' something as a result of encountering a certain musical work, but it is possible to teach them how to identify its tonality, structure, meter, and sonic idiosyncrasies, and to provide them with historical or other contextual details that may ultimately facilitate 'feeling'.

Observation statements are part and parcel of the rational procedures governing belief acquisition. Observation contributes to empirical justification and is, therefore, a basic source for the acquisition of knowledge. On the other hand, as rational agents, we also strive for coherence and consistency among our beliefs. In the absence of observable evidence, we rely on our beliefs being mutually supportive. We also hold beliefs on the basis of good authority. In other words, we rely on the testimony or testimonial evidence of others.

EVIDENCE AND BELIEF: THE IMPORTANCE OF TESTIMONY AND TRUSTWORTHINESS

I referred earlier to problems encountered in relying on observation as a result of access being denied to the viewer for one or other reason. When this happens, we often rely on the evidence of people who happened to see the event and who then convey it to us in a reliable manner. If the evidence we rely on consists at least in part of observation of other people's reports (see Quine and Ullian 1978: 114), then we must be sure that we can trust this evidence. Knowing when to trust someone's evidence is a central concern for anyone who seeks reliable information. Quine and Ullian provide a broad overview of testimony and trustworthiness and discuss these concepts in connection with 'common knowledge' and with justification in science. The role of trust and testimonial evidence in scientific research is discussed in some detail by American philosopher John Hardwig (1991: 693–708).

Under what conditions can testimony be trusted as a source of evidence? Quine and Ullian refer to two basic functions of language, namely persuading others to behave or act in a way we want them to behave or act, as well as to request from others information we need. What is noteworthy about the latter, the 'testimonial' use of language, is that it involves a distinct trust that others not only know what they are talking about but also that they will be telling the truth. It follows that there is strong correlation between testimony, trustworthiness, and truth in the pursuit of knowledge (see Quine and Ullian 1978: 50, 52). I will explore the persuasive use of language, that is, as a means of getting others to do what we want them to do, later in this chapter. My present concern is with what might be called the 'testimonial' or 'information-gathering' use of language. Several important connections should be noted here: between testimony and trust, between testimony and truth, and between trust and truth.

A considerable amount, perhaps most, of what we claim to know is not anything we perceive with our own senses. There are two common types of testimony: oral and written. We normally assume that the oral testimony of others is true unless we have some reason to believe that it is not. Believing others and accepting their claims, unless there is a reason not to, is an enormously time-saving strategy. Trying to find out everything for ourselves would not only be a huge waste of time but would also be irrational. With written testimony (e.g., newspapers, magazines, encyclopaedias, or relevant books), similarly, we tend to accept claims as true unless we find some reason not to, for example, if a claim conflicts with something else we know. Most of the time, when we accept written testimony, we can learn countless truths that we would have neither the time nor the leisure to observe, or simply could not observe because the event is historically or geographically remote. Again, accepting written testimony is, generally, the rational thing to do.

The medium of both oral and written testimony is language. The basis for veracity (truthfulness or honesty) resides in the mechanisms of language acquisition, as does the basis for credulity (willingness to believe that something is true or real). This leads us back to education. Both the teaching and the learning of a language crucially depend on truthfulness and trust for their success. If young children did or could not believe that certain words uttered by their parents and educators referred or corresponded to objects in the world, they would be unable to acquire linguistic skills. Perhaps we could go so far as to say that truthfulness and trust are essential for making basic sense of the world.

Two conditions for rational trust can be identified: truthfulness and competence. A person who is in the habit of cheating or telling lies is not trustworthy, even if he or she is competent. Similarly, we would not trust a person who is honest, but incompetent. For example, we would surely not trust an honest dentist (or motor mechanic) whom we knew to be incompetent. If a person is known to be truthful and competent, this would give us reason to trust him or her, to accept his or her testimony.

It is one thing to accept the testimony of another, whether he is a passer-by who directs us to the soccer stadium or an authority on some subject. Such testimony sometimes yields justification, sometimes not, depending on the source of information and the subject matter. It is another thing altogether to claim that we *know* the way to the stadium (because we have received directions) or that we *know* about the life of Cleopatra (because we have read an Africanist historian's book on the subject). We may be justified in believing that the stadium is two blocks away or that Cleopatra was black, but do we know? Normally, we would probably admit many well-confirmed examples of testimony as genuine knowledge. If we ask several people for directions or read a variety of books on the subject and all are in agreement about the salient points, then we would normally be credited with knowledge, at least in a sense that does not require objective certainty.

There is a problem with testimonial evidence, a more philosophical problem, which is considered by Hardwig (1991: 697*ff.*). How can we know that someone knows that Cleopatra was black unless we already know that Cleopatra was black (in which case, we do not need to appeal to another's testimony)? It is possible to respond to this problem by shifting the emphasis from knowing that *p* to having good reasons for believing that *p*. In other words, we may not know that a particular historian knows that Cleopatra was black, but we may have good reasons for believing that that historian knows that Cleopatra was black. But what does it mean to have good reasons? Does it mean that we have to be aware of or be able to give our reasons (justification, evidence) in order to know? Scheffler (1965: 74) appears to think so:

> when we judge that someone has adequate evidence, we are judging that he has an evidential argument which he understands. In saying he knows, we are not merely ascribing true belief but asserting that he has proper credentials for such belief, the force of which he himself appreciates.

I next consider the question of how we can use different kinds of reasoning to take us, responsibly, beyond the evidence.

DIFFERENT KINDS OF REASONING: GOING BEYOND THE EVIDENCE

There are two areas in which reasoning goes beyond observational evidence or at least immediately observable evidence. The first one belongs to forms of reasoning that we call deduction (sometimes this is also referred to as logical implication). The other is nondeductive reasoning. Nondeductive reasoning includes induction, reasoning by analogy and reasoning to the best explanation, or reasoning abductively. In dealing with each of these, I will clarify what is meant by reasoning going 'beyond observational evidence'.

The first kind of reasoning I will deal with is that of deduction. What makes an argument or piece of reasoning deductively sound is that there is nothing contained in the conclusion that is not already present in the initial premises. There is another important feature of deductive reasoning to note: if the reasoning is valid, the conclusion follows with absolute certainty. Deductive validity is a matter of certainty, of all-or-nothing. There are no degrees of deductive validity. Deductive reasoning does not need to yield true conclusions in order to be valid. What matters in deduction or implication is whether the conclusion follows logically from or is supported by the premises. It is the relationship between the propositions (premises and conclusion) that counts. Truth, on the other hand, concerns the relationship between propositions and the world. Deductive reasoning is sound if it is *both* valid *and* consists entirely of true propositions. I noted earlier that reasoning that relies on deduction operates by achieving absolute certainty. A discipline in which this commonly occurs is plane geometry, where we arrive at the conclusion to a theorem through a process of reasoning. For instance, to go back to the example of the triangle:

if the angles of all triangles add up to 180°, and we have a triangle in front of us, we know with certainty that its angles will add up to 180°. Deduction plays an important part in this kind of activity, where reasoning is required and that nevertheless hardly relies upon observational evidence for achieving its results.

But what about other areas in education? Most of our substantive beliefs about the happenings in the world, whether they belong to current affairs, science, literature, history, geography, or the arts, do not follow deductively or with logical certainty from the available evidence. Furthermore, if we kept to deduction as the only form of reasoning, we would have little left to talk about besides ways of doing theorems and other mathematical problems, over and above indulging in logical sophistication. We would not get very far in educating for life or comprehensive preparation for work.

This brings us to an alternative kind of reasoning—induction—and its allied forms, reasoning by analogy and abduction. Inductive reasoning is characterized by generalizations that are based on accumulated prior experiences. It involves a finite or limited number of observations that repeat themselves on a number of occasions and provide the basis for the making of wider or even universal claims. Of course, there is a great debate about whether inductive reasoning is reliable.

Besides induction, there are two other kinds of nondeductive reasoning: analogical reasoning and reasoning to the best explanation, or abductive reasoning. These are related to induction because, like induction, they do not require absolute certainty in order to be useful. Reasoning that is based on analogy is the most commonly used type of nondeductive reasoning. Most of our everyday inferences are by analogy. Analogy is at the basis of most of our ordinary reasoning from past experience to what the future will hold. Unlike inductive reasoning, which proceeds from the particular to the general, analogical reasoning always involves inference from the particular to the particular, or from the general to the general. Every analogical inference proceeds from the similarity of two or more things in one or more respects to the similarity in one further respect. But like other inductive reasoning, reasoning by analogy is not certain or demonstratively valid. None of the conclusions arrived at follows with logical necessity from the premises. All that is or that can be claimed in such conclusions is probability. The basic form of reasoning by analogy is as follows:

1. A, B, C, and D all have the properties p and q. (This is the first premise.)
2. A, B, and C all have the property r. (This is the second premise.)
3. Therefore, D probably has the property r.

Note that the conclusion contains the word 'probably'. The premises cannot guarantee the conclusion, although they render it more or less probable. We reason by analogy every day of our lives, like when we purchase the new album of a band or artist we like, or when we go to see the new film of a director or actor we like. This kind of reasoning involves a leap. We assume that because something has happened in the past, it will repeat itself in the future. Yet, in spite of the fact that we frequently use reasoning by analogy, the conclusions do not follow with any degree of certainty or logical necessity. (We may dislike the new album or the new film.) All we can say is that we think it is more or less probable or likely that this will happen, depending on the number of particular instances that serve as the basis for the concluding claim.

Abductive reasoning is similar to induction. It is also known as reasoning to the best explanation, where the situation described by the conclusion would provide a good explanation (perhaps the best) of the circumstances described by the premises. A central feature of abductive reasoning or arguments is that the explanations advanced by their conclusions involve concepts not contained in the premises. Consider this example: 'Dogs must have beliefs since this best explains their behavior of expectation and disappointment.' Expectation- and disappointment-behavior in dogs is best explained in terms of dogs having beliefs. We rely on abductive arguments all the time. We come to conclusions that, on the basis of the available evidence, are the best possible explanations at the time. The test of whether abductive arguments are convincing, therefore, is whether the conclusion is the best possible one available.

Inductive inference is intimately connected with hypothesis. By hypothesis, we generally mean a working assumption, a possible account of something that has not yet been proved or established as correct. We might say that induction or inductive inference involves reasoning from a limited number of observations to a conclusion that goes beyond any finite number of observations. Another way of putting this is that induction involves reasoning from the truth of the consequences of a hypothesis to the truth of the hypothesis itself. Inductive inference not only yields hypotheses but is also instrumental in testing them. Hypothesis involves nondemonstrative inference; it goes beyond basic observational evidence. The following virtues constitute a guide to the framing, and count toward the plausibility, of hypotheses. (In what follows, when I speak of a hypothesis being 'preferable' I generally mean 'more justified'. This equation does not hold all the time, however: there may be a conflict between two or more virtues, and one would have to look at the context to determine which one is to be preferred.)

- Conservatism: A more conservative belief or hypothesis is one that requires fewer revisions in one's belief system as a whole (or in one's total theory).

Other things being equal, the belief or hypothesis involving the least conflict with previous beliefs is to be preferred.
- Modesty: Assumption of as little as will do the job is thought to be a general virtue when one forms a belief or formulates a theory about something.
- Simplicity: Almost all philosophers and scientists accept that, other things being equal, the simpler belief/hypothesis/theory is to be preferred.
- Generality: The hypothesis with the widest range of applicability is to be preferred.
- Refutability: The higher the refutability of a belief/hypothesis/theory, the more informative it is.
- Precision: A belief or hypothesis can be precise in a quantitative ('all', 'no', 'how many'/'how much') as well as qualitative sense (e.g., in the redefinition of terms—giving fuzzy or imprecise terms a sharper definition). The more precise a hypothesis, the more useful it is.

But does inductive support yield genuine justification and knowledge? There is no canon of scientific discovery that would help establish that inductive support yields objective probability. Any argument attempting to do this would have to be deductively valid or inductively strong. But we cannot validly deduce propositions about the future from propositions about the past. This is what has become known in philosophical literature as the problem of induction. Eighteenth-century Scottish philosopher David Hume (1896) has pointed out the principal weakness of induction as a source of knowledge against those who believe that induction is a reliable foundation for all science. His reasoning is as follows: if all of the swans you have personally observed have been white, then it is scientifically very probable that all of the swans in the world are white—until you visit Australia and see a black swan. Hume recognized that all scientific findings based on observation and induction must remain conjectural and temporary. Induction can never provide the kind of certainty that logic can.

Where does all of this leave us in terms of the present discussion? It is clear that every hypothesis is underdetermined by evidence. In other words, the evidence available to us at a particular time may be insufficient to determine what beliefs we should hold in response to it. It follows that the choice between hypotheses requires reference to factors outside or beyond evidence. If our nondeductive practices are reliable (i.e., if they yield true beliefs most of the time), then they arguably yield justification even if their reliability is not set in stone. (I will return to this point later.) The 'common sense' approach supports reliance on inductive, analogical and abductive reasoning. The principle of the uniformity of nature states that, given uniformity of nature, all future events will relevantly resemble past or present events. ('As the laws of nature have been in the past, so they will be in the future.') If we could not rely on something like this principle, everyday life would fall apart. We could not make promises, toast a slice of bread, or open a bank account, let alone plan and organize our teaching, unless we could count on life tomorrow being broadly like life yesterday and today.

EXPLANATION

The question whether a written or spoken passage expresses or is intended to express an argument or an explanation is problematic. Because both may contain identical premise-indicators ('since', 'because', and so on) and conclusion-indicators ('as a result', 'that is why', and so on), it is often difficult to distinguish arguments from explanations. This difficulty is compounded by the introduction of reasoning to the best explanation (or abductive arguments). Normally, if the purpose is to establish the truth of a proposition, then it is an argument that is formulated. If the purpose is to account for something (the truth of which is not in doubt), then it is an explanation that is formulated.

The basic questions of philosophy are asked by the average three- to four-year-olds: 'What is . . . ?', 'How do you know . . . ?', 'Why . . . ?' and so on. Naturally, it is not only young children who demand that something that they do not understand be explained to them. Every one of us does it, every single day. Explanation is generally regarded as a process, the end or goal of which is understanding. In requesting an explanation, however, people are often asking for different things. When I ask a student to explain a certain passage in a poem, I am asking her to paraphrase or clarify it, which, in turn, will provide me with evidence as to whether or not she understands the poem. When I ask a child, 'Why did you make such a mess?' it is not because I fail to understand what the child is doing that I request an explanation. Rather, I want to make the child aware of his behavior. Asking the child to explain himself, in this sense, is both a request for justification and an attempt to raise his awareness. On the other hand, it might be because I do not understand or am unclear about something, or because I do not know what to do in a certain situation, that I request an explanation.

Explanation plays a very important part in the natural and social sciences, including educational research, theory, and practice. We ask for an explanation when we do not understand something, when something is puzzling because of a gap in our understanding or in the information we have received. A successful explanation is one that removes the puzzle by supplying information that fills this gap. I will discuss different kinds of explanation and criteria for distinguishing good explanations from bad or inadequate explanations. Explanations, like arguments, can be good or bad, strong or weak. What counts as a good explanation depends partly on what kind of explanation it is.

A successful explanation, I have suggested, is one that removes a puzzle by filling a gap in our understanding. The gap is often filled by a hypothesis, but not all hypotheses are explanatory. How does a hypothesis serve to remove a puzzle, and what are the characteristics of a good explanatory hypothesis? In his book *An Introduction of Philosophical Analysis,* American philosopher John Hospers (1987) discusses scientific explanation and 'why' questions. He distinguishes between the giving of reasons and the giving of explanations: specifically, explanations of occurrences in nature, be it of a particular event, for example, why the pipes burst (241) or of a certain kind of event, for example, an explanation of the laws of nature themselves that determine the freezing of water. In doing so, he considers this question (240–241): How do the patterns of explanation in these two cases of explanation (of specific events and of natural laws) differ? Although hypotheses are crucial to explanation, they do not always qualify as explanations (241). Ordinarily, a hypothesis is not an explanation (or an account) of a past event, but rather a prediction of a future event (I will say more about this in what follows) or an account of something for which the evidence is not all in yet. A hypothesis is not explanatory unless it suggests a causal connection.

What interests philosophers about explanation is, first and foremost, the possibility of different kinds of explanation. A distinction is commonly made between explanation in the natural sciences and explanation in the social sciences. If the distinction between the different kinds of explanation is valid, there will be different conceptual properties involved (in the former case, the notion of causality, or causal diagnosis; in the latter case, intentionality, or purposiveness). Of further interest are the logical properties of explanation (its form) as well as its pragmatic aspects (in other words, how to do it well).

The content of a good or sufficient causal explanation refers to the cause or causes of the event to be explained. When we seek to explain an event, we are often confronted with a multitude of causes. The trick is to determine which of these causes is or are relevant. What counts as a good or sufficient explanation depends on the context or on the factors singled out as relevant within a particular context as well as on our theoretical interests in the event being explained. On occasion, giving a fuller or more complete explanation may not be pragmatic. (Thus, it may be sufficient to respond to the question of a six-year-old, 'What is sex?', by saying that sex is 'like sneezing, but much nicer'—something we would not get away with in the context of slightly older children.) It may actually be detrimental if it is beyond the grasp of the audience, be it listeners or readers. Pragmatically, an explanation should contain neither too little nor too much.

I have suggested that explanations should be evaluated both in terms of their content and their context. But the form of an explanation is also important, especially (but not only) in the natural sciences. What is called the form of explanation is constituted by its structure: that is, the elements that make up an explanation. Explanation in the natural sciences must be expressible in argument form. An argument, when stated in proper form, is made up of premise- and conclusion-statements. The classical argument form is

(1) If p, then q
(2) p
(3) Therefore, q

According to the deductive-nomological model of explanation (sometimes also called the hypothetico-deductive model), the premise-statements would be

- the statement of a law (this could be a universal statement involving reference to 'all' or 'any', or it could be a conditional statement rendered in terms of antecedent and consequent, that is, an 'if-then' statement)
- the statement of antecedent conditions.

These are followed by the conclusion-statement, in the form of the event to be explained.

The 'deductive' part of this model refers to 'deductive validity'. 'Nomological' refers to laws. Laws are statements of regularities governing natural events. They refer to the necessary or nonaccidental connection or connections of events, which usually, if not invariably, means the causal relationship or relationships between events. Where a law is stated in terms of antecedent and consequent, it involves a conditional or hypothetical statement. Take the following example: a child asks, 'Why did I get a shock?' The response might be, 'Because you touched an unshielded copper wire.' Written in argument form, our explanation will look like this:

- All metals act as conductors of electricity. (This is a statement of a universal law.)
- If (or whenever) you touch an unshielded copper wire, you will get a shock. (This is a conditional statement.)
- You touched an unshielded copper wire. (This is a statement of antecedent conditions, conditions that have prevailed or had to prevail for the event to occur.)
- You got a shock. (This is the 'conclusion' statement: the event to be explained.)

The child, knowing that he did touch an unshielded copper wire, will probably not be satisfied with our response, and will ask again, 'But why did that give me a shock?' The child would be entitled to do so. After all, he may have touched an unshielded copper wire the previous day and nothing happened. We will now embark on a lengthy explanation detailing the causal relationship between the events in question, mentioning electricity, the fact that copper (being a metal) acts as a conductor and that only a live copper wire will cause a shock. Our modified explanation, in argument form, will now include not only a general but also a precise statement of the relevant law as the first premise. The second premise, too, will have been made more precise: You touched an unshielded copper wire that had an electrical current running through it.

In the social sciences, on the other hand, there are—strictly speaking—no such laws. Thus, the form of explanation in the social sciences can have no premise containing the statement of a law. At best, it will include a premise containing the statement of a general trend or characteristic behavior. Explanation in the social sciences (psychology, sociology, social anthropology, and so on) involves reference not to causes but to purposes, intentions, motives, reasons, beliefs, and the like. There is some ambiguity here. When I ask why something happened as it did, I am asking for an explanation of some event or (type of) process in the course of nature. On the other hand, when I ask someone why she believes that a certain proposition is true, I am asking her to provide reasons (evidence, justification) in support of her belief. Of course, the reasons that person provides may include reference to causes, but they will still be that person's reasons for believing what she does believe.

This is, however, not what is normally meant by 'explanation in the social sciences'. This kind of explanation is usually called teleological explanation, or explanation in terms of a purpose, end, or goal. When we explain to learners why the Xhosa cattle killings and destruction of crops occurred in South Africa in 1856, we will refer to Nongqawuse's reasons, the beliefs of the Gcaleka Xhosa, and the motives and purposes of the Eastern Cape administrators. When we explain the ebb and flow of the property market, we will refer to buyers' and sellers' expectations or levels of confidence. When we explain a poem, we will refer to the poet's intentions. Similarly, when I explain to a learner or to that learner's parents why he received a low mark, I am not providing a causal explanation of the event. I will mention the learner's bad performance, perhaps his inability to concentrate, the undesirable influence of the learner's peers, perhaps even the effects of peer pressure on him; but none of these *caused* me to give the learner a bad mark. The mark did not result as a matter of causal necessity. I could have done otherwise. I had reasons for giving the learner the mark you did. My intention or motive may have been to sound a wake-up call. My belief may have been that giving the learner a better mark would have been tantamount to sending him the wrong message. My purpose may have been to respond to a bad performance with a deservedly bad mark. (I may, of course, also dislike the learner intensely, and his bad performance may have provided me with a welcome opportunity to give my dislike rational expression. This reason, of course, will presumably not feature in my explanation.)

With regard to these different kinds of explanation, the virtues guiding the framing of hypotheses remain significant. In other words, teleological explanation, like causal explanation, must be guided by simplicity, refutability, precision, and so on, if it is to be 'done well'. In the case of explaining to the child why he received a shock, we are guided by the virtues of generality and precision. Similarly, when we explain the Xhosa cattle killings, we will set out the concomitant reasons, beliefs, and motives modestly and simply, but also in detail. We will not just refer to some 'really bad vibes' between Nongqawuse, the Gcaleka Xhosa, and the Eastern Cape administrators.

Given our role of parents and educators in belief formation, explanation is often not enough to nurture appropriate beliefs in children or learners. We may, for example, explain to them the dangers of drug abuse or unprotected sex, but what we want to achieve arguably goes beyond merely accounting for something. After all, explanation is of value primarily if the truth of what is accounted for is not in doubt or if children or learners do not (yet) have any intense or passionately held beliefs, let alone an idea of the truth, with regard to the dangers of drug abuse or unprotected sex. With older children and learners, it may be different. Nurturing appropriate beliefs in them, and getting them to change their minds, may require rational persuasion. Similarly, we will be aware that we normally have to provide persuasive arguments for having failed a student, for using particular classroom materials or for designing a learning program in one way rather than another.

INDOCTRINATION AND RATIONAL PERSUASION

Why is persuasion an issue in education, and what kind of persuasion is appropriate? Apart from the development of knowledge education is also concerned with the acquisition of skills, dispositions, and certain values. How do we instill dispositions in learners? Which values should we promote? And how do we instill these values in learners without resorting to indoctrination? Even if there is general agreement on the values that ought to be promoted, the question remains, how are they to be promoted? How do we instill them in learners or—more generally—in those who have not previously been exposed to these values? Can we avoid indoctrination in this regard? What, if anything, is wrong with indoctrination anyway?

Education in the sense of personal development refers to a particular kind of human achievement that is considered to be an intrinsically valuable development of the individual. Education is not merely a tool or instrument for getting a job or improving your earning capacity. Education is valuable in itself and for its own sake. The knowledge and understanding obtained as well as the corresponding emotions and attitudes acquired become features of a person's personal identity. They shape that person's sense of what is valuable. Education in this sense is desirable because it provides worthwhile ends or goals in life. It constitutes the basis for self-improvement and individual autonomy as well as for personal responsibility.

Educative teaching necessarily includes rational persuasion, as opposed to indoctrination. The exact meaning of the word 'indoctrination' has been the subject of considerable controversy. However, there appear to be two points on which there exists agreement: first, the sense in which the term is used today (but not necessarily how it was used in the past) has negative connotations and indicates a moral transgression; second, it has to do with beliefs and belief formation. We might attempt to argue that the pejorative sense of the word 'indoctrination' is not always justified. There may be instances of indoctrination (with regard to political and moral education) that are justified: persuading children to be good citizens, vegetarians, or vegans, environmentally aware, and so on. On the other hand, we might argue that indoctrination is undesirable, by definition, because it fails to engage the recipient's capacity for reason and reflection. For example, indoctrination could be described as a form of miseducation (see Horsthemke, 2014b: 38; Crittenden 1972: 146). There are at least three criteria for indoctrination as a form of miseducation: teaching may be judged to be indoctrination in terms of method, content, or intention (see Crittenden 1972: 146; Callan and Arena 2009: 105, 107–109)—that is, *how* it occurs, *what* is being taught, and *why* something is being taught. Indoctrination commonly occurs when

- an educator employs a pedagogical method that is inconsistent with the requirements and principles of inquiry, via tendentious chains of reasoning or systematic distortion, for example, by suppressing or bypassing critical evaluation of reasons and evidence, and/or by proceeding coercively;
- an educator presents content in a way that violates the criteria for inquiry, when certain doctrines or propositions whose epistemic status is questionable are deliberately presented as true and unassailable, or when content has been intentionally and systematically distorted;
- an educator's intention is to foster intense beliefs in the learner, to get her to believe something even against her better judgment and contrary to available reasons and evidence.

While doubts have been expressed about these criteria being sufficient or even necessary for indoctrination, notably by American educational philosophers Eamonn Callan and Dylan Arena (2009), it is usually extremely difficult to separate these criteria; that is, it is almost impossible to speak about indoctrinatory methods without also referring to the content of what is being taught, and the intentions behind this. Indoctrination commonly occurs when there is a confluence of relevant method, content, and intention.

Educators arguably have a responsibility to rely on rational persuasion (an aspect of which is constituted by argumentation, as I will explain below), and *not* indoctrination, in attempting to develop appropriate beliefs, values, and dispositions in learners. Rational persuasion engages both the intellect of the learner (her capacity for effective thinking and for understanding) and her feelings. It is desirable neither that learners be guided solely by their feelings or emotions nor that they be guided exclusively by their intellects. Feelings on their own are not a trustworthy guide because they change, often quickly and radically. Yet, to expect learners to rely on their intellects alone would be to treat them as intellectual robots. The idea of mass-producing intellectual robots acting solely on principle or on the basis of cost-benefit analyses, and who dismiss the rational significance of feeling and caring, is not an attractive one.[5] Rational persuasion plays an important part in changing beliefs and values. The crucial feature of both rational persuasion and argumentation, but not of indoctrination, is that they aim at truth, not at consensus or—what appears to be worse—intellectual dependence, subordination, or oppression.

While there may be justifiable instances of what appears to be indoctrination (think of White's example of the fearful girl and her parents at the beginning of his chapter on 'Beliefs' in his book *The Child's Mind*; White 2002[6]), the important distinction here is that indoctrination usually has little or no regard for the recipient of indoctrination (unlike in the case of the child in White's example) and is not usually aimed at securing only short-term or temporary benefits (like calming the child's fear). Indoctrination commonly occurs in order to safeguard the political, religious, social, and economic *status quo* in the longer term, often at the expense of those who are at the receiving end of the process of indoctrination. Educational examples of such long-term securing of the *status quo* might be instilling in learners an inferior self-image through Bantu education or a superior self-image through Christian National Education, teaching creationism in biology classes, and how the doctrines of Hitler, Stalin, and Mao doctrines pervaded all education and schooling in Germany, the Soviet Union, and China at the time (see Horsthemke 2014b: 38–39; a contemporary example is of course constituted by the Kim dynasty in North Korea).

Rational persuasion plays an important part in changing beliefs and values. In their book *The Web of Belief*, Quine and Ullian give an account of how persuasion bears on belief formation. Assuming a common frame of reference is useful with regard to argument, but not always advisable for teachers. Assuming a common frame of reference means sharing relevant beliefs and assumptions, as well as certain skills, like the capacity to make certain logical connections or inferences. Educators should be aware that they cannot take as much for granted from learners as they can from their colleagues. It is advisable that educators take learners through each of the steps required for informed decision-making, the recognition and evaluation of arguments, language learning, the acquisition of mathematical skills, and so on.

In Plato's theory of education, there is a notion that we do not actually learn anything, but that what we call learning is recollection. The spontaneous recovery of knowledge, too, is nothing but recollection (Plato 1970a: 43). The soul or mind has passed through a previous series of embodied and disembodied states, and the knowledge from these previous cycles needs merely to be awakened, so Socrates says. Everyone is born with such knowledge. It only has to be drawn out by the process of education. Socrates appears in the midwife role, eliciting the Pythagorean Theorem from a slave boy without any formal education. Socrates contends that this knowledge will not come from teaching, but from questioning (ibid.). Like Socrates (and Plato), Quine and Ullian (1978: 174–175) suggest a practice of continuous questioning as appropriate for educators or—as they suggest—in training. As they point out, part of our responsibility to our learners is to school them in critical and rigorous thinking. This is achieved in part by continuous questioning, which is exactly what Socrates is doing and advocating.

Quine and Ullian part company with Socrates (and Plato), presumably, with regard to the doctrine of recollection, which states that learning is remembering. According to Socrates, education consists in eliciting knowledge; in drawing out knowledge that already exists in the learner. Quine and Ullian would arguably maintain that education consists (or should consist) in instilling or inculcating knowledge, skills, and values in learners. In other words, no one is born with knowledge. It is acquired, which is precisely what Socrates is contesting. In conclusion to the cave parable, Socrates claims that "certain professors of education must be wrong when they say that they can put a knowledge into a soul which was not there before, like sight into blind eyes" (Plato 1970b).

Plato's theory of recollection is controversial. To a large extent, it depends on the plausibility of the doctrine of metempsychosis (transmigration of souls). Someone who is not impressed by the idea of a disembodied soul may be similarly unimpressed by the idea of innate knowledge waiting to be recovered. Furthermore, if innate knowledge is remembered from an earlier life, then the relevant source of justification is memory. But memory is often unreliable and, therefore, a somewhat dubious source of knowledge. Of course, the idea of innate knowledge does not depend on the possibility of reincarnation. But even if it is considered as separate from the doctrine of metempsychosis, there is a further problem. How did this knowledge originate? The hypothesis that human beings are born with an intact and complete body of knowledge, just waiting to be tapped, is at best unscientific (because nothing could possibly disprove it, or prove it, for that matter) and at worst false. Interestingly, Socrates himself says—immediately after the last comment quoted above—that the power and capacity of learning exist in the soul already. This is relatively uncontroversial. But the claim that the power and capacity of learning already exist in the soul is very different from the claim that knowledge already exists in the soul. That human beings are educable, that human beings are born with the power and capacity to learn, makes instilling or the inculcation of knowledge, skills, and values possible in the first place. We need not opt for the considerably more controversial view of knowledge as recollection or remembering and of education as elicitation of this knowledge.

How would you go about convincing someone of something? Quine and Ullian suggest the following strategies of rational persuasion:

- starting from beliefs that people already hold, arguing from these beliefs as premises and arguing toward a conclusion that people (at least initially) have not been able or willing to accept; insofar as beliefs are not shared, this process involves two additional strategies:
  ◦ overwhelming (i.e., supplying such a wealth of evidence, proof, or reasons in favor of one's conclusion that one individual ends up convincing another, or others, in spite of their initial belief/s to the contrary)
  ◦ undermining (i.e., directly challenging the other person's belief/s to the contrary; for example, attacking what appears to be the most influential among the beliefs that one seeks to change) (see Quine and Ullian 1978: 130–132).

Quine and Ullian suggest that a combination of overwhelming and undermining is commonly the best strategy of all, that is, for changing people's minds. A particular form of rational persuasion is what American philosopher Alvin Goldman (1994) characterizes as "argumentation."

ARGUMENT AND ARGUMENTATION

Goldman distinguishes between two senses of the term 'argument'. We might say that the first refers to argument as product, while the second refers to argument as process. The first concerns the logical or abstract sense of argument. The second concerns what Goldman calls the social or interpersonal sense and goes on to refer to as argumentation.

Goldman works with a "conception of social epistemology that focuses on the extent to which social and interpersonal practices promote true or false belief" (Goldman 1994: 28, fn. 1). He calls argumentation "a complex speech act in which a thesis is presented and defended with reasons." In other words, the quality of argumentation depends in part on the justification that is offered in the process. The norms of good argumentation flow from what Goldman (28) calls "the epistemic situation of cognizers" (i.e., the social and interpersonal practices of all those working with knowledge and justification), "and are best seen as a social quest for true belief and error avoidance." (This is an important point to which I will return shortly.) Argumentation aims to persuade others of a truth or dissuade them from a falsehood. It does not aim at consensus or agreement. Note that 'consensus', or agreement, *as such* does not amount to truth. This is why Goldman presupposes a 'realist' conception of truth.

The "epistemic situation of cognizers" is characterized partly by what has been called "the epistemological division of labor" (30), a notion very closely related to what has been established by Hardwig (1991). Given that it is impossible for a single person to have epistemic access to all information, even to all of the information relating to a particular domain, we benefit from sharing and exchanging information, and from other people correcting our beliefs. This has to do with a second feature of our epistemic situation, namely that we are all fallible. Even with the best intentions, we might believe and assert falsehoods. Others may, on the basis of possessing knowledge and information that we do not have, help to identify and correct these mistakes. A third feature is people's tendency to deceive, in other words, to make and defend claims they know to be false. This is phenomenon that has come to characterize, for example, politics in the so-called 'post-truth' era with its insistence upon 'alternative facts' (see Horsthemke 2017b).

What Goldman refers to as "norms," "rules" or "principles of good argumentation" constitutes part of a practice aimed at encouraging "the exchange of truth through nonnegligent, mutually corrective and sincere speech" (30). He distinguishes between two different cases of argumentation: "core" and "noncore" cases (33), before providing two examples of noncore cases: "playing the devil's advocate" and "trying on an argument for size." The former occurs when a speaker defends a view or position without actually subscribing to it (in fact, he may actually hold the exact opposite view). In other words, he is merely trying to elicit a strong reaction or response from his audience. The latter involves following an argument where it leads, without the person involved having made up his or her mind about his or her own position.

Goldman lists the following rules of core argumentation (34–43):

(1) A speaker should assert a conclusion only if she believes it.
(2) A speaker should assert a premise only if she believes it.
(3) A speaker should assert a premise only if she is justified in believing it.
(4) A speaker should affirm a conclusion on the basis of stated premises only if
   (a) those premises strongly support the conclusion,
   (b) she believes that they very strongly support it and
   (c) she is justified in believing that they strongly support it.

In the final two sections of Goldman's article (44–49), he draws a distinction between "folk principles of argumentation" and "principles at work in various specialized institutions and disciplines of our culture" (44), a distinction that resonates with that between 'continuous questioning' and 'assuming a common frame of reference' referred to in the previous section.

The first thing to notice about these rules is that Goldman combines the standard form of an argument or inferential reasoning (premise or premises and conclusion) with components of the traditional understanding of propositional knowledge (belief and justification; as we have seen above, in the discussion of the "realist conception of truth," he deals with the truth component independently). Consider the following rule of argumentation: "A speaker should assert a premise only if she is justified in believing it" (34). Goldman goes on to modify it (rule 3*): "A speaker should assert a premise only if she thinks she is justified in believing it" (35). What is the difference? The latter formulation (3*), unlike the former (3), implies that good argumentation requires a person to be aware of his or her justification.

Can young children already be credited with knowledge? Or can a person be said to know only if he knows that he knows? Suppose we ask a learner to provide reasons for a correct answer he has given. Perhaps the learner will be able to provide such reasons, perhaps not. If not, would this mean that the learner does not know even if he invariably manages to give the right answer to similar types of questions? This leads to the debate about knowledge and justification as it is waged between internalism and externalism. From an educational perspective, my main question is this: Under what circumstances can educators properly ascribe knowledge to learners? In other words, when can we say that a learner knows something?

EPISTEMIC INTERNALISM AND EPISTEMIC EXTERNALISM

The traditional view is that awareness of one's justification is required for knowledge. The traditional theory of justification is an *internalist* theory.

According to *epistemic internalism*, all aspects or factors required for a belief to be justified must be *internal*, that is, cognitively available or accessible, to the believer. Must a person *be aware of* or be able to *provide justification* (*evidence* or *reasons*) in order to know? It is possible for a person to have access to evidence that logically supports one of her beliefs even though it plays no psychological role in sustaining the belief. In such a case, one would (probably) say that the evidence does not justify the person in her belief, and that she does not know. However, the fact that someone may not be able to provide her reasons or justification for her beliefs does not *necessarily* imply faulty reasoning.

It is possible to believe something because of evidence that strongly supports the belief without being aware of it. Here are three examples that illustrate this case:

1. My dog believes that I am about to take her for a walk because she hears me getting her leash from the drawer, but she presumably does not think, 'This is evidence for that'.
2. The secretary in our department is talking to my colleague. After a while, he starts to think, 'She is attracted to me', although he does not know why he thinks this. He just cannot help thinking it. In fact, she has given him subconscious signals by means of 'body language', and these clues cause his belief even though he is not consciously aware of them.
3. If I remember that the date of my friend's death was November 28 without being able to quote evidence, one would ordinarily say that I know this (provided that my memory is reliable).

Such beliefs are to some degree justified. Are they knowledge? If awareness of one's evidence is required for knowledge, much of what we ordinarily regard as knowledge, including 'perceptual knowledge', is not knowledge. Internalism demands that the factors on which the justification of a belief depends be accessible to the consciousness of the believer. But this is because internalists have tended to put themselves into the position of the believer, emphasizing '*my* reasons for believing that *p*'. Of course, to be able to answer questions like 'Do I in fact know what I am inclined to think I know?' or 'Are my beliefs really justified?', I must be aware of my justification. But is such awareness required *to be justified* or *to know*? Consider the following questions: *Does my dog know that I am about to take her for a walk, or does she just believe it?*, and *Is my colleague's belief that the secretary is attracted to him in fact justified?* Must my dog or my colleague be aware of their evidence in order for us to answer these questions?

Externalists, who emphasize '*the* reasons for *my* believing that *p*', would say no. It is sufficient, they would say, that the reasons my dog and my colleague could be recognized by *us*, that is, by those who *are* aware of the requisite fit between belief and justification. *Epistemic externalism* argues that the basis of much of what people know might not be available or accessible to their consciousness. Some of the justifying factors or aspects are or could be *external* to the believer, such as beliefs produced by a reliable mechanism. In other words, a reliable process of belief formation may yield knowledge even if people have no conscious justification for the belief concerned. Externalism, but not internalism, would therefore ascribe cognitive states to animals and young children.

To return to my earlier questions: Can young children already be credited with knowledge? Or can a person be said to know only if he *knows that he knows*? If so, an infinite regress threatens: *I know that I have passed the entrance exam* only if *I knows that I know that I have passed the entrance exam*, and I know this only if I *know that I know that I know*, and so forth. Perhaps one might speak of *levels* of knowledge and distinguish between *reflective* and *nonreflective knowledge*. One might say then that nonreflective knowledge requires no awareness of one's justification, while reflective knowledge requires some awareness of it. I will return to this and related issues shortly.

TRUTH

I suggested earlier that both rational persuasion and argumentation, as contrasted with indoctrination, aim at truth, not at consensus. Goldman's article also contains a useful discussion of consensus and truth (31–33). His arguments against a "pure consensus conception" of truth are the following:

- If consensus were the sole aim of argumentation, then it would be permissible "to suppress evidence in the interest of consensus" (31). Think of a creationist teacher in this regard, and biological, anthropological, and paleontological evidence for the evolution of humankind.
- It would be undesirable to introduce evidence that would threaten to undermine (preexisting) consensus (32). Again, in a strongly religious school context, scientific evidence for the origin and development of humankind is unlikely to be covered.
- Finally, it would be legitimate to secure consensus through artificial means, even by (latent threat of) force (32). This, of course, characterizes any totalitarian society or (education) system whose continued existence crucially depends on suppression of dissent or dissension and critical interrogation of the *status quo*.

Not only may what everyone (or the majority) agrees on be false (think of a fundamentalist educational institution or a flat-earth society in this regard), but the above implications also render the sole focus on consensus both epistemically and pedagogically undesirable. (This does not mean that consensus is not ever worth seeking. Think, for example, of learners agreeing on certain rules to be followed in the classroom or school, rules that will then be binding on everyone and ensure classroom or school discipline.)

Up to now, I have discussed in considerable detail only two of the three conditions of knowledge stipulated in the traditional philosophical definition: belief and justification. I have said little about the nature of truth, other than that it refers to what 'is' the case, what is in agreement with fact or reality. What follows is a brief sketch of the pertinent views.

The first theory of truth, the so-called "correspondence theory," holds that a criterion for truth is correspondence with reality. In other words, a belief-statement or knowledge-claim is true if it corresponds with the facts or if it corresponds with some actual state of affairs in the world. This is the common sense view. Most dictionary definitions of truth are versions of this theory. Other theories have been advocated, however, like the consensus theory discussed by Goldman: truth, according to this theory, is whatever is (or might come to be) agreed upon by relevant parties. A third candidate is the coherence theory of truth, according to which the only absolute truth is the whole. Anything less than that can only furnish degrees of truth. In other words, a belief-statement or knowledge-claim is true only insofar as it is part of a coherent and consistent body of mutually supporting statements or claims. Fourth, according to the pragmatic (or pragmatist) theory of truth, a belief-statement or knowledge-claim is true if it 'works', that is, if accepting it would be more beneficial in the long run than accepting any competing statement or claim. Fifth, the constructivist theory of truth states that truth is constructed by social processes, that it is culturally and historically specific, and characteristically shaped by the power struggles within a particular community. A sixth conception does not involve a theory of truth so much as a dismissal of truth. The so-called redundancy theory holds that the concept of truth is redundant since, for example, 'It is true that p' expresses exactly the same thing as 'p'. According to this theory, the concept of truth can be bypassed in the traditional philosophical definition of knowledge

Without being able to elaborate on the matter and to critique rival conceptions of truth (consensus, coherence, pragmatism, and so on), I am suggesting here that the common sense account of truth assumes that there is at least some correspondence between the statements we utter and the world as it exists: that is, independently of us. The central element of correspondence theories of truth is that other things being equal, the truth or falsity of what is said has something to do with a reality that is independent of the statements made about it. We might legitimately describe the world in many different ways for different purposes. But in order for those descriptions and distinctions to stick, there must be features of the world that enable them to be made. We cannot get away from reality and from the truth or falsity of statements that give an account of it (see Horsthemke 2010c: 89–90). Consider the following claims:

- 'There is no such thing as (universal) truth.'
- 'What is true for you is not necessarily what is true for me.'

It makes good sense to take issue with these statements. It makes sense to deny what is said here, and to do this is to concede that what has been said might be wrong and that its negation would be correct. Otherwise, what is the point of disagreeing or arguing? Or what is the point of asserting a point of view? This leads to the unavoidable position that statements (insofar as they are meaningful) are either true or false.

David Bridges (1999) has argued, quite compellingly, that different theories of truth might be seen to fit different areas of knowledge or (educational) research models—without implying relativism about truth. For example, the correspondence theory of truth seems to have its natural home in at least some of the empirical sciences, while the coherence theory of truth pertains, for example, to mathematics and symbolic logic. The pragmatist theory of truth (with utility as its characteristic mark; i.e., a proposition is true if it is useful to believe) is appropriate for technology and certain applied sciences, whereas the consensus conception of truth has a distinct appeal in the realm of social and political decision-making and is also relevant in matters of aesthetics and taste.

In essence, this sums up our discussion of the conditions of knowledge: belief, justification, and truth. Each of these conditions appears to be necessary (the redundancy theory of truth notwithstanding), but are they really jointly sufficient (as it had been assumed for the longest time since Plato)? In other words, does the presence or confluence of these three conditions guarantee that a particular knowledge-claim is, in fact, knowledge? In the section that follows, I will examine some of the difficulties encountered by the traditional philosophical definition of knowledge.

JUSTIFICATION AND CONTEXT

If someone has a justified true belief, does that person have knowledge? Here, following Gettier's influential arguments (which appeared in what has become one of the best-known articles in modern philosophy; 1963: 121–123), I will give some examples that show that these conditions are not jointly sufficient for knowledge.

Consider the following situation: I am sitting in the staffroom of my school. I look at my watch at exactly 8 o'clock. I have excellent reasons for thinking that my watch is reliable. It has never let me down and since its hands are in the 8 o'clock position, I believe that it is 8 o'clock. In fact, however, my watch stopped working exactly twelve hours earlier. I have a justified true belief that it is 8 o'clock. According to the traditional philosophical definition of knowledge, therefore, I know that it is 8 o'clock. But do I know? Surely not: my belief, though justified, is only accidentally true. My justification involves the false belief that my watch is working. We might, therefore, modify the definition of knowledge by adding a fourth condition, namely that a person's justification for believing something to be the case involves no false beliefs among those that are pertinent.

Now consider another situation: I enter the multipurpose room at my school. The first person I see is one of the older boys, who is carrying a knife and a gun. I naturally form the belief that the boy is armed (in the sense of carrying real weapons) and I am justified, given the evidence. My belief is also true: the boy is carrying real weapons. But all of the other boys in the room, who appear to be armed, are actually carrying toy knives and toy guns. In fact, the boys are rehearsing a school play about violence in the townships (shantytowns, *favelas*, or *banlieues*). I have not yet seen any of these boys and have formed no general belief to the effect that all the boys who appear to be armed are, in fact, armed. I have a justified true belief that the first boy I have seen is carrying real weapons. My justification involves no false beliefs. Therefore, according to the modified definition of knowledge, I know that the boy is armed. But do I know? It would appear not. My justification for my belief is not suitably connected with its truth. In this situation, appearing to be armed and being armed are unconnected. An analogous diagnosis holds in the broken watchcase. My justification for my belief is not suitably connected with its truth. The fact that the watch indicates 8 o'clock and that it actually is 8 o'clock are unconnected.

To what extent, if at all, are knowledge and justification context-dependent? The main purpose in the remainder of this section is to deepen and perhaps challenge the ordinary understanding of the relationship between context, justification, and knowledge, with special reference to educational practice. Earlier, I considered the question of when an educator can say that a learner knows something. I now revisit this question, but from a different angle.

What degree of justification must a true belief have in order to be knowledge? As I explained earlier, logical or objective certainty seems too much to require, as it would rule out all kinds of knowledge claims that seem to be true. On the other hand, minimal or weak justification is plainly not enough. For example, we would not accept the following argument: 'I know that older boys are carrying knives and guns because I have a hunch (or had a dream about it or heard it from the staffroom gossip, who has been known to exaggerate).' A hunch does not amount to justification. (Although a hunch may be reason enough for you to investigate the matter.)

In practice, the degree of justification required for attributing knowledge to a person varies with the context. For example, we would normally accept that I know that the boy I see in front of me is armed because I am aware of the knife and gun he is carrying. Yet, if there is a possibility that the boy is carrying toy weapons (as in the case of a school play about township violence), we might deny that I know what I claim to know. In a situation such as this, the reasons or justification provided for my belief are defeated or undermined by possible counterevidence. The implication of this example and others like it is that when we determine whether or not another person knows something, we must be mindful of possible defeating evidence. To do this, we need to take the particular circumstances or context of knowledge claims into account. Indeed, it may even be suggested that perhaps all knowledge is 'relative' to a context of discussion and evaluation.

KNOWLEDGE, CONTEXT, AND EPISTEMOLOGICAL RELATIVISM

American philosopher Stewart Cohen's verdict that the "social component" of knowledge is best seen as indicating that "attributions of knowledge are context-sensitive" (1986: 574) is related to what Scheffler says about adequate justification.[7] Scheffler argues (1965: 57) that the idea of adequacy is

> a matter of appraisal, involving standards of judgment that may differ from age to age, from culture to culture, and even from person to person. The variability of such standards does not, however, imply that assessments of knowledge are arbitrary or that the would-be assessor is somehow paralyzed. He needs to assess in accord with his own best standards at the time, but he may hold his assessment subject to change, should he later have cause to revise these standards.

These standards may be applied more strictly in some cases, more approximately in others, "thus giving rise to multiple interpretations of *knowing*" (58). Thus, the justification component permits some kind of leeway. What counts as adequate or suitable justification in the case of a young child, or learner, or person from a remote rural area, with limited opportunities, resources, or access to information, differs from that required of an older, more mature child, or learner, or person from an industrialized, technologically advanced or privileged, urban background. "As the child grows," Scheffler notes, "and as his prior learning takes hold, his capacity increases, allowing us to tighten the application of our standards in gauging his current performance" (57). Thus, with this growth in the child's cognitive capacity, "the same subject may thus come to be known under ever more stringent interpretations of *known*" (ibid.). Yet, in all the various cases, the justified belief must be true. In the absence of truth, one cannot meaningfully speak of, or ascribe, knowledge. Scheffler suggests a subtle shift from examining beliefs to examining the *contexts* in which beliefs are advanced as knowledge claims. In other words, he suggests that we distinguish the question concerning justification (of a belief) from the "question of *appraisal of the believer*" (64). "To speak of the right to be sure is, in the present context, to appraise the *credentials* of belief from the vantage point of our own standards; it is to spell out the attitude of these standards toward specific *credentials* offered for a belief," Scheffler contends[8] (ibid.).

Like Scheffler, Cohen argues that the suitability of justification, or having good reasons, depends on the relevant epistemic community. He advances his argument through an analysis of what it means to have good reasons for believing something. The concept of *defeasibility* is crucial to Cohen's argument. One's reasons for believing something are *defeasible* if there is something else that could count against them, that is, something that could *defeat* them or undermine their feasibility.

I have already given an example of a situation that could defeat my reasons for believing that the boy in front of her is armed. Here is another example, borrowed from Cohen's article. Suppose a person walks into a room and sees a table that looks red. Let us assume further that the table is in fact red. On the face of it, the person has good reasons to believe that the table is red. But suppose someone who is trustworthy, that is, both honest and competent, says that there is a concealed red light shining on the table. This is a defeater. It counts against the person's other reasons. Suppose two people, one aged six and the other aged sixteen, both look into a room and see a red table. They both say that they know there is a red table in the room because they can see it. A third person, a physical science teacher, says to them, 'Perhaps the table isn't red at all; it might only look red because it has a red light shining on it.' What the teacher says counts as a defeater. While this may be obvious to the sixteen-year-old once it has been pointed out, it is unlikely to be obvious to the six-year-old. The six-year-old does not yet have the concepts and level of reasoning needed for seeing why the presence of a red light could count against his reasons for believing that the table is red. So should we conclude that the six-year-old does not have good reasons for believing that the table is red? No. According to Cohen, we can say that someone (in this case, the six-year-old) has good reasons if, given his reasoning ability, it is (epistemically) permissible for him to believe that something is the case (in this case, that the table is red). In other words, we would be inclined to attribute a right to be sure, to apply our standards of adequacy of justification, more leniently in the case of the six-year-old and more strictly in the case of the sixteen-year-old.

The important point for educators is that what counts as a good reason depends on who is giving the reason and in what context. One of the responsibilities of an educator is to assess learners' knowledge in a way that is sensitive both to their level of understanding and to the context of assessment. Again, I am not talking about logically conclusive justification or *perfect* reasons: I am talking about *good* reasons. An important feature of what constitutes *good* reasons is that they can function as adequate or suitable justification for one's belief/s. What does such adequacy or suitability involve? For one thing, one's sense organs must be intact, one's sense experiences must be appropriately connected with the world, and so on. For another, one's reasoning must be correct. This analysis of good reasons indicates why reference to them is context-sensitive. Neither our sense experiences nor our reasoning is infallible. Nonetheless, as Cohen says (1986: 575), they "can be permissible grounds of belief, . . . even if they are not ideally correct."

Take the case of a timid student. Such a person, according to Scheffler (1965: 65), may be someone "generally lacking in self-confidence, or he may have a history of poor work in related subjects, or he may have had some bad experience in the course of learning that *p*." Although "he lacks strong conviction that *p* . . . he may have grasped the essentials of the subject and fully mastered its techniques." He "may offer his uniformly correct answers or solutions with considerable diffidence." Yet, even in the absence of strong conviction on the part of the student, we may be strongly inclined to credit him with knowledge that *p*, "that he has . . . the right to be surer than he is" (65).

If reference to good reasons is context-sensitive, does this mean that the criteria for knowledge-ascription change with the respective individual, or social or cultural group? Is knowledge itself relative? In Plato's cave parable (1970b), whatever the enlightened person knows about 'reality' stands in stark contrast to the (majority) view that what the prisoners in the cave claim to know is reality. Does this indicate that *knowledge* is ambiguous between various concepts, each based on a different standard? Is this knowledge context-dependent? Scheffler's and Cohen's arguments suggest that it may be better to say that attributions of knowledge are *context-sensitive*. This is because the term 'context-*sensitive*' does not offer an open invitation to epistemological *relativism*.

What is epistemological relativism, and why is it problematic? To be a relativist about knowledge is to maintain that there is no objective knowledge of reality (or better: of realities) independently of the knowers from relevant social or cultural groups. The difficulty for relativists is to avoid the inconsistent claim that the relativistic thesis is itself an item of objective knowledge. (This is only a caricature of the case against relativism. I will return to relativism at various points throughout the book, with the aim of providing a considerably deeper analysis.) By contrast, the term 'context-sensitivity' indicates that the standards of knowledge-attribution may be determined by the context of attribution as well as the intentions of those who attribute or ascribe knowledge. It does not imply that (the concept of) knowledge itself is relative to a particular standard, is unstable or is changing (see Horsthemke 2007: 25).

Regarding the different knowledge claims we are likely to encounter in our own teaching practice, these are likely to cover moral, scientific, and emotional knowledge claims, among many others. Thus, we might encounter different claims about the goodness or badness of certain practices (like the eating of animal flesh, polygamy, male and female circumcision, and so forth), different levels of mathematical reasoning, different (more and less sophisticated) claims about, for example, climate change, and examples of introspection ('This poem makes me feel sad') and literary analysis ('This poem is meant to evoke feelings of sadness in the reader, by means of the following . . . ').

Note that a small child's claims are accepted as 'knowledge' only if they are true and the same—obviously—goes for the claims of older persons. Truth does not vary according to particular individuals, social or cultural groups, and societies or ethnicities. This serves to indicate why, as educators, we are more lenient in some cases than in others, but our leniency does not extend to condoning untruths or falsehoods.

SKEPTICISM

Of course, there is still the possibility that although we may seek to know how things really are, this knowledge cannot be found. This extreme position is called skepticism.

While it is difficult, perhaps even impossible, to disprove skepticism, we can criticize it as being contrary to common sense. We conduct our lives in ways that appear to contradict the central claims of skepticism. Our common sense leads us away from skepticism. We can also criticize extreme skepticism as being incoherent. The extreme skeptic claims that we can never be sure of anything. But then how can the extreme skeptic consistently be sure of the skeptical thesis?

What makes skepticism objectionable has partly to do with the fact that it undermines responsibility. Indeed, it could be said to invite irresponsibility. If skepticism were true (bearing in mind that this is something the skeptic could not coherently argue for because he or she would be making corresponding knowledge claims), then no one could be sure or certain of anything. This would create a climate of epistemic insecurity as well as of perennial distrust. It would make deception and lying that much easier, and it would undermine any striving for epistemic competence. (I will later examine arguments both against and in favor of the idea of epistemic responsibility.)

The idea of context-sensitivity may provide a way of avoiding both skepticism and relativism. To show how, we will consider the examples constructed earlier to illustrate problems with the traditional philosophical definition of knowledge. There are at least three types of skeptical response regarding the problems encountered in the broken watch and the school play rehearsal examples that I discussed earlier. The first is that we should never agree with anything because we cannot be justified in believing anything. The second is that because our beliefs are not adequately justified, we know nothing, even though our beliefs may be true. The third is that we cannot be sure that we have the reasons necessary for knowing anything.

Let us look once more at the examples presented earlier as a challenge to the definition of knowledge. My justification involves the false belief that my watch is working. My justification for my belief that the boy in front of me is armed is not suitably connected with its truth. The likelihood of the watch not working and the likelihood of all the other boys in the room carrying toy weapons are possible alternatives, which are worth considering when considering the ascription of knowledge in the respective cases. Both constitute relevant alternatives, and both are as such intelligible to me as a 'cognizer' or knower. When deciding whether or not to attribute knowledge to a person, we must be mindful of the epistemic context. It would appear, therefore, that the idea of context-sensitivity provides a workable option that avoids both relativism and skepticism.

EPISTEMIC OBLIGATION

What epistemic responsibilities or obligations, if any, do we have? A justified belief is one to which a person is rationally entitled, to which that person has a right. According to Scheffler (1965: 63–65), having adequate justification gives us the right to be sure. (Skepticism, of course, would deny that we could ever have such a right.) An unjustified or insufficiently justified belief, on the other hand, is one that we ought not to hold, on the basis of rational considerations alone. There is a conceptual difference between having a right or (rationally being able) to embrace a belief, if a person so chooses, and having (a duty or an obligation) to embrace a belief, on the basis of rational considerations alone. Honoring our epistemic obligations ultimately comes down to assuming responsibility for the origin of our beliefs. There are two basic epistemic obligations: to pursue truth and to avoid error (although it is obvious that the pursuit of truth is often bound up with committing errors). Goldman says, on a similar note, that the "norms of good argumentation are best seen as a social quest for true belief and error avoidance" (Goldman 1994: 28).

We know from ethical and legal discourse that there is an intimate connection between rights and obligations. If a person has a right, then others have correlative obligations toward that person. But can the same be said to follow from 'the right to be sure'? If a person has a right to be sure, then who (if anyone) has any obligations? And what would be the content of these obligations? One of the responsibilities of educators is to develop learners' understanding of the nature of evidence and their capacity to use evidence appropriately. However, educators have other obligations, too. American philosopher Richard Feldman distinguishes between three kinds of obligation: practical or prudential obligation, moral obligation, and epistemic obligation (Feldman 1998: 235–237).

Epistemic obligations are, at least superficially, distinct from other types of obligations. Educators, for example, have professional or practical obligations to do their work properly, and to make their lessons interesting and informative. Educators' competence would be such an obligation. They also have moral obligations, for example, not to discriminate against certain learners, and to ensure a just and fair approach in the classroom. Educators' trustworthiness would be such an obligation. Epistemic obligations, on the other hand, appear to be different: they concern a person assuming responsibility for his or her beliefs.

What is known as the ethics of belief or achieving epistemic excellence involves normative enquiry. It concerns what we have the right to believe, what we are entitled to believe. Another way of framing the ethics of belief is in terms of enquiring what we ought to believe, what we have an obligation to believe. Questions like 'What is it rational to believe?' and 'What am I justified in believing?' signal an internalist mode of enquiry. They imply a person's awareness of his or her justification.

It is worth noting that the different 'oughts'—in other words, practical or prudential obligation and epistemic obligation—may not coincide. While we may have a practical obligation not to believe something, we may have an epistemic obligation to do so (i.e., on pain of irrationality). For example, a student may have a practical obligation to believe that he will pass the entrance examination (because this will give him valuable self-confidence), but he may have an epistemic obligation not to believe it (given the extraordinarily high failure rate among people taking the exam).

Having an obligation to believe something presupposes having control over your beliefs, in other words, that you are free (not) to believe something. This is what has been called the thesis of doxastic voluntarism. Someone who does not accept doxastic voluntarism may deny the existence of obligatory beliefs. In other words, if we have no control over our beliefs (i.e., if we are not free [not] to believe something), then we cannot be under any obligation to believe something. The argument is the following:

Premise 1: We can have epistemic obligations only if we have control over what we believe. (Another way of expressing this is: If we cannot elect or choose our own beliefs, we cannot be said to have epistemic obligations.)
Premise 2: But we have no control over what we believe. (Or: We cannot elect or choose our own beliefs.)
Conclusion: Therefore, we cannot have any epistemic obligations. (Or: It makes no sense to say that we have epistemic obligations.)

This is clearly a valid argument. The conclusion follows logically from the premises. But is the argument sound? In other words, are the individual premises true, and do they thereby guarantee the truth of the conclusion? At the heart of this argument is the idea that doxastic voluntarism is illusory. We may *think* we are in control of what we believe, that we can voluntarily believe or not believe a certain thing. Doxastic involuntarism states that we are unable to elect or choose what we believe, that we cannot force ourselves to believe anything we like. When we believe or disbelieve something we are reacting only to (changes in) our environment or because we are hardwired to arrive at the beliefs we do.

The first response denies that it is true that we have no control over our beliefs. (In other words, it rejects the second premise.) While it may be correct that we have no direct control over our beliefs, we may have indirect control.

> There are things we can do to alter the ways in which we form beliefs and the kind of information which we receive. I can, for example, study logic or probability theory with the aim of reducing the number of mistaken inferences I draw. I might read the publications of some political or religious groups with the aim of eventually coming to accept the general set of beliefs they support. (Feldman 1998: 238)

Given that we have indirect control over our beliefs, we can therefore have epistemic obligations.

Another possible response (which also denies the correctness of the second premise) is to shift from believing to accepting a belief. The latter signals an action over which we clearly have control. Accepting a belief (like rejecting a belief) is the result of a rational decision, and therefore a voluntary matter. It follows that we can have obligations to accept or not accept certain beliefs or knowledge claims.

The third response accepts, just for the sake of argument, that it is correct that we have no control over our beliefs. However, it rejects what is stated in the first premise, namely that we have epistemic obligations only if we have control over our beliefs. According to Feldman (241), an obligation does not even fall away if we are not free to meet the obligation. Epistemic obligations could be compared legal or financial contexts. My obligation to make a monthly payment for something does not fall away if I am not free to meet this obligation. Of course, the question is whether epistemic obligations *are* relevantly like financial obligations or legal obligations. Nonetheless, it could be argued that contracting out of our epistemic obligations is tantamount to contracting out of rationality.

Is taking responsibility for the formation of our beliefs the same as assuming responsibility for the formation of our values? After all, we cannot have values or act in accordance with values if we have no appropriate beliefs. Values, in a sense, are beliefs: beliefs about what is worthwhile or good. As I mentioned earlier in the chapter, people generally do not readily relinquish or abandon what they believe to be true. It would surely be unreasonable to expect someone to change their values just because a new approach instructs them to do so. Similarly, it would be irrational to adhere to values that have been shown to be questionable. This is part of the problem that we will discuss in the final section. In order to make a discussion of these issues more fruitful, we need to say a little more about an issue that is related to that of epistemic obligation.

EPISTEMIC PARENTALISM

Assuming responsibility for our own beliefs is only one concern in epistemology. Another concerns assuming responsibility for the beliefs of others, through teaching, selection, and control. This involves what Goldman calls "epistemic paternalism" (1992: 209–226). In what follows, I prefer to speak of 'parentalism' rather than 'paternalism'. For many, the latter has generally derogatory associations. Not only is it usually assumed to involve taking care of others while limiting their freedom and responsibility, but it also suggests a social order in which the father is the bearer of formal authority within the family. ('Maternalism' might go some way toward correcting the explicit androcentrism here, in its acknowledgment of informal, crucial, and usually invisible familial authority, but it has a similarly gender-specific connotation.)

Goldman begins by noting that the so-called "requirement of total evidence" (209) may be unacceptable. 'Adequate evidence', we recall, concerns the amount of evidence or justification required for knowledge. One of the chief foci in epistemology is on the person who makes knowledge claims—be it an educator or a learner—who tries to gather as much evidence as possible, and of course appropriate or suitable evidence. Evidence is necessary to ensure the 'grounding' of our beliefs. Yet, Goldman's concern is to show that there may be reasons for doubting the desirability of the "requirement of total evidence."

'Epistemic parentalism' refers, in general, to the idea that certain kinds of information are often withheld or kept from people. Goldman draws an analogy with parents who might keep dangerous toys or other articles away from children, or who might decide not to expose children to certain facts or types of information. In other words, epistemic parentalism is a kind of information (or communication) control. The question Goldman asks (214) is whether epistemic parentalism is "really warranted." A related question is whether epistemic parentalism is "desirable in terms of promoting truth and avoiding error' (214–215, 220).

For our purposes, it is very useful that Goldman chooses to illustrate epistemic parentalism with examples from the realm of education. In particular, he mentions curriculum selection. Curricular materials are selected by school personnel at various levels, not only by educators but also by boards of education and principals. What is involved in curriculum selection? Most pertinent to this discussion, learners are not exposed to all possible views or ideas on a given subject. Not only are they generally exposed only to materials that are relevant and appropriate to their level of understanding (see also Cohen [1986: 575] and what Quine and Ullian [1978: 129] say assuming a common frame of reference), but opinions that are regarded as false or indefensible are also withheld by current educational authorities.

Goldman cites the example of teaching creationism in biology or other science classes. The argument he considers is that experts on science should be allowed to decide that creationism (unlike the theory of evolution) is not a serious contender in terms of scientific theory and should not be taught in science classes. Parents and learners are, generally, not the kinds of authority who need to be consulted in this regard: that is, with respect to promotion of truth and avoidance of error. Goldman and Hardwig argue that since none of us can reasonably hope to assess all evidence for all these personally, we often depend on the authority of others, so epistemic parentalism "is frequently necessary and sometimes epistemically desirable" (Goldman 1992: 220).

Goldman points out that epistemology has traditionally assumed that all those working with knowledge and justification have the same cognitive resources, skills, and opportunities, and that they operate without time constraints and the like. This is an idealized setting, he says, which is endorsed neither by common sense nor by common experience. In

> settings marked by different levels of expertise, by different opportunities for information gathering, by different levels of cognitive maturity and training, and by severe time constraints, idealized principles of communication do not

apply. A social epistemology for the real world needs to take these constraints into account. (224)

EPISTEMOLOGICAL AND FORMAL ACCESS, AND THE PROBLEM WITH CONSTRUCTIVISM

With regard to educational contexts and situations, there are various ways in which marginalization and disadvantage, generally, occur. Education, like virtually all transactions within the "real world," exhibits all kinds of exclusion from those opportunities that ought to characterize epistemic participation, like learning. Among other things, inclusive pedagogy, broadly conceived,[9] might be understood as providing learners with epistemological access (see Horsthemke 2017a). In other words, and importantly, inclusive education is "an issue of how epistemological access is enabled or constrained by the pedagogical choices we make" (Walton and Bekker 2016: 476). "In inclusive education discourse," according to South African educationalists Elizabeth Walton and Tanya Bekker (2016), "'exclusion' is used to describe not only the physical non-presence of children, but also the variety of factors that impede full and fair access to and participation in school activities": that is, "access to the curriculum, learning and teacher attention, access to peer and social interactions, . . . and access to school resources, extracurricular activities and participation in school traditions" (468).

The term "epistemological access" was first coined by Wally Morrow (2009: iv), the late South African educational philosopher who played a significant role in postapartheid educational reform. "Starting from the idea that teaching is conceptually linked to the idea of access," Morrow argues that

> there are two kinds of access—formal and epistemological—not commonly distinguished from each other. Formal access is a matter of access to the institutions of learning, and it depends on factors such as admission rules, personal finances, and so on; epistemological access, on the other hand, is access to [the goods that institutions distribute to those it formally admits and, as the main good distributed by educational institutions, to] knowledge [which must be understood here as encompassing all kinds of practical and theoretical knowledge]. While formal access is important in the light of our history of unjustifiable institutional exclusions, epistemological access is what the game is about. One way of characterising teaching is to say that it is the practice of enabling epistemological access. (Morrow 2007: 2; see also p. 8n.6, and p. 39.)

It follows that the question, "Epistemological access for whom?" (Walton and Bekker 2016: 461), appears to receive the rather uninteresting answer,

'Everyone who is educable'. But this by no means renders the concept redundant. Given that education and classrooms, in particular, are increasingly characterized by diversity and heterogeneity of learners (commonly with vastly different features, competences, learning needs, and learning barriers), it is clear that a 'one-size-fits-all' approach does not (any longer) meet current challenges (ibid.; see also Walton 2016: 524). This will also have a bearing on the breadth and depth of the access in question. On the other hand, responsive educators also need to protect themselves from pedagogical paralysis: if the uniqueness of learners necessitates respectively unique teaching strategies, then an over-emphasis of the individual could soon lead to a culture of overemphasizing difference. It could be argued that it is not so much a matter of diversity in general, but rather of emphasis on pedagogically relevant differences, that is, of judging when and to what extent individual and group differences are pedagogically significant, of planning lessons that are meant to provide access for all, and so forth. The quality of pedagogy, that is, how educators work with knowledge, can be seen either as promoting or as preventing access. Heila Lotz-Sisitka (2009), building on Morrow's ideas and on the basis of several case studies, lists several ways in which teaching practice can *constrain* epistemological access:

- through teachers' failure to bridge the divide between the concrete and the abstract, or between everyday knowledge and school knowledge;
- through teachers' failure to interpret the demands of set curricular standards and subsequent limitation of the scope and level of access in relation to these standards;
- through reliance on teacher knowledge only, which may in itself be limited, and subsequent limitation of the scope and depth of access to new knowledge; and
- through inadequate feedback on tasks, and subsequent failure to enable learners to deepen their understanding or address misconceptions (see also Walton and Bekker 2016: 470–471).

In the remainder of this chapter, I want to discuss a problem I have identified, which also pertains to 'indigenous knowledge' and related ideas. It would appear that a substantial portion of the literature on inclusion understands epistemological access in constructivist terms, that is, in terms of learners being "active participants in the construction of their knowledge" (Bekker 2016: 485). Thus, Bekker writes (494): "Knowledge is frequently presented as contested (in other words, it is not presented as a fixed body of information, but rather as being constructed; contrasting points of view or interpretations and potentially conflicting forms of knowledge are discussed) instead of as universally accepted by all (i.e., as a one-dimensional body of truth)."[10]

What is missing in the pertinent literature is an account, let alone a critical analysis, of the concept of knowledge. An examination of this idea may well demonstrate that the conceptualization of constructivism as an epistemology (see, e.g., Andrej 2015: 62–87) and perhaps even as a pedagogy and as a learning theory, is highly problematic.[11] The common assertion that knowledge is 'contested' seems to draw its strength entirely from this lack of definition and conceptual clarity. Once an account of different uses of the term 'knowledge' and circumspect definitions are furnished, much of the putative basis for 'contestation' will have been eroded. By the time students have completed their undergraduate teacher training, many have been thoroughly indoctrinated with constructivism. (On the purported significance and relevance of constructivist theory in today's classrooms, see for example Delanty 1997; Duffy and Cunningham 1996; George 1999: 84; Richardson 2003; Maturana 1988; Von Glasersfeld 1991, 1995, 1997/2003 and 2000; Windschitl 1999 and 2002.) It is generally assumed that it is only constructivism that provides a compelling account of active, student-centered teaching and learning, and that rival pedagogies and learning theories err in significant respects. According to Duffy and Cunningham (1996) and also Windschitl (1999 and 2002), one of the most difficult underpinnings of constructivism for educators to embrace is that *there are no universal truths* (see also Green 2009: 51, 52) and that constructivism by its very nature is *not compatible with more objective forms of knowing*. No wonder, one might respond—since this can only be apprehended as a "universal truth" itself, or in terms of an "objective form of knowing", respectively. It would appear then that in an important respect, constructivism is self-undermining: either there are no universal truths (or objective forms of knowing), except this particular one; or the statement in question does not itself constitute a universal truth, or objective form of knowing.

There is clearly a grain of truth in constructivism. Some facts are socially constructed, the results of human description and designation—like pass grades in tests or exams, codes of ethics, laws, speed limits, standards of etiquette, culinary recipes, and so forth: contingent facts that emanate from our social practices. Constructivism errs, however, in saying that all facts, including historical and scientific facts, are human constructs. As a pedagogy, I suggest, constructivism has two major, related shortcomings. It degrades a fundamental educational task—that of transmission of knowledge. Furthermore, like postmodernism, constructivism is not only misleading but also potentially dangerous, in that it gives people (educators as well as learners) a false sense of empowerment and authority. Contrary to what their advocates have contended, neither approach is emancipatory. In fact, both as a pedagogy and as a learning theory, constructivism is likely to be disturbingly disempowering. The failure of outcomes-based education in most parts of the world, with its devaluation of subject-based knowledge, knowledge developed in the past and of knowledge for its own sake, is testimony to the plausibility of this judgment.[12] It should be noted that the logic of neither inclusion nor epistemological access requires adoption of a constructivist epistemology.

The presentation of knowledge as 'contested' is also reflected in the verdict, 'Knowledge is regarded as uncertain and changing', that has been bandied about in recent decades, especially within discourses on outcomes-based education.[13] What does this mean? In the cave parable, Plato (through the voice of Socrates) expressed the view that knowledge is certain and unchanging. Which of these two views is correct? Or does it depend on which understanding of knowledge we are working with? A substantial difficulty is, of course, to avoid advancing the proposal that 'knowledge is uncertain and changing' as a knowledge-claim, since this would lead to a paradox. If this is knowledge, then it is itself subject to uncertainty and change (just like the claim that knowledge is contested is itself subject to contestation), in which case it contradicts the statement, insofar as it may at some point turn out to be no longer true (meaning that knowledge may at some point turn out to be certain and unchanging). If, on the other hand, this piece of knowledge is itself certain and not subject to change, then there is at least some knowledge that is not uncertain and changing—which, again, contradicts the statement that it is.

For a long time, the majority of people thought that the universe was geocentric, in other words, that everything revolved around the earth. This was consistent with most religious beliefs and practical observations. With the advent of more sophisticated technology, however, the geocentric world view was gradually replaced by a heliocentric world view, in other words, that the sun is at the center of our universe, with all planets (including our own) revolving around it. Did people in the past possess knowledge that was different from our knowledge now? Surely not: they had certain beliefs about the world, even justified beliefs, but they did not (indeed, could not) have any knowledge in this regard. It simply was not true then, as it is not true now, that the universe was geocentric. You might say now, 'Well, it was true for them that the earth was at the centre of everything, just as it is true for us now that the sun is at the centre.' What this means, however, is that people in the past believed it to be true or to be the case that the universe was geocentric. It was not the way things really were and are. In other words, their belief was false. Consequently, they had no knowledge. It is not knowledge that is 'uncertain and changing'. What is uncertain and changing is people's beliefs, opinions, and attitudes.

A common misconception is that truth is relative, and that truth differs from culture to culture, from society to society, and even from individual to individual (in other words, 'what is true for you may not be true for me').

According to Quine and Ullian (1978: 28), whether an observation statement is true or not is at the very least an intersubjective matter. They take issue with a common and popular view that is as seductive as it is irrational, namely that truth is personal or subjective. This is the view that what is true for you may not be and, indeed, often is not, what is true for me, and that it is generally neither possible nor desirable to reconcile these different 'truths'. The "hoary view" or "irrationalist doctrine" that Quine and Ullian are taking on is relativism about truth. To be a relativist about truth is to maintain that there is no universal, transcultural or objective truth, that 'truth' is in the eye of the beholder or in the mind of the believer: it differs from individual to individual, from society to society, from culture to culture. In other words, according to relativism, truth is particular or relative to a specific personal, social, cultural, historical, or geographic context.

The defense of relativism draws on the central role that Quine and Ullian as well as others have accorded to observation, with regard to belief systems and knowledge formation. Observations are made by individuals. As we have seen earlier in this chapter, our beliefs ultimately rely on observations, including observations of what we as well as others have noted or written down. Whatever evidence we have consists ultimately of what we have accessed and internalized through the use of our senses (see Quine and Ullian 1978: 21). Given, furthermore, that our observations differ, does this not imply that the truth or truths that we access by means of our observations will differ? No, say Quine and Ullian: our observations may indeed differ—they may either contradict each other or they may be different aspects of the same object—but what is actually the case, what is true, does not depend on these observations, nor on any observers.

'Truth is relative to believer.' Is this truth (if it is that) also relative to believer? If so, why should it impress others? If not, then there exists at least one truth that is not relative.

"There's truth for me and truth for you, and their reconciliation is neither possible nor desirable," in Quine and Ullian's characterization of the relativist stance (28). Is this my truth? Or is it also your truth? If the former, why should it impress those who hold a different view of truth? If the latter, this indicates that reconciliation is possible; yet, again at the expense of relativism and in favor of universalism. Either way, the relativist will be caught up in a paradox, in a logical conundrum. At some point, he or she will want to claim that his or her statements about the relativity of truth are, in fact, universally (i.e., nonrelatively) true, which he or she cannot do consistently, given his or her relativism. What may differ from culture to culture, and so on, is not truth but beliefs. This is exactly why beliefs are referred to as the subjective component of knowledge and truth as the objective component. Moreover, this explains why we can compare and evaluate different beliefs and belief systems. We can do so because we have recourse to an objective framework of reference (see Horsthemke 2010: 86). To put it quite bluntly, no respectable philosopher believes that truth is merely a subjective matter. This becomes obvious when we consider that a person's mere belief cannot make it the case she is thin, or pregnant, even if it makes her happy.

Unsurprisingly, these considerations have interesting and important implications for knowledge. Truth, after all, is a necessary condition for knowledge, as are belief and justification. Philosophically, therefore, it would be redundant to speak of true knowledge, or legitimate or valid knowledge, as Goduka (2000: 63), Ndlovu-Gatsheni (2018), and South African anthropologist Lesley Green (2009: 43) do. There is no other kind of knowledge. In other words, to speak of untrue, illegitimate, or invalid knowledge would be nonsensical. It would not square with the conception of knowledge as adequately justified true belief. This is different from speaking of 'ill-gotten' knowledge, knowledge that has been obtained by unethical means. Knowledge that has been obtained through coercion, through treating the experimentees as mere means, and so forth. is not epistemically suspect but rather ethically wrong.

Empirically, too, embracing relativism has undesirable consequences, assuming this would not present insurmountable consistency problems for the advocacy of indigenous knowledge and truth. These become obvious when, for the sake of argument (again, bearing in mind that that assertions to this effect cannot coherently be made in any nonrelative fashion), we take relativism to be true. What would be some of these consequences? First, we could not judge that the beliefs and practices of other societies are epistemically and veritistically inferior to our own. We could not say that something is a false belief or a superstition, or that something is a laborious, time-wasting practice. If knowledge and truth did differ from individual to individual, society to society, culture to culture, then it would be presumptuous to pass judgment on another's knowledge claim. Thus, it would be very difficult to judge (positively or negatively) the 'God-sponsored' segregationist views of White Southerners or staunchly Calvinist-Christian Afrikaners,[14] or to determine the veracity of beliefs in ancestral reward and retribution.[15] Second, we could decide whether beliefs are true or false, and practices are the correct or incorrect ones simply by consulting the standards of our society or epistemic community (we might consider the beliefs of White supremacists in this regard). Third, the idea of progress (scientific and other) is called into doubt, as is the idea of 'reform'. We would not be able to say that a new paradigm constitutes an improvement on the older paradigm it has replaced, whether any progress has been taking place in a society, in terms of advancement in knowledge. Thus, one would be committed to the position that evolutionary theory cannot be held to have contributed to scientific and epistemic progress, *vis-à-vis* religious doctrines like creationism or intelligent-design, or that the heliocentric view of the universe does not constitute a substantial improvement on the geocentric view. Similar considerations would pertain to normative talk about reform and transformation—for example, educational and sociopolitical transformation, in Africa as elsewhere. In view of these consequences, over and above the paradoxicality of denying the objectivity and universality of knowledge and truth,[16] it arguably makes more sense, logically and empirically, to assert that there is considerably less disagreement than is apparent and that social, cultural, and ethnic groups share a considerable body of factual and practical knowledge.

In contrast to constructivism and relativism, a realist epistemology is concerned with a normative account: it deals with processes that ought or ought not to be called 'knowledge'. In other words, 'knowledge' is not ambiguous between various concepts of knowledge. What constitutes knowledge does not fluctuate with differences in people's reasoning abilities or with what their constructs are. This view, it should be noted, is compatible with the insight that people are not all on the same footing as far as cognitive resources, skills, and opportunities are concerned. This insight permits us to talk of different levels of knowledge, without implying relativism.

This chapter has provided a framework in terms of which conceptions of and assumptions about knowledge, belief, truth, and justification can be examined and evaluated. Its aim has been to help develop an understanding of (the concepts of) knowledge and education and how they are connected—and to render possible critical reflection on ideas like 'women's ways of knowing', 'indigenous knowledge' and 'Africanization of knowledge', which is the project of the remaining chapters.

NOTES

1. An intriguing hypothesis suggests that this understanding of knowledge is an inheritance from ancient Egypt. As I will illustrate in the next chapter, a similar conception of knowledge exists in Yoruba.

2. "Opinions" and "beliefs" are treated as synonyms, for present purposes.

3. "An account" and "fastening up . . . ." both refer to justification. "Right belief" is treated as identical to "true belief."

4. This is the title of jazz saxophonist Archie Shepp's 1981 recording for Sackville.

5. To be sure, there may be grounds for contesting the separation of reason and emotion, of thought and feeling. As Julian Barnes (1997: 127) has put it so trenchantly, one can be "sentimental about clarity of thought, emotional about rationality."

6. White describes the attempts by desperate parents to calm their daughter's fear of the atomic bomb. They finally succeed by sprinkling talcum powder on her bed, explaining that it is 'magic dust' that will keep the little girl and her loved ones safe. I do not think that this qualifies as 'indoctrination'. First, the deception occurs for the express benefit of the recipient; and second, it is only a temporary deception: the girl is expected to outgrow this belief, like children are expected to outgrow beliefs in Santa Claus and the tooth fairy.

7. Scheffler initially refers to "evidential adequacy," a notion he later abandons in favor of that of "the right to be sure." For reasons given earlier in this chapter, I take 'justification' to be more comprehensive than 'evidence' and to be consistent with the notion of the right to be sure.

8. The notion of "the right to be sure" is A.J. Ayer's (1956).

9. That is, it concerns not only those living with cognitive and physical impairments but also those who have been historically marginalized, as well as those who experience or who have experienced political and socioeconomical exclusion. In the latter instance 'special educational needs' are defined in terms of a lack of material means as well as a deficit in care, the modeling of empathy, and so forth.

10. The idea is that substantive conversation is needed in multicultural or intercultural contexts, where knowledge is seen as emanating from specific social and cultural histories rather than as 'fixed'. From an inclusive education perspective, Michel Foucault's critique of epistemological hegemony and his analysis of how knowledge and truth are always part of systems of power are considered significant (Bekker; personal communication):

> Each society has its own régime of truth, its 'general politics' of truth: that is, the types of discourse which it accepts and makes function as true; the mechanisms and instances which enable one to distinguish true and false statements, the means by which each is sanctioned; the techniques and procedures accorded value in the acquisition of truth; the status of those who are charged with saying what counts as true. (Foucault 1980: 131)

At least two concerns arise in this regard. The ideas of "régimes of truth" and "'general politics' of truth" not only indicate a category mistake (in treating epistemological matters as necessarily inseparable from matters of social justice), but they are also dangerously close to relativism about truth.

11. The most significant problems are posed by relativism (both about knowledge and about truth) and by the difficulty to distinguish between knowledge and mere belief, between science and nonscience (especially dogma and superstition). See Paul Boghossian (2006a) and Peter Boghossian (2006b), for powerful critiques of constructivist theories of knowledge.

12. This is not the place for a detailed critique of these approaches. My sketchy remarks here are unlikely to persuade anyone that constructivism, for example, should be rejected. They merely serve to underline my misgivings about bestowing special status in education on a theoretical orientation that is deeply problematic. As Lotz-Sisitka claims, "education has a critical role to play in preparing children *to live in the world*" (2009: 71; emphasis added). This arguably requires that those who so prepare children live there, too. Frankly, I cannot see constructivism making a substantial contribution to this preparation process.

13. Department of Education (South Africa) 1997.*Curriculum 2005: Lifelong Learning for the 21st Century*. Pretoria: Government Printer.

14. Jonathan Jansen refers, in this regard, to "divine knowledge" (2009: 157–162; see also 158, 292n.24).

15. For example, George Sefa Dei writes that "the living are emboldened by ancestral knowledge and the wisdom of the dead," and that ancestral spirits are living knowledges. They are acknowledged as guardians of the living. They provide knowledge, wisdom, and advice and regulate living practice. (2004: 356; see also Dei 2002: 6).

16. Thus, Scott Fatnowna and Harry Pickett (2202b: 214, 215) claim,

> Spirituality in an Aboriginal sense is encompassing and holistic in nature. It is the starting point that requires no demonstration or proof; it exists and all truths begin and end there. . . . To look for objectivity in the Aboriginal world is to question one's identity and sense of being. Objectivity as a notion is culturally inappropriate. . . . One does not look for something that is not there. . . . To be just objective requires a dehumanizing process.

This raises the obvious question, from which perspective then are judgments made about Aboriginal truths, and about the 'cultural inappropriateness' of the requirement of objectivity.

Chapter 4

A Critique of Indigenous Knowledge

In chapter 3, I distinguished between three main senses of knowledge: knowledge-that or factual knowledge, knowledge-how or practical knowledge, and lastly, knowledge of persons, places, or things—or knowledge by acquaintance. If discussion of the uniqueness of indigenous people's knowledge interprets it in the third sense, it is fairly uncontroversial. Familiarity with persons and situations, with "stories, legends, proverbs, folklores, rituals, songs, etc." (Kaya 2013: 136; see also Kaya and Seleti 2014: 33, 35; Kaya 2014: 91), and acquaintance with different mentalities, states of affairs, geographical terrain, and the like, differ from individual to individual, society to society, culture to culture. Take, for example, my knowledge of my family and friends. Or consider Vietcong, Afghan, or Iraqi familiarity with their own jungles, mountainous regions, or deserts, knowledge not characteristically shared by foreign soldiers. Acquaintance- or familiarity-type knowledge is often what gives guerilla fighters and revolutionary forces the edge in armed conflicts.

However, in the discussion that follows, I will concentrate primarily on the first two as the senses of knowledge that are relevant here. It is my suspicion that many, if not most, indigenous knowledge projects focus on either knowledge-that or knowledge-how, or both, rather than on acquaintance- or familiarity-type knowledge. The understanding of 'indigenous knowledge' as 'indigenous practice, skill or know-how' is reasonably unproblematic. It makes good sense to acknowledge that (different individuals in) different cultures or societies possess skills or know-how not shared by others. Of course, there is often a close connection between practical and factual knowledge. If a traditional healer knows how to cure people, then this implies that she presumably knows that certain roots, berries, or barks have the requisite disease-curing properties, and perhaps also what these properties are. The

"Inuvialuit of one small Arctic community, Sachs Harbor, are able to provide some 25 kinds of evidence of climate change, spanning the areas of physical environmental change; predictability of the environment; travel safety; access to resources; and changes to animal distributions and condition" (Berkes and Berkes 2009: 10). It follows that the Inuvialuit have both certain skills (they are able to produce and work with various forms of evidence) and factual knowledge, namely about climate change. The Inuit who knows how to distinguish between several shades of white as well as between several different types of snow will be able to orientate himself accordingly, will know that an animal is at a certain distance from him, upwind or downwind, and will know that a certain stretch of snow or ice will support his weight. The problem arises when the two senses of knowledge are treated as if there is no distinction between them, and when knowledge-that is understood as 'indigenous', 'local', or 'traditional'.

I consider the conception of theoretical, factual, or propositional knowledge developed in chapter 3 to be not only plausible but indispensable for clearing up some of the confusions in the debate around indigenous knowledge. In other words, the philosophical account of the nature of knowledge should be used as a yardstick. Thus, the onus will be on anyone who is opposed to the analysis presented here to propose not only an alternative but also a more feasible definition, one that is sufficiently unambiguous and comprehensive to meet the challenges raised in this chapter and the ones that follow.

The way I see it, in cases where 'indigenous knowledge' is taken to refer not to practical knowledge and skills but to knowledge-that, and where it is contrasted with nonindigenous, mainstream or cosmopolitan knowledge, problems are rife. One needs to be clear about what the notion of indigenous knowledge implies in such cases. Current usage by theorists generally suggests several things, all equally problematic. In some instances, 'indigenous knowledge' is taken to cover all kinds of beliefs, with little or no reference to truth or justification. This elevates to the status of knowledge not only mere assumption and opinion, but also superstition, divination, soothsaying, and the like (as Semali 1999: 98; Kunnie 2000: 168; Crossman and Devisch 2002: 117, attempt to do). In the absence of any explicit mention of truth, then, the applicable idea would be that of 'indigenous beliefs'. Beliefs, indeed, vary between individuals, communities, and cultures. Given the philosophical definition of knowledge, however, belief—even justified belief—does not amount to knowledge.

What about justification?[1] Could observation, testimony, memory, different kinds of reasoning, and so forth, be 'indigenous'? There may well be some leeway with regard to justification, to enable greater leniency in assessing (the justification for) Seneca, Ju'hoansi, or Palikur knowledge-claims and greater stringency in assessing those of university graduates.

The appraisal of the suitability of justification may vary with different contexts. Yet, the implication that truth differs in similar ways, that there are (or could be) different indigenous truths, is highly problematic. Truth is neither a matter of personal belief nor of social or cultural consensus. As chapter 3 has shown, there are well-known problems with this kind of relativism. First, the relativist cannot logically and consistently claim universal validity for the thesis that knowledge differs radically across societies and cultures or that truth is local or context-dependent. Furthermore, if accepted—albeit bearing in mind the inconsistency involved, relativism has certain undesirable implications or consequences. First, it would be not only presumptuous but also impossible to evaluate or judge the knowledge- and truth-claims of others. Of course, this is something that may be welcomed by many, if not most, defenders of indigenous knowledge systems and postcolonial theorists. However, this kind of relativism is symmetrical. If it can be employed by the historically disenfranchised against the judgments and interpretational sovereignty of the powerful, then it can also be used to immunize those in power from criticism by the disempowered. Moreover, in order to decide what is true or false, it would be sufficient merely to canvas and then to align oneself with opinions prevalent within one's own society or cultural group. (This, like the previous problem, also raises the issue of superstition, which I will address below.) Finally, one could not really say whether any progress has been made in a society in terms of advancement in knowledge. Nor could one make sense of the ideas of epistemic transformation or reform.

Crossman and Devisch (2002: 17) claim that "differential knowledge-practices are particular to authoritative knowledge-bearers in culture-specific roles and status, such as healers, bards, soothsayers, diviners, messengers or even judges, journalists and so on." And according to Hountondji (2002: 23), "Respected and sometimes renowned physicists and chemists, once they leave their laboratories, do not hesitate to consult local rainmakers to ensure that their guests will not be rained upon during, for example, marriage, burial or other family celebration they wish to organize." The problem with the blurring of boundaries between what is knowledge and what is not, that is, what is mere belief, with admitting all kinds of fervent beliefs or superstitions, about witchcraft, demonic possession, divination (Asante 2005: 41), ancestral blessing, and absolution, and around "the technique of rainmaking and rain-discarding" (Hountondji 2002: 24), among what counts as 'knowledge', is that this would lead to a dilution or trivialization of knowledge and truth. To equate knowledge of the effectiveness of anti-retroviral drugs and the belief that having sexual intercourse with a virgin will prevent or cure HIV/AIDS is simply and mind-bogglingly irrational.

THE *ESPRIT SORCIER* AND THE AFRICAN RENAISSANCE

The most conspicuous examples of superstition are arguably found in witchcraft beliefs and in witchcraft accusations.[2] President of the Zimbabwe National Traditional Healers Association Gordon Chavunduka sees the July 2006 amendment to Zimbabwe's Witchcraft Suppression Act, which in effect legalizes accusations of witchcraft,[3] as a "step in the right direction towards asserting our culture that has been trampled upon by successive colonial governments" (quoted in Kumar 2006: 26). The amendment, then, is seen as an endorsement of 'African (or traditional) knowledge' worldviews, practices, and values. It also implies a distinction between traditional ways of knowing that are good or beneficial (such as traditional healers' medicinal and herbal knowledge, divination practices, and so forth) and those that are bad or harmful (witchcraft and other occult practices, like the use of human body parts; see Becker 2003, 2006a, b, 2007).

Bartholomäus Grill (2005: 1) quotes Valentin Yves Mudimbe as calling the *esprit sorcier*, belief in witchcraft, one of the greatest obstructions to development. Witchcraft belief, says Grill, pertains to all African peoples, cultures, and strata and levels of society. Witchcraft belief, according to Grill (3), becomes an instrument of social control, of terror, that strengthens power and property relations, that prevents upward social mobility and punishes the industrious, mentally immobilizes people and thus obstructs the development of modern *homo oeconomicus*. Not only outsiders, strangers, and individualists are accused of witchcraft but also those who are successful and good-looking, who happen to be adversaries—be it in sport, romance, or business (and conversely, of course, those who happen to be economically unsuccessful, and who are consequently blamed for the community's misfortune or lack of success; see Becker 2007: 164).

In general opposition to indigenous knowledge apologists, Anthony Holiday (2006: 11) argues that African beliefs and practices, taking for granted traditional customs (*lobola*, or 'bride wealth', initiation rites, and the like), "undemocratic traditional authority and African systems of jurisprudence," treating "the pronouncements of *sangomas* [as] a kind of holy writ," and so forth, are all "inimical to the scientific spirit." He claims that it is a matter of "choice between two antagonistic forms of life. One must die if the other is to flourish."

Elsewhere, Grill (2003: 12) seems to postulate a "third alternative," the possibility of which Holiday denies. Describing an incident involving traditional healing, Grill contends:

> It is beyond our rational world, yet the result achieved validates the old medical adage, 'He who heals is right'. . . . The traditional healer has, in a way, also

healed me—or rather, he has cured me of the occidental obsession with knowledge, the need to penetrate and dissect everything intellectually. In Africa, one learns to live with question marks. One understands what one cannot understand—and over the years one becomes more circumspect and cautious, perhaps even more lenient in one's judgements about the continent. (My translation)

Apart from holding despotic and corrupt governments in Africa responsible for the suffering of ordinary people, Chandra Kumar (2006: 26) also blames "Eurocentric rationalism," the "Men of . . . Economic Reason," and Western rationality for its contribution to witch hysteria, by promoting economic conditions that favor the West. The worse off people are, the more prone they are to beliefs in the occult, the paranormal, "diabolical forces" responsible for their misery. Kumar quotes Chavunduka, who acknowledges the conditions that underlie witch hysteria: for him, "the cause is economic" and "the worse the economy gets, the more political tension there is in society, the more frustrated and frightened people get" (ibid.). True: globalization may well be colonialism's modern heir. Yet, Kumar's equation is as problematic as the one he confronts, namely that it is superstition or African "unreason" that is the major (if not the sole) cause of Africa's misery, and that it is attributable to lack of education or of "basic scientific literacy" (Richard Petraitis, quoted in Kumar 2006; see also Holiday 2006: 11). It is problematic because Kumar falls into the trap of implicitly portraying ordinary Africans as victims and recipients, to whom considerations of agency and responsibility do not apply. Moreover, like Grill, he fails to distinguish sufficiently between 'witchcraft beliefs' and 'witchcraft accusations'. I will address these two problems in turn.

Cameroonian academic and development consultant Axelle Kabou, in her much-maligned book *Et si l'Afrique refusait le développement?* ('And if Africa refused development?'; Kabou 1991[4]), blames not only power-crazy heads of state and the corrupt elites for the plight of the continent but also ordinary people, each and every individual. According to Kabou, Africans still believe that the world owes them salvation of the continent, as belated compensation for past injustices, their victim- and beggar mentality being strengthened by the sentimental humanitarianism of naive white aid workers. Africans should look in the mirror in order to realize their own part in this misery. Yet, writes Kabou, they refuse to do this. It is invariably the others who are to blame, foreign companies, the unjust global system of trade, the World Bank, the debt and poverty trap—not to mention the inherited burdens of colonialism. The black elites and the white helpers are united in their dogma that there exists a century-old plot by the white man against the black man, while they refuse to contemplate the more complex causes of this perpetual crisis.

Many consider Kabou's claim, that 'Africa-this-wonderful-continent-that-was-in-perfect-harmony-before-the-invasion-of-the-colonisers' is an anti-colonialist myth and has nothing to do with reality, downright blasphemous. Certainly, her pamphlet is not without stereotyping, of 'the Africans' as such. She tends to neglect the external factors of this chronic crisis, like the deprivation syndrome that white rule has left behind in the collective psyche. She also forgets that Africa lacks the springboard for the huge leap from agrarian society to industrial society. Modernization was forced onto a continent that was unable to support it, sociostructurally and culturally, while the existing entrepreneurship and infrastructure were systematically undermined and destroyed by the colonial masters (see Grill 2003: 115). There is no room for such historical subtleties in Kabou's general account. Nonetheless, no serious debate about the problems facing Africa can afford to ignore her fundamental thesis. She refers not only to the *failed* modernization of postcolonial Africa but to modernization that was *refused*, Africans being the only people on earth who still think that others must take care of their development. Kabou does not simply intend to condemn her African contemporaries. She wants to rouse them into shaking off their 'unbearable mediocrity'. Indeed, the demand for self-criticism makes her argument compelling. Unlike (for example) Kumar's, it takes ordinary Africans seriously, as agents in their own right, rather than portraying them as will and helpless victims or puppets at the mercy of the powers-that-be (corrupt leaders, the wealthy black elites, foreign companies, the World Bank, and so forth) and as suffering under the unjust global system of trade, the debt, and poverty trap—not to mention the inherited burdens of colonialism.

Stephen Ellis and Gerrie Ter Haar are in agreement with Kumar's contention (2006: 26) that legislation like the amendment to the Witchcraft Suppression Act in Zimbabwe enables the suffering masses to blame "their troubles on diabolical forces rather than on the government and business interests that profit from their misery": "Popular beliefs in witchcraft have become a convenient cover for cynical political manipulations" (Ellis and Ter Haar 2004: 150). Yet, their analysis of the pertinent conflicts is a little subtler than Kumar's. For one thing, they draw an analytical distinction between

> witchcraft beliefs—the content of which, as with other forms of spiritual belief, cannot be empirically tested—and witchcraft accusations that may follow from such belief. Witchcraft accusations, unlike witchcraft beliefs, can be empirically observed, and the ensuing actions analyzed. (149)

According to Ellis and Ter Haar (153), "discussions in Africa on how to deal with witchcraft accusations often take on a culturalist tone that some people feel to be appropriate in a postcolonial age." The common view is that witchcraft beliefs are authentically African, and that witchcraft 'really' exists in Africa. As a consequence, governments in postcolonial Africa should be free to devise mechanisms—both in terms of legislation and policing—for dealing with these phenomena. "In South Africa, only recently freed from the rule of a white minority, this approach is sometimes said to be in keeping with the idea of African Renaissance, launched by the government as a project for the regeneration of the continent" (ibid.). In this regard, Ellis and Ter Haar worry about the proliferation of all kinds of "illiberal attitudes and beliefs that are claimed to be 'authentically African and therefore justifiable in the new age'" (ibid.). So much the worse for liberal attitudes, someone like Kumar would probably respond. It is clear, however, that governments need to take witchcraft fears and their implications and consequences seriously. Neither amendments to existing legislation like in Zimbabwe nor the verdict that these fears should be ignored appear to be an appropriate response to the cause of such considerable personal and social misery.

What to do, then? Ellis and Ter Haar suggest that the

> most desirable course might be for the state to retain the principle of religious freedom, including the freedom of people to believe in witchcraft as in other religious constructs. This demonstrates in concrete terms the importance of making an analytical distinction between witchcraft belief and witchcraft accusations . . . The state would be well advised, thus, to observe debates on witchcraft beliefs with a view to intervening when there seems to be a real risk of a criminal action such as physical assault. (153–154; see also Becker 2007: 165, 166)

Ellis and Ter Haar's appears to be at best a short-term solution—it is a response only to the symptoms of the problem, one that fails to get to its roots. I submit that, in the longer term, nothing short of a radical commitment to the alleviation of poverty and to education for global citizenship (e.g., the teaching of critical thinking skills) will do. If anything, reference to 'African ways of knowing', moves like the July 2006 amendment to Zimbabwe's Witchcraft Suppression Act, and so forth are more likely to contribute to the ongoing underdevelopment of Africa and to its increasing marginalization.

PHILOSOPHY AND INDIGENOUS KNOWLEDGE

In his book *Self and Community in a Changing World*, Kenyan philosopher Dismas Masolo writes that "there appears to be little disagreement that there is knowledge that is indigenous to Africa—that is, knowledge that is unique, traditional, or local knowledge that exists within and develops around the specific conditions of the experiences of African peoples" (Masolo 2010: 51–52). Well, my voice has been, and will be in this book, one of dissent. While I agree that there are beliefs and that there may be skills that are unique and indigenous to Africa, I doubt whether the same can be said about propositional knowledge, or 'knowledge that'. More importantly, I think that the case for indigenous knowledge is helped neither by the Yoruba definition of knowledge presented by Barry Hallen and J.O. Sodipo (1997) nor by Wiredu's epistemological theory of "truth as opinion" (1998b, 2008), sources on which Masolo draws extensively in his book. Consequently, I consider the preoccupation with indigenous knowledge as "a viable tool for transforming the world" (Masolo 2010: 18) to be misguided.

One of "the themes that stand out in the recent history of Africans' philosophical reflections" is "the question of reworking and integrating indigenous knowledge into the new philosophical order." The "issue of the status of indigenous knowledge in contemporary Africa runs through all the matters discussed" (7) in Masolo's book:

> Philosophy is always about the familiar and the indigenous, whatever its form or epistemic status; it interrogates, deconstructs, analyses, interprets and tries to explain it. Philosophy is related to indigenous knowledge as the written is to the oral. (28)

Is this not a false analogy? At least we can be sure that 'the oral' exists. And when Masolo goes on to consider "examples that illustrate philosophy's ties with the ordinary and with everyday language" (ibid.), the rejoinder might be that "the ordinary and everyday language" is not the same as 'indigenous knowledge'.

In chapter 1, I dealt with the reasons for the relatively recent emergence of 'indigenous knowledge', and with what its advocacy meant to achieve. Masolo lists several reasons for the "*re*emergence of interest in indigenous knowledge in recent years" (emphasis mine). First, the effects of industrialization "in the Western sphere or the global North," namely "[o]zone depletion and environmental poisoning, . . . have made once-scorned simpler ways of life and controlled scales of industrialisation more attractive for their stances towards biodiversity and their general friendliness to the environment, at least at the intellectual level" (25–26). Clearly (and here I concur with Masolo), Western industrialization has led to, or have had as a significant goal, the subjugation of nature, and so far has been devastatingly effective. The pursuit of nuclear energy, wholesale deforestation and destruction of flora and fauna, factory farming of nonhuman animals for human consumption, vivisection,[5] and genetic engineering are deplorable and—indeed—*ir*rational (see Horsthemke 2010: 51–104), as is the relentless preoccupation with and pursuit of 'growth'. Second, with the end of the Cold War,

> the politics of numbers in the scramble for alliances and geopolitical spheres of influence is a thing of the past, thus making the sustenance of the dependency of distant nations and peoples a far less attractive policy and a sacrifice for regimes and taxpayers in developed nations. There is neither political nor economic gain for such sacrifice. Consequently, the current focus of aid agencies . . . is on helping the disadvantaged governments of economically and technologically disadvantaged nations establish self-reliant and internally sustainable programs. (Masolo 2010: 26)

I am not altogether clear about the intended force of this argument: after all, aid provision has a substantial downside that is well documented (see Kabou 1991; Seitz 2009). Nonetheless, there are additional factors that account for the (re?)emergence of interest in indigenous knowledge systems. With the rise of multiculturalism, the inferiorization of indigenous peoples' practices, skills, and insights has, to a large extent, been unmasked as arrogant and of dubious 'rationality'. There has also developed a strong tendency to view current attempts by industrial and high-tech nations to (re)colonize or appropriate for commercial gain these practices, skills, and insights as exploitative and contemptible.

With regard to the question what the focus on indigenous knowledge is hoped to achieve, we saw that there are several related ideas that appear again and again (see Semali and Kincheloe, eds. 1999 *passim*; Odora Hoppers, ed. 2002 *passim*; and De Sousa Santos, ed. 2007 *passim*): reclamation of cultural or traditional heritage; decolonization of mind and thought; recognition and acknowledgment of self-determining development; protection against further colonization, exploitation, appropriation, and/or commercialization; legitimation or validation of indigenous practices and worldviews; and condemnation of, or at least caution against, the subjugation of nature and general oppressiveness of nonindigenous rationality, science, and technology.

To return to the question initially raised in chapter 1: What actually *is* 'indigenous knowledge'? "Inspired by the claim that knowledge takes place in and reflects the social worlds of its creators in expression and use," according to Masolo (2010: 18), "formerly suppressed systems liberated themselves from foundationalist claims and monolithic canons and called for different, more rigorous, and comparative approaches to the epistemological enterprise in the latter part of the twentieth century."

> Like its cognates (local, native, original, old, or insider) and its antonyms or counterparts (migrant, alien, new, settler, or outsider) the term 'indigenous' is

used to define the origin of an item or person in relation to how their belonging to a place is to be temporally characterized, especially in comparison to other contenders in claiming belonging. . . . The term 'indigenous' has not always had positive connotations for those to whom it was intended to introduce and create awareness of distant worlds. . . . Implications of diversity persist even as the idea of indigeneity acquires more positive connotations. As pluralism takes center stage in contemporary thought and practical orientations in both the public and private realms, indigenous systems are not only encouraged to remain and show more autonomy, they are also thought to have the capacity to sustain themselves. (21)

In chapter 1, I noted a general failure among theorists to appreciate and engage with the ramifications of the concepts of knowledge and epistemology, and also the somewhat indiscriminate use of 'indigenous knowledge' as an umbrella concept for all kinds of practices, skills, customs, worldviews, perceptions, as well as theoretical and factual understandings. Happily, Masolo does not shy away from this philosophical challenge. In fact, he draws on two sources, the Yoruba definition of knowledge presented by Hallen and Sodipo, as well as Wiredu's epistemological theory of 'truth as opinion'. In what follows, however, I will attempt to show not only that neither account helps to render the idea of 'indigenous knowledge' plausible but also that Masolo fails to bring these two conceptions into conversation with one another.

IMÒ AND *IGBÀGBÓ*: THE YORUBA DEFINITION OF KNOWLEDGE

In their book *Knowledge, Belief, and Witchcraft: Analytical Experiments in African Philosophy* Hallen and Sodipo explore the contrast between 'knowledge as justified true belief' and the Yoruba concept of knowledge. Masolo provides the following sketch of Hallen and Sodipo's account:

> When an ordinary Yoruba speaker—one who is not an *onísègùn* [an indigenous cultural expert or traditional healer]—says that she can '*gbàgbó*' (believe) rather than '*mò*' (know) that [*p*, on the basis of a well-placed source's testimony], it is probable (and indeed is often the case) that she says so only because that is how any Yoruba speaker would be expected to correctly deliver that kind of judgement. . . . [I]f pressed on why she only 'believes' that [*p*, despite the well-positioned source asserting so] the Yoruba speaker may, upon the demands of the Yoruba language alone, correctly respond that she has no firsthand knowledge of the situation herself and so can only believe but not claim to 'know' the state of the matter. (Masolo 2010: 30)

This appears to be perfectly in keeping with the traditional (Platonic) definition of knowledge: the source's testimony offers some degree of justification for the speaker's belief, but it does not guarantee 'knowledge'. But there is more to Hallen and Sodipo's distinction:

> According to the analysis, the Yoruba concept of *mò* (knowledge) exacts stringent conditions under which belief (*gbàgbó*) can qualify as or become knowledge (*mò*). It is not enough, as appears in the Anglo-American rendition of this epistemological problem, that one be justified in believing, for example, that *p* for one to know that *p*, even if *p* were to be true. (45)

Hallen and Sodipo observe that in Yoruba

> *Gbàgbó* that may be verified is *gbàgbó* that may become *mò*. *Gbàgbó* that is not open to verification and must therefore be evaluated on the basis of justification alone (*àlàyé, papò*, etc.) cannot become *mò* and consequently its *òótó* [truth] must remain indeterminate.[6]

> The point of difference between the two systems that we find of greatest significance is the relative role of testimony or second-hand information. In the Yoruba system any information conveyed on the basis of testimony is, until verified, *ìgbàgbó*. In the English system [by contrast] a vast amount of information conveyed on the basis of testimony is, *without verification*, classified as 'knowledge that'. (Hallen and Sodipo 1997: 81; quoted in Masolo 2010: 45; emphasis added)

As I explained in chapter 3, reliance on testimony and second-hand information arguably renders possible progress in the natural and social sciences. Yet usually, unverified claims are not classified as propositional knowledge. Take the Nonqawuse case referred to in chapter 3: historians entertain certain hypotheses, but they claim knowledge only of certain aspects of the story. Thus, it is taken to be a historical fact that her account of having been spoken to by her ancestors, and in the process receiving pertinent instructions as to how to free her people from the colonial yoke, led to the cattle-killing and crop-burning among the Gcaleka Xhosa in the middle of the nineteenth century. Yet, there is insufficient evidence that she was on the payroll of the Eastern Cape settlers at the time, that the Eastern Cape government deliberately deceived her, that she suffered from delusions and hallucinations, that she was waging a personal vendetta against her people, and so forth.

Furthermore, the "English system" is mindful of the problems surrounding verification. Either way, it is as yet unclear in what way/s the distinction between *ìgbàgbó* and *ìmò* is meant to contribute to establishing the plausibility of *indigenous* knowledge. Indeed, when Masolo lauds the

Yoruba understanding of knowledge for requiring "first-person experiential (verifiable) testimony and not *mere justification*" (Masolo 2010: 46; emphasis mine), "direct, first-hand experience" (47, 48), and when he acknowledges that the "*ìmọ̀-ìgbàgbọ́* distinction does not privilege tradition or any other form of received information" (48), the same question arises: Where does this leave 'indigenous knowledge'? "In fact," Masolo contends,

> it is so sceptical of untested claims that it even robs science of its predictive strength. Above all, it makes a mockery of the English-language (analytical) definition of knowledge based on *mere justification of belief*. (Ibid.; emphasis added)

This is surely a red herring: I am not aware of any card-carrying representative of the analytical tradition subscribing to this 'definition' (see previous footnote).[7] More seriously, because. In addition, such experience would have to be immediate, not remembered—since memory can and often does fail us and falsify or exaggerate events. Finally, even direct, firsthand experiential knowledge claims are potentially problematic. As I explained in chapter 3, a problem that pertains to observation, albeit not to sensation, is that of fallibility. Not only may observations be deceptive and therefore, but there is also the possibility of different interpretations of, or our vantage points affecting, what we observe. Indeed, we may focus on different aspects of a given observed event—which explains why the accounts of several eyewitnesses often diverge, if not contradict each other. In addition, we do claim to have knowledge about things that we might not be able to observe. Lastly, much of what we observe occurs against the background of some or other theory we have about what it is we are observing.

The Yoruba rejection of received information as a source of knowledge (second-person testimony) may not only be mistaken but also in conflict with a cherished African traditional principle in education. I think Hardwig (1991: 693–694) is correct when he says:

> Modern knowers cannot be independent and self-reliant, not even in their own fields of specialisation. In most disciplines, those who do not trust cannot know; those who do not trust cannot have the best evidence for their beliefs.

The role of trust in knowledge, on this account, indicates a noteworthy communalist or relational orientation, which I characterized in chapter 2. To denigrate the epistemic significance of trust, and of epistemological division of labor through reliance on other people's testimony, may well be in contradiction of African communalism and relationalism.

I suggest, then, that a reduction of 'indigenous knowledge' to firsthand, direct, experiential knowledge claims—that may, indeed, be mistaken!—strips the case for indigenous *knowledge* of much of its intended force. This leaves Masolo's claim (echoing Thomas Kuhn, Sandra Harding, Bruno Latour, and Paulus Gerdes[8]; Masolo 2010, 22, 23, 60) that *all* knowledge is local. On the subject of scientific knowledge in particular,

> according to Sandra Harding, all sciences are local knowledge systems. . . . Because all sciences are locally grounded, they are ethnosciences. . . . all knowledge claims are only points of view, some at the individual level (such as those who profess relativist[9] stands) and others (such as those that incorporate stern and open modes of inquiry) more embedded in culture.[10] (22, 23)

With Harding, Masolo argues that "despite the fact that good science is characterised by strong objectivity, inclusive rationality, and universal validity, the corpus of scientific knowledge remains an aspect of local knowledge" (60). *If* that is so—which is very doubtful—then why insist on retaining the descriptor 'local' (or 'indigenous')? This is as uninformative as to refer to the *Catholic* pope, or to *human* philosophers. Where does all this leave the notion of 'indigenous knowledge'? I want to claim the following: If the important term here is 'indigenous', then it refers either to indigenous practices or skills ('knowledge how'), or to indigenous belief(s). On the other hand, if it actually is meant to refer to 'knowledge' in the factual or propositional sense, then the idea of 'indigenous' knowledge simply fails to make sense. The term 'indigenous' then becomes redundant[11]: what we are dealing with here is knowledge as such. My assumption (shared by the Yoruba definition, it would appear) is that truth (*òótó*) is "a significant component of knowledge" (47). It acts as the objective anchor of our more or less adequately justified beliefs. Or does it?

"TRUTH AS OPINION"

Perhaps the most comprehensive treatment of the notion of truth in African thinking stems from Wiredu. In his book *Philosophy and an African Culture* (1980), he notes that the correspondence theory of truth[12] cannot without circularity be expressed in the Akan language (see also Wiredu 1998b: 235). He adds, "Another linguistic contrast between Akan and English is that there is no word in Akan for the English word 'fact'" (ibid.). He argues that whatever is called the 'truth' is necessarily someone's truth. For an item of information to be considered 'true', it must be discovered, defended, and known by human beings in a particular place, at a particular time. Moreover, he says, as history has shown, and as present experience continues to demonstrate, what human beings consider to be 'true' can be argued to be false from an alternative perspective. Therefore, whatever is referred to as 'truth' is more correctly interpreted as opinion[13] or point of view. This understanding of 'truth' as opinion means that Wiredu rejects what, within academic philosophical circles, is referred to as the "objectivist theory" of truth. He describes this theory as holding that "once a proposition is true, it is true in itself and for ever. Truth, in other words, is timeless, eternal" (Wiredu 1980: 114).

According to Wiredu (115), such an objectivist theory of truth implies that truth is 'categorically distinct' from opinion. But this, in effect, would make truth "as a matter of logical principle, unknowable," since every truth claim would then be reduced to a mere opinion advanced from a specific perspective and therefore "categorically distinct from truth." Truth arises from human agency—from perception and rational inquiry (see Hallen 2004: 107), as opposed to deriving from some transcendent reality. "We must recognize the cognitive element of point of view as intrinsic to the concept of truth" (Wiredu 1980: 115). The fact that truth arises from human endeavor and effort does not mean knowledge will retrogress to the merely subjective or relative. "What I mean by opinion is a firm rather than an uncertain thought. I mean what is called a considered opinion" (115–116). This notion of "considered opinion" is of fundamental significance in Wiredu's overall understanding of truth. Elsewhere, he relates it to the pragmatist idea of 'warrant', although he maintains that these two notions are not identical: "Something is warranted ['well-considered'] not because it is true, but true because it is warranted; better, it is true if and only if it is warranted" (Wiredu, personal correspondence; quoted in Hallen 2004: 107, 138n.16). Truth as opinion must obviously always be held from some perspective. Yet, that opinion becomes warranted (or 'well-considered') when it arises in a genuinely intersubjective context where it is anchored in shared "canons of rational inquiry" (Wiredu 1980: 177). In Wiredu's view, such intersubjective accordance becomes a necessary condition for truth and accounts for his explicit rejection of both subjectivism and relativism.

There is something disturbingly circular about Wiredu's argument. How do I know that what I believe to be true is in fact true? Because it is warranted. But what warrants it? The fact that others believe it too. But what makes their beliefs true? That they are warranted, and so on. At any rate, the idea that truth is the objective component of propositional knowledge and that opinion or belief is its subjective component is the mainstay of classical epistemology.[14] And while there may always exist uncertainty or doubts about scientific, empirical truth (empirically, the truth may well be 'the world's secret'), this does not mean that all truths are unknowable. Logical, mathematical, and analytical truths are perfectly knowable,[15] as are truths about the self and at least *some* empirical or experiential truths: introspective truths and truths of sensation. But even if most empirical (e.g., observational) truths ultimately remain elusive, this is arguably still preferable to the scenario of multiple, perspectival truths—not least because of the 'anything goes' implications this would appear to have.[16] Furthermore, it is difficult to see how Wiredu can avoid logical inconsistency when he advances these claims as having (objective) truth content, for example, that whatever is called the 'truth' is always someone's truth, or that for a piece of information to be called 'true', it must be discovered by, known by, and defended by someone, somewhere, sometime. Masolo explains (2010: 160; see also 175ff.):

> Every individual person has this special relationship to the world as an individual, on the one hand, and an essential relationship to others as the source of meaning-making, on the other. What we 'know' of the world does not and cannot emerge from only one of these sides of our relation to the world. Rather, what we 'know' of the world is a constant striving to reconcile both sides of our relation to the world, namely, reconciling what we (empirically) experience as a stream of physical stimuli with what we have learned these stimuli to be or to mean. This ... is the philosophical-anthropological condition of personhood that grounds the epistemological theory of 'truth as opinion'.

No—I would argue: what this indicates, rather, is that the vast majority of our beliefs arises from our situation as related, relational beings in communities of inquiry, as well the complexity of justification and the interaction of different sources or kinds of justification: sense-experience and observation, on the one hand, and memory, testimony, and deductive and nondeductive reasoning, on the other. Truth is not a social convention, a cultural construct, a matter of meaning-making between consenting adults. So, *if* Wiredu's "position favours a dialogical sense of truth over the objectivist one" (161), I suspect he may be quite wrong. Malawian philosopher Didier Kaphagawani (1998: 241) commits a related error. When he declares that, in his home language Chewa, "What is true is what is seen ... or perceived by either an individual or a collection of individuals," he clearly confuses truth and justification. As I explained in chapter 3, observation and perception are sources of justification and knowledge. Given the possibility of observational error and perceptual relativity, they are not identical with truth as such. Even consensus among all individuals about what they perceive does not amount to truth, the way things really are.

Wiredu explicitly rejects relativism, which in his opinion is 'an absurd doctrine'. He says (1980: 176–177):

> It is the insistence on the need for belief to be in accordance with the canons of rational investigation which distinguish my view from relativism. Truth is not relative to point of view. It is, in one sense, a point of view ... born out of rational inquiry, and the canons of rational inquiry have a universal application.

Yet, I am not sure how Wiredu's position—equating, as it does, truth and opinion—*can* avoid relativism, however much he rejects the doctrine's tendency to make "truth arbitrary, whimsical, and ungrounded in serious gnostic endeavor" (Masolo 2010, 177). The 'truth-is-opinion' advocate will be caught up in paradox, in a logical conundrum. At some point, he will want to claim that his statements about the doxastic nature of truth are, in fact, nondoxastically, universally true (i.e., independently of belief or opinion or point of view)—which he cannot do consistently, given his perspectivalism. Wiredu's position is all the more puzzling in that, elsewhere, he does appear to subscribe to an understanding of truth that avoids any reference to belief or opinion: *nea ete saa*, which is an Akan phrase for "that which is so" (Wiredu 1998b: 235).

The Yoruba definition of knowledge and Wiredu's relational position are not brought into conversation with one another, at least not explicitly, by Masolo. However, there are elements in Wiredu's thought, and also in Yoruba language and culture, that arguably yield weapons against the 'anything-goes' approach implicit in perspectivalist, relativist, and constructivist epistemology. Reiterating his earlier observation that "there is no one word in Akan for truth" (ibid.), Wiredu distinguishes between truthfulness (*nokware*) and truth in the cognitive sense, for which the Akan reserve the expression *nea ete saa*, as explained above. Wiredu is concerned "to make a metadoctrinal point which reflection on the Akan language enables us to see, which is that a theory of truth is not of any real *universal* significance unless it offers some account of the notion of being so" (238–239; emphasis added). He explains, "The opposite of *nokware* is *nkontompo* which means lies. But the opposite of truth is falsity, not lies" (234).

In Yoruba, too, the word *irò* means 'lie' and therefore primarily has a moral meaning (see Bello 2004: 271). It is the opposite of *òtitó*, that is, 'truthfulness'. The significant feature is the affinity both the Yoruba and the Akan languages share with the English language in the matter of truth and truthfulness. Though distinct, there is clearly a conceptual dependence of 'truthfulness' on 'truth'. In the absence of *nea ete saa*, it would make little sense to refer to *nokware*. Similarly, *òtitó* draws its conceptual and normative strength from *òótó*. While the opposite of truth is falsehood, untruth, or error, the opposite of truthfulness is lying, untruthfulness, or fabrication—an intentional misrepresentation of *that which is so* as *that which is not so*. This is all that is required to undermine the putative force of a culturalist, perspectivalist, or constructivist orientation. Truth commissions offer a useful illustration of the assumption that the pursuit of impartial, objective truth is not only possible but that it is also fundamentally desirable (see chapters 8 and 9; see also Posel and Simpson 2002: 1; Posel 2004: 5). Either way, it remains doubtful whether Wiredu's theory can do the requisite work for a defense of 'indigenous knowledge'.

Sometimes, 'happily', Masolo says (2010: 11–12),

when we have the opportunity to know the characteristics of other knowledge communities, we may venture to compare them with our own, meaning that there is little (if anything) that impenetrably closes one knowledge system from another. At the minimum, and barring any unwarranted contempt for or dismissal of the unfamiliar, they can be compared.

The question might now be posed whether skepticism about the notion of 'indigenous knowledge systems' does not amount to 'epistemic injustice', is not a matter of inflicting epistemic harm. Or could this be seen as a form of *'warranted* dismissal'? This is a discussion I will defer until the penultimate chapter of this book.

The idea that knowledge (and philosophy) could be originally 'African', while not uncontroversial, is certainly not implausible. On June 7, 2006, Martin Bernal, in a presentation at the University of the Witwatersrand entitled 'Africa in Europe/Egypt in Africa', outlined the central argument in his then-as-yet-unpublished *Black Athena 3*: although Greek is by most accounts an Indo-European language, 60 percent of Greek terminology is not Indo-European but of Afroasiatic origin. In a book supported by the South African Department of Arts and Culture, *I Am an African: Embrace Your Identity, Escape Victimization*, Ngila Michael Muendane, too (after arguing that physical colonialism may have ceased but that mental colonialism continues to this day—and nowhere more starkly than in academia; Muendane 2006: 53–63), contends that Europeans attribute their enlightenment to Greece, but that Greek thinkers were either educated in Egypt or influenced substantially by Egyptian thought and practice (128). If Bernal and Muendane's analysis is correct, then the latter's argument from 'mental colonization' loses much of its intended strength. If all "philosophy and political thinking, . . . mathematics, . . . astronomy, geometry, medicine," and so forth has been "learnt . . . in Africa from Africans" (ibid.) then how could it possibly issue in mental colonization? In other words, the Afrogenesis thesis would render the idea of 'African ways of knowing' even less plausible. For it is one thing to argue that *all* knowledge originated in Africa initially (this is a moot point): it is quite another to argue that there are distinctly and uniquely 'African' ways of knowing. In other words, one can acknowledge Africa's contribution to 'world' knowledge, without being committed to (embracing) the idea of African indigenous knowledge systems. Similar observations pertain to so-called 'diverse epistemologies' or 'epistemological diversity'. Does recognition of cultural (ethnic, sexual, etc.) diversity also require recognition of epistemological diversity? The key to a compelling response to this question is arguably not the definition of 'diversity', but what is understood by 'epistemology', as the following section will show.

MAKING SENSE OF 'EPISTEMOLOGICAL DIVERSITY'

In his discussion of the ways and possibilities of preparing doctoral students for 'epistemological diversity', American sociologist/educationalist Aaron Pallas (2001: 6) writes: "Experienced researchers and novices alike find it hard to keep up with the cacophony of diverse epistemologies . . . positivism, naturalism, postpositivism, empiricism, relativism, feminist standpoint epistemology, foundationalism, postmodernism." Other appeals to 'epistemological diversity' and 'knowledge diversity' relate not to different normative theories of knowledge, but to diversity across ethnicities, cultures, and so forth, and subdivisions within these, as in so-called 'epistemologies of the South' (De Sousa Santos 2014) and 'multicultural epistemologies' (see chapter 2; see also Phillips 2012; Levisohn and Phillips 2012; Horsthemke 2017e). To this "cacophony," De Sousa Santos (2014) adds a few more: "epistemology of blindness" and "epistemology of seeing" (154–157), "epistemology of absent knowledges" (157ff.), "epistemology of absent agents" (159ff.) and "epistemologies of absence"/"epistemology of absences" (160–163), before introducing the notion of "ecologies of knowledges" (188–211; he refers also to "ecologies of knowledge" and "ecology of knowledges").

De Sousa Santos, Nunes, and Meneses relate their appeal to "the epistemological diversity of the world," which "is immense" (De Sousa Santos et al. 2007: xix, xlviii), not to different normative theories of knowledge (which are concerned with determining the grounds and criteria for 'knowledge'), but rather to diversity across ethnicities, cultures, and so forth. They argue that although "there has been a growing recognition of the cultural diversity of the world" over the last few decades, "with current controversies focusing on the terms of such recognition [. . . ,] the same cannot be said of the recognition of the epistemological diversity of the world, that is, of the diversity of knowledge systems underlying the practices of different social groups across the globe" (xix).

Beginning with the assumption that "there is no global social justice without global cognitive justice" (De Sousa Santos 2014: 42; De Sousa Santos et al. 2007: xix), De Sousa Santos appeals to "a more just relationship among different kinds of knowledge." He deems it "imperative to start an intercultural dialogue and translation among different critical knowledges and practices: South-centric and North-centric, popular and scientific, religious and secular, female and male, urban and rural, and so forth" (ibid.). This intercultural dialogue and translation of "the immense diversity of oppositional ideas and practices" (43) is "at the roots" of what De Sousa Santos calls "the *ecology of knowledges*" (42). His reference to "[t]his potentially unconditional inclusiveness" (43), however, is arguably a *contradictio in adiecto*. Either the model is potentially (i.e., conditionally) inclusive of all "knowledges" or it is unconditionally inclusive. Presumably, and not unreasonably, he wants to deflect the charge of admitting any and all ideas and practices—but then what would have to be in place to enable the shift from potentiality to actuality? The problem seems to reside with the 'unconditionality' of inclusion, which—as we will see—advocates of multicultural epistemologies typically seem to want to retain.

The author's intention is to show that "the ecology of knowledges confronts the logic of the monoculture of scientific knowledge and rigor by identifying other knowledges and criteria of rigor and validity that operate credibly in social practices pronounced nonexistent by metonymic reason"[17] (188). "Such an ecology of knowledges permits not only the overcoming of the mono-culture of scientific knowledge but also the idea that nonscientific knowledges are alternatives to scientific knowledge" (189). De Sousa Santos is quick to point out that this

> ecology of knowledges does not entail accepting relativism. On the contrary, from the point of view of a pragmatics of social emancipation, relativism, considered as an absence of criteria of hierarchy among knowledges, is an unsustainable position, for it renders impossible any relation between knowledge and the meaning of social transformation. If all the different kinds of knowledge are equally valid as knowledge, every project of social transformation is equally valid or, likewise, equally invalid.... The point is not to ascribe the same validity to every kind of knowledge but rather to allow for a pragmatic discussion among alternative, valid criteria without immediately disqualifying whatever does not fit the epistemological canon of modern science. (190)

De Sousa Santos (192) presents "the ecology of knowledges" as "basically a counterepistemology," which "implies renouncing any general epistemology." Or as De Sousa Santos et al. (2007: xx) put it, it "is an invitation to the promotion of non-relativistic dialogues among knowledges, granting 'equality of opportunities' to the different kinds of knowledge engaged in ever broader epistemological disputes aimed both at maximizing their respective contributions to build a more democratic and just society and at decolonizing knowledge and power."

This approach exemplifies the increasingly popular view that ethnic or cultural groups (and subgroups within these) have their own distinctive epistemologies and that these have been ignored, belittled, or rejected by the dominant social group. A corollary of this approach states that educational research is pursued within a framework that represents particular assumptions about knowledge, knowledge production, and ignorance that reflect the interests, historical and indeed (mono-)cultural traditions of this dominant group. This has led to an emphasis on decolonization of knowledge and epistemology, recognition of indigenous, local, or subaltern knowledge systems and "radically different" epistemologies within academic research and academic practice. Thus, Odora Hoppers (2002b: 12) laments universities' "lack of responsiveness to diversity (of knowing, seeing, and interpreting the world." "The challenge," she contends, "becomes one of how to operationalize empowerment itself in a context in which diverse knowledges are barely tolerated and exist only in sufferance and subjugated deference to a mainstream, essentially Western form of knowledge" (14). Her stated aim is "a more inclusive democratic practice that takes full cognizance of the plural manifestations of epistemology and cosmology" (18).

For the remainder of this section, I will focus my attention on the arguments advanced by De Sousa Santos et al. (2007): "Conceptions of knowledge, of what it means to know, of what counts as knowledge, and how that knowledge is produced are as diverse as the [different] cosmologies and normative frameworks [. . .]." They assert that all "social practices involve knowledge" and that the "production of knowledge is, in itself, a social practice" (De Sousa Santos et al. 2007: xxi). The authors consider "recognition of the epistemological diversity of the world" to be "inseparable from the diversity of the cosmologies that divide and organize the world in ways that differ from Western cosmology and its offshoot, modern science" (ibid.). They contend that epistemological diversity is "neither the simple reflection or epiphenomenon of ontological diversity or heterogeneity nor a range of culturally specific ways of expressing a fundamentally unified world." There exists "no essential or definitive way of describing, ordering, and classifying processes, entities, and relationships in the world." In fact, "different modes of knowing, being irremediably partial and situated, will have different consequences and effects on the world." The authors take the "very capacity of the modern sciences to create new entities and in this way to enact an ontological politics [. . .]—with the effect, intentional or not, of increasing this heterogeneity of the world—[. . .] to support this conception." De Sousa Santos, Nunes, and Meneses understand this to give "shape to a robust realism and to a strong objectivity, a clear awareness of the need to accurately and precisely identify the conditions in which knowledge is produced and its assessment on the basis of its observed or expected consequences." This, they contend, "allows a rigorous account of the situatedness, partiality, and constructedness of all knowledges, while rejecting relativism as an epistemological and moral stance" (xxxi).[18]

It is not at all clear how an appeal to "the situatedness [. . .] of all knowledges" *can* avoid the charge of relativism,[19] how "partiality" is to be reconciled with "strong objectivity," or "constructedness of all knowledges" with a "robust realism." "That which exists—knowledge, technological objects, buildings, roads, cultural objects—exists *because* it is constructed through situated practices," according to the authors. They see the pertinent distinction to be "not between the real and the constructed, but between that which is well constructed, which successfully resists the situations in which its consistency, solidity, and robustness are put to the test, and that which is badly constructed, and hence vulnerable to criticism or erosion." They take this to constitute "the difference that allows a distinction to be made between facts (well constructed) and artifacts (badly constructed)" (ibid.). I have already articulated my concerns about constructivism, both as a pedagogy and as an epistemology (see chapter 3). But suppose we accept this constructivist framework: Could we not then distinguish between knowledge (well constructed) and superstition (badly constructed), between science (well constructed) and pseudo-science (badly constructed)?

More often than not, however, in such arguments for different, diverse, alternative, decolonized, or demasculinized epistemologies, some relevant philosophical issues remain unresolved, if not unaddressed altogether. What exactly do these claims about ecologies of *knowledges* and *epistemological* diversity mean? Do these ways of establishing knowledge stand up to critical interrogation? Moreover, how do they relate to traditional epistemological distinctions, for example, between knowledge and belief and between descriptive and normative inquiry, and to epistemologically essential components like warrant/justification and truth?

American philosophers Jon Levisohn and Denis Phillips explain that, especially in the educational literature on multicultural reforms, the language of epistemology has been employed in some kind of rhetorical inflation, thus obscuring rather than clarifying important issues and distinctions (Levisohn and Phillips 2012: 40). Traditionally, 'epistemology' refers to 'theory/logic of knowledge' (*episteme*—knowledge; *logos*—word). Over the centuries, arguably beginning with Socrates and Plato, epistemologists have reached a general agreement about a basic division, that between knowledge and belief.[20] The present concern is not just whether or not a word ('epistemology') is being misused but also (and importantly) whether or not the issues dealt with in epistemology (a complex field that has evolved over a long period of time) are being given short shrift, if not ignored altogether. A related distinction has been made between descriptive and normative inquiry, regarding beliefs and knowledge. "If these distinctions are blurred," the authors write, "then all rational argument is potentially undermined, including the very arguments multiculturalists employ" (42). In order to establish some kind of conceptual clarity, Levisohn and Phillips draw the following distinctions:

1. epistemology as a normative field of inquiry
2. epistemology as a normative theory of knowledge
3. epistemology as a descriptive account of how people acquire beliefs
4. epistemology as a description of a set of beliefs

The first of these refers to the traditional philosophical understanding of knowledge—which, we saw, is not an exclusively Western conception. Relevant distinctions are made here between knowledge and belief, between mere belief and well-warranted (or adequately justified) belief, and between true belief and justified true belief. The inquiry here is essentially normative, for example, evaluating beliefs and belief strategies, investigating what beliefs are trustworthy enough to be acted on, how researchers should validate their findings, what forms of argument and what kinds of justification are acceptable, who (if anyone) counts as an epistemic authority, and so forth

The second point concerns different epistemologies within the philosophical tradition. Levisohn and Phillips distinguish between foundationalist (e.g., empiricist, rationalist, and positivist) and nonfoundationalist (e.g., pragmatist) epistemologies. Here, too, the inquiry is normative. As the authors inform us, all these coexist because philosophers still disagree about them, even though they are in agreement that only one position can be right. This is not the case with appeals to subaltern or "multicultural epistemologies"—which (as their defenders contend) are all equally respectable and valid.

The third general use of 'epistemology' serves an essentially descriptive function—and belongs less in philosophy than in the so-called 'sociology of knowledge' (which might be called, more fittingly, the 'sociology of belief') and perhaps in the psychology of learning. The fourth sense of 'epistemology' is also descriptive, in that it is

> sometimes extended to . . . encompass description of the specific *content* of beliefs that are held, or are accorded the status of being knowledge, by ethnic or cultural groups . . . In this . . . usage, then, multicultural epistemologies are simply *those differing sets of beliefs held by different communities.* (Levisohn and Phillips 2012: 54)

The authors point out, plausibly I think, that within the *descriptive* senses, the notion of multicultural epistemologies is unproblematic—given the interpretation of 'epistemologies' as 'beliefs' or 'belief systems'. There is, however, no coherent *normative* sense in which the existence of diverse epistemologies (multicultural or otherwise) can be affirmed.[21]

A Critique of Indigenous Knowledge 119

American philosopher Harvey Siegel (2012) examines a number of senses in which 'epistemological diversity' is often used:

- beliefs and belief systems
- methodological diversity; diversity in research method(ologie)s
- diversity of research questions
- diversity of researchers and their cultures
- epistemologies and epistemological perspectives

Although the use of 'epistemology' in the first four of these examples is arguably inappropriate (in that philosophers do not understand 'epistemology' in any of these ways), the use of 'diversity' is uncontroversial. Beliefs and belief systems vary, as do research questions and research methods (although Siegel is quick to point out that this should not be taken to imply some kind of methodological relativism, as advocated—for example—by Dani Nabudere[22]). Similarly, there is considerable variation in researchers' backgrounds, their individual, ethnic, and cultural identities, their personal and professional interests, objectives, and priorities. The 'diversity' in question becomes more controversial, and indeed problematic, in relation to "epistemologies and epistemological perspectives." This, says Siegel, goes to the "heart of the matter" (73).

According to advocates of subaltern and multicultural epistemologies, critical evaluation of these different epistemological perspectives is impossible, and—if it *were* possible—undesirable or inappropriate. The question is *why* this should be so. Siegel examines this from a variety of angles.

- Is it *epistemologically suspect* to criticize the epistemology of a particular community of practice, approach to research, or subordinated group? (75) Not obviously. According to Siegel, epistemologies

    that deserve to count as legitimate epistemological alternatives must prove their mettle in the give-and-take of scholarly disputation. Some will survive such disputation, others will not. (75)

    Furthermore, it is doubtful whether epistemologies can be attributed to such communities or groups in a straight-forward one-to-one fashion, given the considerable variation within these communities, groups and subgroups. Siegel perceives a "problematic essentialism" in any such mapping. (78)
- Is it *morally suspect* to criticize the epistemology of a particular community of practice, approach to research, or subordinated group? (78) Even if we *could* attribute epistemologies to different communities, groups, and subgroups, Siegel does not consider criticism to be morally problematic: treating members' ideas with respect means taking them seriously, by subjecting them to due critical consideration and interrogation, rather than ignoring

them. Moreover, if disputation and evaluation follow relevant moral principles, if they are fair-minded, nonquestion-begging, neutral (in the sense not of "global" but of "local neutrality") and rational, then it is difficult to see how such criticism could be morally suspect.
- Is it inevitably an *abuse of power* to criticize? (79) In other words, are these moral principles or criteria not themselves the creation and stipulation of the dominant social group? According to Siegel, hegemonic abuse of power is rejected on the basis of critical evaluation and compelling argument. It is not clear how any rejection of hegemonic imposition, any critique of dominant social power (for an example of such rejection and critique, see Code 2012: 93), can be coherent and consistent without advocates of alternative epistemologies employing these "tools of mainstream philosophical thought" (Siegel 2012: 80).
- Is it *pragmatically suspect* to criticize the epistemology of a particular community of practice, or approach to research, or subordinated group? (81) Should education researchers, to the greatest extent possible, not be able to interact with all available research—mainstream and alternative alike? Siegel considers such all-inclusive engagement worth rejecting for "equally pragmatic" reasons—lack of truth-content, lack of relevance, time constraints, and so forth.

The call for epistemological diversity becomes problematic when it conflates epistemological pluralism and epistemological relativism, "which can only hamper the important project of rethinking the graduate education of future education researchers" (83). For example, while Wajcman (2004) does recognize the dimension of epistemological relativism, she does not problematize it. Instead, she pleads both for epistemological diversity and for allowing several truths to exist alongside each other. Siegel provides a characteristically no-holds-barred response to Ruitenberg's question, how "the field of educational research" should "respond to claims about indigenous African women's epistemologies" (during a roundtable discussion held in San Francisco in April 2010; see Code et al. 2012: 137): "They're not epistemologies. If students don't understand that by the end of their graduate education, they haven't been well educated" (138). The following section examines the problem of relativism in the light of feminist critiques of epistemology, and feminist standpoint epistemology in particular.

FEMINIST CRITIQUES OF EPISTEMOLOGY AND THE PROBLEM OF RELATIVISM REVISITED

"The starting point of standpoint theory," writes Harding (2002: 357), "is that in societies stratified by race, ethnicity, class, gender, sexuality, or some other such politics shaping the very structure of a society, the *activities* of those at the top both organize and set limits on what persons who perform such activities can understand about themselves and the world around them." She asserts that "the standpoint claims that all knowledge attempts are socially situated and [. . .] some of these objective social locations are better than others as starting points for knowledge projects challenge some of the most fundamental assumptions of the scientific world view and the Western though that takes science as its model of how to produce knowledge" (359). Standpoint theorists argue that thought, for example, educational research, should start off "from the lives of marginalized peoples; beginning in those determinate, objective locations in any social order will generate illuminating critical questions that do not arise in thought that begins from dominant group lives." The idea is starting off research from the lives of women "will generate less partial and distorted accounts not only of women's' lives but also of men's lives and of the whole social order." The lives and experiences of women "provide the 'grounds' for this knowledge, though these clearly do not provide foundations for knowledge in the conventional philosophical sense" (359–360).

Harding does not illustrate or provide further argument for her claim that starting off research from women's lives "will generate less partial and distorted accounts [. . .] also of men's lives and of the whole social order." In a related move, she maintains that "standpoint theory does not advocate—nor is it doomed to—relativism." It takes issue with "the idea that all social situations provide equally useful resources for learning about the world and against the idea that they all set equally strong limits on knowledge." In opposition to universalist thinking, "standpoint theory is not committed to such a claim as a consequence of rejecting universalism." It "provides arguments for the claim that some social situations are scientifically better than others as places from which to start off knowledge projects, and those arguments must be defeated if the charge of relativism is to gain plausibility" (364). Harding goes on to distinguish between judgmental (or epistemological) relativism and sociological relativism. The former "is anathema to any scientific project, and feminist ones are no exception," whereas the latter "permits us to acknowledge that different people hold different beliefs." According to Harding, what is "at issue in rethinking objectivity is the different matter of *judgmental* or epistemological relativism."[23] She maintains that "standpoint theory does not advocate" nor is it "doomed to [judgmental or epistemological] relativism" (ibid.). Harding claims that both "moral and cognitive forms of judgmental relativism have determinate histories; they appear as intellectual problems at certain times in history in only some cultures and only for certain groups of people." However, she does not consider relativism to be "fundamentally a problem that emerges from feminist or any other thought that starts in marginalized lives; it is one that emerges from the thought of the dominant groups" (365).

It may be correct that this problem does not *emerge* from feminist and other thought, but this does not mean that it does not present a *challenge* to these. Harding continues: "Judgmental relativism is sometimes the most that dominant groups can stand to grant their critics—'OK, your claims are valid for you, but mine are valid for me'" (ibid.). In a footnote (382n.39), she approvingly refers to Mary G. Belenky and her colleagues (Belenky et al. 1986), who have pointed out that the phrase 'It's my opinion . . . ' has different meanings for the young men and women they have studied. For men this phrase means 'I've got a right to my opinion', but for women it means 'It's just my opinion'. Even if this study is accepted as providing 'evidence',[24] it is hardly enough to make any sweeping global claims about the social situatedness of knowledge and truth. As Levisohn and Phillips have pointed out, "Even for a self-proclaimed standpointist like Harding, the most we can say is that while different cultural standpoints play a significant role in the construction of knowledge, fundamentally *we all play by the same normative epistemic rules*" (Levisohn and Phillips 2012: 61).

Lorraine Code (2012: 91) asserts that "Feminist critiques of epistemology, of the philosophy of science, and of social science have demonstrated that the ideals of the autonomous reasoner—the dislocated disinterested observer—and the epistemologies they inform are artifacts of a small, privileged group of educated, usually prosperous white men." This is not at all obvious, one might respond. First, there is no such homogeneous group, nor has there ever been one; second, one of the few matters (if not the only matter!) epistemologists have reached agreement about is the basic distinction between knowledge and belief, where the former (propositional knowledge or 'knowledge-that') is anchored by the objective component of, that is, the truth condition. Could feminists coherently and consistently reject this distinction?

Code presents the case against "traditional 'S-knows-that-p' epistemologies, with their ideals of pure objectivity and value-neutrality" (85, 86),[25] on the grounds that epistemology would look quite different if it took as its starting focus cases of 'knowledge by acquaintance', where the subjectivity and positionality of the knower might turn out to be epistemically relevant. But *are* subjectivity and positionality really relevant in most epistemologically important inquiries? Without wishing to belittle the sometime significance of 'knowing a person', and so forth, I suspect not.

According to Code, "A realistic commitment to achieving empirical advocacy that engages situated analyses of the subjectivities of both the knower and (where appropriate) the known is both desirable and possible" (97). Code's own case study, John Philippe Rushton's empirical investigation into the purported superiority of Orientals over whites, and of whites over blacks, arguably fails to illustrate what she intends (see Rushton 2000). Contrary to what she asserts, 'Rushton knows that blacks are inferior' does *not* invalidate the '*S*-knows-that-*p*' formula—quite simply *because he does not know this.* 'Rushton *claims* to know that blacks are inferior' would be a more appropriate rendition.[26] It is a knowledge claim that is fairly swiftly disposed with, on the grounds of adequacy of evidence (or lack thereof), as well as arbitrary construction of a scale of superiority/inferiority.

INDIGENIZATION AND ISLAMIZATION

A different kind of challenge arises with the calls for 'Islamization' of knowledge and education (see IIIT 1987; Al-Faruqi 1988; Nasr 1991; Dangor 2005), which first gained momentum in the 1980s. The idea of Islamization of education—that is, the inclusion of certain disciplines within an Islamic school curriculum or the provision of an Islamic perspective on syllabus content and curriculum choice—makes sense and is fairly uncontroversial within Islamic educational settings. These are trends and initiatives that also exist in other religious and devotional educational contexts, and school choice is largely determined by parents' or caregivers' beliefs and interests. That is, there are certain expectations of Muslim, Christian, or Jewish educational institutions it is not unreasonable to meet. However, it would be unreasonable to expect Muslim, Christian, or Jewish doctrines to be included in secular school curricula and syllabi in subjects or learning areas other than religion education. There are several additional issues that beg critical interrogation. These are

- the conception of knowledge and epistemology that informs past and present calls for Islamization;
- the explicit or implicit critique of 'modern secular' education (Dangor 2005: 520), especially Western education's purported value-neutrality and failure to provide moral guidance (521); and
- the attempt by Muslim scholars to present Islamization of knowledge as an indigenous knowledge system (525).

I will address each of these issues in turn.
According to South African Muslim scholar Suleman Dangor (520),

> The theologian, philosopher, and mystic Abu Hamid al-Ghazzali (d. 1111) classified knowledge into *al-'ilm al-'aqli* (knowledge acquired through human reason and intellect) and *al-'ilm al-naqli* (transmitted knowledge). The latter is

obtained from Divine Revelation (*wahy*), accepted by Muslim scholars as the primary source of knowledge in Islam.

The term '*ilm* literally means 'knowledge' and "encompasses all facets of life: intellectual, material, and spiritual" (522). Dangor (523) laments secular education's "scientific approach to knowledge, in terms of which non-empirical knowledge is proscribed, [and which] generates an empirical attitude in learners and a corresponding marginalization of the transcendental, viz. divine principles, norms and values, which have no place in the pursuit of knowledge, techniques, and skills." He adds (ibid.),

> In the Islamic epistemology, revelation occupies a fundamental place. In addition to reason, sensory perception, intuition, and experience (including experimentation and observation), revelation is a primary source of knowledge. Any attempt to understand human behavior without reference to revealed knowledge is considered inadequate by Muslim scholars.

But what makes revelation a source of knowledge (see also Nasr 1991) and not merely a source of belief? Given what was established in chapter 3, there is a powerful argument against accepting "*al-'ilm al-naqli* (transmitted knowledge)" as *knowledge*. At the most, it yields belief in the form of faith, frequently acquired as a result of uncritical and unquestioning rote memorization. There are several disturbing features of the Islamization of knowledge project as characterized by Dangor and other scholars (IIIT 1987; Al-Faruqi 1988; Nasr 1991), in its demand of "the development of a new epistemology, paradigm of knowledge, and methodology" (Dangor 2005: 526). For Ismail Al-Faruqi (1988: 54–62), it means "a systematic reorientation and restructuring of *the entire field of human knowledge* in accordance with a new set of criteria and categories derived from and based on the Islamic worldview" (IIIT 1987: 15; emphasis added). Apart from being epistemologically dubious, there is both a normative and a meta-ethical problem here. The normative problem is simply the application of a narrow and coercive, authoritarian yardstick. The meta-ethical problem concerns the fundamentalist creationist pitch made here. If "education is intended to produce a God-conscious and righteous individual who lives in accordance with the Divine mandate" (Dangor 2005: 522), this raises the question of why divine authority should be accepted as a *moral* authority. If what God commands determines what is moral, then this makes morality wholly arbitrary. God could have commanded anything, and it would be unassailable *qua* "Divine mandate." (The ramifications are manifest in the profound differences in interpreting God's commandments, in all three major monotheistic religions.) If, on the other hand, God commands what is already moral (the corollary being that "Divine mandate" would never be immoral, that God would not never command anything that is not moral), then morality exists outside and independently of God's authority, and individuals could adhere to its standards without being "God-conscious."

This leads to the second problematic issue I referred to earlier. Dangor suggests that "moral or spiritual development is not among the objectives modern secular education," in that it "makes no provision for intuition, contemplation, spiritual values, or moral development" (521). This is plainly false and offers at best a caricature of so-called 'Western' education as being "based on a purely materialistic philosophy of life, its emphasis being essentially on intellectual progress for the material well-being of the individual and society" (523). Far from being 'value-free', the educational system prevalent in the 'West'—while certainly "designed to provide career opportunities" and to meet the "needs of the marketplace" (521)—also aims to contribute to the development of empathetic, caring, open-minded, and respectful persons committed to dialogue and democratic debate. I cannot think of a single respectable contemporary educationalist who has "proposed that education should be neutral to values" (523). When Dangor speaks of moral or ethical values derived from and based on Qur'anic revelation as not being "considered relative, but absolute and eternal," he makes two philosophical mistakes, over and above facing the aforementioned dilemma faced by divine command (or "Divine mandate") theory. The first is the semantic error of contraposing 'relative' and 'absolute'. The opposite of 'relative values' is not 'absolute' but, rather, 'universal values'. One can be opposed to both relative and absolute values—indeed, such opposition is rational and logically coherent. Thus, commitment to the universal values of preservation of life, truth-telling, or respect for property does not mean that there are no exceptions. There may be extraordinary circumstances in which the taking of life, lying, and stealing are morally permissible. This does not in any way bear on the universality of the values in questions. Nor does it mean that they are 'relative'. Second, the implication that secular values are susceptible to relativism is simply false. Rather tellingly, the relativist approach characterizes not (Western) secular education but, rather, advocacy of indigenous knowledge systems. This leads to the third problem facing 'Indigenization of knowledge'.

Most glaringly, 'Islamization of knowledge' cannot—even in the most fertile imagination—be portrayed as being relevantly like indigenous knowledge or 'indigenization' of knowledge. Islamization of knowledge, quite apart from its questionable use of 'knowledge', simply is not 'indigenous' in any relevant sense other than covering a variety of orientations and interpretations. Moreover, its propagation and voracious proselytizing situate it closer to the hegemonism rightly criticized by theorists and defenders of the subaltern. When Dangor asserts that the "division between traditional and modern secular education that now obtains in the Muslim world is a later development—a legacy of colonialism" (521), he seems to be wholly unaware of the interjection that the spread of Islam across the globe (like the earlier spread of Christianity) involves something relevantly like colonialism.

THE VALUE OF DIVERSITY FOR KNOWLEDGE

More recently, Emily Robertson has argued (2013: 300) that diversity is both an epistemic and a moral virtue, but that this argument "does not support alternative epistemologies, cognitive relativism, or the replacement of truth as an epistemic goal by, for example, beliefs that have progressive consequences." The value of diversity for knowledge resides in the possibility of different groups having "different experiences that lead them to know or believe things that escape others' attention": reports of their experiences may function as data that allows researchers to examine the social system or structure from their social location (304).

While postcolonial theory arguably errs in postulating the existence of diverse knowledges and truths (see also Odora Hoppers 2002b: 12, 14, 18, 19), the diversity in question is conceivably generated by prioritizing certain epistemic practices—practices that emanate from different lived experiences, individual as well as social and cultural. A plausible view seems to hold that knowledge and truth do not vary, that they remain constant across individuals, societies, and cultures, but that there may well be distinctive sets of epistemic concerns that arise within particular personal, geographical, historical, and sociopolitical contexts. If it is correct to assume that practical epistemic and educational priorities will emerge from life experiences and from the ways these are socially articulated, then one might assume that, given that the different life experiences of people across the globe, the practical epistemic and educational priorities will also differ.

For example, as Elizabeth Anderson has put it (2002: 325), "No one disputes that personal knowledge of what it is like to be pregnant, undergo childbirth, suffer menstrual cramps, and have other experiences of a female body is specific to women." Gynecology has made substantial progress "since women entered the field and have brought their personal knowledge to bear on misogynist medical practices." According to Anderson, the "claims get more controversial the more global they are in scope." Some writers "claim that women have gender-typical 'ways of knowing', styles of thinking, methodologies, and ontologies that globally govern or characterize their cognitive activities across all subject matters." For example, "various feminist epistemologists have claimed that women think more intuitively and contextually, concern themselves more with particulars than with abstractions, emotionally engage themselves more with individual subjects of study, and frame their thoughts in relational rather than an atomistic ontology." Anderson contends, quite plausibly, that there is "little persuasive evidence for such global claims" (ibid.). Interestingly, too, she does not "suppose that women theorists bring some shared feminine difference to all subjects of knowledge" (326).

Given, to use a further example, the experience of 'indigenous' Africans of a wide-ranging credibility deficit, it stands to reason that they would have as priorities matters of epistemic transformation and redress. If epistemic and educational concerns and priorities arise from different forms of social life, then those that have emerged from a social system in which a particular race or group has been subordinate to another deserve special scrutiny. Given the (especially vicious) history of physical and psychological colonization, it is plausible that one of the epistemic and educational priorities will be to educate *against* development of a subordinate or inferior mindset, as well as *against* a victim and beggar mentality, despite the continuing economic crisis and low level of economic growth. An additional priority arises with Africa's low literacy quotients. In many countries, the language of conceptualization and education is the official language of administration: English, French, or Portuguese, in which the majority of children and learners are not primarily competent.[27] Consequently, there exist few successes in learning, quality and efficiency suffer, and high repeat and dropout rates mean a squandering of available resources. While it does not follow that particular historical and socioeconomic circumstances yield or bestow automatic validation or justification of (the content and objectives of) an 'African epistemology', an idea like 'decolonization of the African mind' has a particular resonance here. Rather than implying a 'post-truth' epistemology, it involves 'going back to one's language' in 'thinking about thinking', examining one's 'own ways of conceptualization'—in short, 'philosophizing' (Wiredu 2008).

If what has been established above is cogent, it follows that so-called 'epistemological diversity' refers neither to a multitude of truths nor to an 'anything goes' conception of justification, but rather to different experiences connected to particular social locations, or—as Robertson puts it—to different social pathways to knowledge (note the singular!). In this sense, reference to 'epistemolog*ies*'—like reference to "plural systems of knowledges" (De Sousa Santos et al. 2007: xxxix) or to indigenous, local or subaltern ways of knowing—is not only unhelpful but also misleading.

EDUCATIONAL IMPLICATIONS

If knowledge is understood in the epistemologically relevant sense as adequately justified true belief, then what is there to be said about ideas like epistemicide, and epistemic or cognitive injustice, and what are the implications for education?

'Epistemicide' is a notion that has achieved widespread articulation and less-than-critical support (see Horsthemke 2020a). Thus, there is a tendency to apply it in a rather undifferentiated manner to all kinds of beliefs—irrespective of whether they amount to knowledge. Does rejection of views underlying rainmaking and ancestor agency amount to the 'killing of knowledge systems'? Is the failure to allow flat-earth and geocentric worldviews in geography classrooms a matter of epistemicide? What about the refusal to teach creationism in biology? Or the unwillingness to allow the counsel of active drug dealers in career guidance sessions? Similar considerations pertain to the ideas of cognitive justice and epistemic injustice. As I will argue in chapter 9, surely there is a difference between rejecting someone's knowledge-claims on the mere grounds that she is black or a woman (this would be both ethically reprehensible and epistemologically problematic), and rejecting the claims held or expressed by someone who happens to be black or a woman, because they are unjustified and/or false, or because they result from faulty or fallacious reasoning. Nonsense is not geographically, ethnically, culturally, racially, or sexually locatable or specific.

What, then, are the implications for education? Which aspects of so-called 'indigenous', 'local', 'alternative', 'informal' and 'traditional' knowledge should be taught or included in the curriculum? Which aspects should be left out? On what grounds? The question as to what should be left out is fairly easily answered. Not included in natural and social science curricula, at least not under the guise of 'knowledge', should be beliefs or opinions that are not anchored by reason or reasons as well as bald assertions, superstitions, prejudice or bias; in fact, anything that involves myth and fabrication, and constitutes an infringement on the rights of learners. However, it may be pedagogically and epistemically useful to teach these as examples of insufficiently justified or even irrational beliefs, opinions, assertions, as superstitions, prejudice, and bias. Of course, literature, poetry, art, and so forth, occupy a different curricular terrain in that there is a strong emphasis here on creative imagination and interpretation. But here, too, 'knowledge' should not be misused or misapplied. Similarly, religion education can be handled via both the presentation of established (historical and geographical) facts and the comparison of different interpretations and exegeses, *qua* interpretation and exegesis. After all, we learn a lot about our own and about other cultures when we examine the origin and nature of people's beliefs.

The question as to which aspects of indigenous knowledge should be included probably requires a more comprehensive response than I am able to provide here. Briefly, indigenous skills and practical knowledge are worthy of inclusion, as are traditional music, art, dance, and folklore (namely as examples of folklore). Moreover, it follows from the account provided in this chapter that anything that meets the essential requirements for knowledge could in principle be included, for example, traditional African knowledge of agriculture and environment, insights into conflict resolution, and the like. Naturally, the context and environment of learners should be taken into account here. That is to say, learners should be taught only what is appropriate for their age or, more correctly, for their cognitive and affective capabilities. Similarly, they should be taught primarily what is relevant or what is likely to be relevant to their lives—*primarily*, but not *exclusively*, for there is significant educational and cognitive value in being exposed to knowledge and information one would not normally be moved or inclined to seek out.

A traditional healer's insight that one should only use a limited amount of bark from a given tree, or that one should harvest no more than one-tenth of a given natural resource (i.e., harvest a plant only if it is one of ten such plants growing in the vicinity), constitutes an insight that may not be shared by many, but it has universal value and application—and there is no reason why these insights should not be included in a comprehensive educational curriculum. There is a surprising amount of common ground between cultures not only in terms of factual knowledge but also in terms of values (the moral premium placed on truth-telling and preservation of life, other things being equal, comes to mind here). A *rapprochement* between so-called 'indigenous' and 'nonindigenous' insights is not only possible but desirable—on educational, ethical, as well as political grounds (see Horsthemke 2004a: 43).

I do not want to believe or be able to say things that are then passed-off as 'my truth', or that are considered to be 'true for me', or 'true for or within my society or culture'. If I say something that I consider to be true, that I believe sincerely and intensely, but that contravenes basic common sense and reason or that involves certain blind spots or blank spots on my part, this should be pointed out to me, criticized and rejected on the basis of available evidence, and of norms and rules of argumentation that apply to all language users, all those participating in relevant discursive exchanges. Epistemic justice demands nothing less than this. (On the same basis, I want to be able to engage critically with what is believed or stated within and also outside of my society or culture, and not to have to accept it merely because of majoritarian consensus, or for spurious reasons of 'political correctness'.) When I abandon or change my beliefs, as a result of such criticism or rejection, this arguably constitutes a qualitative change, indeed progress—just like the transition from a geocentric to a heliocentric worldview constitutes progress, something a rigorous relativism would reject, at least implicitly. What I (have come to) know is different from faith, superstition, bias, and prejudice. My knowledge may have a particular historical and geographical source, a particular origin both in time and in space, but once I know something, once it qualifies as 'knowledge', it is no longer 'local', or 'aboriginal', or 'indigenous'—it is, purely and simply, knowledge.

NOTES

1. Burkhart (2009: 20) dismisses the Western philosophical notion of justification as being counterintuitive to American Indian thinkers, before characterizing the knowledge of the Seneca, for example, as

> lived knowledge that came from what was directly around them and at their feet. The knowledge concerned how the people should best live. It was not based on question-formulation or hypothesis-testing, but rather on patient observation and contemplation. (22)

Observation and contemplation are clearly general forms of epistemic justification not unique to the Seneca.

2. Take, as examples of witchcraft practice, the cases of '*muti* murder' and the use of human body parts that Becker has reported on and analyzed in considerable detail. There are at least three distinct kinds of superstition that pervade these practices (and these are beliefs that are held not only by the practitioners but also by the majority of the population of sub-Sahara Africa; see Becker 2007: 165): (1) that this kind of *muti* (or 'medicine') works; (2) that the vocalization of the victim—which expresses his/her 'life essence'—enhances the power of the 'medicine' that is ideally taken from the (still) living person; and (3) that the discovery of the body (after the requisite parts, bones, or organs have been removed, and the victim has—as is common—been left to bleed to death) secures additional effectiveness (159).

3. Given pertinent 'evidence', the amendment permits the state to convict and punish a person when it considers her witchcraft harmful (see Kumar 2006: 26). The South African Witchcraft Suppression (No. 3 of 1957, last amended in 1997) only mentions "the practice of witchcraft and similar practices." It also fails to make a sufficiently clear distinction between *using* "witchcraft" or "supernatural means" and *pretending* or *professing* to do so.

4. Interestingly, the German title is *Weder arm noch ohnmächtig* ("Neither poor nor powerless").

5. Apart from being profoundly suspect ethically, vivisection (or experimentation on living animals) is also *bad science* (see Horsthemke 2010a: 91–104).

6. To elaborate on the Yoruba understanding: the distinction between *igbágbò* and *imò* is also a distinction between heart (trust/faith in authority) and intellect. Moreover, while justification can also be rendered in terms of *ìfídìmùlè*, *òótó* means 'It is so'.

7. It might be contended that Masolo's reference to "mere justification of belief" is just shorthand for the 'justified true belief' account, especially in the light of his awareness of the truth condition (Masolo 2010: 30, 45). Yet, the inclusion of the word 'mere' certainly gives the impression that he is setting up a straw person here for easy demolition.

8. Doubts about the argumentational plausibility of these sources have been articulated in Horsthemke 2004a, Benson and Stangroom 2006: 50–55, 55–59, and Horsthemke and Schäfer 2007, respectively.

9. The preferable and more accurate term here would be 'subjectivist', rather than 'relativist'.

10. *This* would be a (cultural) relativist stance.

11. One might point out, of course, that 'indigenous' ought to be understood as referring to geographical origin, or source, rather than the scope of validity. Thus, knowledge about the thirst- and appetite-suppressing properties of the *!khoba* cactus (*Hoodia gordonii*) originated with the San, before it became global (and commercially exploited) knowledge (see chapter 1). This is uncontroversial and, indeed, plausible. My problem arises with the demarcation of 'indigenous' knowledge as 'unique' and 'distinct' (see Masolo 2010: 51) and with its purported viability as a 'tool for transforming the world' (18).

12. What has often been considered the 'common sense account of truth' assumes that there is *at least some* correspondence between the statements a person utters and the world as it exists, that is, independently of the speaker. The central element of correspondence theories of truth is that, other things being equal, the truth/falsity of what is said has something to do with a reality that is *independent* of the statements made about it. A person might legitimately for different purposes describe the world in many different ways. But for those descriptions and distinctions to stick, there must be features of the world that enable them to be made. The idea is that one cannot get away from reality—and from the truth/falsity of statements that give an account of it. I have argued in chapter 3 that the assumption of correspondence truth being the default conception within the Western philosophical canon is rather narrow and, in fact, mistaken.

13. This is a point Wiredu made on more than one occasion during the International Society of African Philosophy and Studies (ISAPS) fifteenth Annual Conference which was hosted in April 2007 by the Rhodes University Philosophy Department in Grahamstown, South Africa.

14. 'Classical epistemology' refers, in particular, to the traditional understanding of knowledge as justified true belief that is already found in Plato's dialogues *Meno* (99c–100a) and *Theaetetus* (200e–202d). See chapter 3.

15. A common culturalist, perspectivalist, or constructivist sleight-of-hand is to invoke Albert Einstein's Special and General Theory of Relativity, Kurt Gödel's incompleteness theorems, and Werner Heisenberg's uncertainty principle as casting doubt on any commitment to truth (see, e.g., Peat 1996: 44–50; Ntuli 2002: 55–58). Going into detail here is beyond the scope of this chapter. Suffice it to say that while literary scholars with a weakness for deconstruction may be impressed by this tactic, it does not work with people who actually know something about Einstein, Gödel, and Heisenberg. Paul Gross and Norman Levitt (1998: 51–52) point out that if these scientists had opted for less suggestive names, this would have forestalled a considerable amount of misinterpretation and prevented misconceptions. They characterize, for example, the uncertainty principle as

a predictive law about the behavior of concrete phenomena than can be tested and confirmed like other physical principles. It is not some brooding metaphysical dictum about the Knower versus the Known, but rather a straightforward statement, mathematically quite simple, concerning the way in which the statistical outcomes of repeated observations of various phenomena may be interrelated.... when viewed as a law of physics, the uncertainty principle is a very certain item indeed. *It is an objective truth about the world.*

16. I use the phrase 'appear to have' advisedly. Given Wiredu's explicit commitment to universalism (1998a), his identification of truth as opinion is either a deliberate provocation or he is genuinely unaware of the internal tensions and inconsistencies within his theory.

17. "Metonymic reason" refers to "a kind of reason that claims to be the only form of rationality and therefore does not exert itself to discover other kinds of rationality or, if it does, it only does so to turn them into raw material" (De Sousa Santos 2014: 165).

18. On the "social construction of indigenous knowledge" and the "colonial construction of Western knowledge," see Shizha 2006: 21–23, 25–27.

19. Similarly, it is unclear how the relevance of incommensurability of knowledges (De Sousa Santos 2014: 208) could conceivably be compatible with "intercultural translation" and "dialogue" between different 'knowledges'.

20. See chapter 3. I have acknowledged the possibility of an African (i.e., Egyptian) genesis of this distinction, which is also present in Yoruba.

21. This is also the argumentational thread that runs through Phillips's chapter (2012), where he provides a critical review of several representative accounts of 'multicultural epistemology' that actually constitute misuses of the term 'epistemology'.

22. Nabudere asserts that the "establishment of the Pan-African University should have as its overall goal the provision of opportunities for higher and advanced education for students and adult learners in the context of a new African-based epistemology and methodology" (Nabudere 2003: 1; see also pp. 8ff. and 23). The point Siegel wishes to make, I think, is that compelling judgments can be made about the quality of competing research methodologies. Some are better than others, and some are plainly invalid.

23. Harding (2002) claims that a multicultural, multiracial, and ethnically diverse science will be more 'strongly objective' than its 'malestream' academic counterpart. Given, however, her uncritical acceptance of many of the unfounded or insufficiently justified claims in Ivan Van Sertima's edited volume *Blacks in Science, Ancient and Modern* (1983; see Harding 1991), she is vulnerable to the criticism that 'strong objectivity' in her case amounts to little more than strong gullibility.

24. There are substantial reasons for doubting this. It has been pointed out by Susan Haack (1998: 125) that the authors informed their subjects prior to the interviews that they would be participating in a study dedicated to finding out more about their unique 'women's ways of knowing'. This makes it virtually impossible to know whether the responses given were not biased by the authors' suggestion.

25. For a sophisticated critique of Code's argument, see also Siegel 1998: 23–26.

26. Either way, it would appear that this is an incorrect attribution. When Rushton was asked during a live televised debate at the University of Western Ontario in 1989 whether he believed in racial superiority, he denied this emphatically. He added (quoted in Knudtson 1991: 187),

> from an evolutionary point of view, superiority can only mean adaptive value—if it even means this. And we've got to realize that each of these populations is perfectly, beautifully adapted to their own ancestral environments.

27. For similar considerations regarding linguistic and cultural continuance, see Lagunas 2019. The concern is with the introduction of an indigenous language policy (in this case pertaining to Nahuatl, which was once the dominant language of Coatepec de los Costales, a small village in Guerrero, Mexico, and now threatens to be eclipsed by Spanish. See also Wilder et al. 2016, for a study of the Comcaac (Seri people) in northwestern Mexico, and suggestions as to how the loss of language might be curbed.

Chapter 5

Ethnomathematics

"When I start a basket," says Reuben Ndwandwe from the Hlabisa area of KwaZulu-Natal in South Africa, who is widely acknowledged as a master weaver, "I don't know what it will look like when it is finished" (Van Heerden et al. 2006). Once he has woven the base of the basket Ndwandwe counts the knots he makes, so that the patterns he weaves with the dyed strands of *ilala* are perfectly symmetrical. Beadwork maker Alexia Mkhize is famous for her craft in the Durban area of KwaZulu-Natal. Using a variety of different styles (like brickstitch and netting) in developing her innovative pieces of jewelry and three-dimensional objects like beaded animals, she is committed to the upliftment of her community and its members and hosts workshops on a regular basis, during which she shares her skills.

Ndwandwe and Mkhize are just two of the artists whose work has been showcased not only for their aesthetic appeal but also for the pedagogical value of the mathematical reasoning manifest in their craft. In the early 2000s, South African academics Helene Smuts, Jannie Van Heerden, and Chonat Getz put together teaching resources that consist of a book and a film, *Africa Meets Africa—Making a Living through the Mathematics of Zulu Design*. Aesthetic enjoyment of the baskets and the beadwork, according to the authors (ibid.), involves bringing our own sense of order and design to it: we see shapes and colors in relation to one another. That is, we find general mathematical ideas and principles reflected in them—like triangular and quadrangular numbers and patterns, geometric series, superimposed triangles, and the like. "Because of the integrity of their design, general mathematical conclusions can be recognized in and taught with particular pieces of beadwork, pots and woven baskets." The authors are concerned with offering educators and learners "a familiar context within which to explore visually, mathematical ideas on numbers, tessellations and symmetry." The accompanying film also "explores how, through various entrepreneurial initiatives, the indigenous knowledge contained in the objects—the ideas and design knowledge that generated them—are finding a place within the free market system."[1] The endeavor is to facilitate the teaching of mathematical concepts and constructs with reference to physical, cultural objects, and artifacts with which the learners are familiar.

Mathematical thinking in traditional African cultures is not confined to the manufacture of baskets and beadwork, or pottery (see also Armstrong 2005).[2] The *sona* (sand drawings) of Angola, the Democratic Republic of Congo, and Zambia created by the Chokwe are well-documented examples of "culturally informed mathematics" (Horsthemke and Schäfer 2007: 3). These drawings are complex arrangements of dots and lines that separate the dots from one another. Most are representational, depicting proverbs, riddles, dwellings, animals, and insects, but some drawings show purely decorative, nonrepresentational fractal patterns. The drawings are visually appealing 'reflector curves': that is, curved lines running through arrangements of dots and typically deflecting off 'mirrors' situated symmetrically between some of the dots, sometimes leaving behind a closed trail. The Chokwe aesthetic, then, strongly favors a symmetric layout of dots separated by reflector curves that generate monolinear circuits.

In this chapter, I will interrogate the notion, based on these and other examples, that indigenous peoples have their own mathematics, their own ways of mathematical reasoning. According to Gerdes, in his Stieg Mellin-Olsen Memorial Lecture presented in Bergen, Norway, on August 31, 2005, indigenous (e.g., African) mathematics embodies forms of valuing that include, or are contained in, understanding, recognition, sources of inspiration, as well as (African) renaissance. Explaining its central concerns, he quoted Mellin-Olsen: "To this day it has not been questioned at all whose culture, or which intellectual material, should be the basis for mathematics education" (Mellin-Olsen, Proceedings of the Conference on Mathematics and Culture, Bergen, September 1995; quoted in Gerdes 2005). Using a concrete example of the value and distinctness of ethnomathematics, Gerdes explained that the 'right angle' (*'epopera'*) in Mozambican basket weaving is not 90° but 60°—that is, the only angle that permits continuous folding, weaving, and stability within the woven structure. Appealing though this example might be, Gerdes is clearly conflating two senses of the term 'right' here: the stipulative definition within plane geometry of a right angle (90°) and the theoretical definition as pragmatically correct or advantageous (60°). 'Right angle' may receive additional interpretations from photographers and rugby or soccer players charged with taking free-kicks, none of which bears testimony to mathematical knowledge and reasoning skills.

On this note, the 'classic' form design of the soccer ball (hexagons and pentagons) first introduced in the 1970 World Cup in Mexico may have already been in use in Thailand and Cambodia for some 2,000 years, as Gerdes claimed, but this arguably indicates the transcultural value and validity of design involving mathematical insights, rather than unique and distinct knowledge. Gerdes's reference to 'knowledge', throughout, concerns 'practical' experiential knowledge or skills—so, invoking "complicated," prepractice "calculations" (say, by indigenous basket weavers and bead workers) appears to be no more than another way of describing a process of learning from trial and error. What about Gerdes's "examples of exclusively oral transmission of pottery design patterns" (by practitioners who had not engaged in pottery for years, as a result of the displacement forces of modernization)? Do these indicate complex, extra-practice 'calculations'? Hardly: they might, rather, be said to indicate postpractice recollection.

Moving on to Chokwe *sona* sand drawings, Gerdes explained that the chief values in these drawings are considered to be symmetry and monolinearity, exceptions to which, however, do exist: asymmetry and bilinearity. Again, this indicates skills and creativity, certainly. Yet, the ability of so-called 'innumerate' (or to use Gerdes's term, "unmatherate") people to count and to work with numbers in a broadly abstract fashion does not amount to 'indigenous' mathematics—any more than knitting inventiveness and skills attest to mathematical prowess (see Horsthemke and Schäfer 2007: 4–5).

ETHNOMATHEMATICS VERSUS MAINSTREAM OR ACADEMIC MATHEMATICS

The movement that has become known as *ethnomathematics* involves a study of mathematics that takes into account the social and cultural context in which mathematical reasoning is employed. The term *etnomatemática* was first coined by Ubiratan d'Ambrosio[3] to indicate that mathematics refers not only to symbolic systems but also to concrete physical practices or activities such as "ciphering, measuring, classifying, ordering, inferring, and modelling" (Borba 1990/1997: 265):

> Ethnomathematics is the mathematics practiced by cultural groups such as urban and rural communities, labor groups, professional classes, children of a certain age bracket, indigenous societies, and many other groups that identify themselves through objectives and traditions common to these groups. (D'Ambrosio 2001: 9)

It is used specifically with regard to the thinking and practices in small-scale indigenous societies. Yet, in a broader sense, the prefix 'ethno' has been used to refer to any sociocultural group, that is, labor communities, traditional religious groups, professional classes, and so forth. D'Ambrosio also emphasizes the political nature of the enterprise:

> Beside this anthropological character, ethnomathematics has an indisputably political focus. Ethnomathematics is imbued with ethics, focused on the recuperation of cultural dignity of human beings. The dignity of the individual is violated by social exclusion that often prevents one from passing discriminatory barriers established by the dominant society, including, and principally, the schooling system. (Ibid.)

It is clear, then, that ethnomathematics is a movement that has emerged with multiculturalism and postcolonial discourse, with profound educational as well as epistemological implications:

> Ethnomathematics consists both in this reflection on decolonisation and in the search for real possibilities of access for the subaltern, for the marginalized and for the excluded. The promising strategy *for education*, in societies that are in transition from subordination to autonomy, is to re-establish the dignity of its individuals, recognizing and respecting their roots. To recognize and respect the roots of an individual does not mean to ignore and reject the roots of the other but, in a process of synthesis, to reinforce one's own roots. (42; emphasis added)

Marcelo Borba contends that "ethnomathematics . . . can be seen as an epistemological approach to mathematics" (1990/1997: 261):

> One way of knowing is mathematics. Mathematical knowledge expressed in the language code of a given sociocultural group is called 'ethnomathematics'. (265)

Arthur Powell takes ethnomathematics to represent "a break with attributes of Enlightenment thinking." "In particular," he contends, "it departs from a binary mode of thought and a universal conception of mathematical knowledge that privileges European, male, heterosexual, racist, and capitalistic interests and values" (Powell 2002: 19; on 'male domination' in mathematics, see also Martin 1997: 165). Powell fails to elaborate on the notions of "binary mode of thought" and "universal conception of mathematical knowledge"— in fact, he fails to provide his preferred definition of "mathematical knowledge," as does Borba. Moreover, Powell's contention that the aforementioned conception "privileges European, male, heterosexual, racist, and capitalistic interests and values" may be 'politically correct'—but it is logically dubious and, as it stands, amounts to little more than name-calling. Mathematics is a formal science, while sexism, heterosexism, racism, and so forth, are empirical phenomena. Powell appears to be committing a category mistake here. If it is his intention to condemn occidental arrogance regarding other mathematical knowledge systems, then it is advisable to separate the moral and political from the epistemological project.

The following is a rather stark example of a conflation of these two kinds of project. In "Toward a Feminist Algebra," a paper presented initially at a 1993 meeting of the Mathematical Association of America and published two years later, Maryanne Campbell and Randall K. Campbell-Wright (1995) conclude that women and other marginalized groups are dissuaded from studying mathematics because "word problems" used to test students' grasp of mathematical concepts refer to situations fraught with sexist, racist, and classist stereotypes. The authors note their disapproval of a particular problem in which a girl and her boyfriend run toward each other—even though the girl's slower speed is explained by the fact that she is carrying luggage—because it described exclusively heterosexual involvement. They object to another problem about a contractor and the contractor's workers—worded so as not to specify their sex—because students would supposedly envision the workers as male. However, they approve of a narrative problem about Sue and Debbie, who are portrayed as "a couple financing their \$70,000 home" (133). The authors conclude their paper by calling for problems "presenting female heroes and breaking gender stereotypes," "analyzing sex similarities and differences intentionally," and "affirming women's experiences." The publication of this paper gave rise to all kinds of jokes: "Why did the feminist fail algebra?—She couldn't solve inequalities." And, "$7x - 4y = 13$. Define x in terms of y. Solution: Only x can define its own identity. y has no right controlling who x is."[4] It is one thing to complain about a lack of relevance (a complaint that is often also made with regard to the teaching of the natural sciences, history, and literature), but quite another to accuse mathematics (an abstract science of number, quantity, and space) and in particular algebra (the branch of mathematics that uses letters to represent numbers and quantities in formulae and equations) of collusion with the sexist, racist, and classist status quo. Either way, while it may be possible (albeit far-fetched) to discover heterosexist bias in formulations like, 'If Randall wants to meet his wife Maryanne at the conference at 6 pm . . . ', it is considerably more difficult to impute (hetero-)sexist intent to a problem like, 'Show that one-point compactification $\mathbb{R}^2$ of is homeomorphic to the 2-sphere.'

Feminists have pointed out that mathematics has had a long history of male bias. One such argument may be that it is men who like to invent abstract formal *systems*, which they then try to impose on the far messier world of human beings and their interactions. Owing to a strict distinction between the *public* and *private spheres*, and the relegation of women to the latter, mainstream math's sole concern (it is alleged) has been with the mathematics of the public sphere, a mathematics characterized by impersonal concerns, bargaining, contractual arrangements, cost-benefit calculations, the ebb and flow of market relations, and economic competition. However, feminists assert, the private or *domestic* sphere, governed as it is by personal concerns and affective transactions, is at least of equivalent mathematical significance. As feminist theorists have pointed out, it is a truth universally acknowledged that mathematical (and, generally, scientific) ideas and systems have all emerged from societies that place women in a subordinate position. If those concerns and activities that have been traditionally associated with women were accorded value and status equal to those traditionally associated with men, then mathematical and corresponding social priorities might become very different. (Other feminist authors, like Harding, haul out the big guns. Thus, Harding asks why it is "not as illuminating and honest to refer to Newton's laws [in *Principia Mathematica*] as 'Newton's rape manual' as it is to call them 'Newton's mechanics'"; 1986: 113, a suggestion she later claims to regret having made. See also Mendick 2006.)

Given these considerations, and assuming just for the moment that the notion of ethnomathematics is a meaningful one, what about the possibility and desirability of a movement called 'gynomathematics' or, indeed—and ideally even joining forces with the former—'Afrogynomathematics'? What about the mathematics of everyone or anyone who has been or still is historically disenfranchised, for example, the mathematics of gay, lesbian, and transgender physically impaired migrants? This seemingly facetious question expresses a concern about the fragmentation of mathematics (see Horsthemke and Schäfer 2007: 6).

The question 'Whose knowledge counts?' can be understood both in terms of power relations and in epistemic and veritistic (or truth-promoting) terms. Concerning the former, Powell (2002: 20) may well be justified in his criticism of "Eurocentric historians of mathematics [who] have largely discounted [the] ideas [of an African elite]." To dismiss any indigenous perspective or traditional practice out of hand, just because it does not match or concur with our own, is prejudice, pure and simple. He may also be correct in feeling that "the general empowerment through critical ethnomathematical knowledge is . . . a very important part of the struggle to overcome the colonized mentality" (27). Yet, it is considerably more problematic to attribute *as a matter-of-course*, as Powell seems to want to do (and as Adam et al. do; 2003: 328, 329), the status of *knowledge* and *truth* to the *beliefs* and knowledge *claims* of indigenous people, members of small-scale communities, and so forth.

This kind of move is problematic because it usually goes hand in hand with an explicit or implicit relativism about knowledge and truth.

It may be worthwhile to examine in some detail Powell's criticism of the "Eurocentric myth . . . and [how] it [a]ffects school curricula" (2002: 22; grammatical correction added). He writes,

> Ethnomathematics challenges the particular ways in which Eurocentrism permeates mathematics education: that the "academic" mathematics taught in schools world-wide was created solely by the European males and diffused to the [p]eriphery; that mathematical knowledge exists outside of and unaffected by culture; and that only a narrow part of human activity is mathematical and, moreover, worthy of serious contemplation as "legitimate" mathematics. Many ethnomathematicians view themselves not as neutral academics, but as activist academics, committed to finding ways to contribute to struggles for justice through our educational work. They [are] not just interested, for example, in the mathematics of Angolan sand drawings but also in the politics of imperialism that arrested the development of this cultural tradition, and in the politics of cultural imperialism that discounts the mathematical activity in creating Angolan sand drawings. Further, they are alert for ways that this contextualised mathematical knowledge can be used in educational settings to contribute to greater social justice. (22, 23; corrections added; on Tchokwe *sona* sand drawings, see Gerdes 1994b: 32–34; Gerdes 1999: 157–160)

At first glance, Powell's central contentions and his characterization of the ethnomathematical enterprise seem to be valid. As portrayed here, the position assumed by "Eurocentric historians of mathematics" appears to be presumptuous, as well as morally and intellectually dishonest. However, one needs to distinguish between three kinds of reasons for discounting a particular cognitive tradition or cultural activity. Thus, a particular cognitive tradition or activity may be deemed worthless, inferior, invalid, and so forth, simply because it is 'indigenous', 'local', 'non-European', 'nonwhite', 'non-academic', 'female', 'nonmale,' and so forth. Or the reason given may be that it does not qualify as (a form of) 'knowledge'. Finally, and most subtly, one might spell out the implications of conceiving and constructing ethnomathematics as a discipline or institution separate and different in kind from mainstream mathematics. One might cite the undesirability of these implications as a reason for skepticism about the ethnomathematical enterprise.

Without wishing to elaborate here, I take it as plain that the first of these 'reasons' is deficient. This kind of approach is, indeed, indicative of a racial, sexual, or cultural hegemonism that is difficult to defend in the absence of discipline-specific and epistemic criteria. Powell and others are right in condemning this mindset as an irrational prejudice. However, insofar as there are, to my knowledge, very few—if any—theorists and writers who still subscribe to this approach, focusing on it strikes me as misdirected. I consider the second and third reasons much more promising and challenging, and it is on these that I wish to concentrate in what follows. Once I have covered the pertinent considerations, this will enable me to respond to the educational challenges enumerated by Powell.

THE DEFENSE OF ETHNOMATHEMATICS

If the predominant identification of ethnomathematics with concrete physical practices is all there is to understanding the project, then it is relatively easy to resolve any disputes that may exist. However much the practices or skills involved may diverge, it is the *results* they produce (and the *consistency* with which these are produced) that count. And if the latter are identical across ethnic, cultural, and social boundaries or divides, there is little ground for debate over which method or practice is valid or legitimate. Thus, whatever the means or methodology, what matters is that the shepherd brings back an identical number of sheep and that the accountant gets her books to balance (or at least finds the error).

However, defenders of ethnomathematics seem to want to make a stronger claim. They have condemned advocates and practitioners of mainstream mathematics at a political level, for violating the sovereignty of an ethnic or cultural group, as well as at a psychological level, on grounds of insensitivity to 'local culture' (see Berry 1985; Gerdes 1994a). The underlying tenet of the defense of ethnomathematics, indigenous science, and related movements is that what is perceived as 'universal' is merely the perception common to those who already share a particular culture and/or historical perspective. In this regard, the most significant questions seem to be

- Is there such a thing as 'mathematical truth'? Or are there many diverse and, indeed, conflicting truths? How does this bear on the idea of universality, commonality, and so forth, of knowledge?
- With regard to ethnomathematics, what does 'indigenous knowledge' refer to? Is it practical knowledge, a (set of) skill(s), or is it (also) theoretical (factual or propositional) knowledge? Under what circumstances, then, does the idea of 'indigenous (mathematical) knowledge' make sense?
- Is ethnomathematics a *discipline* that is not only practically but also conceptually/logically/theoretically distinct from mainstream (occidental) mathematics? Does it involve radically different standards of mathematical reasoning and justification (*if* these apply at all)?

- What is advocacy of ethnomathematics meant to achieve? In particular, what function does the prefix 'ethno' have in this regard?
- Finally, what about Adam, Alangui, and Barton's suggestion that "the role of ethnomathematics in mathematics education is now predominantly an empirical matter" (2003: 327)?

For the purposes of this chapter, I will present the defense of ethnomathematics as involving one or several of the following claims. Concerning the questions about mathematical truth, there appears to be a tendency (perhaps insufficiently considered) among proponents not only toward cultural relativism but toward a more thorough-going relativism about truth and knowledge. According to this position, there is no such thing as 'mathematical truth': there are no universal truths, only truths relative to particular cultural and ethnic groups and modes of inquiry. Similarly, or as a consequence, the conception of mathematical knowledge as universal is mistaken. Regarding the question about knowledge, the notion of 'ethnomathematical knowledge' remains largely undefined in the pertinent literature, apart from being characterized as a cultural activity or tradition, that is, determined by 'social interests'. Despite Powell's assertion, "Our practice confirms that ethnomathematical knowledge increases student self-confidence and opens up areas of critical insight in their understanding of the nature of knowledge" (Powell 2002: 27, 28; see also Powell and Frankenstein 1997: 326), there has been disconcertingly little elaboration on *the nature of knowledge*, let alone how it is understood by students, in the relevant literature. 'Mathematical knowledge', like other knowledge, covers not only skills and concrete practices but also theoretical knowledge. Among defenders of ethnomathematics, the understanding of the latter is arguably relativist.

There also appears to be a tendency, if only implicit, among such advocates to respond affirmatively to the third question, to see ethnomathematics as distinct or different from mainstream mathematics. Moreover, because of this difference, proponents of mainstream mathematics ought not (indeed, *cannot*) judge ethnomathematical enterprises or projects. Thus, if it is true (or at least plausible) that ethnomathematics is separate and distinct discipline, this would strengthen the verdict that it may be beyond the scope of critical assessment and judgment by mainstream ('malestream'?) theorists. At the very least, to embark on such a critical evaluative enterprise could be seen and condemned as hegemonism, arrogance, and neocolonialist meddling.

In what follows, in an attempt to dispel these myths, I will argue the following:

- There is such a thing as 'mathematical truth'. There are transcultural truths in mathematics that function as the objective anchor of mathematical knowledge.

- A relativist conception of knowledge and truth (in mathematics as elsewhere) is indefensible, on logical as well as empirical grounds.
- The view that all mathematical knowledge is 'culturally bounded' and that ethnomathematics is distinct or fundamentally different from mainstream mathematics is deficient. There exist shared standards of mathematical reasoning and justification across mathematical practices and conceptualizations.
- Any dismissal of philosophical engagement with the plausibility and viability of *ethno*mathematics and to suggest that ethnomathematics has shifted toward predominantly empirical matters is to proceed in terms of unwarranted verbal arbitration. Insofar as ethnomathematics continues to involve a questionable understanding of knowledge and truth, any such ruling is likely to beg the question of the very validity and conceptual soundness of the ethnomathematical enterprise. I will illustrate, through an analysis and critique of recent perspectives, that the philosophical debate around ethnomathematics is both alive and warranted—indeed, crucial. I argue that 'ethnomathematics' makes, at best, limited sense, namely insofar as it is understood as describing indigenous mathematical *practices*.
- The problematic component in the project under discussion is arguably the prefix 'ethno'. The emphasis on *ethno*mathematics, clearly and critically seen, has neither the political nor the educational clout its proponents desire. What it seeks to counter, sexism, racism, cultural hegemonism, and neocolonialism, is more successfully opposed in terms of appeals to rights. Opposition to these phenomena is better formulated in terms of rights language.[5]

TRUTH AND KNOWLEDGE

Brian Martin approvingly quotes Judith Grabiner's idea (1974) that there have been "revolutions in thought which changed mathematicians' views about the nature of mathematical truth, and about what could or should be proved" (Martin 1997: 164). Using Grabiner's example of the gradual professionalization of mathematics, Martin takes this to illustrate "how the social organization of the profession of mathematics can affect *views* about the nature of mathematical truth" (ibid.; emphasis added). He also argues that the

> *belief* that mathematics is a body of truth independent of society is deeply embedded in education and research. This situation, by hiding the social role of mathematics behind a screen of objectivity, serves those groups which preferentially benefit from the present social system of mathematics. (168; emphasis added)

Contrasting ethnomathematics with academic mathematics, Gelsa Knijnik (2002: 13) states,

> By legitimizing as mathematics more than just intellectual products of the Academe, and by considering the form of other, non-hegemonic ways of knowing and producing mathematics, ethnomathematics relativizes the 'universality' of (academic) mathematics and, moreover, questions its very nature. . . . In problematizing academic mathematics, ethnomathematics emphasizes not only that mathematics is a social construction but, more than this, that such a construction takes place in a terrain shaped by political dispute around what will be seen as mathematics, around which will be considered the legitimate way of reasoning, and therefore, around which groups are those that can legitimately produce science.

I will say more about the logic and coherence of relativization in the next section. Here I want to comment mainly on Knijnik's challenge to the universality of academic mathematics and her remarks on 'legitimizing . . . mathematics', as well as on Martin's remarks concerning the social embeddedness of (mathematical) truth and his doubts about the 'objectivity' of mathematics. Martin and Grabiner may be right about changes in *views* about the nature of mathematical truth. Yet, contrary to what they both seem to want to argue, this does not establish anything about the nature of mathematical truth as such. Similarly, the *belief* "that mathematics is a body of truth independent of society" may be "deeply embedded in education and research," but this does not mean that mathematical truth itself is so embedded.

Contra Martin and Knijnik, mathematical propositions seem to be universally and unchangeably true, as well as necessarily true. For example, the Pythagorean theorem ('The square on the hypotenuse of a right-angled triangle is equal to the sum of the squares of the other two sides') and arithmetic truths like '2 + 2 = 4' are true regardless of time and place. This is not contradicted by alleged counterexamples (adding two liters of water and two liters of alcohol, adding two cats and two goldfish, and so forth). If one has 2 and adds another 2, then at that moment one has 4. Arithmetic does not tell us anything about natural processes, like molecular interpenetration of two substances and predatorial relations. Similarly, if two things give birth or rise to a million things (amoebas, rabbits), this would not threaten the veracity of '1 + 1 = 2'. Neither does the consideration that adding one drop of water to another drop would produce one slightly bigger drop: in this case, the focus has shifted from numbers to physical substance and empirical observation—which is not the concern of arithmetic. Although arithmetic, and mathematics in general, is a useful tool in science, neither is the subject matter of mathematics physical objects nor is empirical observation the ultimate ground for deciding the truth or falsity of mathematical propositions.

Munir Fasheh (1982/1997: 276) takes the "objective of mathematics teaching [to] be to discover new 'facts' about one's self, society, and culture, to be able to make better judgments and decisions; and to build the links again between mathematical concepts and concrete situations and personal experiences." Unfortunately, the examples that follow this promising suggestion conflate empirical inquiry and conjectures about or interpretations of physical data with 'interpretations' of mathematical facts and truths. Thus, he claims (281, 282),

> 'one equals one' is mathematical fact, but its description and interpretation and application differ from one situation to another and from one nation to another. A fresh and delicious apple is not equal to a rotten apple. A certain chair is not equal to another chair in all its details no matter how identical they seem to be.... Strictly speaking, then, 'one equals one' does not have true instances or application in the real world.

Fasheh's example misses the point. In fact, he has committed a category mistake by changing the subject from numbers and numerical identity to physical objects and material identity. Moreover, his last assertion is clearly mistaken: 'one equals one' could be seen as a statement of self-identity—which is as applicable, albeit uninformative, in the 'real' as in the 'mathematical' and 'logical' world.

Whether or not certain other mathematical axioms (like those in geometry) are true, or whether or not they are to be taken as describing physical reality, there is a shared reliance on the method and principles of deduction. The need of the ancient Egyptians to redraw field boundaries each year as a result of the Nile floods (which is where the practical origin of geometry is arguably located; see Flew 1999: 131), the attempt by the Greeks to turn geometry into a rigorously axiomatized science, and the more recent demonstration by geometers that conventional axioms suffice for ordinary finite distances but will not do for the millions of light years in outer space, because of the 'curvature of space' (see Mlodinow 2002)—all these rely on shared standards of deductive rigor in terms of reasoning and justification. Furthermore, algebraic laws like commutative and distributive laws are not products of convention or a 'social construction' but universal laws underpinning abstract structures.

The fact that all the evidence is 'not yet in' does not jeopardize the universal status of mathematics. If anything, the proofs in number theory and topology furnished in recent decades (Andrew Wiles's proof of Fermat's Last Theorem, confirmed in 1995, and Grigori Perelman's apparently successful attempt to prove Poincaré's conjecture that there is only one way to bend three-dimensional space into a shape without holes—just as a sphere is the only way to bend a two-dimensional plane into a shape without holes) illustrate the objectivity and universality of mathematical propositions and justification.

It would appear that the debate about the nature and status of mathematical truth waged between those who support a 'discovery' approach and those who endorse an 'invention' model (Romberg 2000) misses the point. Obviously, the concepts employed in mathematics are 'human' in origin, yet to what they refer and are applied goes beyond human presence, agency, or 'invention'. That is, while the terms and symbols denoting mathematical phenomena are, in an important sense, not discovered, the events and complex relations to which they refer are, again in an important sense, not invented or socially constructed. They are objectively accessible, transcultural phenomena.

Knijnik's idea (2002: 14) that ethnomathematical "knowledge, impregnated by practice, tends to be devalued by the dominant groups, since it has closer ties to the local world where it is produced than to universal narratives" makes a certain amount of sense in its emphasis on practice, for example, in terms of knowledge-*how (to)*. Yet, mathematics is not just a set of skills, but a collection of (events and phenomena) that relate to each other (Romberg 2000). Mathematical practices need to be checked against the theoretical and conceptual, and the results they yield assessed and evaluated. It follows that inflating the significance of "the local world" and making short shrift of ties to "universal narratives" is bound to be counterproductive. In effect, it lessens (if not obliterates) the epistemic and veritistic (or truth-promoting) features of this project.

Similarly, Knijnik's remarks about the "legitimization" of alternative mathematics contain a conceptual error (see also Martin 1997: 156, on 'valid knowledge'; Borba 1990/1997: 267). If something is 'knowledge' in a theoretical or propositional sense (e.g., knowledge-*that* 2 + 2 = 4, that the ratio of the circumference of a circle to its diameter is a constant, that a negative integer multiplied by another negative integer gives a positive integer, and so forth), then one of its necessary components or conditions is justification. It follows that to speak about its legitimization involves a tautology. Mathematical knowledge, *qua* knowledge, *cannot but* be legitimate or valid. In other words, suppression of nonacademic mathematics *is* a problem *only if* the latter amounts to 'knowledge'. It then becomes an issue of social (in) justice, apart from being logically and epistemically indefensible.

MATHEMATICS, 'SOCIAL INTERESTS' AND THE PROBLEM OF RELATIVISM

"In Third World countries," warns Fasheh (1982/1997: 285),

> we should be careful not to follow the Western way of interpreting objective knowledge as being purely abstract, absolute and detached. In teaching a

mathematical concept or 'fact', we should ask for examples where that concept or fact is applicable or true and where it is not; we should ask about some of the uses, misuses, and abuses of that concept or fact.

Apart from pointing to a relativism about mathematical knowledge and truth, this passage contains a further, somewhat confused reference. The 'examples' Fasheh provides have more to do with the misuse and abuse of teacher's authority, and basic professional, pedagogical incompetence, than with misuse and abuse of mathematical concepts and facts.

In a similar vein, Martin (1997: 156) argues that "there is no overarching rational method to decide what is valid knowledge: scientific knowledge depends, on some level, on the vagaries of history and culture." Approaching mathematics from the 'social interests' perspective of the sociology of knowledge, Martin (156, 157) takes 'interests' to refer to

> the stake of an individual or social group in particular types of actions or social arrangements. . . . 'Social interests' are those associated with major social groupings such as social classes, large organizations, occupational or ethnic groups.

What tools does the sociology of knowledge offer for conceptualizing mathematics?

> The dynamics of knowledge involve social, economic, political, religious, biological, and all sorts of other factors. Rather than assuming that content and structure of knowledge are 'given' by logic or the nature of reality—a transcendental explanation of knowledge—the sociology of knowledge looks for a more mundane explanation. (157)

The key features here are that knowledge is explained "in causal terms," that "explanations (are) impartial and symmetrical with respect to the truth or falsity of the beliefs being explained, and that the theory (is) applied to itself" (ibid.; see also Barton 1999: 32). Martin (1997: 162) continues, "The studies in the sociology of knowledge *initiate* the case that mathematics is connected with social interests, by refuting the view that mathematical knowledge always springs antiseptically from the nature of logic, from physical reality or from mathematicians' heads." Perhaps unsurprisingly, sources of patronage (funding), professionalization (and bureaucratization), male domination, and specialization are seen to constitute "the social system of modern science" and to be indicative of the connection between "pure mathematics" and social interests (163–167).

It is not only the practitioners of "pure mathematics" who are to blame, contends Martin (167): "One may judge the mathematics by the same criteria used to judge (its) application. It is not adequate to say that the killer is guilty while the murder weapon is innocent, for in these sorts of application (telecommunication satellites, anti-personnel weapons, solar house design) the mathematical 'weapon' is especially tailored for the job." According to Martin (168),

> The question, 'What is the link between mathematics and social interests?', is usually answered in advance by assumptions about what *mathematics* really is. If mathematics is taken to be that body of mathematical knowledge which sits above or outside of human interests, then by definition social interests can only be involved in the practice of mathematics, not in *mathematics*. This Platonic-like conception sees mathematics as value-free, but is itself a value-laden conception: it serves to deflect attention from the many links between mathematics and society.

Even if Martin is correct in his assessment of the "Platonic-like" conception—which is debatable (Plato sees mathematics as intrinsically valuable)—this would not mean that mathematics itself is value-laden, but only that *conceptions* of mathematics are value-laden. It is clear, moreover, that Martin's own assumptions prejudge the question concerning the necessity of the link between mathematics and social interests, such that they tend to blur the distinction between the practice of mathematics and mathematics proper, the application and the discipline. The sort of reductivist move involved in connecting any (body of) knowledge essentially with social interests is, at best, uninformative. At worst, it is mistaken. Finally, the question arises whether what Martin and also Bill Barton (1999: 32) enlist here for present purposes as 'sociology of knowledge' is not a misnomer, more accurately rendered as 'sociology of belief' or 'sociology of practice'.

A few additional comments: The search for a "mundane" explanation of the structure and content of knowledge and the demand that knowledge be explained "in causal terms" are not unreasonable. I would argue that an understanding of knowledge as 'adequately justified true belief', with the added proviso that ascription of mathematical knowledge be context-sensitive (see below), fulfills both. Furthermore, as far as 'blaming' the mathematical 'weapon' is concerned, 'innocence' or 'guilt' is not a concept that applies to weapons. 'Harmfulness' would be more appropriate—but can *mathematics* be 'harmful'? Martin seems to be committing a category mistake here.[6] Finally, neither the social interest model nor the 'transcendental' account of mathematical knowledge is very plausible: the latter because of its complete failure to refer to the human components, strength of belief, and context of justification, let alone practices and activities, the former because of its inherent relativism.

Knijnik's assertion that "ethnomathematics relativizes the 'universality' of (academic) mathematics and, moreover, questions its very nature" (2002: 13; see also Knijnik 1999: 186) is clearly contradicted by what she states elsewhere. In an earlier piece, Knijnik characterizes the "ethnomathematical approach" as "the investigation of the traditions, practices, and mathematical concepts of a subordinated social group and the pedagogical work which was developed in order for the group to be able to interpret and decode its knowledge; to acquire the knowledge produced by academic mathematicians; and to establish comparisons between its knowledge and academic knowledge, thus being able to analyze the power relations involved in the use of both these kinds of knowledge" (1997: 405; see also Knijnik 1999: 186; Knijnik 2002: 11). A consistent, coherent relativism *cannot* establish comparisons between, let alone analyze or question the power relations involved in the use of, ethnomathematical and academic knowledge.

Knijnik's "argument that humanity as a whole has the right to gain access to and use knowledge created by human beings" (2002: 12) is manifestly *non*-relativist. Moreover, the *value* it refers to—humanity's *right* to access—is not only presented here as having universal purchase but it indicates an endeavor that is more feasible than advocacy of a project of questionable logic. As I will argue below, given the relativism underlying the ethnomathematics approach, *in*clusion—like in school curricula—is best achieved on the basis of a rights approach.

Knijnik's point about "access" raises the question of relevance of mathematical problems and their solutions. Different individuals and social or cultural groups deem different examples, methods, and approaches relevant. While this consideration appears to strengthen the case for contextual relevance in the initiation into mathematics, it cannot imply shielding learners from anything that is not (considered) relevant. The net result of such information- and knowledge control would be a severely impoverished curriculum.

The teaching and learning of mathematics arguably have a strong contextual component in another sense, and this may influence the ascription or attribution of mathematical knowledge to a person. That is, one takes levels of ability in reasoning and justification into account. For example, in appraising children's mathematical knowledge, there are varying degrees of leniency and stringency in applying standards of evidential adequacy. The consideration that attribution of knowledge is context-sensitive does not imply a relativist understanding of knowledge. What is 'relative' is the justification required or expected: it varies according to different standards of adequacy. I will return to the problem of relativism a little later in this chapter.

FUNDAMENTAL DIFFERENCE AND THE 'CULTURAL BOUNDEDNESS' OF MATHEMATICAL KNOWLEDGE

D'Ambrosio points out that belief in the universality of mathematics is contradicted by recent "evidence of practices which are typically mathematical, such as counting, ordering, sorting, measuring and weighing, done in *radically different ways* than those which are commonly taught in the school system" (1985: 44; emphasis added). Powell and Frankenstein add that "once we abandon notions of general universality, which often cover for Eurocentric particularities, we can acquire an anthropological awareness: different cultures produce *different* mathematics and the mathematics of one culture can change over time, reflecting changes in the culture" (1997a: 6; emphasis added).

Borba concurs (1990/1997: 266): "ethnomathematics should not be understood as 'vulgar' or 'second class' mathematics, but as *different* cultural expressions of mathematical ideas." "The notion of ethnomathematics," he says (266, 267),

> has clear implications for education. If different people produce different kinds of mathematics, then it is not possible to think about education as being a uniform process to be developed in the same way for different groups.

He argues that the ethnomathematical "knowledge developed, for example, by groups of students should be *compared* with the (ethno)knowledge developed by the academic (mathematical) disciplines in a way that this academic knowledge can also be seen as *culturally bounded*" (269; emphasis added).

Knijnik (2002: 14) writes, in a similar vein: "in dealing with mathematics not in an abstract form, but as a cultural artefact, directly connected to traditions, to ways of living, feeling and producing meanings of different social groups, ethnomathematics refers to mathematics in the plural, with academic mathematics—the one we usually call *the* mathematics—being one of these different mathematics." It should be clear by now that the kind of "comparison" Borba rightly deems so important for education is possible only if these different pockets of mathematical activity and insight are, in fact, commensurable. The postulation of radical differences, and of the 'cultural boundedness' of all knowledge, as well as the denial of universality with regard to mathematical knowledge militate against the possibility of transcultural comparison.

In a critical response to Powell (Powell 2002), South African mathematics educationalist Mamokgethi Setati argues that

> ethnomathematics can be defined as the mathematics practiced by a cultural group defined by [a] philosophical and ideological perspective. The question

here therefore is how different is this from mathematics? In my view, mathematics is also practiced by a cultural group defined by [a] philosophical and ideological perspective. (2002: 31; amendments mine)

This contention, while correctly problematizing the purported 'difference' of ethnomathematics, seems to miss the point. The point does not reside in being "defined by a particular philosophical and ideological perspective" but rather in providing a satisfactory definition of knowledge, truth, and whatever else '(ethno)mathematics' refers to. Setati continues (32),

> The question to ask here is, are the philosophical, ideological and discursive norms of ethnomathematics different from those of mathematics? . . . Powell's definition of ethnomathematics . . . suggests that [it] is a special type of mathematics. What does it mean therefore to construct ethnomathematics as an institution separate and different from mathematics? . . . Naming . . . creates boundaries and emphasizes difference and thus can be counter-productive. Naming in this case has created the perception that ethnomathematics is different from mathematics and thus inferior. In my view, ethnomathematics is mathematics and therefore to construct it as separate from mathematics is to marginalize it. It is important that ethnomathematics moves form the margins into the centre of mathematics.

Again, Setati is correct in voicing her concern about the alleged difference of ethnomathematics. Yet, her points about the likelihood of perceived inferiority or marginalization need to be developed in considerably greater detail in order to fulfill the promise they bear. To perceive as inferior and to marginalize, realistically and rationally seen, means having been able to compare. Yet, those who advocate a *fundamental* difference between ethnomathematics and academic mathematics are implicitly committed to denying the possibility of comparison. Thus, they would reject Setati's concerns and her invitation to ethnomathematics to join the mainstream. The chief difficulty remains that advocates of ethnomathematics (like Barton 1999: 32, 34) tend to embrace a relativism regarding knowledge and truth that is highly problematic, not only in terms of logical coherence but also in terms of its implications.

EDUCATIONAL CHALLENGES

The educational challenges of the ethnomathematical enterprise, as they are presented by Powell, concern

- the Eurocentric and androcentric bias of 'academic' mathematics,

Ethnomathematics   153

- the importance of context with regard to mathematical knowledge, and
- issues around the exclusiveness and legitimacy of mathematics.

I have already indicated above that many of the references to 'Eurocentrism' and androcentrism amount to little more than name-calling and have also discussed the importance of context. The third of these 'challenges', Powell's point about the exclusiveness of academic mathematics, is echoed by Borba (1990/1997: 265): "Although academic mathematics may be international in that it is currently in use in many parts of the world, it is not international in that only a small percentage of the population of the world is likely to use academic mathematics." In response to Borba and Powell, one might say that this is true not only of mathematics but of virtually every intellectual activity or field within the natural and social sciences. Yet, it may be useful to examine in some detail Borba's suggestions in this regard.

Borba (267) argues that "mathematics education should be thought of as a process in which the starting point would be the ethnomathematics of a given group and the goal would be for the student to develop a multicultural approach to mathematics." Borba envisages a particular kind of relationship between educator and learner. Problems that are to be solved

> would be chosen by both student and teachers in a dialogical relationship which fosters a critical consciousness . . . Knowledge can be seen as a product of this dialogical relationship. . . . Such a dialogue can allow students to strengthen their sociocultural roots, since their (ethno)knowledge is legitimized (recognized as valuable) in the educational process. . . . This dialogical process has no dichotomy between education and research, between teacher and researcher. The one who educates is also the one who researches the ethnomathematics developed by students. (267, 268; for a critique of these suggestions, see Rowlands and Carson 2002: 85, 86)

'Legitimization', in this sense, as well as value as a researchable field, surely depends both on the practical as well as on the veritistic purchase of the so-called 'ethnomathematics' in question. Furthermore, 'knowledge' is not the same as 'consensus'. The latter may well be the product of a dialogical relationship, and this is what Borba seems to be suggesting: "The teacher/researcher has a particular ability and responsibility to help the students find the intersections between their realms of meaning and the teacher's" (1990/1997: 269; see also Fasheh 1982/1997: 285). However, knowledge clearly goes beyond consensus: there may be consensus about what is false, untrue, not the case.

Finally, just as mathematical beliefs and ideas may differ among or across cultures, the manifestation of mathematical practices and skills may so differ.

However, the former amount to knowledge only if they are true *and* if they are adequately justified. Similarly, while they may differ in their manifestation, activities, and practices like counting, measuring, locating, designing, explaining, and playful experimenting are transcultural, "in that they appear to be carried out by every cultural group ever studied" (Bishop 1988: 182; quoted in Borba 1990/1997: 266). It follows that the term 'indigenous' has, at best, limited applicability. A similar point could be made about the prefix 'ethno'. If ethnomathematics constitutes knowledge in the propositional or factual sense, then it is unclear what purpose the prefix 'ethno' is meant to serve—other than artificially severing ethnomathematics from mathematics as such. If it constitutes activities or practices, then—while their actual manifestations may differ among or across cultural or ethnic groups—the fact that these are carried out by *all* cultural or ethnic groups renders them universal. It follows that the term *ethnomathematics* encompasses, at the very most, the different ways in which mathematical activities and practices manifest themselves. These activities and practices need not be treated as anthropological curiosities but can enrich the teaching and learning of mathematics as such, as well as mathematical research. I next turn to the dismissal of critical philosophical engagement with ethnomathematics.

SHIFTS IN DEFINITION AND DIRECTION, AND THE DISMISSAL OF CRITICAL PHILOSOPHICAL ENGAGEMENT

In 1996, Barton writes (1996: 201): "Very little of the ethnomathematical literature is explicit about its philosophical stance," which he considers to be "one of the areas" that "must be addressed if the subject is to gain wider legitimacy in mathematical circles." Seven years later, Barton, Shehenaz Adam, and Wilfredo Alangui (Adam et al. 2003) take issue with a recent, critical investigation of ethnomathematics, especially of its relationship with academic mathematics with regard to teaching and learning. They dismiss the largely philosophical questions raised by Stuart Rowlands and Robert Carson (2002) by suggesting that "the role of ethnomathematics in mathematics education is now predominantly an empirical matter" (Adam et al. 2003: 327).

What has happened in the interim that has contributed to this alleged shift? Is it true, now that the political and philosophical/conceptual questions have been taken care of, that ethnomathematics is used successfully "as a framework in the teaching of mathematics" (334)? This view appears to rely for its plausibility partly on the work discussed in the first two International Congresses on Ethnomathematics (Contreras et al., eds. 1999; de Monteiro, ed. 2002) and by Barton himself (1999b), and partly on the 'promise' of studies in indigenous knowledge. The underlying idea is that a philosophical, conceptual inquiry regarding ethnomathematics is now dated, *passé*—and that any critique must address the empirical issues around curricular reliance on ethnomathematics and evaluate the results.

I argue in this section that any dismissal of philosophical engagement with the plausibility and viability of *ethno*mathematics on the grounds alluded to above smacks of mere verbal legislation. As the discussion above has shown, the philosophical debate around ethnomathematics is both alive and warranted—indeed, crucial. Moreover, *very few* philosophical debates have dated. *Very few* philosophical puzzles and problems have been resolved. (The freedom/determinism debate and the mind-body problem may be among these few.) So, to suggest that ethnomathematics has shifted toward predominantly empirical matters is to proceed in terms of unwarranted verbal arbitration. Insofar as ethnomathematics continues to involve a questionable understanding of knowledge and truth, any such ruling is likely to beg the question of the very validity and conceptual soundness of the ethnomathematical enterprise.

In his 1996 article, Barton (210) traces definitional shifts within ethnomathematics by examining chronologically the work of D'Ambrosio, Gerdes, and Marcia Ascher, respectively. He explores the development of ethnomathematics "into a research programme, with a broader referent," that "now includes: a) the formation of all knowledge (D'Ambrosio), b) mathematics in relation to society (Gerdes); and c) mathematical ideas wherever they occur (Ascher)." Building on these ideas, Barton presents the following definition (214): "Ethnomathematics is a research programme of the way in which cultural groups understand, articulate and use the concepts and practices which we describe as mathematical, whether or not the cultural group has a concept of mathematics'. D'Ambrosio's understanding is strikingly similar but also contains an emphasis on both 'philosophy' and pedagogy: "Ethnomathematics is a research programme in the history and philosophy of mathematics, with pedagogical implications, focusing the arts and techniques (*tics* [from *technē*]) of explaining, understanding and coping with (*mathema*) different socio-cultural environments (*ethno*)" (D'Ambrosio 2006).

Barton's 1999 article constitutes an "attempt to note . . . the current directions in ethnomathematics" and "other well-established developments": the "use of resources derived from other cultures in mathematics education" or what might be called the cultural resource direction, one that appears to have a predominantly practical or empirical focus; D'Ambrosio, Gerdes and the "humanistic mathematics" direction; and "the academic debate concerning the philosophy, legitimacy and relationships with other disciplines and theories," that is, "the critical mathematics direction" (Barton 1999a: 32). These different 'directions' are clearly intimately linked and the boundaries between the cultural resource direction, the humanistic mathematics direction, and the critical mathematics direction overlap, as Barton acknowledges later (2004: 22).

Three years later, Rowlands and Carson (2002) published a critical review of some of the ethnomathematics literature. In response to the question, "What would an ethnomathematics curriculum look like and where would formal, academic mathematics fit in such a curriculum?," they argue that "it is only through the lens of formal, academic mathematics sensitive to cultural differences that the real value of the mathematics inherent in certain cultures and societies be understood and appreciated" (80, 79).

In their response to Rowlands and Carson, Adam, Alangui, and Barton (2003: 327) contend that "debate on cultural issues in mathematics . . . must be based on contemporary writing in the field, and should not focus on extreme views within the political justification for ethnomathematics" and assert that "the role of ethnomathematics in mathematics education is now predominantly an empirical matter." This contention evidently begs the question of the validity and soundness of the concept of ethnomathematics. It mistakenly assumes general agreement on what ethnomathematics *is* and on its "legitimacy in mathematical circles," to use Barton's earlier phrase (1996: 201).

After noting two perspectives on ethnomathematics, the "political perspective," "now more often related to writing on indigenous knowledge" (Adam et al. 2003: 328), and the philosophical perspective (including the question of "mathematical relativity"), the authors assert (330),

> Whether . . . [an ethnomathematical] perspective helps fulfil the aims of conventional mathematics is no longer a question that is debated on ideological lines. For some time it has been regarded as an open empirical question by most of those working in ethnomathematics.

Does this not amount to verbal legislation? The claim that this is the view of 'most of those working in ethnomathematics' fails to establish anything. After all, the majority may simply be wrong, misled, biased, and so on.

The authors state, further (333), that educational

> research is so far demonstrating the success in conventional terms of at least one ethnomathematical approach to the curriculum. Any critique of this field must address such results and evaluate them as research. It must enter current debates. It cannot be ideologically directed, nor is it helpful to address antiquated or extreme positions.

Adam, Alangui, and Barton cite the work done in Alaska (described in Lipka 2002) as an example of "students who have been taught using such an ethnomathematical curriculum [and who] perform better on conventional mathematics tests" (Adam et al. 2003: 333). Yet, they miss one of the essential points of the critique of ethnomathematics: which is to interrogate what is 'culturally specific' or 'unique' about this approach *and*—if indeed it is so specific or unique—whether it *is* 'mathematics'. This critique has little, if anything, to do with 'ideology'. On the contrary, it is informed by a plea for conceptual clarity and argumentational rigor.

Finally, in their endorsement of "an integration of the mathematical concepts and practices originating in the learners' culture with those of conventional, formal academic mathematics" (332), the authors do not address Rowlands and Carson's concerns. The latter do *not* "claim that mathematics should be taught in an artificial setting without relating it to the real-world whatsoever" (333; Rowlands and Carson 2004: 336). Instead, they argue that

> a teacher ought to be sensitive to cultural experience . . . , [but that] to confuse the boundaries between cultural experience and high-order abstract concepts in mathematics is to confuse different cultural systems . . . All good teachers should be aware of the cognitive state of their students, but that awareness can be achieved by how the student responds to the mediation of high-order concepts. This does not mean connecting high-order concepts with cultural experience. (Rowlands and Carson 2002: 96, 97, 98)

Of course, it might be argued (as Alangui did, in conversation with me during the Third International Conference on Ethnomathematics, ICEm3, held in February 2006 in Auckland) that sensitivity to cultural experience and awareness of students' cognitive state are insubstantial and woefully inadequate for addressing the deeper concerns, like the effects of physical and mental colonization. My question is, however, what work does a focus on 'ethnomathematics' do that a rights-based approach does not or cannot do? 'Rights' may be an occidental idea[7] (and certainly not a failsafe one at that), but it is arguably the best tool we have for addressing issues of social justice and redress. I will return to this point towards the end of this chapter.

In a later article, Barton (2004: 22) usefully distinguishes between 'mathematical' knowledge and 'practical' knowledge (e.g., the 'mathematical' practices of artisans):

> There have been many studies done on these issues: studies in ethnomathematics, studies in mathematics education, studies in situated cognition, studies in anthropology, studies in the history of mathematics and studies in indigenous knowledge. . . . [W]riting in one area has been criticised as if it was from another. Rowlands and Carson's (2002) critique of ethnomathematics as if it is an educational movement is a case in point, the rebuttal (Adam et al. 2003)

differentiating between the open educational questions, and the ethnomathematical issue of relativity in mathematical thought.

Rebuttal? Hardly. Again, Barton misses the (meta-)issue here. The critique concerns the very plausibility of *ethno*mathematics and *indigenous* knowledge. In order to make sense of ideas like 'relativity' and 'cultural specificity' in mathematics (education), reference to the distinction between 'mathematical' and 'practical' knowledge is crucial. Yet, such reference is usually unavailable within "studies in ethnomathematics." Tellingly, Barton (23) notes that

> the boundaries between these areas of study overlap—the differences are often ones of emphasis and focus rather than distinct features. Furthermore, many writers deliberately address more than one of these areas in the same article.

The confusion between theoretical and practical knowledge seems to lie at the heart of the defense of ethnomathematics and of indigenous knowledge in general.

After presenting his definition of ethnomathematics (see above), Barton announces (1996: 214), "Both 'mathematics' and 'mathematical' are culturally specific because their referents depend upon who is using the terms." He claims (215) that there are four implications of his definition: "(a) ethnomathematics is not a mathematical study, it is more like anthropology or history; (b) the definition itself depends on who is stating it, and it is culturally specific; (c) the practice which it describes is also culturally specific; and (d) ethnomathematics implies some form of relativism for mathematics."

Before I examine the idea of mathematical relativism in greater detail, I want to comment briefly on Barton's elaborations of points (b) and (c). He writes,

> The definition of ethnomathematics is culturally specific: it is written from the point of view of one culture or social grouping, namely a culture or social grouping which has a conceptual category named 'mathematics'. . . . Part of the purpose of ethnomathematics is to *challenge the universal nature of mathematics*, and to expose different mathematical conceptions. If this is successful, then ethnomathematics is also specific to one particular concept of mathematics. Thus a universal definition is not possible. (216; emphasis mine)

Barton accepts that his preferred definition of ethnomathematics, too, is culturally specific, so he cannot be accused of inconsistency *in this regard*. However, this move renders 'other' mathematics opaque or unintelligible, and perhaps useless, to anyone outside the specific culture. Even more seriously, ethnomathematics is rendered immune to interrogation from without, a sleight of hand I find deeply disturbing intellectually. Yet, Barton is inconsistent *in another regard*. At bottom, he appears to be unaware of the tension between the claim that the definition of ethnomathematics is culturally specific and the claim that part of its purpose is to challenge the universal (or transcultural) nature of mathematics. Is this purpose also culturally specific? Moreover, the verdict that a universal definition is not possible presumably has universal purchase. Or is it culturally specific, too? Barton is silent on these issues. Finally, if it is correct that ethnomathematics is 'more like anthropology or history', it is unclear how its definition *can* be culturally specific. Barton's is a theoretical definition and, as such, subject to transcultural evaluation, can be seen to be more or less useful—and can also be outright incorrect, unlike a stipulative definition.

The assertion that the *practice* described by ethnomathematics is culturally specific makes good sense. However, Barton adds (217), "If the practice of ethnomathematics is carried out with integrity, there will be cognisance of those aspects of the practices and concepts which are other-culture based and which may not, initially, be considered mathematics." Yet, who judges whether "the practice of ethnomathematics" is "carried out with integrity," and on what grounds? Will this not also involve a culturally specific judgment and/or set of criteria? It would appear that those who are universalists (or transculturalists) about definition and judgment find themselves on logically more compelling grounds.

His definition, Barton says (218), "implies two senses in which mathematics is universal, and two senses in which it is relative." I take the former two to be uncontroversial, indeed commonsensical, and will not discuss them here. My focus, rather, will be on the alleged senses in which mathematics is relative. Regarding the first of these, Barton says that

> mathematics must be changing. This change needs to be more than just an evolutionary building on what has gone before, it must be revolutionary. (Ibid.)

There are well-documented problems with this kind of relativism regarding (revolutionary) change, in mathematics as elsewhere (see Horsthemke 2004b: 575, 576). To provide just one example, if successive or 'alternative' paradigms are incommensurable, then a new or 'other' paradigm cannot be established to be superior. Barton writes (1996: 218),

> Ethnomathematics must admit the possibility of other mathematical concepts which are not subsumable by existing ones, or by some new, overarching generalization. This is not to say that all ethnomathematical study will generate alternative mathematics. What is necessary is the idea that it could happen: that new ideas could transform the way mathematics is conceived.

Presumably one wants to still be able to call it mathematics (see Barton's point that mathematics "exists as a knowledge category"; ibid.). It follows from this that there is no such thing as 'alternative mathematics': it either *is* or *is not* 'mathematics' proper. (This will become clearer in what follows.)

Regarding the second sense in which mathematics is relative,

> there must be a recognition that mathematics is not the only way to see the world, nor is it the only way to see those aspects of the world commonly referred to as mathematical, i.e. having to do with number, shape and relationships. What is more, there needs to be a recognition that alternative ways of seeing these phenomena are legitimate and valid. For if they are not legitimate, then there will be no point in trying to study them, there would only be point in trying to "educate" those who do not see it in the 'correct' way. (219)

First, this is no argument *for* seeing alternative ways (of seeing aspects of the world commonly referred to as mathematical) as legitimate or valid. Indeed, one might simply acknowledge that, on epistemological and truth-functional grounds, they are not legitimate and that there is no point in studying them, other than as anthropological curiosities (like witchcraft, and the like). Second, reference to "alternative ways of seeing" seems to be misconceived. If a particular alternative procedure can be shown before "the community of mathematicians" (Barton 2004: 23) to work, then it is not called *alternative* anymore. It is just *mathematics*.

Barton claims (1999a: 34) that the

> use of ethnomathematics as a theoretical tool can be seen as a practical way of acknowledging the reflexivity of [the] relativistic viewpoint: it is the differing conceptions of the field which make it a valuable tool in on-going political and educational debates. We acknowledge that our own conceptions are context-derived, but use that knowledge to continue our work.

Here, as elsewhere, he appears to be unaware of the tension between the "relativistic viewpoint" and universal knowledge, that is, advancing these ideas as universal knowledge claims. He writes (ibid.), "It is an assumption of ethnomathematics that thinking about quantity, relationships and space may vary between cultural groups." Okay—but this does not, indeed cannot, mean that the various views are all equally valid, or that they indicate fundamental differences in mathematical orientation. Barton's final point may indicate a somewhat conciliatory approach, but it contains the mistaken assumption that ethnomathematics is a unique and distinct "field of knowledge."

Adam, Alangui, and Barton (2003: 328) write that the "political perspective on ethnomathematics . . . is now more often related to writing on indigenous knowledge," before claiming that "[p]rivileging some peoples' ideas in the discourse of mathematics while denying others' is colonialism." "Such views," according to the authors,

> justify the need for indigenous mathematicians to engage in ethnomathematics because indigenous knowledge and value systems are under attack. Decolonisation involves reclaiming, protecting and valuing the unique ways of indigenous knowing and doing . . . Indigenous mathematicians engage in ethnomathematics because we know that our peoples have complex knowledge systems that are valuable and could teach the outside world *alternative ways of knowing*. (328, 329; emphasis mine)

The idea of indigenous ways of *doing* being unique is certainly plausible. However, apart from relying on the unwarranted assumption that 'indigenous knowledge' is an unproblematic notion, this perception is mistaken in a further respect. If anything, 'privileging' or 'denying' views happens on the basis of the respective knowledge or truth content, not on the basis of *who* holds them. Moreover, if these *are* genuine "ways of knowing," then they would no longer be alternative. They would be part and parcel of 'knowing' as such. If Adam, Alangui, and Barton wish to preserve the qualification "alternative," then what they are referring to, presumably, is not 'knowing' but 'believing'. When the authors assert (329) that "alternative systems of relationships and their meanings . . . are important to the growth of mathematical knowledge," they take this to indicate not that 'another world is still possible for indigenous people" but that such a world "already exists." Does this mean that all indigenous worldviews, however scurrilous, are equally valid?

According to Adam, Alangui, and Barton (ibid.), the

> political perspective is just one of many in the ethnomathematical field. The philosophical issues are also far-reaching and widely debated. To name just one example, the question of mathematical relativity is implied by ethnomathematics and needs justification.

The authors bring this perspective to bear also on their discussion of 'rationality' (330):

> Greek rationality is only one form of rationality, and . . . the particular form of mathematics that traces its trajectory through a Greek tradition (and a few others) serves particular functions and has particular consequences. . . . However, to use this particular form of mathematics as the standard by mathematics is to be judged misses the point.

What point?, one might ask. Clearly, in the absence of any kind of argument in favor of (for example) culture-specific rationality, the authors' claim here amounts to little more than bald assertion. Moreover, the claim that there are several (equally valid) forms of rationality renders it impossible to evaluate competing knowledge claims. Even more seriously, *any* kind of behavior or worldview could be accounted for and rendered immune to condemnation, in terms of employing or engaging a "different form of rationality."

Barton explains that ethnomathematics "has its focus *firmly fixed* on mathematical knowledge—its aim is the illumination of this knowledge, its methods are to expand the ambit of what can be legitimately regarded as mathematics, *by including* mathematical practices and systems wherever they occur, and, in particular, where they occur in specific contexts" (2004: 22; emphasis mine). Barton's initial emphasis of the distinction between mathematical knowledge and practical knowledge notwithstanding, this statement exemplifies the basic conceptual confusion underlying the defense of both ethnomathematics and indigenous knowledge, namely what is in the final analysis a conflation of theoretical and practical knowledge.

Regarding the question, "How does ethnomathematics extend mathematical knowledge?," Barton points to "some examples of direct contributions from culturally specific knowledge to the general body of conventional mathematics" (23; as an example, he cites Ascher 2002). I suggest that the idea of "culturally specific knowledge" makes sense only with regard to practical knowledge or "mathematical practices"—but *not* when it is taken to refer to theoretical (mathematical) knowledge. Theoretical, factual, or propositional knowledge cannot be culturally specific or relative. Neither can truth. Mathematical truths hold transculturally. My hunch is that when ethnomathematicians and indigenous knowledge apologists speak of culturally specific knowledge or of truth being relative, they are actually referring either to practices or to beliefs.

An evaluation of the research around and application of so-called 'alternative' mathematics is necessarily and correctly conducted against the background of 'formal, academic' mathematics. Having said this, I do not share Rowlands and Carson's view that the "conversation [between critics and defenders of ethnomathematics, . . . i]n addition to purely mathematical issues, . . . involves questions of historical injury and contemporary relationships between *cultural groups whose values are incommensurable*" (2004: 329; emphasis added). In fact, I would suggest that it is precisely the pernicious cultural and ethical relativism invoked here that would make 'conversation' impossible. On the contrary, and my own ICEm3 experience strongly bears this out,[8] the degree of convergence between values and priorities is striking and that, despite some historical and cultural divergence in approaches, there is a common commitment to discussion and argument—as well as to some transcultural standard of correct reasoning in mathematics as in other areas of intellectual life, and about matters that concern us most (see Horsthemke 2006b: 19; Horsthemke and Schäfer 2007: 8).

MATHEMATICS EDUCATION AND RIGHTS

What D'Ambrosio (2001: 42) refers to as "the promising strategy for education, in societies that are in transition from subordination to autonomy," namely "to re-establish the dignity of its individuals, recognizing and respecting their roots," is arguably optimally pursued on the basis of appeals to rights. I therefore agree with De Sousa Santos's identification of "human rights as the new emancipatory vocabulary of progressive politics" (2007a: ix; 2007b).

To use the particular but representative example of South Africa: given the flagrant violation of human rights that occurred under apartheid, the present South African Constitution, which was adopted in 1996, places considerable emphasis on developing a "culture based on human rights." The preamble of the Constitution of the Republic of South Africa states: "We . . . adopt this constitution . . . so as to heal the divisions of the past and establish a society based on democratic values, social justice and fundamental human rights." By being 'fundamental', human rights are also seen as being 'universal'. Yet, a crucial feature of rights is that they are required and invoked to protect individual differences.[9]

This last point is significant in the present context, as far as education and mathematical knowledge are concerned. Part of what ethnomathematics endeavors to achieve has to do with attainment of recognition, acknowledgment that indigenous mathematical practices and insights are of value, as well as redress—compensation for past misrecognition, nonrecognition, and exploitation or intellectual theft, that is, wrongful appropriation of intellectual property.

Apart from providing a basic framework for grounding the need for education and cognitive emancipation, as well as in terms of intellectual property rights, rights language has both a richness in application and a political effectiveness that are lacking in advocacy of ethnomathematics and other 'indigenous knowledge' projects. It can do justice to a multiplicity of approaches to the teaching and learning of mathematics, accommodate particular requirements, ensure personal opportunities and availability of resources, and safeguard the continuing survival of those insights, customs, practices, and values of ethnic and sociocultural groups that deserve acknowledgment and respect.

NOTES

1. http://www.africameetsafrica.co.za/makingaliving.html (retrieved April 29, 2020).

2. Traditional mathematical thinking is obviously not confined to the African continent; see Embong et al. (2010) for examples and illustrations of the application of basic mathematical concepts and principles in Malay *songket* weaving, and Laurens et al. (2019) for an account of activities like selling and trading, weaving, and crafting involving knowledge of, for example, geometry and fractions.

3. At the *Third International Conference on Ethnomathematics* (ICEm3)*: Cultural connections and mathematical manipulations*, held in Auckland in February 2006, D'Ambrosio acknowledged that the first mention of the term 'ethnomathematics' presumably occurred in a review of Claudia Zaslavsky's book *Africa Counts*, a review he himself read only many years later. At the very least, D'Ambrosio can be credited with giving intellectual and ethical substance as well as worldwide currency, and with lasting commitment, to this idea.

4. https://www.reddit.com/r/Jokes/comments/3hgj29/why_did_the_feminist_fail_algebra/ (retrieved April 27, 2020).

5. C. Shiv Visvanathan (2002: 49) complains that "within the current discourse on democracy, all we have to resist" the destruction and museumizing of "alternative knowledge-forms" is "the language of rights," but does not provide further arguments for maintaining that the "defense of nature and the defense of dying cultures are inadequately conceptualized within such a notion of rights."

6. In his ICEm3 address D'Ambrosio stated, "History shows that mathematics is *intrinsically* involved with . . . the denial of the essence of the phenomenon [of] life" (2006; emphasis added). 'Intrinsically'? Surely not. 'Instrumentally' or 'derivatively', perhaps—but it appears to be a mistake to blame the weapon or instrument of destruction (*if* it is that!) along with the agent of destruction. (Compare the banning of handguns, nuclear weapons, and so forth. and the banning of mathematics.) Both D'Ambrosio and Barton might argue that mathematics, *as a social construct*, has been and continues to be used in such 'denial of life'. If we accept that mathematics is indeed, at least in part, a social construct, does this *intrinsically* so implicate mathematics? I would argue that it does *not*—and that there is no compelling reason for accepting that mathematics *is*, exclusively, socially constructed.

7. See De Sousa Santos 2007a: ix, x, 2007b.

8. On this note, I wish to reiterate (see Horsthemke 2007b: 19) here my gratitude to Bill Barton and his team for making ICEm3 the intellectual and human success it was. Despite my critical take on their core interest or area of research, I found the openness and friendliness of the delegates with whom I had personal conversations, especially Gelsa Knijnik, Ubiratan d'Ambrosio, Willy Alangui, Bill Barton, Ivan Reilly, and Charoula Stathopoulou, to be quite disarming.

9. Yash Ghai (2007) is aware of the emancipatory potential of diversity and interculturality, but he issues a warning against the potential dangers of relativism and abuse by authoritarian political leaders eager to invoke cultural specificity in order to justify human rights violations.

Chapter 6

Indigenous Science

COSMIC AFRICA

The film *Cosmic Africa*, by South African brothers Craig and Damon Foster and concept originator and key researcher Anne Rogers, documents the journey of South African astrophysicist Thebe Medupe. His mission is to connect occidental science and astronomy to the cosmological models of some of the oldest civilizations on earth. 'Astronomy' survives in these ancient societies despite the eroding effects of colonialism and its modern heir, globalization. Medupe emphasizes that 'astronomy' has never just been a science in these cultures. For them, it is an "intimate tapestry merging into their prayers, their lives, their dreams and their deaths."[1] Occidental culture, on the other hand, has separated astronomy from daily experience and turned it into "pure science." Medupe's mission is stated at the very beginning of the film: "I need to discover whether my science has a place in Africa, and whether Africa has a place in my science." His journey leads him to the Ju/'hoansi in northeastern Namibia, the Dogon in Mali, and finally to Nabta Playa in the southern Egyptian Sahara, to what is conceivably the site of the first solar observatory (see also Rogers 2007: 19).

During his visit to Namibia, Medupe learns not only of Ju/'hoansi reliance on the stars as to when to plant and to harvest but many of the stories connected to the sun, moon, and stars:

> One memorable night, Kxau Tami and /Kunta Boo, two elderly shamans demonstrated how they would throw burning sticks in the direction of a very bright meteor—as they threw the sticks into the air, they uttered swear and curse words which they said would help to divert the meteor's path and thereby prevent its dangerous potential. They believe that bright shooting stars with fiery tails are

invested with very powerful *!nom* (extreme potency) and that they have the potential to cause sickness. (Ibid.: 21)

Medupe's visit to the Ju/'hoansi coincides with a total solar eclipse. He worries about whether he should tell the people about what is going to happen but decides not to: they would want to know how he knows. Instead, he sets up his equipment. When the eclipse happens, people talk about the return of winter and blame the intruder and his equipment: "The telescope is eating up the sun." After the eclipse and subsequent reconciliation, Medupe says, "For the first time I see how the stars affect the way people live. My science and my Africa are beginning to come together."

This impression is deepened with the visit to the Dogon, whose knowledge of the stars is legendary.[2] Their daily and seasonal activities, routines and customs are guided, for example, by the appearance of what we call Venus (for which the Dogon have "a number of different names . . . , depending on its station in the sky"; ibid.), 'Toro Jugo' (the Pleaides; 20), and so forth. One of the elders, spiritual leader Annayé Doumbo, claims, "In our Dogon way, the man who makes technology is the sorcerer of the sun." Given the harsh conditions under which they live, to the Dogon, knowing the stars can mean the difference between life and death. Does the elder know that human beings have walked on the moon? "There is no gate to the moon," is the reply, "it is not possible for anyone to go there, unless they are the little brother of God."

The last leg of Medupe's journey is what is presented as the origin of astronomy, Egypt. (There is no mention of the innovations and discoveries of the Maya and Aztecs.) In the southern Egyptian desert, near the border of Sudan, he discovers what is conceivably the oldest observatory, conceived and constructed by the Nabtans, nomadic pastoralists, now long dead. Predating Stonehenge in England by almost 1,000 years, it consists of countless stones emanating from a center, in order to trace the rising and setting of the sun during the year, as well as the passage of the moon and stars (23): "The origin of astronomy, its measuring and predicting, is in Africa . . . Stones took the place that my computer takes now."

It is unfortunate that, throughout the film, Medupe and the research team never explored any of the tensions between traditional, indigenous, and scientific worldviews. They seem satisfied with just noting the different perceptions and appear to assume that there is no problem of reconciliation of myth or legend with scientific fact. At the end of the film, Medupe states that he has come "full circle," that his journey has served to (re)unite 'his science' and 'his Africa', without so much as an attempt to account for the contradictions he has encountered between spirituality and astronomy.

One of Medupe's intentions is to create an African star chart. His long-term goal is to develop a database and to set up a formal ethnoastronomy research group. The pertinent questions, for present purposes, are: Does the idea of 'ethnoastronomy' make sense? What, if anything, distinguishes 'ethnoscience' from mainstream, academic science? Is it a contextual, cultural, and/or spiritual element?

NATIVE AMERICAN CREATIONISM VERSUS ARCHAEOLOGY

In 1995, Vine Deloria Jr., legal scholar and history professor at the University of Colorado and prominent Native American advocate, published *Red Earth, White Lies: Native Americans and the Myth of Scientific Fact*, for which he won a Colorado Book Award. One of Deloria's chief targets in the book was the theory, embraced by a vast majority of archaeologists, that America's original, 'indigenous' inhabitants originally came from Asia across the Bering Strait more than 10,000 years ago. Dismissing this account as "scientific folklore," Deloria presented a version of the popular creationist view that Native Americans have always lived in the Americas, after emerging onto the earth's surface from a subterranean world of spirits.

"We never asked science to make a determination as to or origins," Sebastian LeBeau (repatriation officer for the Cheyenne River Sioux, a Lakota tribe based in Eagle Butte, South Dakota) was quoted as saying in a front-page article published in *The New York Times* on October 22, 1996[3]:

> We know where we come from. We are the descendants of the Buffalo people. They came from inside the earth after supernatural spirits prepared this world for humankind to live here. If non-Indians choose to believe they evolved from an ape, so be it. I have yet to come across five Lakotas who believe in science and in evolution. (Johnson 1996: 1)

Perhaps unsurprisingly, many Native American archaeologists say they doubt the ability of science to yield new, compelling information about their origins. According to Larry Benallie, who is part Hopi and part Navajo and an archaeologist for the Navajo Nation,

> There's a real feeling that we've been here forever... The Bering Strait theory makes logical sense, but it doesn't override the traditional belief at all. That comes first. (2)

Benallie added that his people considered archaeology "a necessary evil" (ibid.).

Deloria, similarly—employing arguments strongly reminiscent of those advanced by Christian fundamentalists—rejects the theory of evolution (like the Bering Strait hypothesis) as unsubstantiated dogma. "Science is the dominant religion," he said in an interview. In attempting to salvage their own dogmatic accounts, he said, archaeologists "are fudging considerably so that their general interpretation does not give us much confidence, and some Indian accounts may be more accurate" (reported in ibid.).

The aforementioned *New York Times* article was occasioned by a dispute over the discovery of ancient human hairs in a 10,000-year-old archaeological site in Montana,[4] which exemplified a long series of active, physical, and legal clashes between Native Americans and archaeologists conducting research on prehistoric remains.

> Most archeologists agree with the tribes that historical remains, some taken in wars with the Government and shipped to museums, should be given to their relatives for reburial. But in case after case, Indian creationism is being used to forbid the study of prehistoric skeletons so old that it would be impossible to establish a direct tribal affiliation. Under the repatriation act,[5] who gets the bones is often being determined not by scientific inquiry but by negotiation between local tribes and the Federal agencies that administer the land where the remains are found. (1)

While some archaeologists were reported as

> reacting to challenges from the tribes with anger, others are straining to put the best possible face on a difficult situation. Privately some say they are afraid that if they take too strong a stand on favor of scientific inquiry, they will be denied even more research opportunities. (2)

What is even more remarkable is that, "pulled between their scientific temperaments and their appreciation for native culture, some archeologists have been driven close to a postmodern relativism in which science is just one more belief system" (2, 3). Thus, Roger Anyon, a British archaeologist who has worked for the Zuni tribe, is quoted as saying that science is "one of many ways of knowing the world." The Zunis' worldview, he said, is "just as valid as the archeological viewpoint of what history is about" (3). Larry Zimmerman, an anthropologist at the University of Iowa, said there was a need for

> a different kind of science, between the boundaries of Western ways of knowing and Indian ways of knowing. . . . I personally do reject science as a privileged way of seeing the world. . . . That's not to say that it isn't an important way

that has brought benefit. But I understand that as a scientist I need to constantly learn. (Ibid.)

The questions around ownership of the past, and around the adequacy of, for example, the Native American Graves Protection and Repatriation Act are important. However, at least in the present chapter, my interest in the conflict between science (archaeology) and Native American worldviews does not revolve around issues in social justice, intercultural conflict resolution, and the like. It is predominantly epistemic—that is, I am interested in the conceptual tenability of different 'ways of knowing' and worldviews, the epistemic validity of different ways of 'seeing the world' (see also Horsthemke 2011).

It might of course be argued that, especially with regard to indigenous knowledge, issues in social justice are inseparable from issues in epistemology. As we saw in chapter 4, the emphasis on "diverse epistemologies" or "knowledge diversity" (see De Sousa Santos et al. 2007; Green 2008, 2009) is fairly easy to explain, especially when one considers the denigration, suppression and exploitation of so-called 'traditional knowledge systems' during and even after colonialism (for compelling historical narratives and analyses of 'how the West was lost', see Dee Brown, Peter Farb, and Alvin M. Josephy Jr.'s accounts; Brown 1971; Farb 1988; Josephy 1995). The reclamation project that underlies this renewed focus is not only (or even primarily) epistemological but essentially political, and concerned with social justice and (revisions in) legislation.

Nonetheless, I will argue below that to analyze and evaluate epistemological considerations as *necessarily* having a social justice dimension, to the extent that questions around knowledge and truth are seen, necessarily, to raise questions around power and authority, is to commit a category mistake.[6] When one account is true and another false, or one is adequately justified and another only insufficiently so, it is fairly clear which one ought to be favored, on epistemic grounds. I will contend, further, that the position defended by Green (like the accounts on which she bases a substantial portion of her argument, Nelson Goodman and Catherine Elgin's[7]—at least on Green's interpretation) has the awkward implication of being unable to determine which account or theory, for example, the scientists' or the creationists', is *epistemically* preferable. On the view I am defending here, which is in essence a thoroughgoing realism, it is possible *at once* morally to support, to empathize and sympathize with the plight of, indigenous people (and to condemn and lobby against 'Western' denigration, suppression, and exploitation) *and* to reject some of the epistemological, metaphysical, and ontological foundations of their worldviews.

'KNOWLEDGE DIVERSITY', TRUTH AND CONTEXT-DEPENDENCE: POSTMODERNIST AND POSTCOLONIAL TURNS

According to Green (2008: 157),

> An ethical post-modern and post-colonial anthropology . . . requires a commitment neither to a dogma of secularism nor to the practice of professional distance. In their place, what is needed is a rethinking of what it means to be a Self among Others; a way of engaging with difference that does not require the effacement of belief, or histories of belief.

Clearly, an "ethical anthropology" needs to give consideration to the feelings of the people whose ancestors it so eagerly studies. In the words of Douglas Owsley, a forensic anthropologist at the Smithsonian Institution's Museum of Natural History, "collections" that relate

> to the recent past . . . should not have been acquired in the first place. But we're seeing irreplaceable museum collections that can tell us so much about the *prehistoric past* lost and lost forever. (Johnson 1996: 1; emphasis added).

Owsley's last statement indicates where and how postmodernism and postcolonial relativism err, while Green's argument exemplifies the category mistake to which I referred earlier. According to the view that I am defending here, there is clearly a difference between requiring "the *effacement* of belief, or histories of belief" and arguing, for example, that critical engagement with (histories of) belief is not only *permissible*, but also *mandatory*—on epistemic and veritistic grounds, that is, in terms of promoting truth (and the acquisition of true beliefs) and impeding error (and the acquisition of false beliefs).

Green focuses on "knowledge diversity" (which refers both to "knowledge practices" and to "knowledge traditions"; Green 2008: 149), in a critical response to realist and "universalist" conceptions of rationality, knowledge, and truth (Green 2009: 42, 43; for a target of such a critique see, e.g., Horsthemke 2008b):

> While recognizing the flaws in universalism and the need to value knowledge diversity, there is a need to reject the idea of knowledges as mutually exclusive. . . . In recognizing a wider range of cognitive practices and diverse moral economies of knowledge, scholarship on the commensurability of the sciences and [indigenous peoples'] knowledges . . . can and will impact on far more than village schoolrooms. . . . The focus on epistemically acceptable practices, rather than universal truths (which can never be satisfactorily demonstrated) suggests

that the division of [indigenous knowledge] and the Sciences is spurious, without resorting to a universalism in Science. (Green 2009: 51–52)

Green (2008: 144) argues that

> diverse epistemologies ought to be evaluated not on their capacity to express a strict realism but on their ability to advance understanding. Such an approach allows for the evaluation of the advancement of understanding without necessarily requiring the expression of the literal truths that divide 'belief' from 'knowledge'.

Apart from how—in the absence of such truths—one could make sense of "understanding" (I return to this point below), a question that remains largely unaddressed is whether the ideas of "diverse moral economies of knowledge," "epistemological equality of all the existing paradigms" and of "diverse epistemologies," and "different ways of knowing" (see also Asante 2005: 40; Fatnowna and Pickett 2002b: 211), make any sense. As I pointed out in chapter 4, the central problem appears to be the lack of clarity about the meaning or understanding of 'knowledge' and 'epistemology'. Defenders of the ideas of 'diverse epistemologies', or 'knowledge diversity', and the idea of 'indigenous knowledge' characteristically distinguish between 'skills' and 'knowledge'—which suggests, in the absence of any definition, that at least part of the understanding concerns propositional (or theoretical, or factual) knowledge. Insofar as 'knowledge' in this sense includes reference to 'truth', this invites the perception that a similar 'diversity' exists in the realm of truth (or, perhaps more appropriately on the present view, 'truths').

Indeed, this is the view that Green seems to favor. Acknowledging Goodman's influence, she writes (2008: 147; see also Green 2009: 46):

> Whether one is justified in asserting that 'the sun always moves' or 'the sun never moves' (Goodman 1978: 2) depends wholly on the context in which knowledge is sought: the architect is interested in how the sunlight moves around the building; the climate scientist in how the sun moves from one angle to another in the course of the seasons; the planetary scientist in how the sun is constantly flaring and vibrating, and the astronomer in how our entire galaxy is flying through space at approximately 600 kilometers per second.

The examples presented here miss the point: the architect and the respective scientists would not, indeed *could not*, reasonably advance these as knowledge claims, as representing the world as it *is*. These are examples of figurative or metaphorical speech, more or less useful fictional shorthand. It is generally taken for granted that they do not constitute literal truths. The commitment to truth therefore remains intact.

According to Goodman, unsurprisingly, "Truth . . . pertains solely to what is said, and literal truth solely to what is said literally" (Goodman 1978: 18). This, he says, also has a bearing on the nature of knowledge, insofar as

> knowing cannot be exclusively or even primarily a matter of determining what is true. . . . Much of knowing aims at something other than true, or any, belief. . . . Such growth in knowledge is not by formation or fixation of belief but by the advancement of understanding. (21, 22)

Not only is it unclear how one might make sense of understanding, and indeed of knowledge, in the absence of belief and truth; it is also far from evident how Goodman can avoid (as he wishes to do; 94) the conclusion that 'anything goes', that science is indistinguishable from superstition, as fact is from fiction, and truth from falsehood. When he asserts that "we make worlds by making versions" (ibid.), by "versions" he means sets of descriptions of the world. Indeed, in referring to the (human) "fabrication of facts" and to their description-dependence, he indicates that there is no way the world is, independently of how it is described. In other words, the way the world is depends on our descriptions: this is what he means by "worldmaking." In a later publication, Goodman argues that there is no such thing—objectively, really—as a "constellation." It is only our picking out and designating activity that makes a random group or collection of stars a particular constellation (Goodman 1996: 156). This is neither very controversial nor problematic for someone of a realist persuasion. The problem for Goodman, on the other hand, is that the stars are in and of themselves, not dependent on human choices, designations, or descriptions. To attempt to salvage his position, he would presumably have to resort to increasingly counter-intuitive claims—for example, that the molecules making up the stars, and the atoms that make up the molecules, and so forth, are themselves dependent on (human) designation, and description. "Did the sun set a while ago or did the earth rise? Does the sun go around the earth or the earth around the sun?" The answers do not, as Goodman states, "depend on the framework" (Goodman 1978: 93). The truth of claims like 'The sun moves around the earth' and 'The earth moves around the sun' does not vary with one's frame of reference (2, 3), with the context in which the statements are made. The latter, unlike the former, is simply false.

"On the point of . . . *context-dependence*," Green writes (2008: 150), "—or the idea that (traditional knowledge) is only relevant to a specific context— Agrawal points out that the sociology of scientific knowledge demonstrates the extent to which *scientific truths are context-dependent*" (see Agrawal 1995: 425; emphasis added). This, too, is a misconception: it is different beliefs and perhaps the justification that is given for them that may be context-dependent, not truth (see Horsthemke 2008b). While considerations of 'context' are important (I return to this notion below; see also Horsthemke 2007: 22–25), an *exclusive* focus on context errs in that it ignores evidence and logic, or at least reduces these to social or cultural factors and extraneous interests and agendas. It also involves fundamental misconceptions about truth.

But what about *understanding*? And is it correct that truth is context-independent? The suggestion is that an absolute standard of truth may be (even epistemically) undesirable. In Elgin's words (2004: 115):

> Consensus has it that epistemic acceptability requires something like justified and/or reliable true belief. The justification, reliability, and belief requirements involve thresholds. . . . But truth, unlike the other requirements, is supposed to be an absolute mater. Either the belief is true or not. I suggest, however, that the truth requirement on epistemic acceptability involves a threshold too. . . . My point is . . . that epistemic accessibility turns . . . on whether [a sentence] is true enough—that is, on whether it is close enough to the truth. 'True enough' obviously has a threshold.

According to Green (2008: 153), "Elgin argues for an evaluation of models of knowledge on a very simple principle: their efficacy in producing understanding that is appropriate to context (see Elgin 2004: 121)." Following Elgin's gradational or quantitative conception of truth, Green says, "Knowledge . . . is constituted by what is 'true enough' for the task at hand (Elgin 2004), rather than by access to an absolute truth" (Green 2008: 147). Arguing for a way of regarding scientific laws and models that moves away from the assumption of literal truth, Elgin points out that in the sciences, precision, accuracy, and falsehood are a *matter of context*. "[A] theory may be composed of both factual and fictional sentences" (Elgin 2004: 128). Green (2008: 154), for her own purposes, welcomes Elgin's argument "that scientific laws are not 'true' in the strict sense of the term, but 'true enough'."

There is a sense in which scientific theories might, quite plausibly, be seen as approximations of truth (I return to this point below), and/or as attempts to avoid error. But does this invite something like the 'threshold' analysis of truth? I do not think so: the present analysis appears to conflate 'true enough' and justification/reliability, and in effect to divorce it from the truth criterion. It is unclear what work the phrase 'true enough' is meant to do, over and above establishing grounds for, or the reliability of, knowledge claims.[8] Truth *per se* is the nongradational condition of knowledge: it is not a matter of degree. (The question 'How true must a claim be/How much truth must a belief have in order to qualify as knowledge?' makes no sense. Yet, one *can* ask these questions with regard to justification.) To argue, as Elgin does, for a quantitative or gradational conception of truth (in its revised or 'relaxed' version, like belief and justification), is to misunderstand what it is, that is, its objective.

More to the point, even if one grants—for the sake of the present argument—the plausibility of the notion of 'true enough', it would still not salvage Green's account of indigenous knowledge and epistemological diversity. "In Palikur astronomy," Green writes (ibid.; see also Green 2009: 45),

> the annual movements of specific constellations are related to seasonal rains in a way that describes those constellations as the boats of shamans who bring the rains. The constellations, in other words, are given material form, and cause is attributed to them. If one were to reject as unscientific any explanatory model of the world that does not operate within a *strict realism*, one could not accept this narrative as knowledge.

Precisely; but, as I will show below, even on Elgin's account, with its 'relaxed' truth criterion,[9] this particular explanatory model would not pass muster. "Yet," Green continues (2008: 154; see also Green 2009: 47),

> there is certainly a correlation between the appearance of specific constellations in the hour before dawn, and specific seasons. . . . Is this narrative that attributes causal agency to inanimate objects really that different to the immunologist's metaphors of attack and defence that attributes agency to cellular processes as if they are soldiers in a war? In other words, science does not operate within a framework of strict realism in using its own models. Why judge a different knowledge as false where it uses narrative models?

The difference is that an immunologist is fully aware of the metaphorical nature of the language employed, whereas the Palikur astronomer actually fully believes that inanimate and fictional objects have not only *causal agency* but also a *purposive role* in natural events. Unlike mainstream scientists, the Palikur claim *non*fictional status for fictional elements—that is, they do not (*cannot?*) distinguish between fiction and reality (what is really/actually the case). Elgin herself would probably argue that the Palikur theory (like Native American creationism) is not 'factually defeasible', and therefore neither scientifically tenable nor epistemically desirable. (I return to this point below.) Green (156) contends that "no scientist believes that Scorpius and Orion are literally an arachnid and a human, but the constellations remain known by those names." Without doubt; the importance, however, is not constituted by the *naming*, but by the accompanying beliefs, and the extent to which they reflect *what is actually the case*.

"If 'true enough' is valid for the purposes of communicating understanding in the laws of physics," Green suggests,

> the model of the relationship between the stars and the rains is adequate to the task of communicating understanding of the complex movements of stars in relation to the seasons. It is 'true enough' in its context. One might believe in the shamanic guiding of the star boats, or one might accept that these sentences of the model are metaphorical: either way, they do not need to be eliminated in order for the model of the sky to be valid, which is to say that *such models can be taught in school curricula*, and included in the corpus of knowledge promoted by the state in the task of extending citizenship to people who explain the ecosystem with reference to the rains that come at the same time as certain stars.' (155; emphasis added)

Again, this analysis misses the point—namely that some 'models' are false (they do not even come close to 'true enough') and should not be taught. There is no obvious reason the star boat narrative should be taught in astronomy, although it might be taught in cultural studies or classes on the history and function of myth. Similarly, creationism (whether Christian or Native American) should not be taught in biology classes, although it arguably has a place in dedicated religious instruction.

According to Green (158), "all knowledge, including Newtonian physics and Palikur astronomy, is produced with relevance to specific contexts and questions, and it is within those contexts of use that knowledge, along with the cognitive devices such as models, laws, narratives and metaphors, must be evaluated." To correct Green, all knowledge *claims* are made within specific contexts. Truth itself is not context-dependent. The difference between Newtonian physics and Palikur astronomy is that the former, but not the latter, is *factually defeasible*. Newtonian physics, unlike Palikur astronomy, to use Elgin's words (2004: 129), is a "theory or system of thought" that "accommodates the epistemically accessible facts." What this means is that the "usual considerations about evidence, simplicity, scope, and so forth come into play" (see also Horsthemke 2008b). Even though not all of the components of a theory may be factual (some may be fictional), "the way the world is constrains the acceptability of the theory they figure in":

> An acceptable theory must be at least as good as any available alternative, when judged in terms of currently available standards of cognitive goodness. So such a theory would also be discredited by a theory that better satisfied those standards. *Neither a defeated nor an indefeasible theory is tenable.* Because it is indifferent to evidence, claptrap is indefeasible. Hence it is untenable. . . . A factually defeasible theory has epistemically accessible implications which,

if found to be false, discredit the theory. So a defeasible theory, by preserving its commitment to testable consequences retains a commitment to truth. (Elgin 2004: 129; emphasis added)

Because it is indifferent to evidence, Palikur astronomy, like Native American creationism, is indefeasible. Therefore, on Elgin's (plausible) analysis, it is not scientifically tenable. The factually defeasible theories that make up 'science', on the other hand, may constitute a "privileged way of seeing the world" (Zimmerman; quoted in Johnson 1996: 3), but they also have epistemically *accessible* implications. The scientific method may be considered 'privileged' because of its many virtues. It is evidence-guided and, because it is open to (and usually actively seeks out) *counter*evidence, science is revisable. Defeasibility matters not only because of its proximity to truth,[10] but also because it is essential for the revision of scientific theories—which in turn makes for greater reliability. Unlike Palikur astronomy, which arguably has some predictive force, the scientific account of seasonal rains offers explanations, predictions, and hypotheses that constitute part of a coherent theory of worldwide seasonal weather patterns and changes. As its scope and reliability increase, scientific meteorology matures and improves with time.

When Green (2008: 156) proposes "that in evaluating knowledges, critics of '[indigenous knowledge]' should neither assume that (a) all 'sentences' of a proposition are held to be equally true, nor that (b) a model or a metaphor should always be evaluated within a paradigm of strict realism, but rather they should be judged on their ability to advance understanding," the obvious response is that 'understanding', if it is to have any meaning at all, requires reference to an *objective* framework, to *facts* (whether natural or social), *truth, the way things are*, and so forth. 'Understanding', admittedly, is context-dependent because it has a characteristically subjective component. Nonetheless, it obtains its meaning, its cognitive force, from its additional, essential connection with truth: it is directed toward truth, *toward the way the world is*.

INDIGENOUS SCIENCE AND THE PROBLEMS OF SUPERSTITION AND RELATIVISM

In some instances, "indigenous science" is taken to cover all kinds of beliefs, with little or no reference to truth or evidence. This elevates to the status of knowledge not only mere assumption and opinion but also superstition (as in the case of belief in witchcraft, in the *tokoloshe* or *mantindane* [see chapter 7] or that sexual intercourse with a virgin prevents or cures HIV/AIDS), divination, soothsaying, and the like. In the absence of any explicit reference to truth, then, a more appropriate idea would be that of 'indigenous beliefs'. Given the Platonic as well as the Yoruba understanding of knowledge, belief—even belief that is based on evidence—does not amount to knowledge. The major problem here is that, in the absence of truth, emphasis on "indigenous science" does not appear to render possible a distinction between science and nonscience.

Writers often also refer to the (need for) "validation" or "legitimization" of indigenous science, or to "warranted" and "valid" scientific knowledge (see Semali and Kincheloe 1999: 35; Odora Hoppers 2002b: 7; Odora Hoppers 2005: 24), especially in terms of its inclusion in tertiary educational curricula. All these references are tautologies. Considering the centrality of evidence, scientific knowledge is necessarily valid, legitimate, warranted. There simply could be no other knowledge, knowledge that is invalid, illegitimate, or unwarranted. It would not be knowledge then. This is not to deny that knowledge can be and often is subjugated. A pertinent consideration here would concern the impact of the first significant astronomic discoveries on a flat-earth, geocentric worldview, or of the theory of evolution on an orthodox, theocentric mindset, and the subsequent suppression of these views. But here the emphasis has changed, subtly, to incorporate truth. (It should be noted that reference to "true knowledge," too, involves a tautology.)

In other instances, reference to truth is explicit, the underlying assumption being that there are multitudinous truths, that with a multiplicity of indigenous cultures and subcultures there exists a multiplicity of truths, none of which are superior to any other (see Semali and Kincheloe 1999: 27, 28; Odora Hoppers 2002b: 14; Odora Hoppers 2005). This kind of view leads directly to epistemological relativism and to relativism about truth, with all their attendant difficulties. Relativism in science, in particular, is problematic in that one would not be able to compare and evaluate competing knowledge claims, theories, and/or hypotheses. Of course, many theorists would welcome this implication. South African academics Gilbert Onwu and Mogege Mosimege, for example, are worried about the "gate-keeping" mechanisms set up by "Western" science to determine "what is to be included or excluded as science" (Onwu and Mosimege 2004: 4, 6, 11). If relativism were true, for the sake of the present argument, then there would be no epistemic or veritistic grounds for choosing between the claim that "rain is the result of evaporation and so on and so forth" and the belief that "rain can arise at will as a result of human action," that "the rain by-passes the farm/field of the person who stands while drinking during the ploughing season" (7). Or to use an example given by Nigerian scholar Olugbemiro Jegede (1999: 130, 131), there would be no basis for choosing between the teaching of "Western science" that "a rainbow is caused by the refraction of a beam of light by droplets of water" and the "traditional explanation" of "the appearance of the rainbow as a python crossing a river or a sign indicating the passing away of an important traditional chief." Second, one would not be able to speak of scientific 'progress', even within a particular society or culture. Most disturbingly, this kind of approach would thwart all scientific inquiry into, or curiosity about, phenomena for which there already exists a traditional, folkloric account or explanation.

On the present analysis, either "indigenous science" refers to indigenous practices, skills, or beliefs, whether or not these are "scientific," or it is not characteristically or essentially "indigenous." Without doubt, scientific practices, skills, and beliefs vary across history and across cultures and societies. It also makes sense to say that human values and expectations have an important bearing on scientific practice or procedure. However, the consideration that science is not "value-free" or "value-neutral" (see Visvanathan 2007) has nothing to do with whether or not science is universal. Scientific knowledge and truth are not culturally specific, or relative to particular social circumstances or cultural contexts. While the ascription or attribution of scientific knowledge may vary according to personal, social, or cultural context, scientific knowledge and truth as such do not so vary. It is this insight, and not adherence to a questionable idea, that also has profound implications for education and educational curricula.

If something is referred to as "indigenous scientific knowledge" in the sense of theoretical, factual, or declarative knowledge, it must meet the requisite criteria: belief, evidential adequacy, and truth. If it does, it is relevantly similar and, indeed, equal to 'nonindigenous' knowledge in a particular area or field. Thus, the traditional healer's knowledge would be as significant, epistemologically, as that of a general medical practitioner, and the knowledge of a naturopath or homeopath.[11] The insights into climate change, animal behavior and plant life cycles of a San, Inuit, or South American Indian would be no less important than those of occidental analysts, climatologists, and biologists. In fact, both could arguably learn from each other. Makgoba (1997: 194, 195) points out, in this regard, that

> [w]e have not brought traditional healers into the system. . . . If our Western doctors were to interact more with traditional healers, we might learn a lot, and we might be able to teach them too. The point is that without the participation of these people, we'll never be able to institute the primary health care system we need.

It is important to bear in mind that there is no question here of different truths (different kinds and appraisals of evidence perhaps, different beliefs almost certainly), no question of (radically) different knowledges. Truth and reality are essentially not in the eye of the beholder.

South African author and educator Livingstone Mqotsi (2002: 168, 169) succinctly explains the distinctions between fact and myth, science and superstition. He contends that "beliefs in witchcraft and sorcery" have "social and psychological functions . . . [T]hey regulate human relationships" and also "buttress the power of those in authority." However, as "a manner of adapting to the environment," these beliefs constitute "an ineffectual technique, for it arises from a failure to understand the true relationship between cause and effect, and assumes an understanding of that relationship based on magic." The kind of schism addressed by Mqotsi exists even in scientists like Makgoba who claims that his

> paternal uncles and aunties are experts in the art of fortune-telling and assessing outcome. They are in the old profession of traditional doctoring, popularly referred to as witch doctors. (Makgoba 1997: 1)

Makgoba (15) nonetheless recognizes that the

> laws of nature or science or for that matter scientific discoveries are not written in any particular language or culture, but transcend these. These discoveries are written in the minds of men and women across these artificial divides, hence scientific principles are in general universal.

According to Ntuli (2002: 55), in an essay entitled "Indigenous knowledge systems and the African Renaissance: Laying a foundation for the creation of counter-hegemonic discourses,"

> Quantum theory permits us to conceive the world in which yes/no and either/or can exist simultaneously. It frees us from the world of binary opposites as an organizing principle so prevalent in European thought. Quantum theory provides us with a conceptual framework with which to examine our world from a new perspective.

The choice of example is doubly unfortunate. For one thing, quantum theory (or quantum mechanics, to use a more current term) does not encourage an 'anything goes'-type of approach to conceptualizing and explaining "the world." It would appear that Ntuli focuses on quantum theory's purported permission of paradox in order to validate or legitimate "African thought's" paradoxes and contradictions (56). On the contrary, quantum mechanics describes physical properties on an atomic scale and, consequently, embodies laws of physics that constitute objective truths about the world. Thus, the Principle of Complementarity holds that objects have certain pairs of complementary properties which cannot all be observed or measured simultaneously.

It does *not* endorse or validate an "African worldview [that] permits endless alliances to be maintained by cultic acts that invoke energies, spirit powers and life forces, through masquerades and carnivals" (57). Given, furthermore, that this conceptual framework originated in Europe, it is hardly useful for promoting decolonization of the (African) mind (53) and Africa's renaissance or rebirth (54, 55, 60), hardly very likely to yield "methods that will help break the stranglehold of Eurocentrism and usher in an African-centred one" (60).

A similar, glaring *non sequitur* appears in theoretical physicist F. David Peat's move from the observation, "Quantum theory stresses the irreducible link between observer and observed and the basic holism of all phenomena," to "Indigenous science also holds that there is no separation between individual and society, between matter and spirit, between each of us and the whole of nature" (1996: 6). *Contra* Peat, the laws and principles governing quantum mechanics are *not* about the relationship between individuals and society, about "matter and spirit." According to Semali and Kincheloe, too (1999: 51),

> If the discourse of Western science is mechanistic, exact, hypothesis driven, and in search of facts, universal generalizations, and grand theories, the discourse of many indigenous knowledge systems is metaphysical, based on the forces that connect people to one another, and inseparable from religion. Often agricultural, culinary, medical, architectural knowledges in indigenous discourses are intricately intertwined with the theological realm. . . . Once individuals come to believe that Western science is not the only legitimate knowledge producer, then maybe a conversation can be opened about different forms of research and knowledge production that take issues of locality, cultural values, and social justice seriously.

Setting aside the questionable uses of "knowledge" and "science" in the latter regard, arguably only an approach striving for universality *can* take cultural values and social justice seriously.[12] Any other approach will relocate them to the realm of the local and particular, where no value judgments are possible, at least not translocally or transculturally—including judgments about the evils of colonization, "Western practices of oppression" of indigenous peoples (29, 47), or "Western science's destruction of the earth" (16).[13] I next turn to the idea of traditional ecological (or environmental) knowledge.

NOTES

1. In what follows, unreferenced quotations refer to excerpts I transcribed from the film (see also Horsthemke 2008a: 333–335; Horsthemke 2017de: 586–587).

2. See also Van Sertima (1999: 310–314), Seepe (2000: 125), Zulu (2006: 40).
3. The page numbers refer to the online version of the article.
4. The archaeologists doing the excavations were naturally aware of the enormous scientific value of studying the hairs' DNA for clues about the origin of the prehistoric inhabitants of the area. However, as soon as the discovery was made public, two nearby Native American tribes demanded that the research stop. After a two-year battle, the regulations by which the Federal Bureau of Land Management was guided were revised to exclude naturally shed hair. Nevertheless, at the time the article appeared the team of scientists was still waiting for permission to perform the requisite chemical analysis (Johnson 1996: 1).
5. U.S. Congress passed the Native American Graves Protection and Repatriation Act in 1990.
6. This error appears in a wide range of contributions. Thus, Mahia Maurial (1999: 64) states categorically that "Power defines knowledge." Prakash (1999: 163), similarly, asserts that "Power decides what is and what is not knowledge" (see also Semali and Kincheloe 1999: 28, 29). Perhaps. But this does not make something knowledge or bar something from being knowledge, objectively. It only indicates that mistakes are frequently made in attempts to determine what is and what is not knowledge. Donald Trump's decisions on what is and what is not the case may be examples of strong-arm tactics, of wielding power from a position of political authority, but they have no bearing at all on knowledge and truth.
7. Elgin is well aware of the objections that might be raised against the position she defends here, namely that it might "make the world safe for postmodernist claptrap," that we "lose a valuable resource if we can't simply say" that something is false (Elgin 2004: 128). While I find Elgin's quantitative account of truth problematic, I think she moves in the right direction with the defense she mounts for her own position, namely that a theory has to be factually defeasible, in order to be scientifically tenable and epistemically desirable. A theory is factually defeasible if "there is some reasonably determinate, epistemically accessible factual arrangement which, if it were found to obtain, would discredit the theory" (Elgin 2004: 129). For reasons that will become clearer later, I do not think that Elgin's account can be used to buttress Green's arguments.
8. The dilemma is brought out in the following telling passage:

I am not saying that truth itself is a threshold concept. . . . My point is rather that epistemic acceptability turns not on whether a sentence is true but on whether it is *true enough*—that is, on whether it is close enough to the truth. 'True enough' obviously has threshold. (Elgin 2004: 115; emphasis added)

The process of approximating truth is one of justification and/or reliability: 'true enough' would mean little more than 'adequately justified', or 'as reliable as can be reasonably expected'. Furthermore, if truth is not a threshold concept but 'true enough' is, then the latter cannot do the work of the former. If this is correct, the notion of 'true enough' has been rendered superfluous.
9. Elsewhere (2002: 14; see also Green 2009: 47), Elgin argues,

If epistemology is concerned exclusively with the context of justification, and the context of justification is concerned exclusively with questions like whether evidence concerns a given hypothesis, then . . . aesthetic factors [like metaphor, fiction, and exemplification, which provide alternative ways of seeing, representing, and understanding phenomena] have no epistemological role. But we need not accept this view.

Indeed, we need not and do not subscribe to such an exclusive notion of epistemology and justification. As I made clear in chapter 3, epistemology is concerned not only with the context but also with the degree as well as different kinds of justification. Moreover, while justification in the natural sciences is concerned with evidence, justification in mathematics and logic deals with proof, and justification in ethics and politics involves reasons. Aesthetic factors may well have an epistemological role—provided that one is aware of their metaphorical or fictional character. "Knowledge can be presented in fiction" (Green 2009: 49), but this does not mean that the fiction and metaphors themselves ("the story of a monkey's journey through the night sky," "shamans driving boats," and so on; 43, 45) necessarily constitute knowledge.

10. On this view, scientific theories are concerned with "real states and structures of nature, and succeed" and build on "each other as successive approximations to the full truth" (Flew 1984: 320). It should be noted that the relationship between defeasibility and truth resembles that between justification and truth.

11. On traditional medical practices and their marginalization in South Africa and Mozambique, see also Xaba (2007) and Meneses (2007), respectively. Quite fascinatingly, the prevalent Chinese conception is that the competence of a medical practitioner is not measured in terms of healing people, but rather in terms of people not falling ill, that is, remaining healthy.

12. Siegel (2002) provides a very thoughtful account of what 'universalism' does and does not involve. In exploring possible common ground between universalism and multiculturalism in science education, he considers the justification of multicultural science education. This justification, he contends, is *moral* (rather than epistemological) in nature. Moreover, "if science education is indeed obliged to embrace multiculturalism, that obligation must itself be understood to be a culturally transcendent one" (803).

13. This anti-relativist approach, incidentally, also renders possible condemnation of unethical scientific practices, irrespective of their scientific worth and contribution to knowledge production. Thus, Nazi doctor Josef Mengele's experiments on Jewish twins at the Institute for Heredity Biology and Racial Hygiene in Frankfurt and later, from May 1943, in the concentration camp of Auschwitz, purportedly yielded a few insights into genetic inheritance, but their putative scientific merits are vastly outweighed by the profound inhumanity and immorality of the 'research'. https://www.bbc.com/news/magazine-30933718 (retrieved 18 June 2020).

Chapter 7

Traditional Ecological (or Environmental) Knowledge

ISILWANE/THE ANIMAL

In 1996, Credo Mutwa[1] published *Isilwane/The Animal*, essentially an account of "the reverence in which animals are held according to African ritual and tradition" (1996: back cover blurb). Among the many fascinating 'traditional tales' contained in the book is Mutwa's account of why the cat is "more than just a pet" (30): "treating a cat properly guarantees that it will protect you against the *tokoloshe* and the *mantindane*" (31). He goes on to provide the following account, which is worth quoting in virtual entirety:

> From the Cape right up to Zaire, there is a fearful creature known as the *tokoloshe*. It is short, thickset, round-headed and furry, with a round snout and a pair of glowing, bright red eyes. It has pointed ears and a thick, bony ridge extending from above its forehead to the nape of its neck. This creature, short though it is, is extremely aggressive and viciously cruel. It specializes in sexually assaulting women and challenges benighted travellers to stick fights which it triumphantly wins. (Ibid.)

Mutwa writes that in the course of his career as a traditional healer, he has "come across many women who have been sexually molested and even raped by this terrible creature, which moves in the shadowy field where the real and the unreal, the visible and the invisible meet" (ibid.). "As a *sanusi*," Mutwa has

> treated many men who have been beaten and frightened out of their wits by the *tokoloshe*. However, there are some people, especially white sceptics, who

183

believe that the *tokoloshe* is nothing more than a figment of African superstition and fertile imagination. (32)

Referring to the fact that he possesses "over fifty years of experience," Mutwa feels impelled to

> appeal to these sceptics to think again. The *tokoloshe* is real—it does exist. I have seen the way it injures men and women who are unfortunate enough to fall into its clutches. When Africans fear the *tokoloshe* they are not fearing a figment of their imaginations. Instead of being laughed off by sceptics, the *tokoloshe* deserves investigation. (Ibid.)

"There is another creature," he reports,

> which is not unlike the *tokoloshe* in its love of inflicting bodily harm, and which is also greatly feared. . . . Like the *tokoloshe*, the *mantindane* stands about three-and-a-half feet tall. Unlike the *tokoloshe*, which is a powerfully built, almost chimpanzee-like creature, it appears extremely frail. It has a large, bald, egg-shaped head which can be as large as a fully grown watermelon, and it has very weak-looking jaws. Its mouth is little more than a slit and the nose is rudimentary, with nostrils like comma-shaped holes. The creature's eyes are very strange and resemble beans. They are slanted and covered with what looks like thick, jet-black plastic or horn. It has a very thin neck, narrow shoulders and long, thin arms, and its hands, although resembling those of a human being, are very thin and long. Its long, thin and bony fingers have more joints than those of a human being. The creature's two spindly legs end in long, delicate feet. The *mantindane* is civilized and highly intelligent, and unlike the *tokoloshe*, which appears stark-naked, it always wears some type of garment that reaches from its neck and covers its limbs completely. The color of this creature's skin is a strange greyish white with slight pink overtones. Like the *tokoloshe*, the *mantindane* treats human beings who fall into its hands cruelly and with utter contempt. It kidnaps males and females and scoops out flesh from their legs, thighs and even buttocks and upper arms. Unlike the *tokoloshe* which is solitary, *mantindane* operate in groups. There can be as many as twenty of these vicious creatures in one group.
>
> Sometimes a gang of *mantindane* will kidnap a person and ill-treat him or her. They will then release the person, only to kidnap them again a few months or even a few years later. (Ibid.)

Mutwa states that he has "met many black men and women throughout Africa who have been kidnapped by these creatures several times, and who bear scars on their bodies that testify to their terrible ordeals at the hands of these strange and fearful beings" (ibid.). "I have personally fallen victim to *mantindane*," he reports, "not once, but three times—and I still carry scars on my body that testify to the truth of what I say" (ibid.).

Mutwa's account is noteworthy, in the present context, for its implicit acknowledgment of the conditions that are generally assumed to have to be in place when we make knowledge claims: belief, truth, and appropriate justification ('experience', evidence, testimony). Clearly, "many black men and women throughout Africa" believe that the *tokoloshe* and *mantindane* are real, that they exist. Equally clearly, beliefs in these creatures might be put to educational use in terms of comparative studies of cultural creativity and myth-making (see Lillejord and Mkabela 2004). Do these beliefs constitute 'African ways of knowing', however, and can (and should) they be taught as 'African knowledge'? Before one can even begin to answer these questions, one ought to be clear about what is involved in judging others' knowledge claims, especially if these 'others' adhere to what would appear to be substantially different epistemological traditions. Am I inflicting 'epistemic harm' on someone when I judge her beliefs to be untrue and/or lacking in adequate justification? When I refer to the *tokoloshe* or *mantindane* as "a figment of African superstition and fertile imagination," does this constitute 'epistemic injustice' toward those who hold the beliefs in question? The problem of epistemic injustice will be addressed in chapter 9 below. Evidently, the most desirable way of proceeding would be by trying to understand how those who have certain beliefs could see them as plausible, to grasp the concepts they use. What, exactly, is 'traditional ecological knowledge', and what is the invocation of such knowledge meant to accomplish?

"WE SEE NATURE DIFFERENTLY AND SPEAK TO AND ABOUT IT DIFFERENTLY"

According to Zimbabwean novelist Chenjerai Hove,

We have neither catalogued nature nor pinned it down and preserved it in formaldehyde. We see it differently and speak to and about it differently. (Grill 2003: 363; my translation[2])

Hove is arguably correct about one thing. Practices like large-scale dissection, vivisection, and, generally, all scientific experimentation involving nonhuman animals appear to have been pioneered and exported all over the globe by monetarily inclined 'Westerners'. The same goes for the so-called 'scientific' factory farming and mass slaughter of food animals. That indigenous peoples' custodianship would serve the Amazon rain forest far better than Brazilian president Jair Bolsonaro's short-sightedly capitalist and autocratic, exploitative rule is so obvious that it barely requires mention. Of course, this subjugationist and expansionist mindset and drive claimed countless human victims, too—which may explain the accusations made by or on behalf of indigenous people, Africans, indigenous Americans and Australian aboriginal people, accusations like Hove's. But is Hove correct when he claims, "We see [nature] differently and speak to and about it differently"?

Hove's view is shared by many writers and theorists. Semali and Kincheloe (1999: 16) refer to the

> use of indigenous knowledge to counter Western science's destruction of the earth. Indigenous knowledge can facilitate this ambitious project because of its tendency to focus on relationships of humans to both one another and to their ecosystem.

Later in their chapter, again echoing Hove, the authors contend that in "indigenous knowledge systems the Eurocentric epistemology of studying, knowing (mastering), and then dominating the world seems frighteningly out of place, as it upsets the sacred kinship between humans and other creations of nature" (43). Viergever (1999: 335) adds that the "alternative solutions" proposed in indigenous systems of knowledge are often "equally effective and environmentally more sustainable" (see also Senanayake 2006; Eyong 2007; Ng'Asike 2019; Tom et al. 2019),[3] while Goduka (2000: 67, 68) enumerates the "principles reflective of indigenous philosophical ways of knowing": "collective responsibility of caring for Mother Earth," "interrelatedness, interconnectedness and interdependence among humans, living and non-living creation." In what follows, I present examples of both the relational understanding of indigenous environmental knowledge (also noted by Daes 1997: 3; Corntassel and Hardbarger 2019: 104–110; Crazy Bull and White Hat 2019) and compatibilist approaches, that is, the idea of a possible synthesis between traditional knowledge and modern science in regard of ecology and the environment.

Both types of approaches can be found in an essay by Fikret Berkes and Mina Kislalioglu Berkes (2009: 6), National Resources Institute of the University of Manitoba in Canada. They indicate that

> some indigenous groups have resource-use practices that suggest a sophisticated understanding of ecological relationships and dynamics . . . Such practices tend to be backed up by worldviews that see human beings as part of the ecosystem, based on relationships of respect for the land and for living beings.

Furthermore, referring to the First Salmon ceremony of several indigenous groups of the Pacific Northwest of North America, they suggest that the "qualitative assessment of a sufficient number of mature fish (spawners) swimming upstream to perpetuate the population" made by an experienced ritual leader "can produce results similar to one achieved by a biological management system with population models, counting fences, daily data management, and harvest quota enforcement—but without the whole research infrastructure, quantitative data needs, and associated costs" (7). Berkes and Berkes refer to the capturing and integration of local and scientific knowledge as being governed by "fuzzy logic," "an approach that may help understand, or provide insights, on the question of how local and indigenous knowledge systems may be dealing with complexity" (ibid.).

Peruvian anthropologist Mahia Maurial (1999: 62) associates indigenous knowledge with indigenous "peoples' cognitive and wise legacy as a result of their interaction with nature." Indeed, they "and their territories may teach . . . Western teachers and researchers . . . a way to be *ecologically* literate or how to read the world in a dialogical relationship with nature" (ibid.). The settings for such indigenous education, teaching, and learning, are "homes, rivers, gardens, and forests" (65). Trinidad-born science educator June George (1999: 79) considers the "growing interest in indigenous knowledge" to be "perhaps directly related to growing concerns about degradation of the environment," yet this is "only one of the areas in which good use can be made of indigenous knowledge." She envisages the "inclusion of students' prior knowledge in the school curriculum" (84) to generatively supplement conventional science. Le Grange (2004: 88) concurs:

> (South) Africa has to use the good of Western science and also recognize its negative side that has destroyed natural environments and denigrated the cultures of African people. Invoking the term indigenous knowledge can engage Western science deconstructively so as to overcome the binary opposition between Western science and indigenous knowledge.

Yet, not all authors share the idea of a possible synthesis. Madhu Suri Prakash (1999: 157, 158), after mentioning the claim to universality and objectivity of modern science and its propagators, states that, given "cultural and ecological damage being perpetrated by [modern science] on a global scale, critics have postulated the existence of two distinct and incompatible types of science or knowledge systems" (160). He refers to the incommensurability and fundamental difference between modern scientific and other knowledge systems (167, 168). It should be clear that, on this characterization, there is no basis for comparing and evaluating different types of science and knowledge systems.

In terms of such a contrast, Odora Hoppers (2005: 3) refers to traditional knowledge as

> the totality of all knowledges and practices . . . used in the management of socio-economic, spiritual, and ecological facets of life. In this sense it can be contrasted with 'cosmopolitan knowledge' that is culturally anchored in Western cosmology, scientific discoveries, economic preferences, and philosophies.

She continues (4–6):

> The relationship between people, the knowledge and the technologies for its application are under-girded by a cosmology, a world view. . . . Relationships between people hold pride of place, expressed in the various philosophies across Africa, and best captured by the African concept of *Ubuntu* . . . In the context of such a philosophy, IKS [indigenous knowledge systems] practice does not seek to conquer or debilitate nature as a first impulse. This can be contrasted, for instance, with . . . the mechanistic conception of reality . . . IKS stresses instead the essential interrelatedness and interdependence of all phenomena—biological, physical, psychological, social, and cultural. Indigenous cosmology centres on the co-evolution of the spiritual, natural, and human worlds. . . . Experiences from indigenous communities in other parts of the world emphasize the fact that knowledge is relationship, and relationship brings with it responsibilities and obligations and extends into ecological practice.

Odora Hoppers's contribution is one of numerous attempts to extend the African idea of *ubuntu, botho,* or *hunhu* (Ramose 2002b: 325, 326; Ramose 2009: 309, 312) beyond the realm of moral concern for our species. Thus, Makgoba, Ramose, and Le Grange, respectively, employ *ubuntu* as a locus for "fostering human respect for the environment" (Makgoba 1996: 23), an orientation "towards balance and harmony in the relationship between [human beings] and the broader be-ing or nature" (Ramose 2002b: 326; hyphenation in the original text), and as "an expression of interconnectedness between people themselves, and between people and the biophysical world" (Le Grange 2012: 63). "Humanness" (*ubuntu, botho,* or *hunhu*—in IsiZulu, SeSotho, and ChiShona, respectively), Ramose explains,

> regards being, or the universe, as a complex wholeness involving the multi-layered and incessant interaction of all entities. . . . The principle of wholeness applies also to the relation between human beings and *physical or objective nature*. To care for one another, therefore, implies caring for *physical nature* as well. Without such care, the interdependence between human beings and physical nature would be undermined. Moreover, human beings are indeed an

intrinsic part of physical nature although possibly a privileged part. Accordingly, caring for one another is the fulfilment of the natural duty to care for physical nature too. The concept of harmony in African thought . . . conceives of balance in terms of the totality of the relations . . . between and among human beings, as well as between human beings and physical nature. (Ramose 2009: 309; emphasis added)

Goduka (2000: 69), too, name-checks the "guiding principles" embedded in "the languages of the indigenes" that "reflect this interconnectedness": "*Mitakuye oyasin*—of the Lakota tradition—*we are all related* . . . and the principle of *yobuntu* [*ubuntu*]—*I am we*; *I am because we are*—we are because I am, in other words, we are all related because *I am in you*—*you are in me*" . . . are examples of unity in diversity."

North American educational theorists Bryan McKinley Jones Brayboy and Emma Maugham (2009: 13) contend, similarly, that indigenous knowledge systems are premised on a "circular worldview that connects everything and everyone in the world to everything and everyone else, where there is no distinction between the physical and the metaphysical and where ancestral knowledge guides contemporary practices and future possibilities." This fundamental holistic or circular understanding does not distinguish between the mind and the body, "between human and other earthly inhabitants, and among generations" (ibid.). It is also "central to how many indigenous people view their own places within the larger cosmos of all living things": when everyone and everything is connected, "a person has a responsibility to act according to her surroundings"—that is, she "understands that her actions affect everything else, and she is invested in maintaining necessary balance." As Arapaho scholar Michael Marker has put it (2003: 105–106),

> This emphasis on relationships puts animals, plants, and landscapes in the active role of *teacher* and therefore results in a more holistic and integrated understanding of phenomena. This kind of holism resists constrictive and contrived taxonomy as well as disciplinary boundaries. It also produces a state of consciousness in the Aboriginal intellectual that makes on separation between scientific and moral understandings.

Diné scholar Brian Yazzie Burkhart (2004: 25) provides an indigenous version of the Cartesian *cogito*: "We are, therefore I am." He argues (16–17) that there is

> no world, no truth, without meaning and value, and meaning and value arise in the intersection between us and all that is around us. . . . The idea is simply that the universe is moral. Facts, truth, meaning, even our existence are normative.

In this way, there is no difference between what is true and what is right. On this account, then, all investigation is moral investigation.

It follows from this that community-based knowledges require individuals to be concerned both about their own and others' well-being (see Brayboy and Maugham 2009: 16).

Is the claim that the universe is moral any more illuminating than it would be to say that it is 'non-moral', that all so-called 'norms' and 'values' are physically, chemically, or genetically determined or 'fixed'—or indeed that the universe is 'selfish', that there is no world, no truth, without or beyond self-interest, and that everything in the universe is geared toward self-preservation and self-perpetuation? 'I am, therefore we are.' Is this *obviously* wrong? Who is to say that *Mitakuye oyasin* is not essentially determined by genetic selfishness, or at least by anthropocentrism? Burkhart (23) argues that "American Indian philosophy is concerned with the right road for humans to walk in relation to all that is around them." If "what is right is true and what is true is right," then what would preclude the addition of 'for humans' in each instance? Burkhart's own question (17)—"if acting in a certain way leads to the wrong path, creates the wrong truth, how do we *know* when a certain way of acting will lead to the right path or even which is the right path?"—indicates not only the difficulty of determining the right course of action but also the logical incoherence of such a reductionist enterprise. What could "the wrong truth" possibly mean, beyond the nonsensical 'the wrong right' or 'the false truth'?

What about *ubuntu*? Are Makgoba, Ramose, Odora Hoppers, Le Grange, and Goduka right about the capacity of *ubuntu* to accommodate concern for nonhuman nature in and for itself? In what follows the account given above, Ramose refers in the main to "human dignity" (312) and our relevant choices and duties. The African principle of human interdependence states that a person becomes a person through other persons. Or, in other words, a human being depends on human beings to be a human being: *Umuntu ngumuntu ngabantu*, or *Motho ke motho ka batho*, or *Munhu munhu navhanhu*. It would appear, then, that the envisaged concern for nonhuman nature and the environment could be fostered only on the basis of human benefits and would therefore not amount to any acknowledgement of the inherent value of nature or the environment, let alone of nonhuman animals. Nor could the principle in question constitute a basis for "respect" or a "harmonious relationship" (at least in any deeper or more meaningful sense) with members of other-than-human species. That is, the immediate and direct beneficiaries of such a relationship or "respect" must be human beings, whether as agents or recipients. In fact, in focusing exclusively on human beings, *ubuntu* is by definition anthropocentric, as is the popular Sesotho slogan *batho pele*—"people first."[4] This essential human-centredness of *ubuntu* is suggested explicitly by Odora Hoppers (2002a: 6) who, as we saw earlier, claims that "Relationships between people hold pride of place—best explained by the concept of Ubuntu." A similar relational-anthropocentric concern emerges in slain Black Consciousness leader Steve Bantu Biko's famous essay exploring certain African cultural concepts (2004: 46):

> We regard our living together not as an unfortunate mishap warranting endless competition among us but as a deliberate act of God to make us a community of brothers and sisters jointly involved in the quest for a composite answer to the varied problems in life. Hence in all we do we always place Man first and hence all our action is usually joint community-oriented action rather than the individualism which is the hallmark of the capitalist approach.

At best, then, the principle(s) in question yield what is generally referred to as an "indirect-duty view" or an account of "indirect concern" for nonhuman nature, including animals. Our duties and obligations regarding other animals cannot be duties and obligations "to" them because they lack the prerequisite humanness. Yet, insofar as the ill-treatment of these creatures may have an impact on our dealings with human beings (that is, it may make us "raw" or "insensitive" in our interactions with fellow humans), as well as on the feelings of the latter (to whom, after all, we have direct duties, because of our shared humanity), it is advisable that we refrain from maltreating the former. Again, this is advisable *not* because of any duties to animals—who, after all, exist only as part of "physical or objective nature" (Ramose 2009: 309), that is (by implication) lacking mental life and "subjectivity." Referring to our "duties" to them (even following Ramose, of our "natural duty to care") is only a roundabout way of speaking of our actual duties to human beings. It follows that *ubuntu* does not, indeed *cannot*, concern animals directly—obviously not as moral agents, but not as moral recipients either. I do not, therefore, share South African library archivist and animal rights activist Michelè Pickover's opinion (2005: 171) that "Animal liberation is . . . a natural progression of our humanity, embodying the powerful concept of *ubuntu*."

South African educational philosopher Moeketsi Letseka (2000: 186) has, however unwittingly, pointed out the chasm that exists between *ubuntu/botho/hunhu* and concern for animals:

> Consider . . . the case of an offence on which everyone agrees that it is heinous and an affront to *botho* or *ubuntu*, such as repeatedly raping an eighty-year-old grandmother or a six-year-old girl. To express their displeasure community folk might utter statements like: "He is not a person but a dog" [or] "Oh God, he is an animal."

The dubious move of equating rapists and animals like dogs might be excused as reporting an unreflective popular view, but it arguably indicates something more profound—namely the perception that animals occupy a territory untouched by ordinary moral considerations and concerns: indeed, an amoral realm.

Perhaps it is uncharitable to focus exclusively on *ubuntu* (I will return to this and related ideas in the next chapter)—which constitutes an improvement on egoism, and maximization of self-interest, but is still decidedly anthropocentric—as exemplifying African ethical attitudes toward animals and the environment. According to moral theorists, Africa has additional conceptual resources that might help address questions around direct ethical responsibility regarding nonhuman nature, resources that involve an extension of the traditional ideas of 'relatedness' and 'relationality'. Whereas some thinkers emphasize African holism, "solidarity with creation as a whole" and "cosmic community" (Bujo 2009: 284, 296), an ethic of "nature-relatedness" (Ogungbemi 1997) or "eco-bio-communitarianism" (Tangwa 2004), others draw on the notion of *ukama* originating in Zimbabwe (Murove 2004 and 2009: 315–316; Le Grange 2012: 61–62). Unlike *ubuntu*, *ukama* asserts that a person can be a person in, with and through not just other people (those who are still alive as well as ancestors) and but also in, with and through the natural environment. As Zimbabwean philosopher Munyaradzi Felix Murove explains, *ukama* (meaning "relatedness"; 2009: 302)

> is a Shona word implying relationship and an understanding of reality in terms of interdependence. Grammatically *ukama* is an adjective constructed *u-kama*. . . . *Kama* becomes a word meaning to milk a cow or goat. In Shona thought the idea of milking suggests closeness and affection. (316)

Tellingly, the 'closeness' in question derives from an animal being used, first and foremost, for human ends and purposes. Indeed: "*Umuntu* [man] is always in need of others and these others, as suggested in *ukama*, also imply the natural environment" (324). Just insofar, one might add, as the "natural environment" (which may be taken to include animals) meets and satisfies *umuntu*'s needs—personal, cultural, or other. Murove continues (316):

> In its adjectival form, *ukama* means being related or belonging to the same family. However, in Shona, as in many other African languages, the meaning of *ukama* is not restricted to marital or blood ties. This culture tends to see all people as *hama* (relatives).

"All people"—which effectively excludes nonhuman animals and the environment. Tellingly, however, the "closeness" in question derives from an animal being used, first and foremost, for human ends and purposes. Congolese philosopher Bénézet Bujo's notions of "cosmic community" (2009) and of the relationality of all life, and of holism *tout court*, too, remain perfectly compatible with a largely instrumental view of nonhuman nature.[5] Nigerian environmental philosopher Segun Ogungbemi's ethic of "nature-relatedness" is located in the "ethics of care" (1997) that characterized traditional African society. It recognizes that human existence necessarily depends on the natural world, and it is because of this reliance that humans must treat the environments in which they live with due respect—for the sake of current human and future well-being, not because of any intrinsic value or dignity animals and the natural environment may possess. Similarly, although Cameroonian environmental ethicist Godfrey Tangwa speaks of a tendency toward cosmic humility and cautiousness "in their attitude to plants, animals, and inanimate things" (2004: 389) on the part of ordinary Africans, and although the "traditional worldview . . . does not suppose that human beings have any mandate or special privilege, God-given or otherwise, to subdue, dominate, and exploit the rest of creation," he mentions "frequent offerings of sacrifices to God" (389–390). What do these offerings of sacrifices comprise, if not "plants, animals, and inanimate things"? How is the traditional "live and let live"-attitude to be squared with the anthropocentrism of ordinary Africans and their "contribution to environmental hazards," as identified by Ogungbemi (1997: 204)?

A further, important question concerns *umuntu*'s actual responsibilities with regard to nonhuman nature. The mere moral injunction to harmonize humanity's behavior with the natural environment does not tell much about *umuntu*'s concrete, specific responsibilities and duties. In fact, the imperative of 'harmonization' could be—and indeed has been—considered compatible with, perhaps even to require, the bare-handed slaughtering of bulls,[6] for the sake of 'good relations' between *umuntu* and *amadlozi* (the ancestors) or *abaphansi* (the living dead), and even 'future generations'. Murove's account (2008: 85) of visiting and dining with a friend's relatives in a rural area 40 kilometers from Harare in Zimbabwe (an event he takes to illustrate cordial relations even between strangers on the African continent) provides further telling information:

> A live sheep was presented to us according to custom. After we clapped our hands in gratitude, the sheep was taken away for slaughter.

There is no acknowledgment at all that there may be a moral issue here. Insofar as *ubuntu* and *ukama* have any action-guiding content at all, this is unlikely to have any primary, direct beneficiaries other than human beings. Therefore, like *ubuntu* and most of the environmentalist positions it engenders, *ukama* remains essentially and explicitly anthropocentric.

If this is plausible, if not correct (see also Enslin and Horsthemke 2004: 548; Horsthemke 2010a: 125–127, 2015: 78–85), then the difference between African knowledge systems and the 'Western', 'mechanistic', subjugationist conception of nature and reality is not radical but one of degree, not qualitative but quantitative. One is left to wonder whether, given comparable economic and military powers, so-called 'IKS practice' would not have led to a similar kind and extent of abuse and exploitation, in the name and for the sake of "human solidarity" (Odora Hoppers 2005: 4). Similar considerations apply to native American ideas like *mitakuye oyasin* and *wahkohtowin*.

INDIGENOUS RIGHTS VERSUS ANIMAL RIGHTS

In 1988, a roundtable debate was held between native American trappers and animal advocates.[7] William Cronon was the moderator. David Monture, Bob Stevenson, and Alan Hersovici represented the trappers, while Michael O'Sullivan and Patrice Greanville argued in defense of animal interests. The focus of the debate was the conflict between the rights of indigenous peoples to continue a traditional way of life and the rights of animals. The animal rights advocates found themselves in the awkward position of trying to help one oppressed class—animals—by hindering another—native Americans. The trappers, on the other hand, faced the dilemma of emphasizing the subsistence-value and spiritual or cultural value of their practices and, at the same time, urging support of a fur industry that is alienated from any relationship or respect with regard to the fur-bearing animal and guided solely by economic considerations. At one point in the dispute, O'Sullivan stated that animal advocates are

> not interested in imposing a value system on any culture, [but] when we see cruelty to animals within a society we have a right to challenge that society. In focusing on the fur issue, we are concerned about the cruelty caused to animals and not who is causing the cruelty. (*The Animals' Agenda*, December 1988: 56–57)

The fur industry has to a large extent been successful in convincing the public that trapping (like hunting) is necessary for wildlife management, conservation, and rabies control. Even if these reasons were compelling,[8] this line of defense involves a considerable distortion of the facts. Insofar as hunting and trapping are done primarily to supply pelts for the fur market, hunters, and trappers target the species whose skins are most in demand economically. Traps, for example, are set and baited to catch healthy animals as they move about their habitat and forage for food. Weak, sick, and aged animals, susceptible to starvation, are usually neither the actual nor the intended victims of traps. Hence, trapping is at best unsound wildlife management practice, allowing outbreaks of rabies and other diseases to spread. Moreover, the traps used (whether leg-holds, snares, or conibears), are hardly 'humane', contrary to what trapping advocates claim.

The question of elephant management is widely regarded as one of the more intractable problems in South Africa. Generally valued as magnificent and among the most intelligent members of South Africa's wildlife population, admired by South Africans and foreign tourists alike, elephants are also considered to be among the most problematic in that they have a substantial impact on their environment. Mutwa (1996: 109) provides the following account of the elephant:

> African people regard the elephant with a very deep reverence. It is an animal believed to be more than just a beast—it is considered a spiritual entity. The Zulu, Tswana and Tsonga names for the elephant all mean 'the forceful one', 'the unstoppable one'. In Zulu the name for an elephant is *indlovu*, from the verb *dlovu*, which means 'to crash through', 'to pierce savagely', 'to act with extreme brute force'. The Tswana and Sotho word for elephant, *tlou*, and the Tsonga word, *njovu*, also carry this meaning. . . . African people believed that elephants were reincarnations of murdered gods, gods who had been treacherously slain by other gods in the unseen land and who were reborn on Earth as elephants. (Mutwa 1996: 109)

Given a tradition of "deep reverence" for elephants, how is this to be squared with contemporary perceptions and policy around the culling—or 'legal' (that is, government-controlled) killing for purposes of population management? At the Great Elephant Indaba in March 2005,[9] Michael Masuluke spoke on behalf of the communities bordering Kruger National Park, referring to "the olden days when people and animals lived harmoniously together, before fences were erected" (Report on the Great Elephant Indaba 2005: 12). "Now," he said,

> things are different. Human movement and social activities have become restricted. People are afraid to go to their farms because elephants have taken over. They destroy the crops which are the sole source of living for poor communities. The elephants compete with livestock for grazing land and have taken over rivers where once community dwellers would draw water, do their washing, and bring their livestock to drink. Unlike in the past where communities enjoyed peaceful co-habitation, there have recently been a number of cases, documented and undocumented, of human mortality caused by elephants.

These and related concerns are also discussed by Farieda Khan, long-time researcher in the field of South African environmental history:

> [T]he acceptance and implementation of environmental justice has not been a smooth process, nor has it been without conflict, given the persistent legacy of a conservation ideology which rates the survival of endangered indigenous fauna and flora above that of the poor. The persistence of this legacy may clearly be seen in the following responses to animal rights issues. The first is from the representative of a poor rural community, who stated, 'I strongly caution the animal rights groups that they do not colonise our minds. Gone are those days. It would be better if you aim your ideals toward the balancing of animal rights and human rights' (Makuleke 1997). The second statement is extracted from a newspaper editorial which gave voice to the feelings of many people when it criticized the moral priorities of a society in which far more publicity, public sympathy, and support followed an exposé of the abuse of young elephants than ever greeted the many instances of torture and murder of human beings, most of them poor and black: 'Those facing the brutality of everyday existence find it difficult to feel strongly about animal suffering. . . . The animal rights lobby might gain even more widespread support for their cause if they were at least as active in voicing their protest against cruelty to people' (*Sunday Argus* 10 July 1999). (Khan 2000: 42, 43)[10]

What makes the issue of 'culling' different from cases of abuse and cruelty, as in the Tuli elephant case referred to in the excerpt above[11] is that culling is characteristically seen to require justification, whether in terms of resources, health, welfare, or interests. I will briefly discuss the cultural argument in favor of hunting and culling.[12]

"The expressions of African values and judgments on the issue of elephant management, particularly on the issue of culling, have been largely neglected," according to environmental researchers David Cummings, Angela Gaylard, Guy Castley and Ian Whyte (n.d.: 356): "There is a clear need to rectify this situation and to reliably establish what those values and views may be—particularly from park neighbors." There are various formulations of what might be called the 'cultural' argument in favor of culling. What they arguably share is a diagnosis of human/elephant conflicts and the emphasis that such conflicts ought to be decided, unequivocally, in favor of human beings. Any over-riding concern for elephants is misplaced, an example or expression of 'Western'/'Eurocentric' bias, racism and ethical colonialism. In an interview with the South African weekly newspaper *Mail & Guardian* on the issue of land use, Makuleke leader Gilbert Nwaila is reported as saying:

> You should tell these people who like wildlife that they should come and speak to us before they make statements about how our land is used. And when

they come, they should remember we suffered greatly when our villages were destroyed, and our homes burnt down so that Kruger [National Park] could be made bigger. . . . Now that we have a chance to get some wealth from that land, we are being told to put even more animals there. It will be very difficult to convince our people that wildlife is better than mining. (*Mail & Guardian*, 18–24 August 1995; quoted in Khan 2000: 40)

Nwaila's frustrations are made even more touching by the understatement in his complaints. It is difficult not to sympathize with the feelings and perceptions of, say, small-scale communities and farmers whose livelihood and very existence is threatened by roaming elephants. At the Great Elephant Indaba, Masuluke and Mzwandile Mjadu (who spoke on behalf of the community of Addo Elephant Park in the Eastern Cape, South Africa) discussed the problems they face in their communities, mostly poor rural communities that border on the national parks and that "bear the brunt of unchecked elephant invasions and, as a result, suffer economic and social upheaval, destruction of their crops and the very real threat of conflict from elephants and other species which follow in their wake" (op. cit.: 12). Elaborating on some of the problems that community dwellers face, Masuluke contended that

> urban dwellers can call for assistance if they find a rodent in their house, but in the rural areas, if you walk out one morning and find an elephant munching away at your roof, there is to one to call for help. There are also the problems caused as a result of fence breaking which allows the dispersal of other species, resulting in crop raiding, threats to livestock, and the possible spread of disease. (Ibid.: 13; on the links between elephants' destruction of fences and the spread of disease, see also Cummings et al. n.d.: 358)

The occidental image of the 'noble savage' living in complete harmony with the fauna and flora around him [*sic*] has been shown to be hopelessly romantic. The forces of the market-driven economy favor neither indigenous communities nor 'wildlife', contrary to what Nwaila is suggesting, in anything other than an instrumental sense. They are guided by the dictum, 'If it pays, it stays'. If human and nonhuman communities (note: not individuals, but groups) happen to benefit from these economic arrangements, so much the better, but such benefits are not among the priorities of big business. These impoverished rural communities, as Julian Sturgeon of Resource Africa pointed out at the Great Elephant Indaba (op. cit.: 12),

> are not usually involved in what is going on inside the conserved areas and this causes feelings of being excluded; not being important in the greater scheme of things. They may have suffered land losses or grazing ground. They are subject

to conflict, attacks and destruction of property through broken fences which are not maintained or repaired. This leads to poaching and border problems, and general dissatisfaction amongst communities.

Having noted this fundamental lack of parity, I want to make three comments in response to the scenario presented by Khan, comments that also bear on the community representatives' queries. First, consistency in one's concern for animals' rights requires commitment to the rights of humans. Being for animal rights and being for human rights are not mutually exclusive but, on the contrary, part of the same moral fabric. One cannot consistently reject speciesism if one does not also vehemently oppose racism and sexism. Indeed, opposition to racism and sexism is superficial without any commitment to end at least some of the wrongs suffered by countless numbers of animals each day (see Horsthemke 2010: v, 66–67; Horsthemke 2015: xi). Second, public outcry against abuse, cruelty, torture, and murder is characteristically fired by putting a face and (where available) a name to the individual victims of violence and brutality, irrespective of whether they are human or nonhuman. Faceless and nameless crimes do not generally elicit publicity, and public sympathy and support. Third, cautions like Makuleke's (see above; Makuleke 1997; Khan 2000: 43) have also been directed toward feminists and women's rights groups. Are objections to polygamy, unrelenting human procreation (especially among the poor) and environmental degradation, virginity testing and female genital excision also examples of mental colonization and hegemony? I want to suggest here that one can be a consistent opponent of both social injustice and questionable cultural beliefs and practices. What is envisaged here is an arrangement that accommodates the intrinsic value of both rural community members and elephants. Real concern about the control and preservation of elephants reflects the fact that they—like human beings—are complex, intelligent, and social individuals, subjects of a life that can be better or worse for them, who can be harmed and benefited, and—other things being equal—for whom the cutting short of that life constitutes a substantial, irreversible, and irreparable harm (see Horsthemke 2018: 540).

In response to the widely held belief that indigenous knowledge is biocentric or ecocentric and characteristically endorses an ethic of care and responsibility for all creation, an inherently benign and holistic view of nature and the web of life, American educational theorists Deborah Barca and Alberto Arenas (2010: 14) observe that "having a cosmology that celebrates nature as alive and humans as an integral part of nature did not prevent many indigenous groups from destroying the very ecosystem that sustained them." This has been documented by British historian and environmentalist Clive Ponting (2007). His comprehensive study of the relationship between the environment and human history examines precolonial and preindustrial civilizations from

Sumeria to ancient Egypt, from the Maya to the original inhabitants of Easter Island. He argues that human beings have repeatedly not only transformed their environment but built societies that expanded and prospered by means of exploitation of natural, ecological resources. Invariably, these resources proved unable to sustain the growing populations, leading to an ecological breakdown and subsequent collapse of the societies in question.

A well-known and rather dramatic example of the "overuse of local resources" (Andrej 2015: 51), or more accurately: the indiscriminate slaughter of countless sensitive and intelligent animals, by native Americans is the so-called 'Head-Smashed-In Buffalo Jump' in Alberta, Canada. The HSIBJ Info Guide (2010: 3)[13] offers the following description of the killings, practiced by the Blackfoot and other First Nations for over 7,000 years:

- Buffalo jumping is such a sophisticated hunting technique that modern science is only beginning to understand its workings.
- The hunt began with a spiritual ceremony in which medicine women and men would go through detailed rituals to ensure a safe and successful hunt.
- During the ceremonies, the 'buffalo runners' were sent to locate and herd the animals. These were young men who possessed skill to move the bison herds.
- The buffalo runners, disguised under animal hides, would pass near the herds and try to lure them toward the cliffs, using their intricate knowledge of buffalo behavior.
- Ingenious V-shaped drive lanes were used to channel herds to the most dangerous point on the cliffs. These lanes were edged with rows of stone cairns which are still visible today. The lanes snake their way across the countryside, following ridges, crossing coulees, and rising across the tops of high hills.
- Near the cliff area of the drive lanes, people hid behind brush stuck into the cairns and prevented the beasts from straying by shouting and waving buffalo hides. Hunters rushed from behind, panicking the animals into a thundering headlong plunge over the cliff.
- After falling, many buffaloes were only stunned or wounded. Hunters waited below the cliff to kill the surviving beasts. The Native People believed that escaping animals would warn other herds of the deadly trap.
- The kill brought a surplus of meat to families and clans participating in the hunt. The people dried the meat, made pemmican, extracted fat from the bones, made tools, and tanned hides. Almost every part of the animal was used.

"Almost every part of the animal"? This is rather doubtful, since the site features a ten-meter-thick layer of bone remains, testimony to the extent of the massacres. Joe Crow Shoe Sr. (Aapohsoy'yiis or Weasel Tail, 1903–1999), a ceremonial elder of the Piikani Nation in southern Alberta, played a vital role in the development of what was declared the Head-Smashed-In World Heritage Site by UNESCO in 1981. He "dedicated his life to bringing cultures together," and to the preservation of aboriginal culture, and in 1998 received the National Aboriginal Achievement Award for "saving the knowledge and practices of the Blackfoot people": "His wisdom and vision helped make Head-Smashed-In a place of understanding, tolerance, and celebration."[14] It is very difficult to interpret the 'knowledge' and 'sophisticated, ingenious practices', not to mention the allegedly 'holistic' ethics of the Blackfoot, as anything other than anthropocentric.

While indigenous peoples and communities have hardly made a significant contribution to the environmental crisis facing the world today, they are not entirely blameless either. Moreover, the wet markets of far Eastern Asia, the African bush meat and trophy animal industries, poaching, and the devastation and despoilment of land, forests, lakes, and rivers even in remote rural areas cannot be blamed on poverty alone (see also Naipaul 2010).

"WHERE THE GREEN ANTS DREAM"

In German filmmaker Werner Herzog's film *Wo die grünen Ameisen träumen*, a huge Australian mining company ('Uran Mining Company') wants to extract uranium in a particular region in rural Australia and, toward this end, employs the services of a young geologist to map the subsoil of the desert area covered with anthills. The region targeted turns out to include a sacred site for indigenous Australians living in a nearby reservation. Wanting to keep everything legitimate and above board, the company offers the aboriginal people either generous compensation or a percentage of the potential revenue. The latter, through their spokespersons, refuse to accept the offer. When asked for the reason for their refusal—after all, the amount offered is perceived to be able to make a major difference with regard to the general upliftment of the community—the company representatives are offered a simple but cryptic answer: "Because this is where the green ants dream, and their dreams may not be disturbed," the implication being that disturbing their dreaming will destroy humankind. Invited on a trip to the city for further negotiation, some of the indigenous people see a military airplane and express the wish to own it. The company buys it and donates it to the aborigines as a sign of good will. A runway is built in the desert and the plane is flown to the location. However, all negotiations concerning the area fail. Irritated by the stubbornness and apparent irrationality[15] of the aborigines, the mining company takes the dispute to a court of the

Commonwealth, where parties and experts are heard—and further obstacles are met. For example, a representation is made by an old aborigine who is the sole survivor of his tribe (and language)—and no one understands what he is saying. Two of the aborigines take off in the plane, despite the fact that there is very little fuel left. The mining company wins the legal battle, and the company sends in bulldozers, trucks, tractors, and the like. Some aborigines arrive from the mountains and speak about a big winged ant that has fallen from the sky.

This scenario appears to offer a classic example of the impasse between Western technology, science, and development projects and indigenous mythology, spirituality, and rootedness, with neither side being able or perhaps even wanting to comprehend the other's rationale. Examined carefully, the aboriginal response in Herzog's film may also be taken to allude to ecological disaster. While its spiritual element may be inaccessible to western developers, the warning concerning devastation of the environment certainly is not. Thus, over and above the blatant immorality of the disregard for indigenous cultural and spiritual heritage, there are cogent objective reasons for resolving this impasse one way rather than another. Herzog is reported as commenting on his film,

> What would you say if we arrived in Rome with bulldozers and pneumatic hammers and began to dig in St. Peter's? . . . We do not own the land, the land owns us. (Herzog 1979: 47; translation mine[16]; see also Horsthemke 2004a: 41, 42; Horsthemke 2014b: 127–128)

In his discussion of concepts and criteria for mapping indigenous territories and the promise of using indigenous maps for the advancement of "a variety of anticolonial politics," Bryan (2009: 24) poses the question whether indigenous knowledge should be represented in the knowledge economy. His worry is that such mapping, like indigenous knowledge generally, would be "rapidly assimilated into development policy" by neoliberal institutions and turned into services or commodities promoting the flow of global capital. The dilemma is as follows. If indigenous peoples did not map their territory and thus assert control over their land, others would do so on considerably less favorable terms. Yet, doing so may force them into "commensurability with Western grids of rationality" (Turnbull 2009: 3). The very idea of mapping as a declaration of ownership is foreign, indeed incomprehensible, to many indigenous or aboriginal peoples. From this point of view, the idea of 'ownership of the land' is not obviously 'rational'. Or, more accurately, its rationality is at least highly questionable. The connections between rationality, morality, and objectivity will be discussed in the following chapter.

NOTES

1. Mutwa, according to the publicity information on the back cover (1996), is a "well-known wise man of Africa and *sanusi* (uppermost *sangoma*) of all *sangomas* [traditional healers] in southern Africa, [and] respected and well-known by people across the world."

2. "Wir haben die Natur weder katalogisiert noch aufgespießt und dann in Formaldehyd aufbewahrt, wir sehen sie anders und sprechen anders mit ihr und über sie." I have not been able to find the original source of this quotation, but I assume that it is an accurate reflection of Hove's view.

3. I have critically interrogated the ideas of sustainability and sustainable development in Horsthemke (2018: 135–143, 188–191), largely because of their anthropocentric orientation.

4. I would even go so far as to say, *contra* Le Grange (2012: 63), that *ubuntu* is speciesist. Animals and the biosphere are essentially defined in terms of human purposes and ends. It may be correct that *ubuntu* "helps us to appreciate . . . that the self is inextricably bound up in relations with the other and the biophysical world" (10)—but then the master, however favorably disposed, is also inextricably bound up in relations with his slaves.

5. This is also apparent in the 'holistic' understandings of the environment shared by the Inuit, Inuvialuit, Cree, and Dene peoples (Berkes and Berkes 2009: 8, 11), understandings that are invariably bound up with fishing, hunting, and trapping customs (7, 8, 9).

6. The annual *ukweshwama* ritual takes place in KwaZulu-Natal, South Africa, during the 'first fruits' festival. The ritual, which involves the barehanded killing of a bull by a group of young Zulu warriors, is traditionally performed to ensure that the Zulu nation has a strong army to defend the king and his subjects. https://www.thenational.ae/world/africa/culture-clash-over-bull-killing-ritual-1.542495 and http://www.onlyonesolution.net/html-versions/ukweshwama.html (both retrieved June 24, 2020).

7. "A new ethic or an end to a way of life?" (*The Animals' Agenda*, December 1988: 6–23, 56–57).

8. As I have argued elsewhere (Horsthemke 2010a, chapter 3) these reasons are hardly persuasive.

9. Report on the Great Elephant Indaba: 12 (PDF 3MB). 2005 (March 8, 2005). http://celtis.sanparks.org/events/elephants/report.pdf (retrieved September 5, 2006)

10. On the significance of indigenous knowledge in the shift from colonial to participatory conservation in Burkina Faso, see Lanzano 2013.

11. http://www.ens-newswire.com/ens/apr2003/2003-04-10-01.html (retrieved May 15, 2020).

12. I also discuss, and dismiss, the scientific, economic, and moral arguments in favor of hunting and killing in Horsthemke (2010a: 67–74; 2018: 530–540).

13. https://headsmashedin.ca/sites/headsmashedin/files/editor_files/HSIBJ%20INFO%20GUIDE%202010.pdf (retrieved June 30, 2020).

14. https://headsmashedin.ca/visit (retrieved June 30, 2020); see also Peat 1994: 28–31.

15. This seems to be what Berkes and Berkes (2009: 6) mean when they suggest that "indigenous knowledge approaches complex systems by using simple prescriptions consistent with fuzzy logic."

16. In conversation with Hans Günther Pflaum, Herzog asked, "Was würden Sie sagen, wenn wir mit Bulldozern und Presslufthämmern in Rom in die Peterskirche kämen und anfingen zu graben? ... Wir besitzen nicht das Land, das Land besitzt uns."

Chapter 8

Morality, Knowledge, and Local Values

Cynthia Ngewu's son was killed in an ambush by the South African security forces in the township of Gugulethu near Cape Town in March 1986. Seven young men, allegedly members of the armed wing of the African National Congress, *Umkhonto We Sizwe* ('Spear of the nation') were shot execution-style, among them Ngewu's son Christopher Piet. During the Truth and Reconciliation hearings, she gave a tearful response to the plea for forgiveness by the man who had killed her son:

> This thing called reconciliation . . . if I am understanding it correctly . . . if it means this perpetrator, this man who has killed Christopher Piet, if it means he becomes human again, this man, so that I, so that all of us, get our humanity back . . . then I agree, then I support it all. (Translated from Xhosa and quoted in Krog 2008: 356)

This response is a moving illustration of the interconnectedness of all people, which has not only an ethical but also an ontological and an epistemological dimension. As Antjie Krog notes (2004: 8),

> What [Cynthia Ngewu] knew . . . is that the person who kills one's son is doing it because he has lost his humanity. What she knew . . . is that it is in her (and his) interest to help the perpetrator get his humanity back. What she knew . . . is that if you kill the perpetrator, you destroy your own opportunity to get your humanity back. You freeze your society in inhumaneness. So the woman in the shack at Hout Bay did not forgive because she thought now she would get what whites have. She forgave because she saw that whites have lost their humanity and because they are inhuman within all their wealth, she cannot fulfil her full potential of being humane. She forgave in order to humanize whites.

Krog's analysis is interesting for several reasons. First, she invokes what might be called 'moral knowledge'. The mother's understanding or insight, it should be noted, is not 'indigenous'. Rather, it reflects intersubjectively and transculturally accessible reasoning and moral common sense. This does not mean that everyone would or should act the same way in identical or similar circumstances. (I doubt whether more than a small minority were able to do what Ngewu did.) It means, rather, that the decision-making process is comprehensible, open to scrutiny and public or intersubjective appraisal. Second, in Krog's interpretation the mother's act is neither wholly altruistic nor wholly self-interested. Ngewu is solely concerned neither with the perpetrator regaining his humanity nor with keeping her own hands clean and thus retaining her own humanity. Her decision to forgive the murderer of her son is communally oriented, motivated by a concern for society and humanity as a whole—"all of us." Finally, what is emphasized here is our (human) interconnectedness, the interrelatedness of our agency—and presumably also of our omissions. What connects us, as perpetrators, as victims, as executioners and forgivers, and as avengers and compensators, is our humanity—which we can forfeit and which we can also regain.

RELATIONAL ETHICS: *UBUNTU, MAAT, MITAKUYE OYASIN,* AND *WAHKOHTOWIN*

As chapter 7 has shown, the African principle of human interdependence states that a person becomes a person through other persons: 'I am because we are'. Or, in other words, a human being depends on human beings to be a human being: *Umuntu ngumuntu ngabantu*, or *Motho ke motho ka batho*, or *Munhu munhu navhanhu*.[1] In southern Africa, the relevant view would be that expressed by *ubuntu* (a Nguni language group term for common or shared humanity, or humanness; equivalent concepts in other language groups are *botho* or *hunhu*) or *ukama* (a Shona concept that emphasizes the interrelatedness of humans, the environment, God, and the ancestors). The basic idea is that the individual and her well-being depend essentially on the community, understood here as a web of relationships. Parallels can also be drawn between *ubuntu* (and its cognates) and the ancient Egyptian idea of *maat*, which emphasizes harmony, righteousness, and the need to locate and understand oneself and one's actions "in the context of the larger whole," something that "has great significance for both social and environmental ethics" (Karenga 2004: 181). Among Native Americans, this view finds expression in the Lakota phrase *Mitakuye oyasin* or the Cree concept of *wahkohtowin* ('All is related'; 'We are all related'), both of which refer to the self in relation, the self being defined relationally.[2] Lakota scholars Cheryl Crazy Bull and Emily White Hat (2019: 11) note that

> Indigenous education and philosophy are rooted in our understanding of relationships. In that context, our ecological knowledge can be constructed from our belief in the sacred circle, *Cangleska Wakan*, which represents all of creation.

"The sacred circle, *Cangleska* [circle] *Wakan* [mystery] in Lakota," they point out (119), "is symbolic of the interrelatedness of all things." In chapter 7, I suggested that this "interrelatedness" is contradicted by a pervasive anthropocentrism that characterizes many indigenous practices and customs. One might also ask whether the assertion made in *ubuntu* and related notions, 'I am because we are', is correct. It appears to make at least as much, if not more, sense to assert that 'We are because I am'. Rastafarians' use of the expression 'I and I' for 'we' constitutes an interesting twist in this regard.

THE TRUTH AND RECONCILIATION COMMISSION

What made the Truth and Reconciliation Commission (TRC)[3] unique was the decision to grant "amnesty to individuals in exchange for a full disclosure relating to the crime for which amnesty was being sought" (Tutu 1999: 34). Tutu, who had been appointed Chair of the Commission by then-President of South Africa Mandela, points out (34–35) that this

> way of conditional amnesty was consistent with a central feature of the African *Weltanschauung* (or worldview)—what we know as *ubuntu* in the Nguni group of languages, or *botho* in the Sotho languages. What is it that constrained so many to choose to forgive rather than to demand retribution, to be so magnanimous rather than wreaking vengeance? *Ubuntu* . . . speaks of the very essence of being human . . . We say, 'a person is a person through other people'. It is not 'I think therefore I am'. It says rather: 'I am human because I belong'. I participate, I share. A person with *ubuntu* is open and available to others, affirming of others, does not feel threatened that others are able and good; for he or she has a proper self-assurance that comes from knowing that he or she belongs in a greater whole and is diminished when others are humiliated or diminished, when others are tortured or oppressed, or treated as if they were less than who they are . . . Forgiveness gives people resilience, enabling them to survive and emerge still human despite all efforts to dehumanize them.

Ubuntu means, says Tutu (35), that

in a real sense even the supporters of apartheid were victims of the vicious system which they implemented and which they supported so enthusiastically. Our humanity was intertwined. The humanity of the perpetrator of apartheid's atrocities was caught up and bound up with that of his victim whether he liked it or not. In the process of dehumanising another, in inflicting untold harm and suffering, the perpetrator was inexorably being dehumanized as well.

Tutu's exposition illustrates the attractiveness of twinning the ideas of *ubuntu/botho* and reconciliation, as well as their compatibility. Lesiba Joe Teffo (1998: 5), similarly, suggests that the philosophy of *ubuntu* or *botho* is transcultural and, if embraced, would enable South Africans to succeed in their quest for reconciliation and nation building. In a closely related development, the closing paragraphs of the interim Constitution of 1993 express the constitution-makers' ethical vision of human beings and the social order which is to guide policy and legislation "in education as in all other sectors":

> The pursuit of national unity, the well-being of all South Africans and peace require reconciliation between the people of South Africa and the reconstruction of society . . . [The divisions and strife of the past] can now be addressed on the basis that there is need for understanding but not for vengeance, a need for reparation but not for retaliation, a need for ubuntu but not for victimization.[4]

Reference to *ubuntu* is excluded from the new (South African) Constitution, Act No. 108 from 1996. Mogobe Ramose questions the wisdom of this exclusion on political and philosophical grounds and argues that as a result the Constitution, inconsistent as it now is with the "basic political, legal and ethical exigencies of *ubuntu*," is both impoverished and flawed (Ramose 2004: 155). I would suggest that, on the contrary, the decision to excise reference to *ubuntu* constitutes a wise move, for reasons given in what follows. As far as twinning this notion with the idea of reconciliation is concerned, the problem is not only that *ubuntu* fails to address or take care of the weaknesses pointed out in connection with reconciliation; it has its own, potentially damaging flaws.

What is *prima facie* disturbing about claims like *ubuntu* being "the invisible force uniting Africans worldwide" (Makgoba 1996: 23) is the implicit superiority over other ethical and political considerations that are commonly attached to *ubuntu*. Characterizing the *ubuntu* bandwagon over the past twenty-five years is, among other things, the artificial/contrived opposition of 'vicious' (Western, Northern, Eurocentric) individualism and 'virtuous' (indigenous) communalism or communitarianism, or the relationalism of the global South. Not only is it mistaken to equate individualism with egoism or selfishness, but individualism in Northern societies like Germany is perfectly compatible with a socially conscious, mutually trustful, and altruistic orientation. Examples abound: neighborhood book exchanges; 'help-yourself' fruit and vegetables stalls replete with cash boxes; cleaning up after oneself, or one's dog, or cleaning up litter others have left behind in public places; adherence to social injunctions against jaywalking and other everyday norms (the idea is that jaywalking, for example, will set a negative and potentially dangerous example for children who might be witnessing this); social solidarity in times of far-reaching pandemics: for example, instituting 'bring-and-take' or 'gift' fences, where bags containing—preferably nonperishable—food, hygiene articles, and clothes are tied to fences for people in need to take with them. If a claim like Makgoba's has an evaluative purchase, it is dangerously close to racial or cultural hegemonism. If it is an empirical, descriptive claim, it is contradicted by the actual traditions, customs, and practices of many Africans. A serious problem is constituted, in this regard, by the patriarchal practices that have come to be associated with *ubuntu* in southern Africa: polygamy, *amaqhikiza* (a type of mentorship program among older and younger girls "to ensure sexual abstinence" until the latter are "ready to take full control of their affairs"), and *inkciyo* or *ukuhlolwa kwezintombi*—that is, 'virginity testing' in girls, a ritual in which girls undergo routine hymen inspection by designated female community elders, a practice that "seeks to achieve the goal of purity in the context of the spread of HIV/AIDS" (Ntuli 2002: 61, 62). In her Master of Public Health thesis, South African Zolisa Swartbooi-Xabadiya (2010) conducted research among girls from rural areas in South Africa on their perceptions and attitudes on this traditional practice. She reports that, contrary to arguments that the practice constitutes a violation of girls' rights, a significant number of the girls interviewed perceived it as a way of gaining self-respect and the affirmation of their community. In several instances, the girls referred to additional benefits, such as the prevention of HIV and other sexually transmitted diseases. There is very little in Swartbooi-Xabadiya's account that indicates any kind of self-determination on the part of the girls. They seem instead to be reacting to community pressure, which is perfectly understandable—given the nature of small-scale rural communities, gender-based division of labor and recreational activity, and discouragement of any kind of critical engagement, especially in rural African communities (see Adeyemi and Adeyinka 2003, on the principles and values of traditional African education). What arguably makes practices like *amaqhikiza* and *inkciyo* objectionable is not only that similar testing is not applicable (and consequently never done) with regard to boys, but also that it is women who are implicitly held responsible for the spread of HIV/AIDS. Furthermore, regarding the compatibility of *ubuntu* and polygamy, Ramose states (2002: 329), "That marriage should not of necessity be monogamous is one of the ancient practices of *ubuntu* philosophy." Given the reality of (especially

South) African polygamy, this declaration is tantamount to an endorsement of *'ubuntu* for men'. The kind of relationality that is envisaged here follows androcentric and patriarchal ideas and precepts.

It may be pointed out, of course, that *ubuntu* is a regulative principle, and that it furnishes a basis for the critique of extant states of affairs, like inhumane behavior on the African continent. On this view, it would be a weak argument against the *principle* to refer to the staggering incidence of genocide, torture, despotism, corruption, sexism, xenophobia, and generally cruel practices. On the contrary, one depends on *ubuntu* in order to highlight the inhumanity of such practices. But *does ubuntu* constitute a 'regulative' principle? How exactly does the philosophy of *ubuntu* promote 'good' human relationships and increase human value, trust, and dignity? What happens if two or more of the values associated with *ubuntu*, like generosity, hospitality, friendliness, care, and compassion, are in conflict? It would appear that *ubuntu* may on occasion tell us what kinds of persons we should *be* but that it provides insufficient guidance as to what we should *do*, especially in cases of conflict. In other words, one might doubt the value and efficiency of *ubuntu* as a practical action- and policy-guide. According to Tutu (1999: 45), the link between the TRC and *ubuntu* is made explicit in "a postscript that became the constitutional underpinning for the Truth and Reconciliation Commission: . . . there is a need for understanding but not for vengeance, a need for reparation but not for retaliation, a need for ubuntu but not for victimization." Yet, how would an appeal to *ubuntu* respond to demands around educational redress, reparation and—indeed—transformation? Thus, appeals to *ubuntu* often not only fail to resolve conflicts and problems but frequently even exacerbate these, by 'tackling' them in terms of verbal legislation.

An option that is available to defenders of *ubuntu* and related ideas[5] may be to claim some kind of cultural immunity for their favored value and to point out that critics and skeptics are unable, empirically or normatively, to grasp what is at stake here or to make cross-cultural judgments about the values and morals of a culture, society or group of individuals to which they do not belong. After I discuss, and dismiss, the case for the latter kinds of particularity and perspectivalism, I advance the argument that, like the ideas of 'knowledge' and 'truth', ethical values have universal purchase and that candidates for such values are transculturally examinable and evaluable.

CULTURAL RELATIVISM

Cultural relativism is the view that right and wrong, good and bad, and so on, are determined by the standards of particular cultures or societies. In other words, what is morally right or good is what meets the approval of a particular culture or society and what is morally wrong or bad is what is disapproved of. Cultural relativism thus goes beyond personal relativism, which emphasizes (dis)approval by the individual. (Only extreme relativists would embrace personal relativism. See Horsthemke 2016b.)

A key idea in late nineteenth/early twentieth-century American sociologist William Graham Sumner's work is that of "folkways." Human beings share a common ancestry with other animals, from whom we have inherited certain instincts that guide their attempts to satisfy their needs through a process of trial and error, "channels of habit and predisposition along which dexterities and other psychophysical activities would run easily" (Sumner 1906: 2). Characteristically for social beings dwelling in groups, they all adopted similar ways for similar purposes, which then "turned into customs and became mass phenomena." It is in this way, according to Sumner, that "folkways" arise (2-3). "Ethnocentrism," he explains, "is the technical name for this view of things in which one's own group is the centre of everything, and all others are scaled and rated with reference to it" (13). Each ethnic group considers itself superior and regards outsiders with contempt. Each group considers its own folkways to be

> the only right ones, and if it observes that other groups have other folkways, these excite its scorn. Opprobrious epithets are derived from these differences. 'Pig-eater', 'cow-eater', 'uncircumcised', 'jabberers', are epithets of contempt and abomination. . . . For our present purpose the most important fact is that ethnocentrism leads a people to exaggerate and intensify everything in their own folkways which is peculiar and which differentiates them from others. It therefore strengthens the folkways. (Ibid.)

With the ability to generalize philosophically and ethically about the welfare of the group or society, the "folkways" develop into "mores." They become prescriptive, indicating what everyone belonging to the particular social group ought to do.

> [T]he mores can make anything right. What they do is that they cover a usage in dress, language, behavior, manners, etc., with the mantle of current custom, and give it regulation and limits within which it becomes unquestionable. The limit is generally a limit of toleration. (521)

Sumner points out that the mores vary not only from society to society, culture to culture, but also over time within a particular society or culture. Morality, the "standards, codes, and ideas of chastity, decency, propriety, modesty, etc." (418), is simply what is required by the mores at a particular time and place. "Immoral" simply means "contrary to the mores of the time and place" (ibid.). There is no objective standard of evaluation, "no permanent or universal standard by which right and truth in regard to these matters can be established and different folkways compared and criticized" (ibid.). In an attack on the discipline of philosophy, Sumner claims that philosophy and ethics merely follow changes in living conditions while claiming, frequently and illegitimately, that they were the cause of the changes.

Early twentieth-century social anthropologist Ruth Benedict writes:

> The very eyes with which we see the problem are conditioned by the long traditional habits of our own society . . . We do not any longer make the mistake of deriving the morality of our locality and decade directly from the inevitable constitution of human nature. We do not elevate it to the dignity of a first principle. We recognize that morality differs in every society and is a convenient term for socially approved habits. Mankind has always preferred to say, 'It is a moral good', rather than, 'It is habitual'. . . . But historically, the two phrases are synonymous. The concept of the normal is properly a variant of the concept of the good. It is that which society has approved. (2000: 631; emphasis added).

Many people find cultural relativism intuitively appealing. But is it plausible? Sumner's attack notwithstanding, philosophy provides us with the tools necessary for rational analysis, and for recognizing and evaluating arguments. Like all theories, cultural relativism can be subjected to critical scrutiny. When we analyze the theory, we find that it is not nearly as convincing as it initially appears. For Sumner and Benedict (and many others), morality is simply whatever a society or culture deems to be normal behavior. At the heart of their theory is the claim that what is right and true is so by virtue of the fact that it is approved by a particular society or culture at a particular time. There is no morality that is universal and that exists nonempirically, outside of a particular historical and institutional context, and outside or beyond social or cultural tradition. But different societies or cultures have different conceptions of 'normal'. It follows that there is no universal standard or set of principles in morality.

How do Sumner and Benedict defend the claim that what is right and true is relative and varies from society to society, from culture to culture? Sumner provides little by way of illustration, apart from citing numerous examples of different social or cultural groups who consider themselves superior to others. This in itself does not amount to much. After all, they may simply be exhibiting an unwarranted arrogance and, what is worse, they may be mistaken. However, examples can be found. Benedict cites numerous examples of different standards of normality or (un)congenial types of behavior. About her own case studies, she writes that "they are travelling along different roads in pursuit of different ends, and these ends and these means in one society cannot be judged in terms of those of another society, because essentially they are *incommensurable"* (Benedict 1934: 223; emphasis added). Corporal (and indeed capital) punishment, homosexuality, and the amassing of property are practiced and permitted in some societies, but not in others, as are infanticide, female circumcision or clitoridectomy (clitoral excision), honor killings, tribally sanctioned rapes, and euthanasia. Different cultures have different customs and practices of interacting with neighbors as well as different ways of dealing with their dead. Cows are revered in the Hindu religion but ritually slaughtered in most parts of Africa. Thus, social and cultural traditions differ. But does morality differ with these traditions? And, importantly, would this indicate that there is no objective 'truth' in morality, that morality and ethics are not universal? Most glaringly, consider the dilemma contained in the statement, "Cultural relativism in its extreme form argues that we should respect diverse customs and abstain from moral judgements regarding other cultures" (Barca and Arenas 2010: 20[6]). The dilemma is the following. If cultural relativism is true, then the requirement of respect and abstention cannot itself be universal and can therefore happily be ignored by everyone outside the culture of those who issued it. If, on the other hand, it is meant to be a normative priority for everyone, then there is at least one imperative that is not relative. And if this is so, then why could there not be others?

THE CULTURAL DIFFERENCES ARGUMENT

Let us examine what might be called the "cultural differences" argument (Rachels 1995: 18–20). It is expressed in the following form of reasoning:

Premise 1: In some cultures, corporal punishment is seen to be cruel and wrong, and to be avoided at all cost.
Premise 2: In other cultures, corporal punishment is seen to be an essential part of child-rearing and education.
Subconclusion: Therefore, whether corporal punishment is moral or immoral is merely a matter of opinion, and opinions differ from culture to culture.
Conclusion: It follows that corporal punishment is neither objectively (universally) right nor objectively (universally) wrong.

Stated in the form of a more general argument:

Premise: What is right and true is so by virtue of the fact that it is believed to be right and true by a particular society or culture at a particular time.

Subconclusion: Therefore, there is no morality that is universal and that exists nonempirically outside of a particular historical and institutional context, and outside or beyond social or cultural tradition.
Additional premise: But different societies or cultures have different conceptions of 'right' and 'true'.
Conclusion: It follows that there is no objective truth in morality.

The first important thing to be noted is that the cultural relativist moves from considerations of what people believe to be right and true to what is in fact right and true. This is an illegitimate move and serves to cast doubt on the claim made in the first premise. For the same reason, the subconclusion that constitutes the second premise in the overall argument does not appear to follow. The claim advanced in the third premise, again, concerns people's conceptions of right and true. The conclusion, however, concerns what is really the case. Given that the second premise is unsupported and given that the third premise concerns what people believe to be right and true, the conclusion does not follow logically from the premises. To test the logic of this argument, we might try substituting the term 'morality' with 'geography' or 'biology' and the moral issues by examples drawn from geography and biology, and the logical inadequacy of the argument will be glaringly obvious.[7]

The relativist may now reply that morality is unlike geography, biology and the like in that it does not draw on any (provable) facts. The following might be called the "provability" argument (Rachels 1999: 25):

Premise 1: If there were such a thing as objective truth in ethics, we would be able to prove that some moral beliefs are true and others are false.
Premise 2: But in fact we cannot prove which moral beliefs are true and which are false.
Conclusion: Therefore, there is no such thing as objective truth in ethics.

What can be said in response to this argument? Unlike the "cultural differences" argument, it is valid: the conclusion receives logical support from the premises. But is it also sound? No, because we can, and usually do, compare divergent moral beliefs and judgments by reference to the reasons that are advanced to support them. In short, we provide and demand justification and, in so doing, seek to avoid error (see the comments below on the objectivity of morality). While this may not amount to evidence in any scientific sense, or proof in any logical sense, it does provide rationally persuasive grounds for treating some moral beliefs as more compelling than others. In ethics, as in the natural sciences and in logic, there is a premium on standards of correct (in other words, error-free) reasoning. So while the 'cultural differences' argument is neither sound nor valid, the 'provability' argument, although valid, is not sound: the second premise is false. Now let us assume, however, that it is possible to modify the 'provability' argument in such a way as to make its defense plausible.

What would be the consequences of taking cultural relativism seriously? We could no longer say that the customs of other societies are inferior to our own. We could no longer criticize or condemn the policies of other nations. (Take a nation or society that permits, indeed requires, brutal forms of corporal punishment in educational institutions.) Cultural relativism would prevent us from saying that these kinds of castigation are wrong.

Furthermore, we could decide whether actions are right or wrong just by consulting the standards or traditions of our society. (Consider the case of someone living in a society like apartheid South Africa, pondering whether segregationist schooling as in Bantu education is morally correct.) Cultural relativism would not only imply that these standards and traditions (regardless of whether they are democratic or undemocratic) are right and worth emulating; it would also imply that we cannot criticize or condemn the policies of our society or culture. It is exceedingly conservative in that it endorses whatever moral views happen to be current in a society. But many believe that their society's moral code is mistaken. Are these would-be reformers wrong?

Finally, the ideas of moral progress and social reform would be called into doubt. It is generally felt (the surge in crime, corruption and also school violence notwithstanding) that changes in South Africa since 1994, for example, from apartheid to integrated education, have been for the better. If cultural relativism is correct, however, we cannot think of the educational developments in South Africa as moral progress. There is no standard by which we could judge the new ways or current social and educational policies to be better. To say that we have made progress is to make just the sort of transcultural judgment that cultural relativism considers impermissible. Similarly, the idea of social 'reform' could only apply in the case of a society not living up its own ideals, not to challenging the ideals themselves. After all, they are by definition morally correct.

Apart from the unsavory implication that a value like human rights, too, is culturally specific, an additional problem with the view embraced by Benedict (and by many others) turns on the issue of logical consistency. Is the relativism contained in the claim, "The very eyes with which we see the problem are conditioned by the long traditional habits of our own society" (Benedict 2000: 631), not applicable to Benedict's own position? Second, surely the descriptive aspect of anthropological investigation is separable from the prescriptive aspect of evaluating cultures. Relativism may be committed to the former, but it cannot be committed to the latter, in terms of advocacy of a 'hands-off' approach, since it would then violate its own relativist stance. Benedict's conclusion (1934: 251ff.) in her book *Patterns of Culture* that anything one group of people is inclined toward doing is worthy of respect by another illustrates the dual logical inconsistency of deriving a universal value judgment from a set of culturally specific factual observations. Almost without exception, as Benedict's book was reprinted and re-edited, it was lauded as "a gateway to tolerance" (Antrosio 2013). Apart from the fact that Benedict elevates at least one moral value (namely tolerance) above what is relative to a particular culture (namely to a universal value), she hardly adheres to her own counsel; for example, when she sharply criticizes the Dobu culture of New Guinea (Benedict 1934: 131–132, 171) for their "lawlessness," "treacherousness," and "nastiness," or the Kwakiutl of the Pacific Northwest (220) for their "megalomaniacal tendencies."

So, if the basic arguments underlying cultural relativism are logically faulty and if the theory has disturbing consequences, how can we respond to it in a constructive manner? Three points are worth making. First, there is not nearly as much disagreement between cultures as is commonly suggested (Rachels 1995: 23–25). Different cultures frequently and characteristically disagree, not only on matters of etiquette (or manners, in other words, what constitutes 'good behavior'; I will return to this point later) but also in many of their factual and religious beliefs, that is, in their beliefs as to what is the case, how a certain state of affairs is to be brought about, what is to be done to avoid certain things and so on. There is considerably less disagreement in terms of their ethical beliefs. Thus, in sub-Sahara Africa, it is a sign of respect toward elders, senior citizens, and persons in authority for a person to lower his or her gaze, in other words, not to look them in the eye. In most occidental societies and cultures, on the other hand, behaving respectfully toward these people demands the very opposite: that is, to look them in the eye and to hold their gaze. This has significant educational implications, for example, regarding classroom behavior. Although its manifestations (the factual beliefs) may differ, the underlying ethical belief (namely that elders, senior citizens and persons in authority deserve respect) is the same and is shared across societies and cultures.

Second, all cultures share many significant values (25-26). For a society to function properly, certain rules must be adhered to. This is true of any society. Without rules against murder, theft, and lying (to mention only a few transgressions), society on any large scale could not function and would in all likelihood break down completely. Without such rules, the social fabric would simply be eroded, or society would not be possible in the first place. There are some moral rules that all societies have in common because those rules are necessary for society to exist and for social relations and interaction and to be possible.

Third, the initial appeal of cultural relativism is not completely illusory. Even if it is ultimately rejected, the following can be learned from the theory. Near the beginning of her book, Benedict (1934: 10–11) offers a statement that is no less relevant today than it was in 1934, when the book was first published:

> Modern existence has thrown many civilizations into close contact, and at the moment the overwhelming response to this situation is nationalism and racial snobbery. There has never been a time when civilization stood more in need of individuals who are genuinely culture-conscious, who can see objectively the socially conditioned behavior of other peoples without fear and recrimination.

There is something profoundly insensitive, and arguably even wrong, about basing all of our preferences, judgments, and the like on some absolute standard. (Note: This is not the same as basing them on a universal or objective standard.) Some practices are cultural products (and these are very often matters of etiquette; think of demonstrations of respect, nudity, and table manners, but consider also matters of religious observance, and so on). Cultural relativism errs crucially in claiming that all practices are products of culture. Furthermore, cultural relativism teaches us to keep an open mind. (It clearly cannot do this explicitly because to do so would be to elevate at least one ethical belief, namely open-mindedness, above what is relative to a particular culture, namely to a universal value.) We may come to realize that our preferences and judgments "are not necessarily perceptions of the truth" (Rachels 1995: 28). They "may be nothing more than the result of cultural conditioning" (ibid.). We would do well to be mindful of this possibility in order to avoid bias and prejudice. When it is suggested to us "that some element in our social code is not really the best and we find ourselves instinctively resisting the suggestion" (ibid.), we would do well to stop and remember this. Then we may become more open to discovering the truth, whatever that might be (ibid.).

This last point bears on the current debate concerning multiculturalism, something of a buzzword in education, politics, the arts, and so on. Cultural relativism owes its appeal to the genuine insight that many of the practices and attitudes that have been considered natural are really only cultural products. Moreover, keeping this insight firmly in view is important if we want to avoid nationalistic and ethnocentric arrogance or racial snobbery and have an open mind. Sensitivity toward context, recognition of the culture and history of different ethnic groups, and acknowledging, respecting, and perhaps even celebrating cultural differences, as envisaged by multiculturalists, is compatible with a basic requirement of reason, impartiality, and universal justice.

Notwithstanding the existence of a wealth of cultural differences, there are significant moral values and principles that carry weight in virtually every human community. Among these are not only a general prohibition of murder, lying, theft, and so on, but also obligations on members of a family to support their kin, constraints on sexual relationships (especially a taboo on incest), and obligations of reciprocity. The obligation of reciprocity, to return favors done and gifts received, culminates in the Golden Rule, which remains to this day a cornerstone of religious and secular ethics and morality (as in Kant's "categorical imperative" and the principle of universalizability). Kenyan legal scholar Yash Ghai (2007) recognizes the emancipatory possibilities of both diversity and interculturality, but he cautions against the twin dangers of relativism and abuse by authoritarian political figures keen to invoke cultural specificity in order to legitimate gross human rights violations.

Two important considerations emerge from the discussion of cultural relativism. The first concerns the inescapability of reason and indeed good reasoning. Reason informs us not only of what is, but also of what ought to be the case. Moral judgments, or for that matter all value judgments, must be supported by good reasons. A moral judgment is more likely to be correct when it has the weight of reason on its side. Conflicting moral views and judgments are evaluated essentially in terms of the reasons produced in their support and the arguments that are advanced for or against them. The second important point concerns the objectivity of morality. Moral truths are truths of reason. A moral truth (unlike a personal preference, which is a matter of taste) is a conclusion that is backed up by reasons. While it is clear that moral truths and moral knowledge are not like or reducible to empirical facts, they are objective in the sense that they transcend what an individual, group of individuals, or even a majority of people want, feel, approve, or decide. What makes morality objective is in part the requirement of reason and rationality. Morality is also objective in another sense, namely in that it requires impartiality. When we make moral judgments or moral decisions, we should as far as possible take an objective or external view. I turn next to considerations of justice and rights, as applied to knowledge and epistemology.

NOTES

1. See Letseka (2000: 182–183): "a person depends on others just as much as others depend on him/her."

2. The insight that *ubuntu* is conceptually and practically associated with a long and profound tradition of humanist concern, caring, and compassion, also prominent in Western thought, is echoed by Mamphela Ramphele:

Ubuntu as a philosophical approach to social relationships must stand alongside other approaches and be judged on the value it can add to better human relations in our complex society. . . . The refusal to acknowledge the similarity between *ubuntu* and other humanistic philosophical approaches is in part a reflection of the parochialism of South Africans and a refusal to learn from others. . . . We have to have the humility to acknowledge that we are not inventing unique problems in this country, nor are we likely to invent entirely new solutions. (Ramphele 1995: 15)

3. In this section I discuss the ethical endeavors and goals of the Commission. The following chapter deals in part with the epistemological underpinnings.

4. https://peaceaccords.nd.edu/provision/truth-or-reconciliation-mechanism-int erim-constitution-accord (retrieved 30 June 2020).

5. A further option, of course, is to imbue the idea of *ubuntu* with normative teeth, as philosopher Thaddeus Metz has done. Since 2005, he has produced an impressive body of work on and within African philosophy, notably African ethics. His endeavors have not met with unanimous approbation and acclaim from African philosophers. Given the nature of philosophy and philosophical discourse, this is unsurprising. What is noteworthy, however, is that the reasons for the dismissal of Metz's work have tended to have little to do with philosophical substance, the critique more often than not amounting to thinly veiled *ad hominem* attacks on the U.S. immigrant and non-African-language speaker. Nonetheless, Metz's contribution must stand out as a systematic and far-reaching attempt to make African philosophy analytically compelling and normatively sound, by providing a sympathetic but never sycophantic (re-)interpretation of some of its central concepts and concerns. Metz seeks at once to highlight African philosophy's distinct contribution to global, academic philosophy and to strengthen it in instances where it may appear wanting. His work on the possible normative value of *ubuntu* is a case in point (Metz 2007a, b, 2009a, b, 2012).

6. This is not a view to which the authors subscribe.

7. Visvanathan, too, postulates a relevant similarity, but reaches a wholly different conclusion: "Morality, like science, has to be invented individually" (2002: 51). This indicates a fundamental misconception on Visvanathan's part. In fact, neither science nor morality are individual inventions. Individuals are initiated into both and perhaps (ideally!) attain moral and scientific autonomy as a result, or in culmination, of this initiation process.

Chapter 9

Epistemic Justice, Recognition, and Rights

Is the critical interrogation of the ideas of 'indigenous' knowledge (systems), of distinctly and uniquely "African ways of knowing," and of diverse, multicultural epistemologies not part of a hegemonic, colonialist discourse? Take, as an example I already mentioned earlier in the book, Siegel's response to Ruitenberg's question regarding "indigenous African women's epistemologies" (during a roundtable discussion held in San Francisco in April 2010; see Code et al. 2012: 137): "They're not epistemologies. If students don't understand that by the end of their graduate education, they haven't been well educated" (138). Could this possibly constitute some kind of epistemic harm *vis-à-vis* indigenous African women? In other words, is this not a case of epistemic injustice?

Well, do indigenous African women have a theory of knowledge? It seems exceedingly unlikely that they do. They have knowledge in the acquaintance, practical, and propositional senses, but hardly an epistemology in the philosophically relevant sense that sets them apart as indigenous African women. In maintaining this, of course, Siegel and I might now be accused of Western or Eurocentric arrogance, and of epistemic violence[1] (see also Marker 2004; Heleta 2016), in the sense of deliberate, principled nonrecognition, if not discursive infliction of harm on subjects. In the section that follows, I address a few of the responses to my own work before I tackle the all-important issue of epistemic (in)justice.

"WESTERN ARROGANCE," "EUROCENTRISM," "WHITE DOUBTS" AND FEARS, AND "EPISTEMIC VIOLENCE": THE RESPONSES

The charge of epistemic violence is certainly serious—if and when it is applicable. I take it, following Savo Heleta (2016: 2), to be directed against

Eurocentrism and the continued "reinforcement of white and Western dominance and privilege," stereotyping, "prejudices and patronizing views about Africa and its people."

Is the "perception of African indigenous knowledge as mere repetition of practices without any theory to explain them" an example of "Eurocentric prejudices" (Kaya and Seleti 2013: 33), of "Western cultural and intellectual arrogance" (31), of a failure to understand the "holistic nature [of] AIKS [African indigenous knowledge systems]" (Kaya 2013: 138) and "African traditional education which does separate theory from practice, especially its community-based nature" (Kaya and Seleti 2013: 36)? The charge of "Eurocentric" or "Western arrogance" is often legitimate, especially when it proceeds without any theory or conceptual framework of its own. I do not think, however, that my critique can be dismissed in this fashion. It constitutes a challenge to defenders of African and other indigenous knowledge systems to engage with my analysis of knowledge and with my concerns and to furnish a relevant and plausible understanding of knowledge and epistemology. Nor do I think that a simple reference to the separation of theory and practice will do.

Masolo (2014: 202–208) takes issue with my skepticism about indigenous knowledge (Horsthemke 2014a), which I expressed during a colloquium on his book, *Self and Community in a Changing World*, held at the University of Johannesburg, South Africa, in March 2012. Among other things, his contentions are the following:

- that I appear "unduly to think that knowledge is only about empirical claims. The world of humans is made of far more than preoccupation with just empirical claims about 'the world', or only with the truth value of such claims. Objects may be the same to a group of people who populate a particular region, but it does not follow that everyone in that region thinks only of the same atomic facts out of such objects even if it would make sense to them when made. Horsthemke's argument rests implausibly on a reductionist definition of 'experience' as pure somatic movements of nerves, muscles, lenses, and so on. In other words, the meaning of 'experiencing objects' would have to be restricted to what occurs when we encounter one in empirical senses alone; but is it? . . . The idea of indigenous knowledge is far broader than how people express concerns or make claims about empirical reality. It is also about people's creative transformation of the physical world around them in response to their needs; and it is also about how people design norms of conduct to regulate their relations as well as access to and distribution of resources." (203–205)
- "that the term 'indigenous' is not a synonym for 'non-Western' or for 'non-modern', although it was given these connotations in colonial language and

literature. Its variant, 'native', is equally common. . . . On the other hand, assuming that it is indeed a form of indigenous knowledge, then what would exempt the definition of knowledge as 'justified true belief' from being an example of indigenous Western knowledge?" (207, 208)

Two quick responses will have to suffice. First, although I consider empirical claims to be of fundamental significance in knowledge, I do not think I have ever advocated any kind of exclusive, reductionist account of experience. I do think, for reasons I cannot go into here that it makes excellent sense to speak of moral knowledge (even of moral truth and facts). Nor do I deny the cognitive force of feelings and emotions. Second, the definition of knowledge as 'justified true belief' resonates with distinctions made in Yoruba and in ancient Egypt (which may well have had a profound influence on Greek and generally occidental beliefs and values). Even if it is accepted, purely for argument's sake, that this definition is an example of "Western knowledge," in the sense that it originated in the "West," it has the immense virtue of being internally consistent and logically coherent. It is, in fact, universally (or at least translocally) applicable.

Against what Constance Khupe and Moyra Keane (2017: 27) have referred to as my "universalist . . . way of understanding knowledge," they propose a "pluralist" view of "knowledge as a sociocultural and historical construction": "From a pluralist perspective, what qualifies as knowledge depends on the ways in which particular societies categorize, code, process, and assign meaning to their experiences." This way of understanding knowledge also has normative implications for research: "research among African people *must* be characterized by flexibility, participation, and negotiated purposes . . . , and *should* seek to interrupt colonizing forms of research by focusing on African though and experience" (emphasis added). It is not at all clear how Khupe and Keane's favored view of knowledge and research can avoid the dual threat of relativism and parochialism—with all the attendant problems.

In Felix Maringe's account of the transformation of knowledge production systems in "the new African university" (2017: 15), he refers to my argument (Horsthemke 2004a) "that IKS involves at best an incomplete, partial, or at worst, a questionable understanding or conceptualisation of knowledge and . . . that as a concept, it has questionable relevance to the debates around real issues of transformation." He then declares that he disagrees "completely with these sentiments, as, in [Maringe's] view, they represent overtures by 'white doubters'—those who are scared of ceding control of the academy and seek to cement the hegemony of the west as the only legitimate players in shaping transformational discourses in the African university." Maringe's characterization of my ("white") doubts is correct. I am indeed skeptical about the idea of indigenous knowledge, for reasons given earlier in this book.

However, these are not "sentiments," as Maringe suggests, but the results of careful reasoning and circumspect argumentation, guided entirely by both philosophical scrutiny and examination of the available evidence—and not by any fear of ceding control or any hegemonic impulses. I am not opposed to transformation, and I have nothing to gain from any such opposition—but I *am* opposed to irrational beliefs, weak justification, dodgy reasoning, and fashionable assertions that parade as liberatory and transformative discourse. To rise above plain name-calling, Maringe would have done well to engage with my philosophical, epistemological analysis and not merely dwell on a set of pat assumptions about critics' and skeptics' motivation.

THE IDEA OF EPISTEMIC INJUSTICE

Having observed that "the really crucial problem for Third World intellectuals is that of being taken seriously" (Masolo 2010: 25), Gayatri Spivak writes:

> For me, the question "Who should speak?" is less crucial than "Who will listen?" . . . The real demand is that, when I speak from that position, I should be listened to seriously. (Spivak 1990: 59–60; quoted in Masolo 2010: 25: see also Spivak 2005)

One might argue that what Spivak is driving at here is the demand for epistemic justice.

"Epistemic injustice," argues Miranda Fricker (2007: 1; see also p. 21), is a distinct kind of injustice. She distinguishes between two kinds, "testimonial injustice" and "hermeneutical injustice," each of which consists, "most fundamentally, in a wrong done to someone specifically in their capacity as a knower."

> Testimonial injustice occurs when prejudice causes a hearer to give a deflated level of credibility to a speaker's word; hermeneutical injustice occurs at a prior stage, when a gap in collective interpretive resources puts someone at an unfair disadvantage when it comes to making sense of their social experiences. (1)

Central to her analysis is the notion of (social) 'power', which Fricker defines as "a socially situated capacity to control others' actions" (4; see also p. 13). Power works "to create or preserve a given social order," and is displayed in various forms of enablement, on the one hand, and disbelief, misinterpretation, and silencing, on the other. It involves the conferral on certain individuals or groups, qua persons of that kind, "a credibility excess" or "a credibility deficit" (21). The primary characterization of testimonial injustice, according to Fricker (ibid.), "remains such that it is a matter of credibility deficit and not credibility excess." This is certainly plausible, although we can think of instances where credibility excess is disadvantageous: an overburdened teacher or lecturer being asked questions by his students that call for a more specialist training. Similarly, promoting someone to a position (e.g., through affirmative action) for which they are not equipped, simply to rectify past wrongs, may be argued to involve epistemic harm.

Fricker's interest resides specifically with "identity power" and the harms it produces through the manifestation of "identity prejudices." The latter is responsible for denying credibility to, or withholding it from, certain persons on the basis of their being members of a certain "social type" (21). Thus, testimonial injustice involves rejecting the credibility of their knowledge claims, while hermeneutical injustice involves a general failure of marshaling the conceptual resources necessary for understanding and interpreting these knowledge claims. An example of testimonial injustice is the rejection of a knowledge-claim made by someone (e.g., a black female educator) on the mere grounds that she is a woman, black or both. An example of hermeneutical injustice is the inability of a person to make sense of what has happened to her because she has not been given the conceptual resources to make sense of her situation. Thus, a female learner who has been sexually harassed by a teacher, but who has no concept or understanding of sexual harassment, suffers hermeneutical injustice. The result is that these people are hindered in their self-development and in their attainment of full human worth: they are "prevented from becoming who they are" (5). In white patriarchal societies, these "epistemic humiliations" (51)[2] carry the power to destroy a would-be (black or female) knower's confidence to engage in the trustful conversations (52–53) that characterize well-functioning epistemic communities. As Fricker suggests (55), they can "inhibit the very formation of self." Although they are experienced (and may be performed) individually, testimonial and hermeneutical injustice constitute not only individual harms: they originate within a social fabric of which the biases and prejudices that enliven and perpetuate them are a characteristic part. Contesting such injustices and harms, according to Fricker (8), requires "collective social political change."

In order to bring about such change, what is required[3] at a testimonial level is "reflexive awareness of the likely presence of prejudice," and this "anti-prejudicial virtue is the virtue of testimonial justice" (91–92). Testimonial justice, says Fricker (124), is "both ethical and intellectual in character, at once a virtue of truth and a virtue of justice." Thus, apart from being able to rely on the competence and sincerity of speakers (72), and apart from sensitivity (ibid.) and empathy (79), "hearers need dispositions that lead them reliably to accept truths and to reject falsehoods" (115). However, there is no guarantee that epistemic and ethical ends will harmonize. If some down-trodden schoolteacher is told in no uncertain terms by the unscrupulous head teacher that when the school inspector visits the classroom, he must ask the pupils a question and make sure that he picks from among the sea of raised hands someone who will come out with the right answer. This epistemic aim might be best served by a policy that is not remotely just. It might be best served, for instance by picking a pupil who, notoriously, always gets her big brother to text her the answers on her mobile. (126)

"Hermeneutical justice, like testimonial justice, is a hybrid virtue" (174), says Fricker. What it is meant to counteract is hermeneutical injustice—which occurs when (members of certain) groups or communities lack the hermeneutical tools to make sense of their own social experience (146). "For something to be an injustice, it must be harmful but also wrongful, whether because discriminatory or because otherwise unfair" (151). When there is unequal "hermeneutical participation with respect to some significant areas(s) of social experience, members of the disadvantaged group are hermeneutically marginalised" (153). Fricker's account, of course, raises the question whether there could be hermeneutical *self*-marginalization. I am thinking in particular of Kabou's own 'inside' understanding in referring to ordinary African women and men as having refused development and modernization (Kabou 1991; see especially Part 2). Fricker (2007: 153) appears to deny this:

> Hermeneutical marginalization is always socially coerced. If you simply opt out of full participation in hermeneutical processes as a matter of choice . . . , then you do not count as hermeneutically marginalised—you've opted out, but you could have opted in. Hermeneutical marginalization is always a form of powerlessness, whether structural or one-off.

Yes, one might respond, but one can be responsible for one's powerlessness, as in the case of Kabou's "ordinary Africans" (1991). It would seem to follow that hermeneutical injustice and hermeneutical marginalization are not identical, insofar as the latter can be seen to include self-marginalization.

Given how prejudice affects various levels of credibility, and given that the critical interrogation of 'indigenous knowledge' has sometimes been part of a hegemonic discourse and constituted epistemic injustice, the question might now be raised whether my critique of this notion is not part of this discourse. Louise Antony suggests the adoption of "epistemic affirmative action" by men as a "working hypothesis that when a woman, or any member of a stereotyped group, says something anomalous, they should assume that it's they who do not understand, not that it is the woman that is nuts" (Antony 1995: 89; quoted in Fricker 2007: 171). By contrast, Fricker (2007: 171) does not believe a policy of epistemic affirmative action across all subject matters to be justified: "the best way to honour the compensatory idea is in the form of a capacity for indefinitely context-sensitive judgement—in the form . . . of a virtue." At what point, then, can a white man judge a woman, or any member of a stereotyped group, to be 'nuts'—if ever? Does epistemic justice require me, as a matter of course, to reserve judgment, to keep "an open mind as to credibility" (172)? As I have indicated above, if 'credibility deficit' is a matter of epistemic injustice, then why should 'credibility excess' (giving previously 'epistemologically humiliated' people or groups lots of credibility) not also constitute epistemic harm? More fundamentally, surely there is a difference between criticizing someone's view on the mere grounds that she is black, or a woman, and criticizing the views held or expressed by someone, who happens to be black or a woman, on the grounds of faulty or fallacious reasoning. Nonsense is not a cultural, racial, or sexual prerogative. Indeed, although she gestures in the direction of a basic "do no harm" principle (85), Fricker herself insists (106) that a "'vulgar' relativist" resistance to passing moral judgment on other cultures "is incoherent."

According to Fricker (102–103; emphasis added),

> any epistemic subject will have a reason to get at the truth. This is not to underestimate the complex and often troubled nature of our relationship with truth. Human beings are obviously subject to all sorts of powerful motivations, and indeed reasons, for shielding themselves from painful truths through mechanisms of denial or repression. On the whole, however, one must see such mechanisms against a background of a more general *motivation to truth.*

Bernard Williams (2002) identifies three collective epistemic needs: first, the need to possess sufficient truths (and not too many falsehoods) to facilitate survival; second, the need to participate in the practice of an epistemic community, where there exists a division of epistemological labor, that is, where information is shared or pooled; and third, the need to promote dispositions in individuals that will stabilize relations of trust. The practical virtue of competence and the epistemic virtues of accuracy and sincerity spring directly from these fundamental epistemic needs. Williams expresses the hope that his "genealogical story" will assist in making "sense of our most basic *commitments to truth and truthfulness*" (19; emphasis added).

'TRUTH AND RECONCILIATION'

According to Masolo (2010: 181),

> Wiredu's theory of truth gives the phrase 'truth and reconciliation', now central as a strategy and process for healing broken trusts and healing from public

conflicts, an important epistemological grounding. Reconciling our different and often conflicting aims and aspirations is the path to a collectively acceptable and workable world.

The Truth and Reconciliation Commission (TRC), as I explained in chapter 8, was set up after the first democratic election in South Africa in order to bring to light and address the injustices and moral wrongs committed under apartheid—and indeed to "heal the divisions of the past" and contribute toward establishing "a society based on democratic values, social justice, and fundamental rights" (Constitution of South Africa: Preamble). One of the principal contributions of the TRC was to turn *knowledge*—in other words, that which so many people already knew—into public *acknowledgment*, allowing the nation to acknowledge atrocity for what it is (see Villa-Vicencio 2003: 15). Asked to name the most significant achievements of the TRC in a national survey, the vast majority of South Africans, irrespective of race, referred to the disclosure of the *truth* about the past.

Let us pause to think about the present use of the terms 'knowledge' and 'truth'. Great care was taken during the TRC hearings, to make room not only for forensic truth but also for "personal or narrative truth, social or dialogic truth," as well as "healing or restorative truth" (Swanson 2015: 34, 35).[4] Truth, like *ubuntu* and knowledge, is understood as communal, relational, and refers to what it means to be a person or fellow citizen and "to be in relationship with an-Other" (34). It is certainly debatable whether the latter three (nonforensic) conceptions actually concern truth—and not, rather, personal opinion, consensus, and reconciliation, respectively. It is clearly important for a truth commission to acknowledge different subjectivities and competing versions of events. This relates to the moral and political imperative of giving voice to those who have been silenced and marginalized in the past. But once these different versions have been registered, the task of truth commissions is to move beyond these multiple narratives, dialogues, and concerns. There is a reason why the TRC was not called '*Belief* (or *Opinion*) and Reconciliation Commission' or '*Consensus* and Reconciliation Commission'. There is a premium here not on personal perceptions (although these are also deemed important by the Commission; see Posel 2002: 150, 154–155; Posel 2004: 9, 17, 20–21), but on factual, historical truth (see Simpson and Posel 2004: 4). It was tasked, first and foremost, with establishing what *actually* took place (or happened or occurred), independently of what people sincerely believed agreed on, and perhaps even found comfort in.

I want to suggest that the use of the terms 'knowledge' and 'truth' in the particular enterprise referred to here cannot be matters of personal opinion or even communal consensus, that knowledge and truth are not dependent on a particular set of cultural relationships or social context. If it did not involve an understanding of truth as transcultural or universal (and as objectively anchoring knowledge), as reflecting what actually happened, that is, facts about South Africa's past, setting up a commission like this would be pointless.

What, then, constitutes "a viable tool for transforming the world" (Masolo 2010: 18)? There is a pervasive view that recognition, protection against exploitation, appropriation, counteracting wholesale subjugation of everything that is deemed subjugatable is best achieved on the basis of appeals to 'indigenization' (like 'Africanization') of, for example, education and knowledge, and to the validity of 'local knowledge' or 'indigenous knowledge systems'. Yet, apart from their frequent proximity to relativism, superstition, questionable customs and traditions, and to a relative lack of agency and autonomy, the ideas of 'indigenization', 'indigenous' or 'local' knowledge, and so forth, tend to have a (self-)marginalizing effect. (For more elaborate argument and illustration, see Horsthemke 2004b, 2006a; see also Rata 2012a, b.) Despite their ostensible contribution to 'independence from colonialism', these ideas are less empowering and have less transformative potential than is commonly assumed. To couch the demand for and the necessity of fundamental changes in education, and so forth, *primarily*, if not *exclusively*, in the language of indigenization (Africanization, and so forth) is not only fanciful but is also to miss the political *and* practical *point* of the project. For one thing, it may create a false or at best a superficial sense of 'belonging'. For another, it may lead to further marginalization or derogation, such as that already contained in ideas like 'African time'. Of course, the question is whether reference is made in the latter instance to the *concept* of time or to the *experience* of time—or both, as in cultural practices regarding 'time management'. Clearly, it may often be detrimental to be so beholden to schedules, to the dictates of our watches and clocks. As Grill puts it so memorably (2003: 347; my translation),

> We learn that [Germans] have clocks, whereas Africans have time. Time in traditional Africa obeys different laws. It is not organized or subdivided into hours and minutes, and even less into seconds, but into natural cycles and cultural rules: rainy season and dry season, sowing and harvest, birth, initiation, marriage, death. Time is connected with events, plans, festivities, rites, symbols or needs: the first rains, the length of shadows, a stroke of luck, a remarkable occurrence, . . . the crowing of a cock, the rumbling of a tummy.

I have urged (see chapter 5, and also Horsthemke 2004a, b, c, 2005, 2009) locating the pleas for recognition, and so forth. in a rights-based framework, with corresponding practical, moral as well as epistemic obligations. A rights-based framework has the potential, and arguably the necessary educational, legal, ethical, and political clout, to initiate lasting changes. Insofar as human rights are anchored in as well as responsive to human agency, rights are essential for the protection of human differences. In essence, taking rights seriously implies taking individual, social, and cultural identity seriously. Perhaps a first set of steps toward transformation (or what Fricker calls "collective social political change"; 2007: 8) is constituted by a process or project that has rights as its backbone.

The conferral and enforcement of rights, however, does not necessarily imply *qualitative* changes, for instance, in our perception of 'others'. Our behavior toward them may change, but our attitude toward them may not. This is arguably due to the fact that by virtue of their appeals to rights, law, and morality have an inescapably coercive aspect. As Karl Marx has pointed out (1987: 142), rights imply the "separation of man from man," or moral atomism. Rights are held by individuals *against* other individuals, society, or the world at large. His own conception, the Marxian idea of revolutionary emancipation, envisages the "union of man with man," a oneness in struggle and, finally, liberation, a union which is social (economic?) rather than legal or political. Marx is surely wrong, however, in linking individualism with egoism and in detecting only egoistic motivation in appeals to rights (147). To some extent, it may be true that the invocation of rights is self-interested, but the extension of rights to the hitherto underprivileged and to those who cannot themselves claim them surely disproves the argument from solely self-interested motivation.

Appeals to the fundamental equal rights of all humans have, more or less gradually, led to the abolition of slavery, child labor, and other forms of abuse and exploitation. Yet, unequal treatment and consideration, ethnocentric and racial prejudice, sexism and heterosexism have not been eradicated. They still occur frequently. Many of us, despite respecting those rights as a matter of necessity, prudence, and expediency, continue to harbor much the same racial prejudice and other preconceptions as before. In other words, we have not yet liberated the Other in our own moral awareness—and therefore not liberated ourselves.

In order to effect any *lasting* changes, then, a viable set of tools for "transforming the world" needs to encompass more than reasons and principles associated with a deontological orientation or rights ethic. It needs to incorporate caring, appeals to kindness, compassion, empathy, and feelings of kinship. There is a possible compromise between the two kinds of approaches that will avoid relativism as well as nurture social, political, environmental, and epistemic literacy and responsibility. It will consist in the adoption of a rights and justice orientation as the basis, without denying the importance of the affective dimension. After all, children are not made moral individuals by appealing first to their intellect and only thereafter, if at all, to their feelings. As American educational philosopher Amy Gutmann observes, "To cultivate in children the character that *feels* the force of right *reason* is an essential purpose of education in any society" (1987: 43; emphasis added). "There are times when people know through feelings, through unexplained inner-most core intuitions," according to Mosha (1999: 220–221): "It is, therefore, imperative that educators, formators, and parents should strive to provide an education that not only challenges and informs the mind but also inspires the heart." An affective capacity for morality provides the 'raw material' for fostering rational self-determination and the use of reason for making choices and decisions. Just as society can indoctrinate or brainwash people into a politics of resentment, xenophobia, and prejudice, it can achieve the opposite, through both the elicitation of care, empathy, and compassion as well as the inculcation of 'moral knowledge', principles, and skills. A child, a person, has to realize that what is wrong for another to do to her is wrong for her to do another. This appears to be the essence of the idea that there is no substitute for a direct concern for others as the basis of morality. Children, people, must learn to cultivate their empathetic and sympathetic imaginations. This is not easy, and it will not be brought about by rational discussion alone. Thus, the ethical significance of feelings is not questioned. What *is* denied, however, is that the motives and ethical beliefs underlying the practice of virtues, care, recognition of responsibilities, and so on, differ from culture to culture. Moreover, it is highly doubtful whether, in the absence of rights and considerations of justice, such empathetic and sympathetic imagination, caring, and so on, can actually provide a sound basis, that is. a guarantee or consistent prescription, for right action.

EPISTEMIC EMPATHY

There is an important sense in which the ideas of cognitive and epistemic justice, and epistemic liberation, concern not only rectification of past injustices and so-called 'epistemic marginalization', that is of the nonrecognition and misrecognition of indigenous people's contributions to 'world' or 'global' knowledge, but also epistemic self-liberation, both by the victims and the perpetrators. The recommendations made in this chapter take the form of a hybrid approach that combines a justice/rights orientation with a conception of reconciliation that foregrounds empathetic and sympathetic understanding, by advocating what might be called epistemic empathy.

The idea of epistemic empathy is a fairly recent addition to discourses within social, moral, and virtue epistemology. According to Julinna Oxley (2011: 6^5), "empathy's most important functions are epistemic": "empathy can be used to acquire justified beliefs about others' mental and emotional states" (12). It

> performs a number of *epistemic* functions that enable us to reflect on our beliefs about others in a new way.... Empathy enables people to understand how others see the world, helps them to appreciate others' perspectives and connect with them emotionally, eliminates the perception of conflict between oneself and others, and makes possible the perception of similarity between oneself and others.
>
> Focusing on empathy's epistemic dimension is an approach that has the resources for explaining how empathy and empathic thinking are relevant to ethical reflection, deliberation, and justification. (5–6)

Perhaps the case might be made that, with regard to empathy in particular, the cognitive and the affective, reason and emotion, are indivisible (see also Slote 2013: 50, 54, 90/91fn.7[6]). The relevant characteristics in this regard are knowledge of another's internal state, including her thoughts and feelings; understanding how another is thinking and feeling; and imagining how one would think and feel in the other's place (see Oxley 2011: 7, 8).

Oxley devotes a whole chapter in her book to the epistemic functions of empathy (35–58), namely gathering information about the other person (42–46), as well as understanding others (46–48). She analyzes the psychological experience of empathy and shows that it makes unique epistemic contributions to our understanding of other people. Since empathy brings information to our attention in a personal way, it has the potential to enrich moral deliberation. Nevertheless, it is not intrinsically moral and does not always lead to moral action. Given its role in helping us understand others, empathy is relevant also to Kantian ethics and contractual ethics,[7] not just to ethical theories that emphasize care and altruism. Citing empirical evidence, Oxley shows that the cultivation of empathy must begin early in life in order for people to be inclined to feel empathy for others in a way that informs their moral decisions. Michael Slote (2013: 52) is concerned with the role that epistemic empathy (empathy with another person's state of belief or knowledge or their intellectual, scientific, or cognitive 'point of view') can play in the reconciliation of moral caring with the admission or recognition that there is such a thing as greater or lesser creativity (or intelligence or talent). He also introduces "the epistemological ideals and intellectual/epistemic virtues of open-mindedness and fair-mindedness" as "(desirable) forms of epistemic empathy and epistemic *respect*" (50, 51). In what follows, I will assume—without additional argument—that open-mindedness and fair-mindedness are part and parcel of 'mindfulness'.

While empathy does not constitute the whole of what makes someone a good person, it is nonetheless instrumental in defining and motivating normative principles and obligations. It is probably at its most generative if it is employed in conjunction with specific principles and directives.[8] This is where respect for rights arguably fulfills a crucial function. Empathy and respect for rights are not identical, but they may well be coextensive. Rights-based moral action and respectful concern without empathy depicts an unlovely, normatively impoverished scenario. Similarly, empathy without emphasis on rights is conceivable, but equally incomplete. My considered intuition about an effective and compelling approach to moral and epistemic interaction[9] sees respect for rights as its backbone, and empathy as its heart.

A discussion of epistemic empathy would also be incomplete without consideration of possible limits. It appears that there is an indirect limit and also a more obviously direct set of limitations. The former consideration concerns the extent to which epistemic empathy and mindfulness will eventually entail consensus or agreement. Given that such empathy will embody a certain favorable attitude toward others' beliefs, thoughts, and ideas, one might ask whether such a proattitude will eventually lead to agreement. I do not think that it will—or that it should, for that matter. As an empathic parent, I may not wish to impose my desires, needs, and ambitions on my child, to force my child to endure the violin, ballet, and other lessons that may lead to the kind of success that has always eluded me, that is, without taking the child's point of view, ideas, desires, and aspirations into account. But this point of view counts for considerably less when there are other parentalistic matters at issue, like a visit to the dentist or doctor, extra mathematics classes, and the like. Relatedly, if someone's belief is mistaken, or someone's point of view involves false assumptions, dodgy justification, and so on, then empathy would not lead to endorsement of such a belief or point of view—quite the opposite. My open-mindedness and fair-mindedness, for example, would not require me to adopt and/or endorse a view or train of thought that, for good reasons, I may disagree with.[10] In fact, my empathic attitude and 'objective listening' may lead me to recognize and understand the kinds of perceptual and conceptual errors that have been committed here—just like it may lead me to change my own mind or outlook. It may—but it need not: epistemic empathy is not sufficient for eventual consensus. Furthermore, just as empathy, in "being instrumental to moral action, . . . must be employed in tandem with specific moral principles and directives to generate a moral response" (Oxley 2011: 5), epistemic empathy is instrumental in the acquisition of knowledge and the recognition of truth—if used in tandem with specific epistemic principles and directives to generate an epistemic response.

The second set of limitations concerns empathy with those who are either unwilling or otherwise unprepared to be empathic, mindful, and so forth, toward the positions, beliefs, thoughts, and experiences of others. "There are limits to epistemic empathy," Slote notes (2013: 91fn.10), just as there are limits to the empathy an empathic person will feel concerning other people's welfare. If people betray you, your empathy for them will likely diminish to the vanishing point, in the wake of the anger you feel toward them, and, more generally, we will tend to have less empathy for those who are themselves lacking in empathic concern for others. In parallel fashion, one will be much less epistemically empathic and open-minded about the views of those who aren't epistemically empathic and open-minded towards one's own views or those of others, and such reactions of understandable epistemic intolerance and of what might therefore even be thought of as mild *epistemic anger* are as much a part of epistemic empathy and open-mindedness as reactions of anger and lesser empathic benevolence towards those who hurt us or others are built into empathic caring as a concept and phenomenon.

There is, however, clearly no precise method for determining when a person's empathy is no longer morally and epistemically appropriate. Some of us seem to have, especially with regard to those we love, sheer inexhaustible empathic resources. As a guide for educators, albeit perhaps not for parents, one might argue that neither too little nor too much empathy is desirable.

NOTES

1. This was, indeed, the response of a young woman to my presentation on way-centered and truth-centered epistemologies at the International Conference on *Migrations of knowledge: Potentials and limits of knowledge production and critique in Europe and Africa*, Carl von Ossietzky University, Oldenburg/Germany, in December 2014.
2. Fricker borrows the notion of epistemic humiliation from Simone de Beauvoir.
3. A link might be forged here with Masolo's reference (2010: 18) to "a viable tool for transforming the world."
4. Referring to participative "indigenous," "African research methodology," Khupe and Keane assert (2017: 34),

> Standard notions of validity are thrown into question. 'Truths' are defined not only as factual truths and representational truths, but also as healing truths. . . . For the research process to be truly participative, respectful challenge needs to be directed across the whole research community's input and assumptions. Such robust engagement guards against romanticizing [indigenous knowledge] systems, helps to acknowledge changing contexts, and allows for multiple truths.

It is difficult to make sense of this understanding of truth, that is, as necessarily constituted by "multiple truths." Can a "healing truth" that is not also a factual truth even have the status of 'truth'? I suspect that what the authors are actually referring to in all these cases is not 'truths' but, rather, 'beliefs'.

5. See also Clark (2010): "Empathy, at its most basic level, is epistemic." An objection that might be raised at this point concerns the apparent redundancy of the term 'epistemic'. Or perhaps we might do away with 'epistemic empathy' altogether, in favor of an idea like 'recognition'. I have argued elsewhere (Horsthemke 2015) that the notion of epistemic empathy fulfils a distinct and irreducible function in epistemological discourse, especially in education.

6. In Slote's view (2013: 91fn.7),

> there are no strictly intellectual opinions. All genuine opinions involve a relevantly favorable attitude, and perhaps this emotional aspect of the opinions facilitates the osmotic transmission of opinions (e.g., from parents to children) and makes it more plausible to accept the common sense view that they can be transmitted or soaked up in this way.

7. Empathy is relevant to Kantian and contractarian ethics in terms of recognizing others as rational agents and as rational (constrained) maximizers of self-interest (e.g., in 'prisoner's-dilemma'-type of situations; see Poundstone 1993), respectively.

8. As Oxley notes,

> empathy alone is insufficient and undesirable as a sole moral criterion; empathy is a psychological experience, not a normative principle. Thus, it cannot serve as a criterion of morally good action. (Oxley 2011: 6)

9. As I have pointed out in chapter 3, like other ideas usually employed in normative discourses, the notion of rights has also acquired an epistemic significance. Having 'the right to be sure' has been used as synonymous with possession of adequate justification (see Scheffler 1965; Ayer 1956).

10. In "cases where one knows [or has good reason to suspect] that someone is defending a position that is absolutely beyond the pale of rational discussion, it seems . . . that open-mindedness and fair-mindedness don't require one to (try to) see what s/he is saying in a favorable light" (Slote 2013: 91, fn. 10).

Chapter 10

An Applied Epistemology for the Real World

Philosophy in all its forms and traditions has always been centrally preoccupied with truth. However, rather suddenly, in the last couple of decades of the twentieth century truth became unfashionable. I cannot help thinking that particular members of the academic community—certain constructivists, postmodernists and postcolonial theorists, even some feminists (see Quale 2008; Hall and Ames 1987, 1998; Maffie 2009, 2014; Rosemont Jr. et al. 2014a, b; Harding 1991, 1996; Code 2013, and the emphasis on locality, subjectivity, and standpoint perspectives)—have contributed to the current climate in which truth, facts and rationality are treated with disdain. For example, the idea that truth is not objective or universal has taken hold not only of popular culture but also of politics, perhaps to the detriment of the latter. However understandable postcolonial and postmodern theorists' initial motivations may be, it appears that they have targeted the wrong ideas. Together with the ethical and the political, they have the ontological and the epistemological in their sights, which accounts for a lot of the confusion and errors. The precedence given to assorted political and ideological agendas, then, along with the rising popularity of certain 'isms' (like anti-foundationalism and standpointism) and also of pseudoscience in academia, has led to a decline both of truth as a serious subject and an intellectual tradition that arguably began with Socrates, Plato, and Aristotle and became a defining characteristic of the Enlightenment.

THE 'POST-TRUTH' WORLD

After much discussion, debate, and research, the Oxford Dictionaries Word of the Year 2016 was *post-truth*—an adjective defined as "relating to or denoting circumstances in which objective facts are less influential in shaping public opinion than appeals to emotion and personal belief".[1] In this case, the 'post-' prefix does not mean "after" so much as it implies an atmosphere in which a notion is irrelevant (see, e.g., Maffie 2009; Rosemont Jr. 2014a, b). Thus, post-truth as an adjective refers to "beyond or superseding the importance of truth; usually in a pejorative sense, uncaring of factual accuracy." As a noun, post-truth signals the "fact or state of being post-truth; a time period or situation in which facts have become less important than emotional persuasion."

As early as 2004, Ralph Keyes coined the term "post-truth era" in his book by the same title:

> In the post-truth era, borders blur between truth and lies, honesty and dishonesty, fiction and nonfiction. Deceiving others becomes a challenge, a game, and ultimately a habit.[2]

The era of truth and facts/facticity has given way to an era where personal feelings, inclinations, and biases become significant in interpreting data.

Post-truth politics (also called *postfactual politics*) refers to a political culture in which debate is framed largely by appeals to emotion disconnected from the details of policy, and by the repeated assertion of talking points to which factual rebuttals are ignored. While post-truth political techniques have long played a role in campaigns worldwide, the contemporary origin of the term is attributed to blogger David Roberts used the term in 2010 in a column for *Grist* (Roberts 2010), where it was defined as "a political culture in which politics (public opinion and media narratives) have become almost entirely disconnected from policy (the substance of legislation)." It became widespread during the 2016 presidential election in the United States and the 2016 referendum on membership in the European Union in the United Kingdom.

When people refer to post-truth, they seem to mean those political statements which are untouched by rational argument, which are held and accepted regardless of (even against) the evidence available. In this sense, they are above and beyond truth, since there is no seeming 'truth maker'. There is no actual state of affairs which can make that idea true or false.

A long list of proven untruths and fabrications characterized the "Leave" campaign prior to the Brexit vote.[3] In a prescient 1967 essay, Hannah Arendt writes that no one "has ever doubted that truth and politics are on rather bad terms with each other, and no one," as far as she knows, "has ever counted truthfulness among the political virtues":

> Lies have always been regarded as necessary and justifiable tools not only of the politician's or the demagogue's but also of the statesman's trade. (1) . . . While probably no former time tolerated so many diverse opinions on religious

or philosophical matters, factual truth, if it happens to oppose a given group's profit or pleasure, is greeted today with greater hostility than ever before (5) ... Truthfulness has never been counted among the political virtues, because it has little indeed to contribute to that change of the world and of circumstances which is among the most legitimate political activities. (13)

Arendt considers "the result of a consistent and total substitution of lies for factual truth" to be "not that the lies will now be accepted as truth, and the truth be defamed as lies, but that the sense by which we take our bearings in the real world—and the category of truth vs. falsehood is among the mental means to this end—is being destroyed" (15). Why is her analysis so topical? A democratic debate requires provable facts about which there exists agreement. The debate then concerns what actually follows from these facts. But what happens when facts themselves are not given their proper due, when there is a constant stream of lies, deflections, and dilutions? The culture of debate then follows the laws of 'like' and 'dislike'. The value of a statement is not measured by its plausibility or facticity but by its potential to accumulate 'likes'.

After the 2017 presidential inauguration in the United States, White House press secretary and communications director Sean Spicer famously declared: "This was the largest audience to ever witness an inauguration, period." When confronted with the obvious inaccuracy of this statement, Trump's counsellor Kellyanne Conway defended Spicer by stating that he had offered "alternative facts." Conway's phrase reminded many commentators of "Newspeak," a dystopian language style that was a key element of the society portrayed in George Orwell's novel *1984*. Even before former U.S. President Donald Trump's CIA speech,[4] Spicer's first press conference, or Kellyanne Conway's attempts to spin Russian hacking, Trump's team had problems with telling the truth. Trump supporter Rudy Giuliani famously declared that before Barack Obama, there had been no notable terror attacks on American soil. (This statement is made even more piquant by the fact that Giuliani was New York City mayor at the time of the 9/11 attacks in 2001.) As *Politifact* noted, Trump made almost 200 statements during the campaign that were deemed 'pants on fire'[5] lies or simply false. In the first thirty-five days of Trump's presidency, *The Washington Post* counted 133 false or misleading claims, which it catalogued and carefully refuted.[6] Trump seems to suffer no negative consequences for making things up. If anything, his popularity has held steady and even increased with every accusation that he has stated a factual inaccuracy, notably his dismissal of the 2020 presidential election as "fraudulent."

The interesting thing is that it is not difficult to identify these statements as lies. Even those who applaud the speakers know, more often than not, that what they have just been offered is untrue. But they do not care—because they like what they have heard. The question whether or not something relates to the facts has become irrelevant. Take Giuliani's statements about terror attacks. They are addressed to people who feel that since Obama became U.S. president, everything has become worse, even terror. The truth of a statement is no longer significant for its value in the political arena.[7] A defining trait of post-truth politics is that campaigners continue to repeat their talking points, even if these are found to be untrue by the media or independent experts. Post-truth politics can also include a claimed rejection of partisanship and negative campaigning. Michael Deacon (2016), parliamentary sketch writer for *The Daily Telegraph*, summarized the core message of post-truth politics as "Facts are negative. Facts are pessimistic. Facts are unpatriotic." Post-truth and alternative-fact politics seem to have received unintended support from postcolonial misgivings about truth.

'WAY-CENTERED' AND 'TRUTH-CENTERED' EPISTEMOLOGIES

Against the understanding of knowledge, facts, and truth developed in this book, and its educational implications, it has been contended that non-Anglo-European traditions place no special emphasis on 'belief', 'evidence', or 'truth'—but that, according to indigenous practitioners, it is rather 'the way' that constitutes knowledge, harmonious interaction, and appropriate models of conduct (Hall and Ames 1987, 1998; Maffie 2009; Rosemont Jr. 2014a, b; Maraldo 2014; Thakchoe 2014). In this regard, John Maraldo refers to Japanese philosopher Wasuji Tetsurō, who associates propositional or descriptive truth (*shinri*) with truthfulness or sincerity and with trust (the connotations of Wasuji's term *makoto* also range from fidelity and honesty to reality and factual truth; Maraldo 2014: 170, 171). It has been argued, further, that cognitive states are (to be) seen as 'maps', as useful and practical action-guides (Deloria Jr. 1995, Deloria et al. 1999, Hester and Cheney 2001). This is why (so the argument for "polycentric epistemologies" or "polycentric global epistemology" goes) divination, rain-making, rain-discarding, shamanism, sorcery, ceremony, ritual, mysticism, and so forth, must be acknowledged as ways of knowing alongside animal husbandry, botany, medicine, mathematics, tool-making, and the like (Maffie 2009: 60).

David Hall and Roger Ames argue that those epistemologies that might be called "way-seeking," as opposed to "truth-seeking,"

> are concerned neither with truth, true belief nor truthful representation. Rather, they are concerned with identifying the *proper path* or *appropriate model* of conduct that will enable humans to live the kind of life suitable for human

beings. (Maffie 2009: 57, emphasis added; see Hall and Ames 1987, Hall and Ames 1998)

James Maffie refers to the Mexica (Aztec) concept of *neltiliztli* (rootedness) as being "embedded within a larger philosophical conception of human endeavours that [he sees] as path-seeking or 'praxis-guiding' (to borrow from Rosemont [2014: 155]) rather than truth-seeking" (Maffie 2014: 161–162). For many (if not most) indigenous Africans, Asians, and Oceanians, for example, this involves

> living harmoniously with one's social surroundings. Correspondence truth plays no role in this endeavour. One aims for a life of authenticity, genuineness, rectitude and wholeness—not knowledge defined as justified true belief. [This kind of] epistemology seeks to identify the kind of practical know-how needed for following this path. (Maffie 2009: 57)

This basic orientation is echoed in a symposium anchored by Henry Rosemont, Jr. (Maffie, Maraldo and Sonam Thakchoe are the other participants; Rosemont Jr. et al. 2014: 150). The argument is that traditions outside the Anglo-European mainstream

> seem to draw on an integrated view of thinking, feeling, and living a human life. For their practitioners, truth is less of a correspondence with a given external reality. In fact, it enables human beings to strike the right path in living good, social lives.

According to Wasuji, the "correspondence between thought and external things . . . does not deserve the name of truth if it does derive from a practiced correspondence between words and acts, a correspondence shared in a community" (Maraldo 2014: 172). Wasuji argues that truth is reached when truthfulness (or sincerity) informs our judgments. Truth for him is more than correct statement, more than conformity of words with facts.

> Wasuji notes that one could intend to deceive but inadvertently describe the facts correctly, and such a description would not constitute truth. Truthfulness depends on preserving a relationship of trust. Put negatively, truth requires not betraying the trust of others. (Ibid.)

Wasuji does not appear to consider the possibility that one can speak sincerely and nonetheless misrepresent the facts.

Speaking about conquest-era Mexica philosophy in particular, Maffie (2014: 161) contends that it lacks such a concept and theory of truth. Truth as correspondence, mirroring, representation, or aboutness plays no role in the Mexica's theory of language. Mexica philosophy embraces instead a concept of well-rootedness . . . that derives its meaning from a conceptual cluster that includes: furthering one's ancestral lineage . . . and inherited lifeway; arranging, ordering, and balancing one's lifeway; as well as appropriateness, rectitude, authenticity, and the ability to be assimilated into one's lifeway.

These responses seem to contain a number of confusions and errors. The first is the failure to distinguish between epistemology, on the one hand, and ethics (in this case virtue ethics) on the other. While there are important connections between the two (as a quick survey of the field of social epistemology will show), and notwithstanding the conceptual dependence of 'truthfulness' on 'truth', there appears to be no awareness on the part of the authors that they may be committing a category mistake here. It is also unclear whether a hard-and-fast distinction between propositional and practical knowledge is possible[8] (I will return to this point below). Furthermore, identification of the 'proper (or right) path', and so forth, will almost certainly involve some beliefs about the appropriateness and correctness of this identification. Surely, there must be beliefs about which paths are '*im*proper', 'wrong', or which models are '*in*appropriate', and what counts as 'correct' identification of proper paths and appropriate models.[9] One can quite coherently aim *both* for "a life of authenticity, genuineness, rectitude and wholeness" *and* "knowledge defined as justified true belief." The two are not mutually exclusive—quite the contrary. A similar response might be given to Maffie's claim (2009: 57),

> Conquest-era indigenous Nahuatl-speaking philosophers in Central Mexico conceived knowing in terms of balance, well-groundedness, moral uprightness, authenticity and disclosingness . . . Correspondence truth played no role in their notions of wisdom, knowledge, or right belief.

Finally, the excessive focus on "correspondence truth" as the standard Western (or Northern) conception of truth may be misguided, as I have indicated in chapter 3. There are different theories of truth, all with distinct strengths and weaknesses. Many theorists would probably contend that only one theory can be correct. Yet, as Bridges (1999) has argued, quite compellingly, different theories of truth might be seen to fit different areas of knowledge or (educational) research models (see chapter 3). It follows that the assumption of correspondence truth being the default conception within the Western philosophical canon is rather narrow and, in fact, mistaken.

> It has been contended (by Deloria Jr., Deloria et al. and Hester and Cheney) that indigenous North American philosophies treat *cognitive states as maps rather*

than as beliefs. Native Americans adopt an agnostic attitude towards the correspondence truth of their maps seeing as they are concerned only with the utility of maps as practical action-guides. Native American philosophy does not focus upon belief and thus worries not about correspondence truth of belief. Native Americans focus upon practices and adopt an attitude of non-belief (i.e. neither belief nor disbelief) towards their practices. Knowing is likewise practical. It is not a species of belief or theoretical attitude towards some abstract proposition, justified or otherwise. (Maffie 2009: 57; emphasis added)

In response, one might point out that there is nothing incoherent about treating beliefs as maps. White does this explicitly in the chapter "Beliefs: Maps by Which We Steer" in his book *The Child's Mind* (White 2002). Moreover, while propositional and practical knowledge are clearly distinct, and one does not collapse into the other, they are considerably more intimately connected than the above-named authors are willing to acknowledge. Surely, Native Americans will almost certainly entertain certain beliefs about, for example, the utility and sustainability of their practices. Similarly, if indigenous "Amazonia philosophy . . . conceives knowledge in terms of the trustworthy, responsible, and careful ordering and arranging of things" and "eschews broad, overarching, abstract conceptions of truth such as correspondence between propositions and the world" (Maffie 2009: 57), it is difficult to see how one is to make sense of trustworthiness, ordering, arranging, and so forth, in the absence of truth-based knowledge—especially given their justificatory role.

Maffie (57–58) is arguably correct in pointing out that "Western truth-seeking epistemologies (beginning with Plato and Aristotle) . . . standardly define knowledge in terms of theoretical contemplation rather than practical application." After all, this is what *makes* them 'epistemologies'. But if one accepts, *merely for the sake of argument*, that there is an undesirable bias involved here, one could direct a similar complaint towards Maffie—who focuses on one (practical knowledge) at the expense of another (propositional knowledge). He keeps returning to this dichotomy:

> it is common for [those working in non-Anglo-European traditions] to reject what they see as Western philosophy's . . . obsession with truth (as correspondence), belief, and worldview. What matters most to indigenous North Americans, for example, is how one lives—*not what one believes.* Indigenous North American philosophy is practice-centred (58–59; emphasis added)

To repeat: it is difficult to see how views about how one lives or ought to live, what one practices or ought to practice, and so forth, *can* be held in the absence of belief (i.e., beliefs about the utility, appropriateness and sustainability of one's practices, life, and so forth) and of the corresponding desire for one's beliefs to be not only justified but also true.

AN APPLIED EPISTEMOLOGY FOR THE REAL WORLD

There appears to be one last avenue open to advocates of "way-seeking" philosophies and defenders of "polycentric global epistemology." "Knowledge" from an indigenous or aboriginal perspective, according to Maffie (59),

> concerns how one conducts oneself in the world. It is not about producing rational arguments or deductive-nomological explanations, and the inability to produce these is not considered an epistemological shortcoming. Indeed, it is precisely the insistence upon rational proofs that is typically considered a shortcoming. Hence the very idea of discursively refuting [Western critics] is misplaced since it appeals to notions of propositional truth and falsity that these philosophies reject.

How can one provide a response here that will not exhibit the much-maligned rationality and discursiveness? Maffie's intended knock-down argument will lead to exactly the kind of impasse illustrated in the following pertinent excerpt from a play by Bertolt Brecht. Although this parable is ostensibly about reality, and our perception of it, it also serves as a fitting epitaph to the discussion of the fate of truth with which I began the last section. In other words, the parable can also be taken to pose questions around the nature of knowledge, realism versus constructivism, and objectivity-versus-subjectivity of truth and truth-claims. The very reason why an answer has not been furnished actually constitutes the answer—and directs us away from subjectivism, relativism, and constructivism.

The teacher: Si Fu, name the central questions of philosophy!
Si Fu: Are things outside of us, for themselves, also without us, or are the things within us, for ourselves, not without us?
The teacher: Which opinion is the correct one?
Si Fu: No verdict has been reached yet.
The teacher: What was the latest tendency among the majority of our philosophers?
Fu: The things are outside of us, for themselves, also without us.
The teacher: Why did the question remain unsolved?
Si Fu: The conference that was supposed to yield the final verdict took place, as it has done for the past two hundred years, in the monastery Mi Sang, on the banks of the Yellow River. The question was: Is the Yellow River real, or does it exist only in people's heads? During the conference, however, there was a melting of snow in the mountains, and the Yellow River rose above its banks

and swept away the monastery Mi Sang and all conference participants. The proof that the things are outside of us, for themselves, also without us, therefore, has not been furnished. (Brecht 1967–1969: 36, my translation; see also Horsthemke 2010c, 2011, 2014a, 2016a)

Contra John Keats, truth is not necessarily beautiful: in fact, it is often brutal, ugly, and disgusting. We also do not always love truth: on balance, perhaps our lives would seem to be more pleasant and perhaps even more bearable without it. What, then, is it about truth that makes it so important and that renders its absence a horrible tragedy? According to Keyes,

> Post-truthfulness . . . erodes the foundation of trust that underlies any healthy civilization. When enough of us peddle fantasy as fact, society loses its grounding in reality. Society would crumble altogether if we assumed others were as likely to dissemble as tell the truth. We are perilously close to that point.[10]

Without an epistemological premium placed on truth and without an ethical premium placed on truthfulness, society on any large scale could not function and would in all likelihood break down completely. If we could not know as a matter of course whether or not someone was telling the truth, the social fabric would simply be eroded—or society would not be possible in the first place. *Imfihlakalo yasemhlabeni iqiniso*—'the truth' may be the world's secret,[11] but we can learn to avoid falsehoods and error and, in so doing, get closer to the way things really are—or were, for that matter.

While postcolonial theory arguably errs in postulating the existence of diverse knowledges and truths, the diversity in question is conceivably generated by (characteristically) practical epistemic priorities—priorities that emerge from different lived experiences, individual as well as social and cultural. A plausible view appears to be that knowledge and truth do not fluctuate, that they remain invariant across individuals, societies, and cultures, but that there may well be distinctive sets of epistemic concerns that arise from personal, historical, and sociopolitical circumstances. If it is correct to assume that practical epistemic and educational priorities will emanate from life experiences and from the ways these are socially articulated, then one might assume that, given the different life experiences of people across the globe, the practical epistemic and educational priorities will also differ.

The promise of an educationally relevant epistemology, an applied epistemology for the real world, then, has in part to do with locality and context-specific relations—but not in terms of any exclusionist, 'hands-off' approach. Rather, it appears to be plausible that the particular historical, geographic, and sociocultural experiences of people give rise to particular priorities that shape their epistemic theory and practice—and also yield conceptual and epistemological tools that are likely to enrich education and educational research as a whole.

NOTES

1. https://en.oxforddictionaries.com/word-of-the-year/word-of-the-year-2016 (retrieved February 13, 2017).
2. http://www.ralphkeyes.com/the-post-truth-era/(retrieved February 13, 2017).
3. http://www.richardcorbett.org.uk/long-list-leave-lies/ (retrieved February 21, 2017). See also http://brexitlies.com/http://brexitlies.com/. Incidentally, this is not to imply that the 'Stay' campaign operated without resorting to lies and fabrications. See Horsthemke (2017b).
4. In January 2017, Trump delivered a largely self-referential speech that included an untruthful claim that his inauguration was better attended than those of Barack Obama. He also made the astounding claim so belied by the evidence—"I love honesty." Here, too, I do not mean to imply that Hilary Clinton's campaign was completely devoid of untruths.
5. http://www.politifact.com/personalities/donald-trump/ 'Liar, liar, pants on fire' is a phrase that children like to use when someone is suspected of lying.
6. https://www.washingtonpost.com/graphics/politics/trump-claims/ (retrieved 23 February 2017).
7. Alexander Gauland of the German right-wing party *Alternative für Deutschland* (AfD) asserted in 2017 that the German government is trying to replace the German people with migrants. It is difficult to prove or disprove this kind of statement. But this does not matter to AfD supporters and sympathizers: what matters is that Gauland has articulated what they are feeling—in this case, what they fear or dislike.
8. According to Maffie (2014: 164), "philosophic reflection for the Mexica is first and foremost a *practical* endeavor concerned with creating a good life, not a *theoretical* endeavor concerned with discovering truth." "Mexica philosophy speaks not of propositional belief ('belief that') and knowledge ('knowledge that') but of '*ohtlatoca*' ('following a path') and 'know how' respectively" (166). "Right-path knowing ('*tlamatiliztli*') . . . is understood in terms of skill, competence, and the ability to make things happen—and not in terms of the intellectual apprehension of truths or states of affairs" (166–167).
9. A similar point can be made about Burkhart's reference to Buddhist philosophy (2009: 21):

In Mahāyāna Buddhism, *prajñā* is the perfection of wisdom . . . One foolish notion is enough to shut off *prajñā*.

But on what grounds is a notion considered "foolish"? Identification of *prajñā* surely requires an objective, independent standard of distinguishing between wisdom and foolishness.

10. http://www.ralphkeyes.com/the-post-truth-era/ (retrieved February 23, 2017; see also Horsthemke 2017b).
11. The IsiZulu proverb can be translated as "The truth is the world's secret."

References

Abdullah, J. & Stringer, E. 1999. Indigenous knowledge, indigenous learning, indigenous research. In *What is Indigenous Knowledge?: Voices from the Academy*, ed. L.M. Semali & J.L. Kincheloe: 143–155. New York/London: Falmer Press.

Adam, S., Alangui, W. & Barton, B. 2003. A comment on: Rowlands and Carson 'Where would formal, academic mathematics stand in a curriculum informed by ethnomathematics? A critical review'. *Educational Studies in Mathematics* 52: 327–335.

Adeyemi, M.B. & Adeyinka, A.A. 2003. The principles and content of African traditional education. *Educational Philosophy and Theory* 35(4): 374–382.

Agrawal, A. 1995. Dismantling the divide between indigenous and scientific knowledge. *Development and Change* 26: 413–439.

Ahenakew, C., Andreotti, V., Cooper, G. & Hireme, H. 2014. Beyond epistemic provincialism: De-provincializing indigenous resistance. *AlterNative: An International Journal of Indigenous People* 10(3): 216–231.

Aikenhead, G.S. 1996. Cultural assimilation in science classrooms: Border crossings and other solutions. *Studies in Science Education* 7: 1–52.

Aikenhead, G.S. 2001. Integrating western and aboriginal sciences: Cross-cultural science teaching. *Research in Science Education* 31(3): 337–355.

Aikenhead, G.S. & Elliott, D. 2010. An emerging decolonizing science education in Canada. *Canadian Journal of Science, Mathematics and Technology Education* 10(4): 321–338.

Aikenhead, G.S. & Jegede, O.J. 1999. Cross-cultural science education: A cognitive explanation of a cultural phenomenon. *Journal of Research in Science Teaching* 36(3): 269–287.

Al-Faruqi, I. 1988. Islamization of knowledge: Problems, principles, and prospective. *In Islam: Source and Purpose of Knowledge/* Proceedings and selected papers of the Second Conference on Islamization of Knowledge 1402/1982. International Institute of Islamic Thought, Herndon.

Anderson, E. 2002. Feminist epistemology: An interpretation and a defense. In *Knowledge & Inquiry: Readings in Epistemology*, ed. K.B. Wray: 312–351. Ontario/New York: Broadview Press.

Andrej, M. 2015. Die Konstruktion von traditional ecological knowledge: Eine kritische Analyse wissenschaftlicher Umwelt- und Naturschutzdiskurse. *Social Ecology Working Paper* 162. Vienna, April.

Andreotti, V., Ahenakew, C. & Cooper, G. 2011. Epistemological pluralism: Ethical and pedagogical challenges in higher education. *AlterNative: An International Journal of Indigenous People* 7(1): 40–50.

Ani, M. 1994. *Yurugu: An Africa-Centered Critique of European Cultural Thought and Behavior*. Trenton/NJ: Africa World Press.

Antony, L. 1995. 'Sisters, please, I'd rather do it myself': A defense of individualism in feminist epistemology. *Philosophical Topics* 23(2): 59–94.

Antrosio, J. 2013. Ruth Benedict, Patterns of culture: From culture to cultures. http://www.livinganthropologically.com/2013/01/23/ruth-benedict-patterns-of-culture/ (retrieved 18 December 2015).

Arendt, H. 1967. Truth and politics. *The New Yorker*, February 25 https://idanlandau.files.wordpress.com/2014/12/arendt-truth-and-politics.pdf (retrieved 14 February 2017): 1–15.

Armstrong, J. 2005. Zulu pottery. *Indilingua: African Journal of Indigenous Systems* 4(1): 340–346.

Asante, M.K. 1987. *The Afrocentric Idea*. Philadelphia: Temple University Press.

Asante, M.K. 2003. *Afrocentricity: The Theory of Social Change*. Chicago: African American Images (revised and expanded edition).

Asante, M.K. 2005. African ways of knowing and cognitive faculties. In *Encyclopedia of Black Studies*, ed. M.K. Asante & A. Mazama: 40–42. Thousand Oaks: SAGE.

Asante, M.K. 2017. The philosophy of Afrocentricity. In *The Palgrave Handbook of African Philosophy*, ed. A. Afolayan & T. Falola: 231–244. New York: Palgrave Macmillan.

Ascher, M. 2002. The Kolam tradition. *American Scientist* 90: 57–63.

Ascher, M. & D'Ambrosio, U. 1994. Ethnomathematics: A dialogue. *For the Learning of Mathematics* 14(2): 36–43.

Ayer, A.J. 1956. *The Problem of Knowledge*. Harmondsworth/Middlesex: Pelican.

Bakari, R.S. 1997. Epistemology from an Afrocentric perspective: Enhancing black students' consciousness through an Afrocentric perspective. http://digitalcommons.unl.edu/pocpwi2/20 (retrieved 19 March 2009): 1–4.

Banks, J.A. 1998. The lives and values of researchers: Implications for educating citizens in a multicultural society. *Education Researcher* 22(5): 4–14.

Barca, D. & Arenas, A. 2010. Words of caution on indigenous knowledge and education. *Educational Practice and Theory* 32(1): 5–28.

Barnes, J. 1997. *Cross Channel*. London/Basingstoke: Picador.

Barnhardt, R. & Kawagley, A.O. 2005. Indigenous knowledge systems and Alaska native ways of knowing. *Anthropology and Education Quarterly* 36(1): 8–23.

Barton, B. 1996. Making sense of ethnomathematics: Ethnomathematics is making sense. *Educational Studies in Mathematics* 31(1): 201–233.

Barton, B. 1999a. Ethnomathematics: A political plaything. *For the Learning of Mathematics* 19(1): 32–35.
Barton, B. 1999b. Ethnomathematics and philosophy. *Zentralblatt für Didaktik der Mathematik* 1999(2): 54–58.
Barton, B. 2004. Mathematics and mathematical practices: where to draw the line? *For the Learning of Mathematics* 24(1): 22–24.
Becker, O.G. 2003. Dein Augapfel lässt mich in die Zukunft sehen. *Frankfurter Allgemeine Sonntagszeitung*, Nr. 13/ Wissenschaft, 10 March: 61.
Becker, O.G. 2006a. Adam—niedergemetzelt für ein blutiges Ritual, 1.Teil. *Spiegel Online/* Wissenschaft, 20 October. http://www.spiegel.de/wissenschaft/mensch/0,1518,443144,00.html (retrieved 3 March 2009): 1–3.
Becker, O.G. 2006b. Adam—niedergemetzelt für ein blutiges Ritual, 2. Teil. *Spiegel Online/* Wissenschaft, 20 October. http://www.spiegel.de/wissenschaft/mensch/0,1518,443144-2,00.html (retrieved 3 March 2009): 1–2.
Becker, O.G. 2007. 'Muti Morde' in Afrika: Töten für okkulte Medizin. In *Witchcraft in Modern Africa: Witches, Witch-Hunts and Magical Imaginaries/ Hexenglauben im modernen Afrika: Hexen, Hexenverfolgung und magische Vorstellungswelten*, ed. B. Schmidt & R. Schulte: 87–212. Hamburg: DOBU-Verlag.
Bekker, T. 2013. Ensuring epistemological access. In *Education Studies*, ed. K. Horsthemke, P. Siyakwazi, E. Walton & C. Wolhuter: 463–485. Cape Town: Oxford University Press South Africa.
Belenky, M.F., Clinchy, B.M., Goldberger, N.R. & Tarule, J.M. 1986. *Women's Ways of Knowing: The Development of Self, Voice, and Mind*. New York: Basic Books.
Bello, A.G.A. 2004. Some methodological controversies in African philosophy. In *A Companion to African Philosophy*, ed. K. Wiredu: 263–273. Oxford: Blackwell.
Benedict, R. 1934. *Patterns of Culture*. New York: Houghton Mifflin.
Benedict, R. 2000. In defense of moral relativism. In *Introduction to Philosophy: Classical and Contemporary Readings* (2nd ed.), ed. L.P. Pojman: 626–633. Belmont/CA: Wadsworth/Thomson Learning.
Benson, O. & Stangroom, J. 2006. *Why Truth Matters*. London/New York: Continuum.
Berkes, F. & Berkes, M.K. 2009. Ecological complexity, fuzzy logic, and holism in indigenous knowledge. *Futures* 41: 6–12.
Berry, J.W. 1985. Learning mathematics in a second language: Some cross-cultural issues. *For the Learning of Mathematics* 5(2): 18–23.
Berry, K.S. 2015. Research as bricolage: Embracing relationality, multiplicity and complexity. In *Doing Educational Research*, ed. K. Tobin & S. Steinberg: 79–110. Rotterdam, Boston & Taipei: Sense Publishers.
Biko, S. 2004. *I Write What I Like*. Johannesburg: Picador Africa.
Bishop, A.J. 1988. Mathematics education in its cultural context. *Educational Studies in Mathematics* 19: 179–191.
Boghossian, P. 2006a. *Fear of Knowledge: Against Relativism and Constructivism*. Oxford: Clarendon Press.
Boghossian, P. 2006b. Behaviorism, constructivism, and Socratic pedagogy. *Educational Philosophy and Theory* 38(6): 713–722.

Borba, M.C. 1990/1997. Ethnomathematics and education. *For the Learning of Mathematics* 10(1): 39–43. Reprinted in *Ethnomathematics: Challenging Eurocentrism in Mathematics Education*, ed. A.B. Powell & M. Frankenstein: 261–272. New York: SUNY Press (page references pertain to the latter).
Borges Coelho, J.P. 2007. The state, the community, and natural calamities in rural Mozambique. In *Another Knowledge is Possible: Beyond Northern Epistemologies*, ed. B. De Sousa Santos: 219–245. London/New York: Verso.
Braidotti, R. 1991. *Patterns of Dissonance: A Study of Women in Contemporary Philosophy*. New York: Routledge.
Braidotti, R. 1993. Embodiment, sexual difference, and the nomadic subject. *Hypatia* 8(1): 1–13.
Braidotti, R. 2006. *Transpositions: On Nomadic Ethics*. Cambridge: Polity Press.
Brayboy, B.M.J. & Maughan, E. 2009. Indigenous knowledges and the story of the bean. *Harvard Educational Review* 7(1): 1–21.
Brecht, B. 1967–1969. Turandot oder Der Kongress der Weißwäscher. In *Stücke*, ed. B. Brecht, E. Hauptmann (Volume 14). Berlin/Weimar: Aufbau Verlag.
Bridges, D. 1999. Educational research: Pursuit of truth or flight of fancy? *British Educational Research Journal* 25(5): 597–616.
Brown, D. 1971. *Bury My Heart at Wounded Knee: An Indian History of the American West*. London: Barrie & Jenkins.
Bryan, J. 2009. Where would we be without them? Knowledge, space and power in indigenous politics. *Futures* 41: 24–32.
Bujo, B. 2009. Ecology and ethical responsibility from an African perspective. In *African Ethics: An Anthology of Comparative and Applied Ethics*, ed. M.F. Murove: 281–297. Scottsville: University of KwaZulu-Natal Press.
Burkhart, B.Y. 2004. What Coyote and Thales can teach us: An outline of American Indian epistemology. In *American Indian Thought: Philosophical Essays*, ed. A. Waters: 15–26. Oxford: Blackwell.
Callan, E. & Arena, D. 2009. Indoctrination. In *The Oxford Handbook of Philosophy of Education*, ed. H. Siegel: 104–121. Oxford/New York: Oxford University Press.
Campbell, M. & Campbell-Wright, R.K. 1995. Toward a feminist algebra. In *Teaching the Majority: Breaking the Gender Barrier in Science, Mathematics, and Engineering*, ed. S.V. Rosser: 127–144. New York: Teachers College Press.
Chan-Tiberghien, J. 2004. Towards a 'global educational justice' research paradigm: Cognitive justice, decolonizing methodologies, and critical pedagogy. *Globalisation, Societies and Education* 2(2): 191–213.
Clark, F. 2010. Empathy and epistemic closure. http://www.patheos.com/blogs/slacktivist/2010/04/30/empathy-and-epistemic-closure/ (retrieved 2 January 2014).
Code, L. 2012. Taking subjectivity into account. In *Education, Culture and Epistemological Diversity: Mapping a Contested Terrain*, ed. C.W. Ruitenberg & D.C. Phillips: 85–100. Dordrecht: Springer.
Code, L., Phillips, D.C., Ruitenberg, C.W., Siegel, H. & Stone, L. 2012. Epistemological diversity: A roundtable. In *Education, Culture and Epistemological Diversity: Mapping a Contested Terrain*, ed. C.W. Ruitenberg & D.C. Phillips: 121–143. Dordrecht: Springer.

Cohen, S. 1986. Knowledge and context. *Journal of Philosophy* 83(10): 574–586.
Contreras, L., Morales, J. & Ramírez, J. (eds.) 1999. *Ethnomathematics and Mathematics Education: Building an Equitable Future/* Proceedings of the First International Conference on Ethnomathematics (ICEM1), CD Rom, Universidad de Granada, Granada, Spain.
Corntassel, J. & Hardbarger, T. 2019. Educate to perpetuate: Land based pedagogies and community resurgence. *International Review of Education* 65: 87–116.
Crazy Bull, C. & White Hat, E.R. 2019. *Cangleska Wakan:* The ecology of the sacred circle and the role of tribal colleges and universities. *International Review of Education* 65: 117–141.
Crittenden, B.S. 1972. Indoctrination as mis-education. In *Concepts of Indoctrination: Philosophical Essays*, ed. I.A. Snook: 131–151. London: Routledge & Kegan Paul.
Crossman, P. & Devisch, R. 2002. Endogenous knowledge in anthropological perspective: A plea for a conceptual shift. In *Indigenous Knowledge and the Integration of Knowledge Systems: Towards a Philosophy of Articulation*, ed. C. Odora Hoppers: 96–125. Claremont: New Africa Books.
Cummings, D., Gaylard, A., Castley, G. & Whyte, I.J. n.d. *Management Charter— Draft Summary/Synthesis* http://celtis.sanparks.org/parks/kruger/conservation/sc ientific/key_issues/9.Management.pdf (retrieved 5 September 2006): 350–366.
Daes, E.-I. 1997. *Protection of the Heritage of Indigenous People*. Human Rights Studies Series 10. New York: United Nations.
D'Ambrosio, U. 1985. Ethnomathematics and its place in the history and pedagogy of mathematics. *For the Learning of Mathematics* 5(1): 44–48.
D'Ambrosio, U. 1990. *Etnomatemática: Arte ou técnica de explicar e conhecer*. São Paulo: Editora Atica.
D'Ambrosio, U. 2001. *Etnomatemática: Elo entre tradições e a modernidade*. São Paulo: Editora Atica.
D'Ambrosio, U. 2006. Ethnomathematics: The scenario 30 years after. Plenary presentation, Third International Conference on Ethnomathematics: *Cultural Connections and Mathematical Manipulations*, Auckland, New Zealand, 12–16 February.
Dangor, S. 2005. Islamization of disciplines: Towards an indigenous educational system. *Educational Philosophy and Theory* 35(4): 519–531.
Deacon, M. 2016. In a world of post-truth politics, Andrea Leadsom will make the perfect PM. *The Daily Telegraph*, 9 July 2016 (retrieved 11 July 2016).
Dei, G.J.S. 2002. Spiritual knowing and transformative learning. NALL (New Approaches to Lifelong Learning) Working Paper #59. http://www.oise.utoronto. ca/depts/sese/csew/nall/res/59GeorgeDei.pdf (retrieved 19 March 2009): 1–13.
Dei, G.J.S. 2004. Learning culture, spirituality and local knowledge: Implications for African schooling. *International Review of Education* 48(5): 335–360.
Delanty, G. 1997. *Social Science: Beyond Constructivism and Realism*. Buckingham: Open University Press.
Delgado Bernal, D. 1998. Using a Chicana feminist epistemology in educational research. *Harvard Educational Review* 68(4): 555–582.

Deloria Jr., V. 1995. *Red Earth, White Lies: Native Americans and the Myth of Scientific Fact*. New York: Scribner.
Deloria, B., Foehner, K. & Scinta, S. (eds.) 1999. *Spirit and Reason. A Vine Deloria Jr. Reader*. Golden/CO: Fulcrum.
De Monteiro, M. (ed.) 2002. Proceedings of the Second International Conference on Ethnomathematics (ICEM2), CD Rom, Lyrium Communacacão Ltda., Ouro Preto, Brazil.
De Oliveira Andreotti, V. 2011. (Towards) Decoloniality and diversality in global citizenship education. *Globalization, Societies and Education* 9 (3–4): 381–397.
De Oliveira Andreotti, V., Ahenakew, C. & Cooper, G. 2011. Equivocal knowing and elusive realities: Imagining global citizenship otherwise. In *Postcolonial Perspectives on Global Citizenship Education*, ed. V. de Oliveira Andreotti & L.M.T. Menezes de Souza: 221–237. London/New York: Routledge.
De Sousa Santos, B. (ed.) 2007. *Another Knowledge is Possible: Beyond Northern Epistemologies*. London/New York: Verso.
De Sousa Santos, B. 2007a. Preface. In *Another Knowledge is Possible: Beyond Northern Epistemologies*, ed. B. De Sousa Santos: vii–xvii. London/New York: Verso.
De Sousa Santos, B. 2007b. Human rights as an emancipatory script? Cultural and political conditions. In *Another Knowledge is Possible: Beyond Northern Epistemologies*, ed. B. De Sousa Santos: 3–40. London/New York: Verso.
De Sousa Santos, B. 2014. *Epistemologies of the South: Justice against Epistemicide*. London/New York: Routledge.
De Sousa Santos B., Nunes J.A. & Meneses M.P. 2007. Introduction: Opening up the canon of knowledge and recognition of difference. In *Another Knowledge is Possible: Beyond Northern Epistemologies*, ed. B. De Sousa Santos: xix–lxii. London/New York: Verso.
De Sousa Santos B. & Meneses M.P. 2020. Epistemologies of the South—Giving voice to the diversity of the South. In *Knowledges Born in the Struggle: Constructing the Epistemologies of the Global South*, ed. B. De Sousa Santos & M.P. Meneses: xvii–xliii. New York/London: Routledge.
Dondolo, L. 2005. Intangible heritage: The production of indigenous knowledge in various aspects of social life. *Indilingua: African Journal of Indigenous Systems* 4(1): 110–126.
Duffy, T.M. & Cunningham, D. 1996. Constructivism: Implications for the design and delivery of instruction. In *Handbook of Research for Educational Communications and Technology*, ed D. Jonnasen: 170–198. Mahwah/NJ: Lawrence Erlbaum Associates.
Egziabher, T.B.G. 2007. People-based globalization. In *Another Knowledge is Possible: Beyond Northern Epistemologies*, ed. B. De Sousa Santos: 417–436. London/New York: Verso.
Elgin, C.Z. 2002. Creation as reconfiguration: Art in the advancement of science. *International Studies in the Philosophy of Science* 16(1): 13–25.
Elgin, C.Z. 2004. True enough. In *Epistemology*, ed. E. Sosa & E. Villanueva: 113–131. Boston: Blackwell.

Ellis, S. & Ter Haar, G. 2004. *Worlds of Power: Religious Thought and Political Practice in Africa.* Johannesburg: Wits University Press.
Embong, R., Aziz, N.M.R., Abd Wahab, Z. & Maidinsah, H. 2010. An insight into the mathematical thinking of the Malay Songket weavers. *Procedia Social and Behavioral Sciences* 8: 713–720.
Enslin, P. & Horsthemke, K. 2004. Can *ubuntu* provide a model for citizenship education in democracy in African democracies? *Comparative Education* 40(4): 545–558.
Enslin, P. & Horsthemke, K. 2015. Rethinking the 'western tradition'. *Educational Philosophy and Theory* 47(11): 1166–1174.
Eyong, C.T. 2007. Indigenous knowledge and sustainable development in Africa: Case study on Central Africa. In *Indigenous Knowledge Systems and Sustainable Development: Relevance for Africa* (Edition: Tribes and tribals) Special Volume 1, ed. E.K. Boon & L. Hens: 121–139. Publisher: Kamla-Raj Enterprises.
Farb, P. 1988. *Die Indianer—Entwicklung und Vernichtung eines Volkes.* Berlin: Ullstein.
Fasheh, M. 1982/1997. Mathematics, culture, and authority. *For the Learning of Mathematics* 3(2): 2–8. Reprinted in *Ethnomathematics: Challenging Eurocentrism in Mathematics Education*, ed. A.B. Powell & M. Frankenstein: 273–290. New York: SUNY Press (page references pertain to the latter).
Fatnowna, S. & Pickett, H. 2002a. Establishing protocols for an indigenous-directed process: Perspectives from Australia and the region. In *Indigenous Knowledge and the Integration of Knowledge Systems: Towards a Philosophy of Articulation*, ed. C. Odora Hoppers: 67–95. Claremont: New Africa Books.
Fatnowna, S. & Pickett, H. 2002b. Indigenous contemporary knowledge development through research: The task for an indigenous academy. In *Indigenous Knowledge and the Integration of Knowledge Systems: Towards a Philosophy of Articulation*, ed. C. Odora Hoppers: 209–236. Claremont: New Africa Books.
Fatnowna, S. & Pickett, H. 2002c. The place of indigenous knowledge systems in the post-postmodern integrative paradigm shift. In *Indigenous Knowledge and the Integration of Knowledge Systems: Towards a Philosophy of Articulation*, ed. C. Odora Hoppers: 257–285. Claremont: New Africa Books.
Feldman, R. 1998. Epistemic obligations. *Philosophical Perspectives* 2: 235–256.
Flew, A. (ed.) 1999. *A Dictionary of Philosophy.* New York: Gramercy Books (revised 2nd edition).
Flórez Alonso, M. 2007. Can we protect traditional knowledges? In *Another Knowledge is Possible: Beyond Northern Epistemologies*, ed. B. De Sousa Santos: 249–271. London/New York: Verso.
Foucault, M. 1987. Truth and power. In *The Foucault Reader*, ed. P. Rabinow: 51–75. New York: Pantheon.
Freter, B. 2020. Decolonization of the west, desuperiorization of thought, and elative ethics. In *Handbook of African Philosophy of Difference*, ed. E. Imafidon: 1–24. Cham: Springer.
Fricker, M. 2007. *Epistemic Injustice: Power and the Ethics of Knowing.* Oxford: Oxford University Press.

George, J.M. 1999. Indigenous knowledge as a component of the school curriculum. In *What is Indigenous Knowledge?: Voices from the Academy*, ed. L.M. Semali & J.L. Kincheloe: 79–94. New York/London: Falmer Press.

Gerdes, P. 1994a. Reflections on ethnomathematics. *For the Learning of Mathematics* 14(2): 19–22.

Gerdes, P. 1994b. *African Pythagoras: A Study in Culture and Mathematics Education*. Maputo: Instituto Superior Pedagógico Moçambique.

Gerdes, P. 1999. *Geometry from Africa: Mathematical and Educational Explorations*. Washington: Mathematical Association of America.

Gettier, E.L. 1963. Is knowledge justified true belief? *Analysis* 23(6): 121–123.

Ghai, Y. 2007. Globalization, multiculturalism, and law. In *Another Knowledge is Possible: Beyond Northern Epistemologies*, ed. B. De Sousa Santos: 383–416. London/New York: Verso.

Goduka, I.N. 2000. African/indigenous philosophies: Legitimizing spiritually centered wisdoms within the academy. In *African Voices in Education*, ed. P. Higgs, N.C.G. Vakalisa, T.V. Mda & N.T. Assie-Lumumba: 63–83. Lansdowne: Juta.

Goldman, A.I. 1992. *Liaisons: Philosophy Meets the Cognitive and Social Sciences*. Cambridge/MA: MIT Press.

Goldman, A.I. 1994. Argumentation and social epistemology. *Journal of Philosophy* 91(1): 27–49.

Goodman, N. 1978. *Ways of Worldmaking*. Indianapolis: Hackett.

Goodman, N. 1996. Notes on a well-made world. In *Starmaking: Realism, Anti-Realism, and Irrealism*, ed. P. McCormick: 151–160. Cambridge/MA: MIT Press.

Grabiner, J. 1974. Is mathematical truth time-dependent? *American Mathematical Monthly* 81: 354–365.

Grill, B. 2003. *Ach, Afrika. Berichte aus dem Inneren eines Kontinents*. Berlin: Siedler.

Grill, B. 2005. Die Macht der Hexen. *Die Zeit* 2005(38), 15 September www.zeit.de/2005/38/Afrika?page=all (retrieved 3 March 2009): 1–7.

Green, L.J.F. 2008. 'Indigenous knowledge' and 'science': Reframing the debate on knowledge diversity. *Archaeologies* 4(1): 144–163.

Green, L.J.F. 2009. Challenging epistemologies: Exploring knowledge practices in Palikur epistemology. *Futures* 41: 41–52.

Gross, P.R. & Levitt, N. 1998. *Higher Superstition: The Academic Left and Its Quarrels with Science*. Baltimore/London: Johns Hopkins University Press (2nd edition).

Gutmann, A. 1987. *Democratic Education*. Princeton/NJ: Princeton University Press.

Gwaravanda, E.T. 2019. An epistemological critique of the African university education system. *Education Systems Around The World*. Intech Open: 1–11. https://www.intechopen.com/online-first/an-epistemological-critique-of-the-african-university-education-system

Haack, S. 2015. *Manifesto of a Passionate Moderate*. Chicago: University of Chicago Press.

Hall, D. & Ames, R. 1987. *Thinking through Confucius*. Albany/NY: State University Press of New York.

Hall, D. & Ames, R. 1998. *Thinking from the Han. Self, Truth and Transcendence in Chinese and Western Culture*. Albany/NY: State University Press of New York.

Hall, B.L. & Tandon, R. 2017. Decolonization of knowledge, epistemicide, participatory research and higher education. *Research for All* 1(1): 6–19.

Hallen, B. 2004. Contemporary anglophone African philosophy: A survey. In *A Companion to African Philosophy*, ed. K. Wiredu: 99–148. Oxford: Blackwell.

Hallen, B. & Sodipo, J.O. 1997. *Knowledge, Belief, and Witchcraft: Analytical Experiments in African Philosophy*. Stanford: Stanford University Press.

Harding, S.G. 1987. Conclusion: Epistemological questions. In *Feminism and Methodology*, ed. S. Harding: 181–190. Bloomington: Indiana University Press.

Harding, S.G. 1991. *Whose Science? Whose Knowledge? Thinking from Women's Lives*. Ithaca: Cornell University Press.

Harding, S.G. 1996. Gendered ways of knowing and the 'epistemological crisis' of the West. In *Knowledge, Difference, and Power: Essays Inspired by Women's Ways of Knowing*, ed. N.R. Goldberger, J.M. Tarule, B.M. Clinchy & M.F. Belenky: 431–454. New York: Basic Books.

Harding, S.G. 1998. *Is Science Multicultural?: Postcolonialisms, Feminisms, and Epistemologies*. Bloomington: Indiana University Press.

Harding, S.G. 2002. Rethinking standpoint epistemology: What is "strong objectivity"? In *Knowledge & Inquiry: Readings in Epistemology*, ed. K.B. Wray: 352–384. Ontario & New York: Broadview Press.

Hardwig, J. 1991. The role of trust in knowledge. *Journal of Philosophy* 88(12): 693–708.

Heleta, S. 2016. Decolonization of higher education: Dismantling epistemic violence and Eurocentrism in South Africa. *Transformation in Higher Education* (1)1. http://www.thejournal.org.za/index.php/thejournal/article/view/9/31 (retrieved 4 January 2020).

Herzog, W. 1979. Herzog im Gespräch mit Hans Günther Pflaum. *Werner Herzog (Reihe Film 22)*. Carl Hanser Verlag: Munich & Vienna.

Hester, L. & Cheney, J. 2001. Truth and native American epistemology. *Social Epistemology* 1(4): 319–334.

Higgs, P., Vakalisa, N.C.G., Mda, T.V. & Assie-Lumumba, N.T. (eds.) 2000. *African Voices in Education*. Lansdowne: Juta.

Higgs, P., Lillejord, S., Mkabela, Q., Waghid, Y. & Le Grange, L. (eds.) 2004. Indigenous African knowledge systems and higher education. *South African Journal of Higher Education* 18(3): 5–341.

Hill Collins, P. 1990. *Black Feminist Thought: Knowledge, Consciousness, and the Politics of Empowerment*. New York: Routledge.

Holiday, A. 2006. Beliefs sap the life of Africa's potential to use science. *Sunday Independent*, 26 March: 11.

Horsthemke, K. 2004a. 'Indigenous knowledge': Conceptions and misconceptions. *Journal of Education* 32: 31–48.

Horsthemke, K. 2004b. Knowledge, education and the limits of Africanization. *Journal of Philosophy of Education* 38(4): 571–587.

Horsthemke, K. 2004c. 'Indigenous knowledge', truth and reconciliation in South African higher education. *South African Journal of Higher Education* 18(3): 65–81.

Horsthemke, K 2005. Redress and reconciliation in South African education: The case for a rights-based approach. *Journal of Education* 37/Kenton 2004 Special Edition: 169–187.

Horsthemke, K. 2006a. The idea of the African university in the twenty first century: Some reflections on Afrocentrism and Afroscepticism. *South African Journal of Higher Education* 20(4): 449–465.

Horsthemke, K. 2006b. Ethnomathematics and education: Some thoughts. *For the Learning of Mathematics* 26(3): 15–19.

Horsthemke, K. 2007. 'Local knowledge', assessment and international standards. *South African Review of Education* with *Education with Production* 13(1): 19–30.

Horsthemke, K. 2008a. Scientific knowledge and higher education in the 21st century: The case against 'indigenous science'. *South African Journal of Higher Education* 22(2): 333–347.

Horsthemke, K. 2008b. The idea of indigenous knowledge. *Archaeologies* 4(1): 129–143.

Horsthemke, K. 2009. The South African higher education transformation debate: Culture, identity and 'African ways of knowing'. *London Review of Education* 7(1), March: 3–15.

Horsthemke, K. 2010a. *The Moral Status and Rights of Animals.* Johannesburg: Porcupine Press.

Horsthemke, K. 2010b. African and Afrikaner 'ways of knowing': Truth and the problems of superstition and 'blood knowledge'. *Theoria* 57(123), June: 27–51.

Horsthemke, K. 2010c. 'Knowledge diversity', truth and schooling: In (cautious) defence of realism. *Journal of Education* 48: 77–98.

Horsthemke, K. 2011. 'Diverse epistemologies', truth and archaeology: In defence of realism. *Science and Engineering Ethics* 17: 321–334.

Horsthemke, K. 2014a. Some doubts about 'indigenous knowledge', and the argument from epistemic injustice. *Quest* 25/1–2 (special issue), ed. T. Metz in collaboration with W. Van Binsbergen, "Engaging with the Philosophy of D.A. Masolo": 49–76.

Horsthemke, K. 2014b. Of ants and men: Epistemic injustice, commitment to truth, and the possibility of outsider critique. *Ethics and Education* 9/1: 127–140.

Horsthemke, K. 2015. Epistemic empathy in childrearing and education. *Ethics and Education* 10/1: 61–72.

Horsthemke, K. 2016a. 'Way-centered' versus 'truth-centered' epistemologies. *Education Sciences* 6(1)/8: 1–11; published online 4 March: doi:10.3390/educsci6010008.

Horsthemke, K. 2016b. Ethics and values in education (revised). In *Education Studies* (2nd edition), ed. K. Horsthemke, P. Siyakwazi, E. Walton & C. Wolhuter: 300–358. Cape Town: Oxford University Press South Africa.

Horsthemke, K. 2016c. Knowledge and education (revised). In *Education Studies* (2nd edition), ed. K. Horsthemke, P. Siyakwazi, E. Walton & C. Wolhuter: 359–438. Cape Town: Oxford University Press South Africa.

Horsthemke, K. 2017a. Access, parentalism and justice: Epistemological reflections on integration and inclusion in education. *Journal of Advances in Education Research* 2/3: 145–156.
Horsthemke, K. 2017b. "#FactsMustFall"? —Education in a post-truth, post-truthful world. *Ethics and Education* 12/3: 273–288.
Horsthemke, K. 2017c. Epistemological diversity in education: Philosophical and didactic considerations. *Forum Pedagogiczne* 7/1, Poland: 265–282.
Horsthemke, K. 2017d. Indigenous (African) knowledge systems, science, and technology. In *The Palgrave Handbook of African Philosophy*, ed. A. Afolayan & T. Falola: 585–603. New York: Palgrave Macmillan.
Horsthemke, K. 2017e. Africanization and diverse epistemologies in higher education discourses: Limitations and possibilities. In *Knowledge and Change in the African Universities: Volume 1—Current Debates*, ed. M. Cross & A. Ndofirepi: 101–120. Rotterdam, Boston & Taipei: Sense Publishers.
Horsthemke, K. 2018. Free-roaming animals, killing, and suffering: The case of African elephants. In *The Palgrave Handbook of Practical Animal Ethics*, ed. A. Linzey & C. Linzey: 525–543. London: Palgrave Macmillan.
Horsthemke, K. 2019. Educational research, culturally distinctive epistemologies and the decline of truth. *European Educational Research Journal* 18/5, special issue edited by David Bridges, "'Rigour', 'discipline' and the 'systematic' in the European educational research community: Fetish or fundamental?": 513–526.
Horsthemke, K. 2020a. The provincialization of epistemology: Knowledge and education in the age of the postcolony. *On_Education. Journal for Research and Debate* 3/7: 1–5. https://doi.org/10.17899/on_ed.2020.7.6
Horsthemke, K. 2020b. Global citizenship education and the idea of diverse epistemologies. *Forum Pedagogiczne* 10/1, Poland: 197–212. https://czasopisma.uksw.edu.pl/index.php/fp/issue/view/559
Horsthemke, K. & Schäfer, M. 2007. Does 'African' mathematics facilitate access to mathematics? Towards an ongoing critical analysis of ethnomathematics in a South African context. *Pythagoras* 65, June: 2–9.
Hospers, J. 1987. *An Introduction of Philosophical Analysis* (2nd ed.). London: Routledge & Kegan Paul.
Hountondji, P.J. 2000. Manufacturing unemployment: The crisis of education in Africa. In *African Voices in Education*, ed. P. Higgs, N.C.G. Vakalisa, T.V. Mda & N.T. Assie-Lumumba: 39–46. Lansdowne: Juta.
Hountondji, P.J. 2002. Knowledge appropriation in a post-colonial context. In *Indigenous Knowledge and the Integration of Knowledge Systems: Towards a Philosophy of Articulation*, ed. C. Odora Hoppers: 23–38. Claremont: New Africa Books.
Hume, D. 1896. *A Treatise of Human Nature*. Oxford: Clarendon Press (Originally published in 1739).
IIIT (International Institute of Islamic Thought). 1987. *Islamization of Knowledge: General Principles and Work Plan*. Herndon: International Institute of Islamic Thought.
Jansen, J. 2009. *Knowledge in the Blood: Confronting Race and the Apartheid Past*. Lansdowne/Stanford: UCT Press/Stanford University Press.

Jansen, J. 2017. *As by Fire: The End of the South Africa University*. Cape Town: Tafelberg.

Jegede, O.J. 1999. Science education in non-Western cultures: Towards a theory of collateral learning. In *What is Indigenous Knowledge?: Voices from the Academy*, ed. L.M. Semali & J.L. Kincheloe: 119–142. New York/London: Falmer Press.

Johnson, G. 1996. Indian tribes' creationists thwart archeologists. *The New York Times*, October 22, A1: 1–3. http://query.nytimes.com/gst/fullpage.html?res=9C06EFD71730F931A15753C1A960958260&sec=&spon=&pagewanted=print (retrieved 30 January 2009).

Josephy Jr., A.M. 1995. *500 Nations: An Illustrated History of North American Indians*. London: Hutchinson/Pimlico.

Kabou, A. 1991. *Et si l'Afrique refusait le développement?* Paris: L'Harmattan.

Kaphagawani, D.N. 1998. Themes in a Chewa epistemology. In *Philosophy from Africa*, ed. P.H. Coetzee & A.P.J. Roux: 240–244. Cape Town: Oxford University Press Southern Africa (1st edition).

Karenga, M. 2004. *Maat: The Moral Ideal of Ancient Egypt*. New York: Routledge.

Kaya, H.O. 2013. Integration of African indigenous knowledge systems into higher education in South Africa: Prospects and challenges. *AlterNation* 20(1): 135–153.

Kaya, H.O. 2014. Revitalizing African indigenous ways of knowing and knowledge production. In *Restoring Indigenous Self-determination: Theoretical and Practical Approaches*, ed. M. Woons, M.: 88–94. Bristol: E-International Relations.

Kaya, H.O. & Seleti, Y.N. 2013. African indigenous knowledge systems and relevance of higher education in South Africa. *The International Education Journal: Comparative Perspectives* 12(1): 30–44.

Keane, M., Khupe, C. & Muza, B. 2016. It matters who you are: Indigenous knowledge research and indigenous knowledge researchers. *Education as Change* 20(2): 163–183.

Keane, M., Khupe, C. & Seehawer, M. 2017. Decolonizing methodology: Who benefits from indigenous knowledge research? *Educational Research for Social Change* 6(1): 12–24.

Keyes, R. 2004. *The Post-Truth Era: Dishonesty and Deception in Contemporary Life*. New York: St. Martin's.

Khan, F. 2002. The roots of environmental racism and the rise of environmental justice in the 1990s. In *Environmental Justice in South Africa*, ed. D.A. McDonald: 15–48. Cape Town: University of Cape Town Press.

Khupe, C. & Keane, M. 2017. Towards an African education research methodology: Decolonizing new knowledge. *Educational Research for Social Change* 6(1): 25–37.

Knijnik, G. 1997. An ethnomathematical approach in mathematical education: A matter of political power. In *Ethnomathematics: Challenging Eurocentrism in Mathematics Education*, ed. A.B. Powell & M. Frankenstein: 403–410. New York: SUNY Press.

Knijnik, G. 1999. Indigenous knowledge and ethnomathematics approach in the Brazilian Landless People education. In *What is Indigenous Knowledge?: Voices from the Academy*, ed. L.M. Semali & J.L. Kincheloe: 179–189. New York/London: Falmer Press.

Knijnik, G. 2002. Ethnomathematics: Culture and politics of knowledge in mathematics education. *For the Learning of Mathematics* 22(1): 11–14.
Krog, A. 2004. African forgiveness—too sophisticated for the West. Opening address of the 4th International Literature Festival in Berlin, 21 September: 1–11 https://www.lit eraturfestival.com/medien/texte/eroeffnungsreden/krog-engl (retrieved 19 May 2020).
Krog, A. 2008. "This thing called reconciliation..." Forgiveness as part of an interconnectedness-towards-wholeness. *South African Journal of Philosophy* 27(4): 353–366.
Kumar, C. 2006. Witches, witch doctors and 'men of reason'. *Mail & Guardian*, September 8–14: 26.
Kunnie, J. 2000. Indigenous African philosophies and socioeducational transformation in 'post-apartheid' Azania. In *African Voices in Education*, ed. P. Higgs, N.C.G. Vakalisa, T.V. Mda & N.T. Assie-Lumumba, 158–178. Lansdowne: Juta.
Kwaa Prah, K. 1999. African renaissance or warlordism? In *African Renaissance— The New Struggle*, ed. M.W. Makgoba: 37–61. Cape Town: Mafube/Tafelberg.
Kwaa Prah, K. 2004. Africanism and Africanisation: Do they mean the same thing? In *Towards an African Identity of Higher Education*, ed. S. Seepe: 93–107. Pretoria: Vista University and Skotaville Media.
Lagunas, R.M. 2019. Nahuatl in Coatepec: Ideologies, practices, and management for linguistic and cultural continuance. *International Review of Education* 65: 67–86.
Lanzano, C. 2013. What kind of knowledge is 'indigenous knowledge'? Critical insights from a case study in Burkina Faso. *Transcience* 4(2): 3–18.
Laurens, T., Ngilawayan, D. & Pattiasina, J. 2019. Ethnomathematics study of islands indigenous peoples in Maluku Provinces. *Jurnal Pendidikan Progresif* 9(1): 113–122.
Lebakeng, T. 2004. Towards a relevant higher education epistemology. In *Towards an African Identity of Higher Education*, ed. S. Seepe: 109–119. Pretoria: Vista University and Skotaville Media.
Le Grange, L. 2004. Western science and indigenous knowledge. *South African Journal of Higher Education* 18(3): 82–91.
Le Grange, L. 2007. Integrating western and indigenous knowledge systems: The basis for effective science education in South Africa? *International Review of Education* 53(5–6): 577–591.
Le Grange, L. 2012. *Ubuntu, ukama* and the healing of nature, self and society. *Educational Philosophy and Theory* 44(S2): 56–67.
Le Grange, L. 2016. Decolonizing the university curriculum. *South African Journal of Higher Education* 30(2): 1–12.
Le Grange, L. & Aikenhead, G.S. 2017. Rethinking the 'Western tradition': A response to Enslin and Horsthemke. *Educational Philosophy and Theory* 49(1): 31–37.
Letseka, M. 2000. African philosophy and educational discourse. In *African Voices in Education*, ed. P. Higgs, N.C.G. Vakalisa, T.V. Mda & N.T. Assie-Lumumba, 179–193. Lansdowne: Juta.
Lévi-Strauss, C. 1979. *Myth and Meaning*. New York: Schocken Books.
Levisohn J.A. & Phillips D.C. 2012. Charting the reefs: A map of multicultural epistemology. In *Education, Culture and Epistemological Diversity: Mapping a Contested Terrain*, ed. C.W. Ruitenberg & D.C. Phillips: 39–63. Dordrecht: Springer.

Lillejord, S. & Mkabela, Q.N. 2004. Indigenous and popular narratives: The educational use of myths in a comparative perspective. *South African Journal of Higher Education* 18(3): 257–268.

Lipka, J. 2002. Connecting Yup'ik elders' knowledge to school mathematics. In Proceedings of the Second International Conference on Ethnomathematics (ICEM2), ed. M. de Monteiro, CD Rom, Lyrium Communacacão Ltda., Ouro Preto, Brazil.

Lotz-Sisitka H. 2009. Epistemological access as an open question in education. *Journal of Education* 46: 57–79.

Macedo, D. 1999. Decolonizing indigenous knowledge. In *What is Indigenous Knowledge?: Voices from the Academy*, ed. L.M. Semali & J.L. Kincheloe: xi–xvi. New York/London: Falmer Press.

Mackenthun, G. 2016. Coloniality of knowledge. https://www.iaa.uni-rostock.de/forschung/laufende-forschungsprojekte/american-antiquities-prof-mackenthun/project/theories/coloniality-of-knowledge/ (retrieved 24 October 2019).

Maffie, J. 2009. 'In the end, we have the Gatling gun, and they have not': Future prospects of indigenous knowledges. *Futures* 41: 53–65.

Maffie, J. 2014. Reflections on Henry Rosemont's "Introductory statement." *Confluence: Online Journal of World Philosophies* 1: 161–167.

Makgoba, M.W. 1996. In search of the ideal democratic model for SA. *Sunday Times*, South Africa, October 27: 23.

Makgoba, M.W. 1997. *Mokoko: The Makgoba Affair—A Reflection on Transformation*. Florida/Johannesburg: Vivlia.

Makgoba, M.W. 2003. An African vision for mergers. *Beyond Matric/Mail & Guardian*, May 2–8: 1–2.

Makgoba, M.W. & Tleane, C. 1998. Africanization and education. Lunchtime presentation; School of Education/University of the Witwatersrand, September 23.

Makgoba, M.W. & Seepe, S. 2004. Knowledge and identity: An African vision of higher education transformation. In *Towards an African Identity of Higher Education*, ed. S. Seepe: 13–57. Pretoria: Vista University and Skotaville Media.

Makuleke, L. 1997. Rural communities as roleplayers and stakeholders in the South African wildlife industries. Presentation at the *Wildlife Utilisation Forum of South Africa* conference, Suikerbosrand Nature Reserve (South Africa), 14 April.

Maraldo, J. 2014. Truth is truthfulness: The Japanese concept of *makoto*. *Confluence: Online Journal of World Philosophies* 1: 168–185.

Maringe, F. 2017. Transforming knowledge production systems in the new African university. In *Knowledge and Change in African Universities: Volume 2—Re-imagining the Terrain*, ed. M.A. Cross & A. Ndofirepi: 1–18. Rotterdam, Boston, Taipei: Sense Publishers

Marker, M. 2004. Indigenous voice, community, and epistemic violence: The ethnographer's 'interests' and what 'interests' the ethnographer. *Qualitative Studies in Education* 16(3): 361–375.

Martin, B. 1997. Mathematics and social interests. In *Ethnomathematics: Challenging Eurocentrism in Mathematics Education*, ed. A.B. Powell & M. Frankenstein: 155–171. New York: SUNY Press.
Masaka, D. 2017a. Challenging epistemicide through transformation and Africanization of the philosophy curriculum in Africa. *South African Journal of Philosophy* 36(4): 441–455.
Masaka, D. 2017b. 'Global justice' and the suppressed epistemologies of the indigenous people of Africa. *Philosophical Papers* 46(1): 59–84.
Masaka, D. 2018. The prospects of ending epistemicide in Africa: Some thoughts. *Journal of Black Studies* 49(3): 284–301.
Masolo, D.A. 2010. *Self and Community in a Changing World*. Bloomington: Indiana University Press.
Masolo, D.A. 2014. The case for communitarianism: A reply to critics. In *Engaging with the Philosophy of Dismas A. Masolo/Quest* 25(1–2), ed. T. Metz: 185–230.
Mataira, P.J. 2019. Transforming indigenous research: Collaborative responses to historical research tensions. *International Review of Education* 65: 143–161.
Matos, N. 2000. The nature of learning, teaching and research in higher education in Africa. In *African Voices in Education*, ed. P. Higgs, N.C.G. Vakalisa, T.V. Mda & N.T. Assie-Lumumba: 12–38. Lansdowne: Juta.
Matthews, G.B. 2009. Philosophy and developmental psychology: Outgrowing the deficit conception of childhood. In *The Oxford Handbook of Philosophy of Education*, ed. H. Siegel: 162–176. Oxford/New York: Oxford University Press.
Maturana, H. 1988. Reality: The search for objectivity or the search for a compelling argument. *The Irish Journal of Psychology* 9(11): 25–82.
Maurial, M. 1999. Indigenous knowledge and schooling: A continuum between conflict and dialogue. In *What is Indigenous Knowledge?: Voices from the Academy*, ed. L.M. Semali & J.L. Kincheloe: 59–77. New York/London: Falmer Press.
Mbembe, A. n.d. Decolonizing knowledge and the question of the archive. https://wiser.wits.ac.za/system/files/Achille%20Mbembe%20-%20Decolonizing%20Knowledge%20and%20the%20Question%20of%20the%20Archive.pdf (retrieved 29 January 2020).
Mendick, H. 2006. *Masculinities in Mathematics*. New York: Open University Press.
Meneses, M.P.G. 2007. "When there are no problems, we are healthy, no bad luck, nothing": Towards an emancipatory understanding of health and medicine. In *Another Knowledge is Possible: Beyond Northern Epistemologies*, ed. B. De Sousa Santos: 352–380. London/New York: Verso.
Metz, T. 2007a. Toward an African moral theory. *Journal of Political Philosophy* 15(3): 321–341.
Metz, 2007b. *Ubuntu* as a moral theory: Reply to four critics. *South African Journal of Philosophy* 26(4): 369–387.
Metz, T. 2009a. The final ends of higher education in light of an African moral theory. *Journal of Philosophy of Education* 43(2): 179–201.
Metz, T. 2009b. Higher education, knowledge for its own sake, and an African moral theory. *Studies in Philosophy and Education* 28(6): 517–536.

Metz, T. 2012. An African theory of moral status: A relational alternative to individualism and holism. *Ethical Theory and Moral Practice: An International Forum* 14: 387–402.
Mlodinow, L. 2002. *Euclid's Window: The Story of Geometry from Parallel Lines to Hyperspace*. London: Penguin.
Molefe, T.O. 2016. Oppression must fall: South Africa's revolution in theory. *World Policy Journal* 33(1): 30–37.
Morrow, W. 2007. *Learning to Teach in South Africa*. Cape Town: HRSC Press.
Morrow, W. 2009. *Bounds of Democracy: Epistemological Access in Higher Education*. Cape Town: HSRC Press.
Mosha, R.S. 1999. The inseparable link between intellectual and spiritual formation in indigenous knowledge and education: A case study in Tanzania. In *What is Indigenous Knowledge?: Voices from the Academy*, ed. L.M. Semali & J.L. Kincheloe: 209–225. New York/London: Falmer Press.
Mqotsi, L. 2002. Science, magic, and religion as trajectories of the psychology of projection. In *Indigenous Knowledge and the Integration of Knowledge Systems: Towards a Philosophy of Articulation*, ed. C. Odora Hoppers: 158–172. Claremont: New Africa Books.
Mudimbe, V.Y. 1988. *The Invention of Africa: Gnosis, Philosophy, and the Order of Knowledge*. Bloomington/Indianapolis: Indiana University Press.
Muendane, N.M. 2006. *I am an African: Embrace your Identity, Escape Victimization*. Johannesburg: Soultalk Publishers.
Murove, M.F. 2004. An African commitment to ecological conservation: The Shona concepts of *ukama* and *ubuntu*. *Mankind Quarterly* 45 (2): 195–215.
Murove, M.F. 2008. On African ethics and the appropriation of Western capitalism. In *Persons in Community: African Ethics in a Global Culture*, ed. R. Nicholson: 85–110. Scottsville: University of KwaZulu-Natal Press.
Murove, M.F. 2009. An African environmental ethic based on the concepts of *ukama* and *ubuntu*. In *African Ethics: An Anthology of Comparative and Applied Ethics*, ed. M.F. Murove: 315–331. Scottsville: University of KwaZulu-Natal Press.
Mutwa, C. 1996. *Isilwane/The Animal*. Cape Town: Struik.
Mwadime, R.K.N. 1999. Indigenous knowledge systems for an alternative culture in science: The role of nutritionists in Africa. In *What is Indigenous Knowledge?: Voices from the Academy*, ed. L.M. Semali & J.L. Kincheloe: 243–267. New York/London: Falmer Press.
Nabudere D. 2003. Towards the establishment of a pan-African university: A strategic concept paper. *African Journal of Political Science* 8(1): 1–30.
Naipaul, V.S. 2010. *The Masque of Africa: Glimpses of African Belief*. London, Basingstoke/Oxford: Picador/Macmillan.
Nashon, S., Anderson, D. & Wright, H. 2007. Editorial introduction: African ways of knowing, worldviews and pedagogy. *Journal of Contemporary Issues in Education* 2(2): 1–6.
Nasr, S.V.R. 1991. Islamization of knowledge: A critical review. *Islamic Studies* 30(3): 393–395.
Ndlovu-Gatsheni, S.J. 2018. *Epistemic freedom in Africa: Deprovincialization and decolonization*. London/New York: Routledge.

Nelson-Barber, S. & Johnson, Z. 2019. Raising the standard for testing research based interventions in Indigenous learning communities. *International Review of Education* 65: 47–65.

Ngara, C. 2007. African ways of knowing and pedagogy revisited. *Journal of Contemporary Issues in Education.* 2(2): 7–20.

Ng'asike, J.T. 2019. Indigenous knowledge practices for sustainable lifelong education in pastoralist communities of Kenya. *International Review of Education* 65: 19–46.

Nkomo, M. 2000. Educational research in the African development context: Rediscovery, reconstruction and prospects. In *African Voices in Education*, ed. P. Higgs, N.C.G. Vakalisa, T.V. Mda & N.T. Assie-Lumumba: 47–62. Lansdowne: Juta.

Ntuli, P.P. 1999. The missing link between culture and education: are we still chasing gods that are not our own? In *African Renaissance—The New Struggle*, ed. M.W. Makgoba: 184–199. Cape Town: Mafube/Tafelberg.

Ntuli, P.P. 2002. Indigenous knowledge systems and the African Renaissance: Laying a foundation for the creation of counter-hegemonic discourses. In *Indigenous Knowledge and the Integration of Knowledge Systems: Towards a Philosophy of Articulation*, ed. C. Odora Hoppers: 53–66. Claremont: New Africa Books.

Odora Hoppers, C. 2000. African voices in education: retrieving the past, engaging the present and shaping the future. In *African Voices in Education*, ed. P. Higgs, N.C.G. Vakalisa, T.V. Mda & N.T. Assie-Lumumba: 1–11. Lansdowne: Juta.

Odora Hoppers, C. 2000. Interview—Renaissance or 'menaissance'? *Agenda* 44.

Odora Hoppers, C. (ed.). 2002. *Indigenous Knowledge and the Integration of Knowledge Systems: Towards a Philosophy of Articulation.* Claremont: New Africa Books.

Odora Hoppers, C. 2002a. Old truths, new realities. *Africa Insight* 32(1), March.

Odora Hoppers, C. 2002b. Introduction. In *Indigenous Knowledge and the Integration of Knowledge Systems: Towards a Philosophy of Articulation*, ed. C. Odora Hoppers: vii–xiv. Claremont: New Africa Books.

Odora Hoppers, C. 2002c. Indigenous knowledge and the integration of knowledge systems: Towards a conceptual and methodological framework. In *Indigenous Knowledge and the Integration of Knowledge Systems: Towards a Philosophy of Articulation*, ed. C. Odora Hoppers: 2–22. Claremont: New Africa Books.

Odora Hoppers, C.A. 2005. *Culture, Indigenous Knowledge and Development: The Role of the University.* Johannesburg: Centre for Education Policy Development (CEPD), Occasional Paper No. 5: 1–50.

Odora Hoppers, C.A. 2008. Culture, language, indigenous knowledge and the role of universities in sustainable rural development. In *Universities in southern Africa as catalysts for sustainable rural development/* Proceedings of the conference hosted by the Centre for Education Policy Development (CEPD) and held at the Kopanong Conference Centre in Johannesburg, 6–7 March: 29–35.

Ogungbemi, S. 1997. An African perspective on the environmental crisis. In *Environmental Ethics: Readings in Theory and Application*, ed. L.P. Pojman: 330–337. Belmont/CA: Wadsworth (2nd edition).

Onwu, G. & Mosimege, M. 2004. Indigenous knowledge systems and science and technology education: A dialogue. *African Journal of Research in SMT Education* 8(2): 1–12.

Owuor, J. 2007. Integrating African indigenous knowledge systems in Kenya's formal education system: The potential for sustainable development. *Journal of Contemporary Issues in Education* 2(2): 21–37.

Oxley, Julinna C. 2011. *The Moral Dimensions of Empathy: Limits and Applications in Ethical Theory and Practice*. Basingstoke/New York: Palgrave-Macmillan.

Peat, F.D. 1994. *Blackfoot Physics: A Journey into the Native American Universe*. London: Fourth Estate.

Peters, R.S. 1970. *Ethics and Education*. London: George Allen & Unwin.

Phillips, D.C. 2012. A critical review of representative sources on multicultural epistemology. In *Education, Culture and Epistemological Diversity: Mapping a Contested Terrain*, ed. C.W. Ruitenberg & D.C. Phillips: 11–38. Dordrecht: Springer.

Pickover, M. 2005. *Animal Rights in South Africa*. Cape Town, South Africa: Double Storey.

Plato 1970a. Meno. In *The Complete Texts of the Great Dialogues of Plato*, transl. W.H.D. Rouse, ed. E.H. Warmington & P.G. Rouse. New York, Toronto & London: Plume.

Plato 1970b. The republic. In *The Complete Texts of the Great Dialogues of Plato*, transl. W.H.D. Rouse, ed. E.H. Warmington & P.G. Rouse. New York, Toronto & London: Plume.

Plato 1978. Theaetetus. In *Plato—Collected Dialogues*, ed. E. Hamilton & H. Cairns. Princeton: Princeton University Press.

Ponting, C. 2007. *A New Green History of the World: The Environment and the Collapse of Great Civilizations*. New York: Vintage Books.

Posel, D. 2002. The TRC report. What kind of history? What kind of truth? In *Commissioning the Past: Understanding South Africa's Truth and Reconciliation Commission*, ed. D. Posel & G. Simpson: 147–172. Johannesburg: Witwatersrand University Press.

Posel, D. 2004. Truth? The view from South Africa's Truth and Reconciliation Commission. In *Keywords. Truth. For a Different Kind of Globalization*, ed. N. Tazi: 1–25. Cape Town: Double Storey.

Posel, D. & Simpson, G. 2002. The power of truth. South Africa's Truth and Reconciliation Commission in context. In *Commissioning the Past. Understanding South Africa's Truth and Reconciliation Commission*, ed. D. Posel & G. Simpson: 11–13. Johannesburg: Witwatersrand University Press.

Poundstone, W. 1993. *Prisoner's Dilemma*. New York: Anchor/Random House.

Powell, A.B. & Frankenstein, M. (eds.) 1997. *Ethnomathematics: Challenging Eurocentrism in Mathematics Education*. New York: SUNY Press.

Powell, A.B. & Frankenstein, M. 1997a. Ethnomathematical knowledge. In *Ethnomathematics: Challenging Eurocentrism in Mathematics Education*, ed. A.B. Powell & M. Frankenstein: 5–11. New York: SUNY Press.

Powell, A.B. & Frankenstein, M. 1997b. Reconsidering what counts as mathematical knowledge. In *Ethnomathematics: Challenging Eurocentrism in Mathematics Education*, ed. A.B. Powell & M. Frankenstein: 193–200. New York: SUNY Press.

Powell, A.B. & Frankenstein, M. 1997c. Ethnomathematical research. In *Ethnomathematics: Challenging Eurocentrism in Mathematics Education*, ed. A.B. Powell & M. Frankenstein: 321–327. New York: SUNY Press.

Powell, A.B. 2002. Ethnomathematics and the challenges of racism in mathematics education. In *Mathematics, Education and Society, Part 1*/Proceedings of the Third International Mathematics Education and Society Conference, 2–7 April 2002; Helsingør, Denmark), ed. P. Valero & O. Skovsmose: 17–30. Copenhagen: Centre for Research in Learning Mathematics.

Prakash, M.S. 1999. Indigenous knowledge systems—Ecological literacy through initiation into people's science. In *What is Indigenous Knowledge?: Voices from the Academy*, ed. L.M. Semali & J.L. Kincheloe: 157–178. New York/London: Falmer Press.

Quale, A. 2008. *Radical Constructivism: A Relativist Epistemic Approach to Science Education*. Rotterdam/Taipei: Sense Publishers.

Quine, W.V. & Ullian, J.S. 1978. *The Web of Belief*. New York: McGraw-Hill (revised 2nd edition).

Rachels, J. 1995. *The Elements of Moral Philosophy* (2nd ed.). New York: McGraw-Hill.

Rachels, J. 1999. *The Right Thing To Do: Basic Readings in Moral Philosophy*. Boston: McGraw-Hill (2nd edition).

Rains, F.V. 1999. Indigenous knowledge, historical amnesia and intellectual authority: Deconstructing hegemony and the social and political implications of the curricular 'other'. In *What is Indigenous Knowledge?: Voices from the Academy*, ed. L.M. Semali & J.L. Kincheloe: 317–331. New York/London: Falmer Press.

Ramose, M.B. 1998. Foreword. In *Black Perspective(s) in Tertiary Institutional Transformation*, ed. S. Seepe: iv–vii. Florida/Johannesburg: Vivlia.

Ramose, M.B. 2002a. The philosophy of *ubuntu* and *ubuntu* as a philosophy. In *Philosophy from Africa*, ed. P.H. Coetzee & A.P.J. Roux: 230–238. Cape Town: Oxford University Press Southern Africa (2nd edition).

Ramose, M.B. 2002b. The ethics of *ubuntu*. In *Philosophy from Africa*, ed. P.H. Coetzee & A.P.J. Roux: 324–330. Cape Town: Oxford University Press Southern Africa (2nd edition).

Ramose, M.B. 2002c. 'African Renaissance': A northbound gaze. In *Philosophy from Africa*, ed. P.H. Coetzee & A.P.J. Roux: 600–610. Cape Town: Oxford University Press Southern Africa (2nd edition).

Ramose, M.B. 2004. In search of an African philosophy of education. *South African Journal of Higher Education* 18(3): 138–160.

Ramose, M.B. 200). Ecology through *ubuntu*. In *African Ethics: An Anthology of Comparative and Applied Ethics*, ed. M.F. Murove: 308–314. Scottsville, South Africa: University of KwaZulu-Natal Press.

Ramphele, M. 1995. *Ubuntu* doesn't mean a friendly greeting to your gardener. What it does mean is another question... *Sunday Independent*, 24 September: 15.

Ramoupi, N.L.L. & Ntongwe, R.N. 2017. Africanization of humanities knowledge in the universities in Africa. In *Knowledge and Change in African Universities*, Vol. 1, *Current Debates*, ed. M. Cross and A. Ndofirepi: 195–215. Rotterdam: Sense.

Rata, E. 2012a. *The Politics of Knowledge in Education*. New York/London: Routledge.

Rata, E. 2012b. The politics of knowledge in education. *British Educational Research Journal* 38(1): 103–124.

Reynar, R. 1999. Indigenous people's knowledge and education: A tool for development? In *What is Indigenous Knowledge?: Voices from the Academy*, ed. L.M. Semali & J.L. Kincheloe: 285–304. New York/London: Falmer Press.

Richardson, V. 2003. Constructivist pedagogy. *Teachers College Record* 105(9): 1623–1640.

Roberts, D. 2010. Post-truth politics. *Grist*. 1 April 2010. https://grist.org/article/2010-03-30-post-truth-politics/ (retrieved 11 July2016).

Roberts, M. 1998. Indigenous knowledges and Western science: Perspectives from the Pacific. In *Science and Technology Education and Ethnicity: An Aotoroa/New Zealand Perspective/* Proceedings of a conference held at the Royal Society of New Zealand, Thorndon, Wellington, May 7–8, 1996, ed. D. Hodson: 59–75. The Royal Society of New Zealand Miscellaneous Series #50.

Robertson E. 2013. The epistemic value of diversity. *Journal of Philosophy of Education* 47(2): 299–310.

Robins, S.L. 2008. *From Revolution to Rights in South Africa: Social Movements, NGOs & Popular Politics after Apartheid*. Pietermaritzburg: University of KwaZulu-Natal Press.

Robinson, R. 1971. The concept of knowledge. *Mind/New Series* 80(317): 17–28.

Rogers, A. 2007. The making of Cosmic Africa: The research behind the film. *African Skies/Cieux Africains* 11, July: 19–23.

Romberg, T. 2000. Changing the teaching and learning of mathematics. *Australian Mathematics Teacher* 56(4): 6–9.

Rosemont, H. Jr. 2014a. Introductory statement. *Confluence: Online Journal of World Philosophies* 1: 151–157.

Rosemont, H. Jr. 2014b. Reply: Truth as truthfulness. *Confluence: Online Journal of World Philosophies* 1: 205–212.

Rosemont, H. Jr., Maffie, J., Maraldo, J. & Thakchoe, S. 2014. Symposium: Does the concept of 'truth' have value in the pursuit of cross-cultural philosophy? *Confluence* 1: 149–217.

Rowlands, S. & Carson, R. 2002. Where would formal, academic mathematics stand in a curriculum informed by ethnomathematics? A critical review. *Educational Studies in Mathematics* 50: 79–102.

Rowlands, S. & Carson, R. 2004. A comment on Adam, Alangui, and Barton's "A comment on: Rowlands and Carson 'Where would formal, academic mathematics stand in a curriculum informed by ethnomathematics? A critical review'." *Educational Studies in Mathematics* 56(2–3): 329–342.

Ryle, G. 1963. *The Concept of Mind*. Peregrine/Penguin Books: Harmondsworth/Middlesex (first published in 1949 by Hutchinson).

Sardar, Z. 1989. Islamization of knowledge: A state of the art report. In *An Early Crescent: The Future of Knowledge and the Environment in Islam*, ed. Z. Sardar: 27–56. London and New York: Mansell Publishing Ltd.

Scheffler, I. 1965. *Conditions of Knowledge: An Introduction to Epistemology and Education*. Chicago: Scott, Foresman and Company.

Scheurich, J. & Young, M. 1997. Coloring epistemologies: Are our research epistemologies racially biased? *Educational Researcher* 26(4), 4–16.

Schroeder, D. 2009. Informed consent: From medical research to traditional knowledge. In *Indigenous Peoples, Consent and Benefit Sharing: Lessons from the Sanhoodia Case*, ed. Wynberg, R., Schroeder, D. & Chennells, R.: 27–52. Dordrecht, Heidelberg, London & New York: Springer.

Schumann, C. 2016. Knowledge for a common world? On the place of feminist epistemology in philosophy of education. *Education Sciences* 6(10): 1–13. http://www.mdpi.com/2227-7102/6/1/10 (retrieved 3 August 2016).

Seepe, S. 2000. Africanization of knowledge: Exploring mathematical and scientific knowledge embedded in African cultural practices. In *African Voices in Education*, ed. P. Higgs, N.C.G. Vakalisa, T.V. Mda & N.T. Assie-Lumumba: 118–138. Lansdowne: Juta.

Seitz, V. 2009. *Afrika wird armregiert oder Wie man Afrika wirklich helfen kann*. München: Deutscher Taschenbuch Verlag.

Semali, L.M. & Kincheloe, J.L. (eds.) 1999. *What is Indigenous Knowledge?: Voices from the Academy*. New York/London: Falmer Press.

Semali, L.M. & Kincheloe, J.L. 1999. Introduction: What is indigenous knowledge and why should we study it? In *What is Indigenous Knowledge?: Voices from the Academy*, ed. L.M. Semali & J.L. Kincheloe: 3–57. New York/London: Falmer Press.

Semali, L.M. 1999. Community as classroom: (Re)valuing indigenous literacy. In *What is Indigenous Knowledge?: Voices from the Academy*, ed. L.M. Semali & J.L. Kincheloe: 95–118. New York/London: Falmer Press.

Senanayake, S.G.J.N. 2006. Indigenous knowledge as a key to sustainable development. *The Journal of Agricultural Sciences* 2(1): 87–94.

Setati, M. 2002. Is ethnomathematics = mathematics = antiracism? In *Mathematics, Education and Society, Part 1*/Proceedings of the Third International Mathematics Education and Society Conference, 2–7 April 2002; Helsingør, Denmark), ed. P. Valero & O. Skovsmose: 31–33. Copenhagen: Centre for Research in Learning Mathematics.

Shay, S. 2016. Decolonising the Curriculum. It's Time for a Strategy. *The Conversation*, 13 June. https://theconversation.com/decolonising-the-curriculum-its-time-for-a-strategy-60598 (retrieved 4 January 2020).

Shizha, E. 2006. Legitimizing indigenous knowledge in Zimbabwe: A theoretical analysis of postcolonial school knowledge and its colonial legacy. *Journal of Contemporary Issues in Education* 1(1): 20–35.

Siegel, H. 1998. Knowledge, truth and education. In *Education, Knowledge and Truth: Beyond the Postmodern Impasse*, ed. D. Carr: 19–36. London: Routledge.

Siegel, H. 2002. Multiculturalism, universalism, and science education: In search of common ground. *Culture and Comparative Studies* 86: 803–820.

Siegel, H. 2012. Epistemological diversity and education research: Much ado about nothing much? In *Education, Culture and Epistemological Diversity: Mapping a Contested Terrain*, ed. C.W. Ruitenberg & D.C. Phillips: 65–84. Dordrecht: Springer.

Slote, M. 2013. *Education and human values: Reconciling talent with an ethics of care*. New York/London: Routledge.

Smith, L.T. 1999. *Decolonizing Methodologies: Research and Indigenous Peoples*. New York: Zed Books.

Spivak, G.C. 1990. Questions of multiculturalism. In *The Post-Colonial Critic: Interviews, Strategies, Dialogues*, ed. S. Harasym, S.: 67–74. New York: Routledge.
Spivak, G.C. 2005. IKS and globalization. *Indilingua: African Journal of Indigenous Systems* 4(1): 38–45.
Stanley, W.B. & Brickhouse, N.W. 1994. Multiculturalism, universalism, and science education. *Science Education* 78(4): 387–398.
Sumida Huaman, E. 2019. Comparative indigenous education research (CIER): Indigenous epistemologies and comparative education methodologies. *International Review of Education* 65: 163–184.
Sumner, W.G. 1906. *Folkways*. Boston: Ginn & Company.
Swanson, D.M. 2015. *Ubuntu*, indigeneity, and an ethic for decolonizing global citizenship. In *Decolonizing Global Citizenship Education*, ed. A.A. Abdi, L. Shultz and T. Pillay: 27–38. Rotterdam, Boston & Taipei: Sense.
Swartbooi-Xabadiya, Z.C. 2010. Attitudes and perceptions of girls in St John's College about the practice of virginity testing. MPH (Master of Public Health) thesis, University of Limpopo. http://policyresearch.limpopo.gov.za/bitstream/han dle/123456789/714/attitudesandperceptionsofgirlsinstjohn%C3%83%C6%92%C 3%82%C2%A2%C3%83%E2%80%9A%C3%A2%E2%80%9A%C2%AC%C3% 83%E2%80%9A%C3%A2%E2%80%9E%C2%A2scollegeaboutthepracticeofvi rginitytesting.pdf?sequence=1 (retrieved 23 June 2020).
Tangwa, G. 2004. Some African reflections on biomedical and environmental ethics. In *A Companion to African Philosophy*, ed. K. Wiredu: 387–395. Oxford: Blackwell.
Teffo, L.J. 1998. *Botho/ubuntu* as a way forward for contemporary South Africa. *Woord en Daad* 38(365): 3–5.
Teffo, L.J. 1999. Moral renewal and African experience(s). In *African Renaissance— The New Struggle*, ed. M.W. Makgoba: 149–169. Cape Town: Mafube/Tafelberg.
Teffo, L.J. 2000. Africanist thinking: An invitation to authenticity. In *African Voices in Education*, ed. P. Higgs, N.C.G. Vakalisa, T.V. Mda & N.T. Assie-Lumumba: 103–117. Lansdowne: Juta.
Tom, M.N., Sumida Huaman, E. & McCarty, T.L. 2019. Indigenous knowledges as vital contributions to sustainability. *International Review of Education* 65: 1–18.
Turnbull, D. 2009. Introduction: Futures for indigenous knowledges. *Futures* 41: 1–5.
Van Heerden, J., Getz, C. & Smuts, H. 2006. *Africa Meets Africa—Making a Living Through the Mathematics of Zulu Design*, ed. H. Smuts. Johannesburg, Cape Town & New York: David Krut Publishing. http://www.africameetsafrica.co.za/makin galiving.html (retrieved 25 January 2011).
Van Sertima (ed.). 1983. *Blacks in Science, Ancient and Modern*. New Brunswick: Transaction Books.
Van Sertima, I. 1999. The lost sciences of Africa: An overview. In *African Renaissance—The New Struggle*, ed. M.W. Makgoba: 305–330. Cape Town: Mafube/Tafelberg.
Vergès, F. 2002. Psychoanalysis, the enigma of human behavior, and the contribution of indigenous knowledges. In *Indigenous Knowledge and the Integration of*

Knowledge Systems: Towards a Philosophy of Articulation, ed. C. Odora Hoppers: 173–186. Claremont: New Africa Books.
Viergever, M. 1999. Indigenous knowledge: An interpretation of views from indigenous peoples. In *What is Indigenous Knowledge?: Voices from the Academy*, ed. L.M. Semali & J.L. Kincheloe: 333–343. New York/London: Falmer Press.
Villa-Vicencio, C. 2003. No way around the past. *Sowetan*, June 23: 15.
Visvanathan, C.S. 2002. Between pilgrimage and citizenship: The possibilities of self-restraint in science. In *Indigenous Knowledge and the Integration of Knowledge Systems: Towards a Philosophy of Articulation*, ed. C. Odora Hoppers: 39–52. Claremont: New Africa Books.
Visvanathan, C.S. 2007. Between cosmology and system: The heuristics of a dissenting imagination. In *Another Knowledge is Possible: Beyond Northern Epistemologies*, ed. B. De Sousa Santos: 182–218. London/New York: Verso.
Von Glasersfeld, E. 1991. Knowing without metaphysics: Aspects of the radical constructivist position. In *Research and Reflexivity: Inquiries into Social Construction*, ed. F. Steier: 12–29 (1–55). London: Sage Publications.
Von Glasersfeld, E. 1995. *Radical Constructivism*. London: Falmer Press.
Von Glasersfeld, E. 1997/2003. Homage to Jean Piaget (1896–1980). *The Irish Journal of Psychology* 18(3): 293–306. http://www.oikos.org/Piagethom.htm (retrieved 14 January 2011).
Von Glasersfeld, E. 2000. Problems in constructivism. In *Radical Constructivism in Action Building on the Pioneering Work of Ernst Von Glasersfeld*, ed. L.P. Steffe & P.W. Thompson: 3–9. New York: Routledge Falmer.
Wa Thiong'o, N. 1986. *Decolonizing the Mind*. Heinemann: London.
Wajcman J. 2004. *Technofeminism*. Cambridge: Polity Press.
Wallner, F. 2005. Indigenous knowledge and western science: Contradiction or cooperation. *Indilingua: African Journal of Indigenous Systems* 4(1): 46–54.
Walton, E. & Bekker, T. 2013. Pedagogy and inclusion. In *Education Studies*, ed. K. Horsthemke, P. Siyakwazi, E. Walton & C. Wolhuter: 440–462. Cape Town: Oxford University Press South Africa.
Walton, E. 2013. Responsive teaching. In *Education Studies*, ed. K. Horsthemke, P. Siyakwazi, E. Walton & C. Wolhuter: 486–510. Cape Town: Oxford University Press South Africa.
White, J. 2002. *The Child's Mind*. London/New York: Routledge/Falmer.
Williams, B. 2002. *Truth and Truthfulness: An Essay in Genealogy*. Princeton: Princeton University Press.
Windschitl, M. 1999. A vision educators can put into practice: Portraying the constructivist classroom as a cultural system. *School Science and Mathematics* 4: 189–196.
Windschitl, M. 2002., Framing constructivism in practice as the negotiation of dilemmas: An analysis of the conceptual, pedagogical, cultural, and political challenges facing teachers. *Review of Educational Research* 72(2): 131–175.
Wiredu, K. 1980. *Philosophy and an African Culture*. Cambridge: Cambridge University Press.
Wiredu, K. 1998a. Are there cultural universals? In *Philosophy from Africa*, ed. P.H. Coetzee & A.P. J. Roux: 31–40. Cape Town: Oxford University Press Southern Africa.

Wiredu, K. 1998b. The concept of truth in the African language. In *Philosophy from Africa*, ed. P.H. Coetzee & A.P. J. Roux: 234–239. Cape Town: Oxford University Press Southern Africa.

Wiredu, K. 2004. Prologomena to an African philosophy of education. *South African Journal of Higher Education* 18(3): 17–26.

Wiredu K. 2008. Social philosophy in postcolonial Africa: Some preliminaries concerning communalism and communitarianism. *South African Journal of Philosophy* 27(4): 332–339.

Wynberg, R., Schroeder, D. & Chennells, R. 2009. Introduction. In *Indigenous Peoples, Consent and Benefit Sharing: Lessons from the San-hoodia Case*, ed. R. Wynberg, D. Schroeder & R. Chennells: 3–10. Dordrecht, Heidelberg, London & New York: Springer.

Wynberg, R. & Chennells, R. 2009. Green diamonds of the south: An overview of the San-*hoodia* case. In *Indigenous Peoples, Consent and Benefit Sharing: Lessons from the San-hoodia Case*, ed. R. Wynberg, D. Schroeder & R. Chennells: 88–126. Dordrecht, Heidelberg, London & New York: Springer.

Xaba, T. 2007. Marginalized medical practice: The marginalisation and transformation of indigenous medicines in South Africa. In *Another Knowledge is Possible: Beyond Northern Epistemologies*, ed. B. De Sousa Santos: 317–351. London/New York: Verso.

Zaslavsky, C. 1979. *Africa counts: Number and Pattern in African Culture*. Westport: Lawrence Hill & Company.

Zaslavsky, C. 1994. 'Africa counts' and ethnomathematics. *For the Learning of Mathematics*, 14(2): 3–8.

Zulu, I.M. 2006. Critical indigenous African education and knowledge. *The Journal of Pan African Studies* 1(3): 32–49.

Index

abduction/abductive reasoning, 59, 61
Abdullah, Jill, 4
aboriginal/Aboriginal, 2, 4, 12, 15, 24, 96n16, 130, 186, 200, 201, 244; beliefs, 24; knowledge, 15, 24, 244
'academic left', 8n1
'academic right', 4
Adam, Shenenaz, 140, 143, 154, 156, 157, 161, 169
Adeyemi, Michael, 209
Adeyinka, Augustus, 209
African holism, 33, 34, 192
Africanization, 18; of knowledge, 14, 15
African renaissance, 14, 15, 32, 40n9, 100, 136
African ways of knowing, 18, 31, 32, 35, 113, 185
Afrikaner/Afrikaners, 28–31, 40n7
Afrocentricity/Afrocentrism, 4, 14, 18
Agrawal, Arun, 25n5, 172
Ahenakew, Cash, 38
Aikenhead, Glen, 4, 17, 24
Akan, 109, 112
Alangui, Wilfredo, 143, 154, 156, 157, 160, 161, 164n8
algebra, 7, 139, 146
Ames, Roger, 237, 240, 241
analogical reasoning, 60, 61

ancestors, 18, 33, 107, 170, 192, 193, 206
Anderson, David, 32
Anderson, Elizabeth, 126, 127
Andrej, Melanie, 90
Andreotti, Vanessa, 36, 38
Ani, Marimba, 4
animals, 104, 136, 183, 189–95; bush meat, 200; dissection, 185; factory farming, 104, 185; scientific experiments on, 104, 185; slaughter of, 199, 213; trophy animal industry, 200; vivisection, 104, 185
anthropocentrism, 7, 190–93, 200, 202n3, 237
anti-foundationalism, 237
Antony, Louise, 226
Antrosio, Jason, 216
Anyon, Roger, 168
Arena, Dylan, 68
Arenas, Alberto, 25n5, 198, 213
Arendt, Hannah, 238, 239
argument, 65, 71, 73, 85
argumentation, 71–73
Aristotle, 237, 243
Armstrong, Juliet, 136
Asante, Molefi Kete, 4, 18, 34, 37, 89, 171

271

Ascher, Marcia, 155, 162
Ayer, Alfred Jules, 95n8, 235n9

Bakari, R. Sentwali, 31, 37
Banks, James, 37
Barca, Deborah, 25n5, 198, 213
Barnes, Julian, 94n5
Barnhardt, Ray, 37
Barton, Bill, 143, 148, 149, 152, 154–62, 164n6, 164n8
basket-making, 17, 135–37
bead-weaving, 135–37
Becker, Oliver, 100, 103, 130n2
Bekker, Tanya, 88, 89, 95n10
Belenky, Mary Field, 37, 122
belief/beliefs, 6, 11, 24, 30, 43–52, 55, 57–59, 68, 69, 71–75, 83–87, 109–12, 118, 128, 129, 140, 170, 172–74, 176–79, 214, 216, 224, 228, 232, 233, 243, 244
Bello, A.G.A., 112
Benallie, Larry, 167
Benedict, Ruth, 212, 213, 215–17
Benson, Ophelia, 131n8
Bering Strait (Theory), 167, 168
Berkes, Fikret, 13, 98, 186, 202n5, 203n15
Berkes, Mina Kislalioglu, 13, 98, 186, 202n5, 203n15
Bernal, Martin, 13, 98, 113
Berry, John, 142
Biko, Steve Bantu, 191
Bishop, Alan, 154
Boghossian, Paul, 95n11
Boghossian, Peter, 95n11
Bolsonaro, Jair, 186
Borba, Marcelo, 137, 138, 147, 151, 153
botho. *See ubuntu*
Braidotti, Rosi, 37
Brayboy, Bryan McKinley Jones, 25n5, 189, 190
Brecht, Bertolt, 244, 245
Brexit, 238
Bridges, David, 77, 242
Brown, Dee, 169

Bryan, Joe, 16, 201
buffalo, 199, 200
Bujo, Bénézet, 192
Burkhart, Brian Yazzie, 25n7, 130n1, 189, 190, 246n9

Callan, Eamonn, 68
Campbell, Marilyn, 139
Campbell-Wright, Randall, 139
Carson, Robert, 153, 154, 156, 157, 162
Castley, Guy, 196
Chan-Tiberghien, Jennifer, 17, 36
Chavunduka, Gordon, 100, 101
Cheney, Jim, 240, 242
Chennells, Roger, 9, 10
Chokwe (Tchokwe) *sona* (sand drawings), 136, 141
Clark, Fred, 235n5
Clinton, Hilary, 246n4
Code, Lorraine, 37, 120, 122, 132n25, 221, 237
cognitive injustice, 128
cognitive justice, 38, 231
Cohen, Stewart, 79–81, 87
colonialism/colonization, 3, 38, 101, 140, 157, 161, 165, 169, 198, 223, 229
compatibilism, 4, 186
constructivism, 8n1, 12, 13, 22, 76, 88–91, 95n12, 112, 117, 132n18, 146, 164n6, 237, 244
context-sensitive realism, 5
Contreras, L., 154
Conway, Kellyanne, 239
Corntassel, Jeff, 16, 186
Crazy Bull, Cheryl, 186, 207
creationism, 124, 128, 169, 175; Native American, 167–69, 174–76
Crittenden, Brian, 68
Cronon, William, 194
Crossman, Peter, 11, 21, 22, 98, 99
Crow Shoe, Joe Sr., 200
'cultural differences argument', 213, 214
culturalism, 4, 8n1, 102, 131n15

Index 273

cultural relativism, 7, 23, 131n10, 162, 210–18
Cummings, David, 196
Cunningham, Donald, 90

Daes, Erica-Irene, 27, 186
D'Ambrosio, Ubiratan, 105, 137, 138, 151, 155, 163, 164n3, 164n6, 164n8
Dangor, Sulieman, 37, 123–26
Deacon, Michael, 240
De Beauvoir, Simone, 234n2
decoloniality/decolonization, 5, 14–22, 39, 127
deduction/deductive reasoning, 59, 60, 65, 111, 146, 244
Dei, George J. Sefa, 31, 32, 34, 37, 40n8, 41n10, 41n12, 96n15
Delanty, Gerard, 90
Delgado Bernal, Dolores, 37
Deloria, Barbara, 242
Deloria Jr., Vine, 167, 240, 242
demonic possession, 99
De Monteiro, M., 154
De Oliveira Andreotti, Vanessa. *See* Andreotti, Vanessa
De Sousa Santos, Boaventura, 17, 24, 36, 37, 39, 105, 114–17, 127, 132n17, 132n19, 163, 164n7, 169
desuperiorization, 17
Devisch, René, 11, 21, 22, 98, 99
diverse epistemologies. *See* epistemological diversity
divination, 18, 19, 99, 176, 240
Dogon, 165, 166
Dondolo, Luvuyo, 12
Doumbo, Annayé, 166
Duffy, Thomas, 90

Egziabher, Tewolde Berhan Gebre, 23
Einstein, Albert, 51, 131n15
elephants, 195–97
Elgin, Catherine, 169, 173–76, 181n7, 181nn8–9
Elliott, Dean, 4, 17
Ellis, Stephen, 102, 103

Embong, Rokiah, 164n2
empathy, 230–34, 235n5, 235n7, 238n8. *See also* epistemic empathy
Enslin, Penny, 26n9, 194
epistemic empathy, 231–34, 235n5
epistemic externalism, 73–75
epistemicide, 39, 128
epistemic injustice, 7, 38, 113, 128, 185, 221, 224–27
epistemic internalism, 73–75
epistemic justice, 7, 221, 224, 231
epistemic obligations, 44, 83–86, 229
epistemic parentalism/paternalism, 86–88
epistemological access, 6, 88, 89, 150
epistemological diversity, 3, 6, 24, 25n5, 35–39, 113, 114, 119, 126, 127, 171. *See also* knowledge diversity
epistemological relativism, 79–83, 120–22, 177
epistemology/epistemologies, 3, 6, 24, 117–20, 218, 221, 245; applied epistemology, 8, 237, 245; feminist critique of, 120–23. *See also* relational epistemology
esprit sorcier, 100
ethical values. *See* moral values
ethnoastronomy, 6, 67, 166
ethnocentrism, 7, 211, 217, 230
ethnomathematics, 6, 7, 15, 135–64
Eurocentrism, 15, 23, 31, 38, 140, 141, 180, 208, 221, 223
evidence, 2, 53–59, 62, 86, 87, 95n7, 130n3, 175–77, 185
explanation/explanations, 176; in the natural sciences, 63–66; in the social sciences, 63, 66, 67
Eyong, Charles Takoyoh, 186

Farb, Peter, 169
Al-Faruqi, Ismail Raji, 123, 124
Fasheh, Munir, 146, 147, 153
Fatnowna, Scott, 4, 12, 17, 21–23, 25n5, 96n16, 171
Feldman, Richard, 84–86

feminism, 4, 7, 8n1, 33, 120–22, 139, 140, 198, 237
feminist epistemology, 114
Fermat's Last Theorem, 146
'first fruits' festival, 202n6
First Salmon ceremony, 187
Flew, Antony, 146, 182n10
Flórez Alonso, Margarita, 23
folkways, 211, 212
Foster, Craig and Damon, 165
Foucault, Michel, 34, 35, 40n6, 95n10
foundationalism, 53, 105, 114, 118
Frankenstein, Marilyn, 143, 151
Freter, Björn, 17
Fricker, Miranda, 224–27, 230, 234n2

Gauland, Alexander, 246n7
Gaylard, Angela, 196
genocide, 210
geometry, 53, 56, 135, 146
George, June, 90, 187
Gerdes, Paulus, 136, 137, 141, 142, 155
Gettier, Edmund, 47, 77
Getz, Chonat, 135
Ghai, Yash, 164n9, 218
Al-Ghazzali, Abu Hamid, 123
Giuliani, Rudy, 239, 240
globalization, 165
Gödel, Kurt, 131n15
Goduka, Ivy, 22, 93, 186, 189, 190
Goldman, Alvin, 71–73, 86–88
Goodman, Nelson, 169, 171, 172
Grabiner, Judith, 144, 145
Greanville, Patrice, 194
Green, Lesley, 28, 90, 93, 169–75, 181n7, 181–82n9
Grill, Bartholomäus, 100–102, 229
Gross, Paul, 4, 8n1, 131n15
Gutmann, Amy, 231
Gwaravanda, Ephraim Taurai, 39n1

Haack, Susan, 132n24
Hall, Bud, 17, 38
Hall, David, 237, 240, 241
Hallen, Barry, 104–7, 110

Hardbarger, Tiffanie, 16, 186
Harding, Sandra, 4, 37, 109, 120–22, 132n23, 140, 237
Hardwig, John, 57, 58, 72, 87, 108
'Head-Smashed-In Buffalo Jump', 199, 200
Hegel, Georg Friedrich Wilhelm, 5
Heisenberg, Werner, 131n15
Heleta, Savo, 29, 221
Hersovici, Alan, 194
Herzog, Werner, 200, 201, 203n16
Hester, Lester, 240–42
heterosexism. *See* sexism
Higgs, Philip, 24
Hill Collins, Patricia, 37
Holiday, Anthony, 100, 101
holism, 96, 180, 198, 202n5
Hoodia gordonii, 9–11, 23, 131n11
Hospers, John, 64
Hountondji, Paulin, 20, 99
Hove, Chenjerai, 185, 186, 202n2
Hume, David, 62
hunhu. *See ubuntu*
hunting, 194, 199, 202n5, 202n12

indigenous knowledge: critique of, 97–133, 221–23; and decolonization, 5, 14–22, 105, 161; and marginalization, 7, 22, 24, 182n11, 226, 228, 229; and protection, 5, 14, 105; and reclamation, 5, 14, 16, 105, 169; and validation/legitimation/ legitimization, 5, 14–16, 22, 105, 147, 153, 177
indigenous science, 5, 15, 165–82
individualism, 21, 208, 230
indoctrination, 67–69
induction/inductive reasoning, 59–61; problem of, 62, 63
injustice, 7, 16, 101, 128, 198, 231; hermeneutical injustice, 224–26; testimonial injustice, 224–26. *See also* cognitive injustice; epistemic injustice
Inuit, 2, 98, 177

Islamization: of education, 123; of knowledge, 37, 123–26

Jansen, Jonathan, 29–31, 40n5, 96n14
Jegede, Olugbemiro, 4, 177
Johnson, George, 170, 176, 181n4
Johnson, Zanette, 17
Josephy Jr., Alvin, 169
Ju'hoansi, 98, 165, 166
justice, 36. *See also* cognitive justice; epistemic justice; social justice
justification, 2, 6, 44–47, 50–62, 73–75, 87, 95n7, 108, 111, 130n1, 173, 174, 181n8, 182n9, 182n12, 224, 233, 235n9; and context, 52, 77–81, 98; degrees of, 52, 54; kinds of, 52–62

Kabou, Axelle, 101, 102, 105, 226
Kant, Immanuel, 5, 102, 105, 226
Kaphagawani, Didier, 111
Karenga, Maulana, 206
Kawagley, Angayuqaq Oscar, 37
Kaya, Hasan, 97, 222
Keane, Moyra, 17, 22, 223, 234n4
Keats, John, 245
Kemp, Kemp J., 40n3
Keyes, Ralph, 238, 245
Khan, Farieda, 196–98
Khupe, Constance, 17, 22, 223, 234n4
Kincheloe, Joe, 4, 11–13, 22, 24, 25n5, 27, 105, 177, 180, 181n6, 186
Knijnik, Gelsa, 145, 147, 150, 151, 164n8
knowledge: acquaintance- or familiarity-type, 5, 6, 33, 45, 97, 221; and context, 52, 77–81, 150; diversity, 3, 5, 7, 38, 169–76. *See also* epistemological diversity; ecology/ ecologies of, 35, 36, 114; kinds of, 35; local knowledge, 3, 4, 12, 13, 31, 39, 103, 128; mathematical knowledge, 53, 138, 143–47, 150–52, 157; moral. *See* moral knowledge; practical knowledge, 5, 6, 12, 35, 45, 97, 221, 243; propositional (factual/theoretical knowledge), 5, 6, 35, 43, 45–48, 97, 110, 122, 123, 142, 147, 149, 162, 221, 243, 246n8; scientific knowledge, 4, 13, 25n5, 82, 148; sources of, 35, 51–63; traditional philosophical definition of, 6, 43–47, 98, 107, 127, 130n7, 131n14, 178, 223, 242; Yoruba definition of, 94n1, 104, 106–9, 112, 130n6, 132n20, 177, 223
knowledge in the blood, 28–31
Koko, Emma, 28
Krog, Antjie, 205, 206
Kuhn, Thomas, 109
Kumar, Chandra, 100–103, 130n3
Kunnie, Julian, 16, 18, 22, 98
Kwaa Prah, Kwesi, 4, 40n9

Lagunas, Rosalva Mojica, 133n27
Lanzano, Cristiano, 202n10
Latour, Bruno, 109
Laurens, Theresia, 164n2
Lebakeng, Teboho, 39
LeBeau, Sebastian, 167
Le Grange, Lesley, 4, 17, 21, 24, 38, 39, 187, 188, 190, 202n4
Letseka, Moeketsi, 191, 218n1
Levisohn, Jon, 114, 117, 118
Lévi-Strauss, Claude, 8n1
Levitt, Norman, 4, 8n1, 131n15
Lillejord, Solveig, 185
Lipka, Jerry, 156
Liyong, Taban lo, 20
Lotz-Sisitka, Heila, 89, 95n12

maat, 206
Macedo, Donaldo, 21, 25n5
Mackenthun, Gesa, 38
Maffie, James, 237, 238, 240–44, 246n8
Makgoba, Malegapuru William, 4, 20, 178, 188, 190, 208, 209
Makuleke, L., 196, 198
Mandela, Nelson, 28, 31, 207
mantindane, 176, 183–85

Māori, 15–17, 24
Maraldo, John, 240, 241
Maringe, Felix, 223, 224
Marker, Michael, 27, 189, 221
Martin, Brian, 138, 144, 145, 147–49
Marx, Karl, 230
Masaka, Dennis, 38, 39
Masolo, Dismas, 103–9, 111–13, 130n7, 131n11, 222, 224, 227, 229, 234n3
Masuluke, Michael, 195, 197
Mataira, Peter, 17
mathematics, 133–64; mathematical knowledge. *See* knowledge, mathematical; mathematical truth. *See* truth, mathematical
Matos, Narciso, 4, 17
Matthews, Gareth, 43
Maturana, Humberto, 90
Maughan, Emma, 25n5, 37, 189, 190
Maurial, Mahia, 4, 181n6, 187
Mbembe, Achille, 17
Medupe, Thebe, 165, 166
Mellin-Olsen, Stieg, 136
Mendick, Heather, 140
Meneses, Maria Paula, 17, 36, 114–16, 182n11
Mengele, Josef, 182n13
Metz, Thaddeus, 219n5
Mexica (Aztec), 15, 241, 246n8
mitakuye oyasin, 189, 190, 194, 206
Mjadu, Mzwandile, 197
Mkabela, Queeneth, 185
Mkhize, Alexia, 135
Mlodinow, Leonard, 146
Molefe, T.O., 29
Monture, David, 194
moral education, 68
moral facts, 7, 189, 223, 231
morality/morals, 10, 21, 24, 54, 68, 112, 116, 119–21, 123–26, 129, 169, 171, 182n12, 188–93, 198, 201, 202n12, 205–19
moral judgements, 214, 218
moral knowledge, 7, 82, 206, 223, 231
moral obligation, 84, 229
moral realism, 7

moral relativism, 7, 162
moral values, 7, 125, 210, 216
Morrow, Wally, 88
Mosha, R. Sambuli, 27, 231
Mosimege, Mogege, 177
Mqotsi, Livingstone, 179
Mudimbe, Valentin Yves, 31, 100
Muendane, Ngila Michael, 113
multicultural/multiculturalism, 15, 37, 95n10, 105, 114, 115, 117–19, 132n21, 132n23, 138, 153, 182n12, 217
Murove, Munyaradzi Felix, 192
muti murder, 130n2
Mutwa, Credo, 183–85, 195, 202n1
Mwadime, Robert, 12

Nabudere Dani, 119, 132n22
Nahuatl, 133n27, 242
Naipaul, Vidiadhar Surajprasad, 200
Nashon, Samson, 32
Nasr, Seyyed Vali Reza, 123, 124
Ndlovu-Gatsheni, Sabelo, 17, 19, 22, 29, 38, 39, 93
Ndwandwe, Reuben, 135
Nelson-Barber, Sharon, 17
Newton, Isaac, 51, 140, 175
Ngara, Constantine, 32
Ng'asike, John Teria, 186
Ngewu, Christopher Piet, 205
Ngewu, Cynthia, 205, 206
Nkomo, Mokubung, 16, 37
nonfoundationalism, 53, 118
Nongqawuse, 66, 67, 107
Ntongwe, Roland Ndille, 29
Ntuli, P. Pitika, 11, 15, 16, 19, 40n9, 131n15, 179, 209
Nunes, João Arriscado, 36, 114–16
Nwaila, Gilbert, 196, 197

Obama, Barack, 239, 240, 246n4
objectivism, 7, 110, 111
objectivity, 32, 38, 96n16, 116, 117, 147, 191, 213, 214, 237, 244
observation, 35, 53–57, 108, 110, 111, 130n1, 145

Odora Hoppers, Catherine, 4, 12, 14, 22, 24, 37, 105, 116, 126, 177, 188–91
Ogungbemi, Segun, 192, 193
Oma, Kxao Moses, 10
Onwu, Gilbert, 177
Orwell, George, 239
O'Sullivan, Michael, 194
Oxley, Julinna, 231, 232, 235n8
Owsley, Douglas, 170
Owuor, Jenipher, 31

Palikur, 15, 98; astronomy, 174–76
Pallas, Aaron, 114
Peat, F. David, 131n15, 180
Perelman, Grigori, 146
persuasion, 67, 68. *See also* rational persuasion
Peters, Richard, 33, 35
Petraitis, Richard, 101
Phillips, Denis C., 114, 117, 118, 132n21
Pickett, Harry, 4, 12, 17, 21–23, 25n5, 96n16, 171
Pickover, Michelè, 191
Plato, 44, 70, 77, 117, 131n14, 149, 177, 237, 243
Poincaré, Henri, 146
polygamy, 198, 209, 210
Ponting, Clive, 198
Posel, Deborah, 112, 228
positivism, 114, 118
postcolonial theory, 7, 19, 99, 237, 240, 245
postmodernism, 90, 114, 168, 170, 237
post-truth, 72, 127, 237–40
pottery, 17, 135, 137
Poundstone, William, 235n7
Powell, Arthur, 138–43, 151–53
Prakash, Madhu Suri, 4, 181n6, 187
priorities, 140, 196; educational priorities, 7, 126, 127, 245; epistemic priorities, 7, 126, 127, 245
'prisoner's dilemma', 235n7
'provability argument', 214, 215

Quale, Andreas, 237

quantum theory/mechanics, 179, 180
Quine, Willard Van Orman, 49, 54–57, 70, 71, 87, 92

Rachels, James, 213, 214, 216
racism, 14, 29, 37, 50, 138, 141, 144, 198, 209, 230
rain-making/rain-discarding, 99, 128, 240
Rains, Frances, 22
Ramose, Mogobe, 4, 40n9, 188–91, 208, 209
Ramoupi, Neo Lekgotla Laga, 29
Ramphele, Mamphela, 218–19n2
Rastafarians, 207
Rata, Elizabeth, 8n1, 25n7, 229
rationality, 6, 7, 14, 24, 32, 50, 52, 86, 94n5, 101, 105, 132n17, 161, 162, 170, 201, 218, 237, 244
rational persuasion, 67–71
realism, 94, 117, 172, 174, 176, 244. *See also* context-sensitive realism; moral realism
reason, 52, 53, 72, 101, 218
reasoning, 163; kinds of, 35, 52, 59–63, 111. *See also* abduction/abductive reasoning; deduction/deductive reasoning; induction/inductive reasoning
reasons, 52, 53, 73–75
recognition, 5, 14, 21–23, 221, 232, 235n5
Reilly, Ivan, 164n8
relational epistemology, 24, 36–37
relationalism/relationality, 21, 108, 186, 206, 207, 228
relativism, 7, 35, 91–94, 95n11, 99, 110–12, 120.123, 125, 126, 131n9, 144, 147, 150, 159, 160, 168, 170, 176, 227, 230, 244. *See also* cultural relativism; epistemological relativism; moral relativism
Reynar, Rodney, 4, 27
Rhodes, Cecil John, 20, 29
Richardson, Virginia, 90

rights, 21, 23, 128, 144, 150, 157, 163, 164n5, 221, 229–31, 235n9; animal rights, 194, 196; indigenous rights, 23, 194
Roberts, David, 238
Roberts, Mere, 40n8
Robertson Emily, 126, 127
Robins, Steven, 25n4
Robinson, Richard, 33
Rogers, Anne, 165
Romberg, Thomas, 147
Rosemont, Henry Jr., 237, 238, 240, 241
Rowlands, Stuart, 153, 154, 156, 157, 162
Ruitenberg, Claudia, 33–35, 41n11, 120
Rushton, John Philippe, 122, 123, 133n26
Ryle, Gilbert, 33, 35

San, 2, 5, 9–11, 15, 23, 25n1, 178
sand drawings. See Chokwe *sona* (sand drawings)
Schäfer, Marc, 131n8, 136, 137, 140, 163
Scheffler, Israel, 48, 53, 59, 79–81, 83, 95n7, 235n9
Scheurich, James Joseph, 37
Schumann, Claudia, 37
science, 2, 4, 6, 12, 14, 139, 165–82, 187, 219n7
science education, 175, 182n12
Seepe, Sipho, 4, 14, 15, 22, 181n2
Seitz, Volker, 105
Seleti, Yonah, 97, 222
Semali, Ladislaus, 4, 11–13, 22, 24, 25n5, 27, 98, 105, 177, 180, 181n6, 186
Senanayake, S.G.J.N., 186
Seneca, 98, 130n1
sensation/sense-experience, 35, 52, 53, 55, 56, 108, 110, 111
Setati, Mamokgethi, 151, 152
sexism, 14, 37, 50, 139, 141, 144, 198, 210, 230
shamanism, 240

Shay, Suellen, 29
Shizha, Edward, 22, 132n18
Siegel, Harvey, 119, 120, 132n22, 132n25, 182n12, 221
Simpson, Graeme, 112, 228
skepticism, 82, 83
Slote, Michael, 232, 233, 235n6, 235n10
Smith, Linda Tuhiwai, 16, 19, 22
Smuts, Helene, 135
social epistemology, 72, 88
social justice, 7, 17, 22, 34–36, 38, 95n10, 114, 141, 169, 180
sociology of knowledge, 118, 148, 149, 172
Socrates, 44, 45, 71, 117, 237
Sodipo, J. Olubi, 104–7
Spicer, Sean, 239
Spivak, Gayatri, 224
standpoint theory/standpoint epistemology/standpointism, 114, 120–22, 237
Stangroom, Jeremy, 131n8
Stathopoulou, Charoula, 164n8
Stevenson, Bob, 194
Stringer, Ernie, 4
Sturgeon, Julian, 197
subjectivism, 110, 244
subjectivity, 21, 32, 122, 191, 237
Sumida Huaman, Elizabeth, 17
Sumner, William Graham, 211, 212
superstition, 95n11, 128, 129, 176, 179, 185
sustainability/sustainable development, 7, 186, 202n3, 243, 244
Swanson, Dalene, 228
Swartbooi-Xabadiya, Zolisa, 209

Tandon, Rajesh, 17, 38
Tangwa, Godfrey, 192, 193
Teffo, Lesiba Joe, 4, 37, 40n9, 208
Ter Haar, Gerrie, 102, 103
testimony, 35, 57–59, 108, 111, 185
Thakchoe, Sonam, 240, 241
Tleane, Console, 20

tokoloshe, 176, 183–85
Tom, Miye Nadya, 186
traditional ecological/environmental knowledge (TEK), 7, 23, 183–201
traditional healer/healers, 129, 178, 183
trapping, 194, 195, 202n5
Trump, Donald, 181n6, 239, 246n4
trustworthiness, 57–59, 243
truth, 2, 3, 6, 7, 22, 30, 31, 44–48, 51, 53, 57, 72, 75–78, 91–94, 99, 109–13, 131n15, 140, 170–79, 181nn6–8, 210, 214, 218, 225, 227–29, 234n4, 237, 246n8; coherence theory of, 76, 77; consensus theory of, 75–77, 153; correspondence theory of, 76, 77, 109, 131n12, 241–43; mathematical truth, 53, 110, 142–47; pragmatic theory of, 76, 77, 110; scientific truth, 2, 172
Truth and Reconciliation (Commission), 29, 40n4, 112, 205, 207, 210, 219n3, 227–29
truth-centered epistemologies, 240–44
truthfulness, 112, 125, 129, 227, 239, 245
Turnbull, David, 4, 13, 28, 37, 201
Tutu, Desmond, 29, 207, 208, 210

ubuntu, 188–93, 202n4, 206–10, 218n2, 219n5, 228
ukama, 192, 193, 206
ukweshwama. See 'first fruits' festival
Ullian, Joseph S., 49, 54–57, 70, 71, 87, 92
understanding, 136, 173–76
universalism, 38, 92, 121, 132n16, 159, 170, 182n12, 223
Uwuor-Anyumba, Henry, 20

Vaalbooi, Petrus, 10
values, 7, 30. *See also* moral values
Van Heerden, Jannie, 135
Van Sertima, Ivan, 132n23, 181n2
Vergès, Françoise, 4, 18
Viergever, Marcel, 12, 23, 186

Villa-Vicencio, Charles, 228
virginity testing, 198, 209
Visvanathan, C. Shiv, 37, 164n5, 178, 219n7
Von Glasersfeld, Ernst, 90

wahkohtowin, 194, 206
Wajcman, Judy, 37, 120
Wallner, Fritz, 4
Walton, Elizabeth, 88, 89
Wasuji Tetsurō, 240, 241
Wa Thiong'o, Ngũgĩ, 19, 20
way-centered epistemologies, 240–43
ways of knowing, 32–35, 132n24, 138, 161, 169, 185. *See also* African ways of knowing
White, John, 49, 50, 53, 55, 69, 95n6, 243
White Hat, Emily, 186, 207
Whyte, Ian, 196
Wilder, Benjamin, 25n6, 133n27
'wildlife management', 194, 195
Wiles, Andrew, 146
Williams, Bernard, 227
Windschitl, Mark, 90
Wiredu, Kwasi, 19, 104, 106, 109–12, 127, 131n13, 132n16, 227
witchcraft/witches, 11, 99–103, 130n2, 176, 179
Woods, Macdara, 29, 30
Wright, Handel, 32
Wynberg, Rachel, 9

Xaba, Thokozani, 182n11
xenophobia, 210, 231
Xhosa, 66, 67, 107, 205; cattle killing and crop burning, 66, 107

Young, Michelle, 37

Zaslavsky, Claudia, 164n3
Zimmermann, Larry, 168, 176
Zulu, 135, 202n6, 246n11
Zulu, Itibari, 37, 181n2
Zuni, 168

About the Author

Kai Horsthemke is an associate professor and has taught philosophy (of education) at the University of the Witwatersrand and the University of the Western Cape, both in South Africa and at KU Eichstätt-Ingolstadt in Germany. He is a visiting professor in the Wits School of Education and a fellow at the Oxford Centre for Animal Ethics, UK. He is the author of three monographs, *The Moral Status and Rights of Animals* (2010), *Animals and African Ethics* (2015) and *Animal Rights Education* (2018), and, together with Peggy Siyakwazi, Elizabeth Walton and Charl Wolhuter, the coeditor of the first two editions of *Education Studies* (2013 and 2016, respectively).

www.ingramcontent.com/pod-product-compliance
Lightning Source LLC
Chambersburg PA
CBHW020111010526
44115CB00008B/787